FUNDAMENTALS OF FORENSIC PHOTOGRAPHY

In *Fundamentals of Forensic Photography*, Keith Mancini and John Sidoriak offer practical techniques for common situations encountered in forensic documentation. Topics include equipment selection, lighting techniques, crime scene and evidence documentation, macro and micro photography as well as aerial, high speed, and computational photography. Techniques for photographic documentation in both the laboratory and the field are discussed.

Keith Mancini is a Forensic Photographer for the Westchester County, NY, Forensic Lab. He has served in that role for approximately 17 years. Keith is a certified Forensic Photographer and Forensic Video Examiner by the International Association for Identification where he also serves on the Forensic Video Certification Board. Keith is a member of the National Institute of Justice's OSAC (Organization of Scientific Area Committees) Video and Image Analysis Subcommittee.

John Sidoriak is the Vice President and Director of Operations for Fisher-Cal Industries, Inc., a photography, graphics, and multimedia contractor to the Department of Defense for over 20 years. John is also the accident and crime scene instructor to the Photodocumentation Series at the National Transportation Safety Board Training Center in Ashburn, VA.

ABOUT THE SERIES

APPLICATIONS IN SCIENTIFIC PHOTOGRAPHY

Like all fields, there are many subspecialties within the broad field of scientific photography. While each is seemingly specialized, there are areas within the individualized fields of science where photography is practiced in generalized ways as well. The **Applications in Scientific Photography** series was produced to become an industry resource, in homage to the seventeen books created for the Time Life Photography series in the 1970s, which outlines various aspects of photography for the working professional and student, including technology, methods, applications, tools, and important photographers.

The second book in the **Applications in Scientific Photography** series is *Fundamentals in Forensic Photography: Practical Techniques for Evidence Documentation on Location and in the Laboratory*. This book offers practical techniques for the most common situations encountered in forensic documentation. The topics include proper equipment selection, effective settings and scientific strategies for forensic documentation. Emphasis is placed on techniques used in both laboratory and field settings to present the factual, true and accurate imagery that is vital in all aspects of forensic science and crime scene investigation. The text concludes with methods for archiving and retrieval of imagery, including scene, injury, autopsy, and evidence documentation; and HDR, high speed, and time-lapse imaging.

Each subsequent title in the series has been designed to share the best practices from each discipline using applied and practical strategies. Each book in the series will deconstruct and emphasize how images are considered scientific data and the end facts of an experiment or photographic documentation/survey.

Titles in the Series

Laboratory Imaging and Photography: Best Practices for Photomicrography & More
Michael Peres, Rochester Institute of Technology

Fundamentals of Forensic Photography: Practical Techniques for Evidence Documentation on Location and in the Laboratory
Keith Mancini and John Sidoriak

FUNDAMENTALS OF FORENSIC PHOTOGRAPHY

Practical Techniques for Evidence Documentation on Location and in the Laboratory

Keith Mancini and John Sidoriak

Routledge
Taylor & Francis Group
NEW YORK AND LONDON

First published 2018
by Routledge
711 Third Avenue, New York, NY 10017

and by Routledge
2 Park Square, Milton Park, Abingdon, Oxon OX14 4RN

Routledge is an imprint of the Taylor & Francis Group, an informa business

Library of Congress Cataloging-in-Publication Data
Names: Mancini, Keith, author. | Sidoriak, John, author.
Title: Fundamentals of forensic photography : practical techniques for evidence documentation on location and in the laboratory / Keith Mancini and John Sidoriak.
Description: New York : Routledge, 2017. | Series: Applications in scientific photography | Includes bibliographical references and index.
Identifiers: LCCN 2017007684 (print) | LCCN 2017008564 (ebook) | ISBN 9781138910812 (pbk : alk. paper) | ISBN 9781138910843 (hbk : alk. paper) | ISBN 9781315693125 (ebk) | ISBN 9781315693125 (Master) | ISBN 9781317435396 (web pdf) | ISBN 9781317435389 (epub) | ISBN 9781317435372 (kindle)
Subjects: LCSH: Legal photography.
Classification: LCC TR822 .M34 2017 (print) | LCC TR822 (ebook) | DDC 778.9/36325—dc23
LC record available at https://lccn.loc.gov/2017007684

ISBN: 978-1-138-91084-3 (hbk)
ISBN: 978-1-138-91081-2 (pbk)
ISBN: 978-1-315-69312-5 (ebk)

Typeset in Photina MT
by Apex CoVantage, LLC

For Product Safety Concerns and Information please contact our EU representative: GPSR@taylorandfrancis.com
Taylor & Francis Verlag GmbH, Kaufingerstraße 24, 80331 München, Germany.

Contents

ABOUT THE CONTRIBUTORS

ADAM HARTLEY is a forensic firearms examiner who has spent the better part of his career working in microscopy and image analysis. In addition to giving presentations on the use of image analysis and photogrammetry in forensics at regional and national training conferences, he is also published in scientific journals such as *Nature* and the *Journal of Neuroscience*. He can be contacted at AdamJHartley@gmail.com.

GEORGE REIS is owner of Imaging Forensics, providing training, consulting, and expert witness services in the areas of forensic image analysis, video analysis, and photography. He can be reached at reis@imagingforensics.com. His website is www.imagingforensics.com.

ACKNOWLEDGMENTS

We would like to wish a special thank you to the following people who contributed to the success of this project:

Michael Peres, Associate Chair, School of Photographic Arts & Sciences, Rochester Institute of Technology

Kunjlata Ashar, M.D., Pathologist/Medical Examiner, Westchester County Department of Laboratories and Research

Robert Adamo, Director, Westchester County Forensic Lab

Mary Eustace, Forensic Science Specialist, Westchester County Forensic Lab

Brandi Clark, Forensic Scientist, Westchester County Forensic Lab

The entire staff of the Westchester County Forensic Lab

Sandra Viens, Toxicology Specialist, Westchester County Toxicology Lab

Lt. Joseph Rainone, Waterbury Police Department

Sean C. Lonergan, Pilot/Police Officer, Westchester County Police Department

Joseph P. Mancini

W. Reid Lindsay, for passing on his vast knowledge of forensic photography.

The NTSB Training Center

Dr. Paul Schuda, NTSB Training Center Director at National Transportation Safety Board

From Keith: My wife Kristen and children Kaitlyn and Alexis.

From John: My wife Barbara and children Dominique, Ivan and Grier for their support and allowing me the opportunity to make this possible.

INTRODUCTION

Documentation of evidence in forensic science and crime scene investigation is a vital component to supporting an investigation. In fact, in some cases getting the "shot" can make or break a case. Advancements in photographic technologies, including digital imaging, have made it possible to document evidence in ways that previously may not have been possible. That being said, it often takes a knowledgeable photographer to successfully capture the details of the evidence so that they may be used as part of the investigation.

True and accurate evidence documentation is vital in all aspects of forensic science and crime scene investigation. This can range from a simple recording of the condition of evidence to enhancing specific details that may not be discernible to the human eye or recognized by the layperson. This documentation of evidence must be done in a way that is true and accurate, reproduces the evidence as fact, and provides the viewer with an unbiased view of the item. This type of documentation presents several unique challenges that do not exist in other disciplines of photography.

It is our purpose to provide readers of this book with the skills necessary to accomplish several common photographic tasks encountered in forensic science. We do not want to provide too much extra information that would only confuse the reader, rather than add to the success of the photograph. We feel there is plenty of technical information available on many of the photographic techniques discussed in this book. It is our intention to only give the information necessary to successfully complete the tasks discussed.

This book offers practical techniques for many of the most common situations encountered in forensic documentation. Topics include equipment selection, effective settings, and the best how-to scientific strategies for forensic documentation. Emphasis is placed on techniques used both in a laboratory and field setting to present factual, true, and accurate imagery.

Since budgets tend to run the gamut in the field of forensic science, we attempted to provide both a best-case scenario as well as inexpensive and resourceful approaches to the challenges of forensic photography.

Chapter 1 Equipment and Technology

Cameras

Undoubtedly the most important piece of equipment for forensic photography is a camera. Evidence documentation is essential and the camera is the forensic photographer's primary tool to preserve a moment in time. As time keeps moving, evidence will as well. The camera stops time and captures evidence in its existing location for analysis.

The camera is essentially a light tight box that contains a sensor, which records light and converts it into electronic signals, and supports a lens that focuses light upon the sensor. The camera will also have a mechanism to control the amount of light striking the sensor, usually a shutter and aperture. All cameras share this same basic design; however, the variety of features beyond this basic design can be overwhelming when deciding upon a camera. Choosing the right camera for you will depend upon its intended use as well as your budget. Recent advances in digital imaging technology have considerably blurred the lines between what is a professional camera and what is a consumer camera, so when deciding what is the right camera for your task it is more important to consider individual features and what your needs are. Nevertheless, there are some general categories of cameras that should be discussed. Generally speaking the following types of cameras go from more advanced to least. However, there will always be exceptions to that rule; for instance, a high-end point-and-shoot camera may outperform a low-end DSLR and this can only be determined by comparing their features. The camera has evolved and the future of camera technology is unknown. Despite the advances cameras have experienced, we still come back to the ultimate goal of a camera, and that is to take a picture and record data and evidence. There are some general categories of cameras that will be covered in this chapter. However, they can only be determined by comparing their features and if possible testing camera systems in a controlled environment.

Components of Cameras

Cameras from the professional level to the everyday smartphone will contain the same parts and mechanical devices. Every part and mechanical device will produce the same effect for the same reasons. The overall idea is to record light during a set time period. The camera housing, or black box, eliminates extraneous light sources from activating the sensor. The light entering the camera housing must be mechanically controlled to create a proper image. A shutter is used to control the light entering the camera at the location of the lens. The lens focuses the light entering through the shutter onto the sensor. The sensor is located at a specific distance from the lens and permits proper focusing of the image.

DSLR Cameras

Short for digital single-lens reflex, these are probably the most common cameras used by forensic photographers. The DSLR is the most versatile camera system available by way of having a multitude of settings, options, lenses, and accessories. DSLR cameras have a mirror that directs light from the lens into the viewfinder allowing the photographer to see what will be recorded once the photograph is taken. The ability to see in the viewfinder what will be the captured images permits the photographer to compose the image and focus on specific information, which is a must for forensic evidence gathering. Once the shutter button is pressed, the mirror moves out of the way allowing the light to expose the sensor.

DSLR cameras accept interchangeable lenses allowing the photographer to select the best lens for the task at hand. Interchangeable lenses also allow the photographer greater control over composition, color, clarity, focus, speed, and depth of field. Environment, location, and the subject will influence the photographer's lens selection. Each photographer may have a "go to" lens that they would use as their primary lens. Additional lenses will aid in expanding the photographer's and camera's capabilities. Each camera manufacturer uses its own mounting system for lenses, called a lens mount, and not all systems are compatible. Therefore it is important to have the correct lenses for your DSLR camera. One way to accomplish this is by purchasing lenses such as Canon, Nikon, Sony, or Leica, made by the same company as your camera; however, there are several lens manufacturers that make lenses in a variety of mounts. An expanded description of lenses will be given later in this chapter.

DSLR camera digital sensors come in a variety of sizes, but tend to be larger than those of cameras in other categories, with the exception of medium- and large-format cameras; however, these tend to be very expensive and are not common to forensic work. The full-frame sensor is currently the largest available sensor for DSLR cameras. It is called "full frame" because of its evolution from 35mm film cameras with it replicating the view within the viewfinder that many trained film photographers are accustomed to seeing. Traditional film photographers are not accustomed to the LCD display on the back of the camera. The full-frame sensor also replicates the field of view many traditional photographers are familiar with by seeing a 1.5 in. × 1 in. area. Larger sensors of the same resolution (or megapixels) tend to produce better-quality images because the larger sensor is capable of capturing more light, therefore reducing noise. Smaller sensors on DSLR cameras will produce a smaller view than a full frame or larger sensor. This effect is called cropping, and depending upon the size of the sensor the effect will be reported as a crop factor; the crop factor compares the sensor to a full-frame sensor. Smaller sensors will have a crop factor larger than that of a larger sensor because they

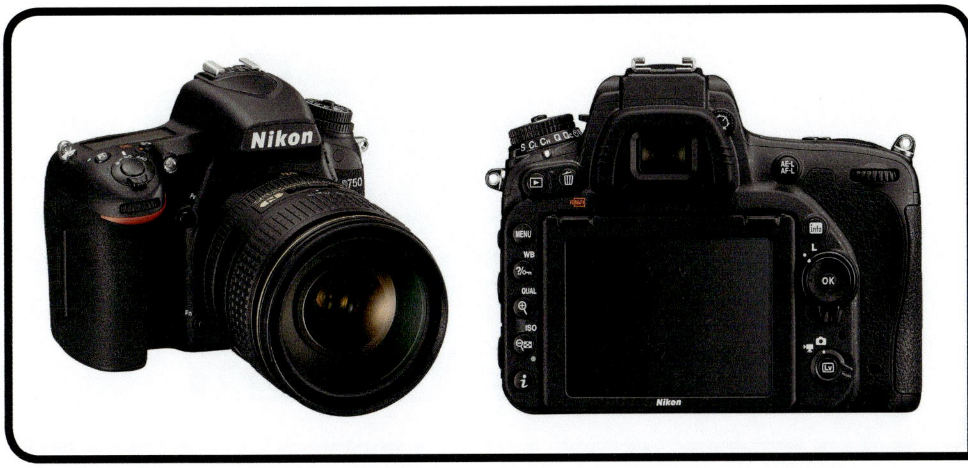

Figures 1.1 – 1.2 Front and rear of a DSLR camera with attached lens

crop more of the image, or a smaller view is seen. The result of this crop is also increased depth of field, the part of the subject that is in focus, which will be discussed in greater detail in Chapter 2.

Another important feature of DSLR cameras is the ability to accept an external flash, while many DSLR cameras do have their own pop-up flash. A flash is a light source used to produce a burst of artificial light to help illuminate a scene, typically where there are less light or dark areas of a scene. An on-camera flash is typically low power and lacks the maneuverability needed for many of the lighting techniques critical to forensic photography. Like lenses, it is important to have a flash specifically designed to work with your camera.

Other notable features of DSLR cameras include more control over the image-making process, video capture, better performance, and faster autofocus then cameras in other categories.

Medium-Format Cameras

Similar in design to DSLR cameras, medium-format cameras contain a much larger sensor then even a full-frame DSLR. Their designs evolved from film cameras that used a film format larger than 35mm, in fact 56mm and larger. The larger sensor in these cameras produces images of far greater quality than the full-frame sensors in other cameras. However, medium-format cameras tend to be too bulky for fieldwork, or even hand holding in the lab setting, and their high cost may make them unattainable for some publically funded facilities and operations.

Medium-format camera manufacturers include Phase One, Hasselblad, Leica, Mamiya, and Pentax. Each one has individual characteristics but all will maintain the larger sensor size to capture evidence in greater detail. The new medium-format camera systems have been better designed to be mobile and ergonomic for ease of use in the field and on location. It creates another option and advantage for the forensic photographer as a legitimate camera system. The photographer is able to produce high detail and quality images to document

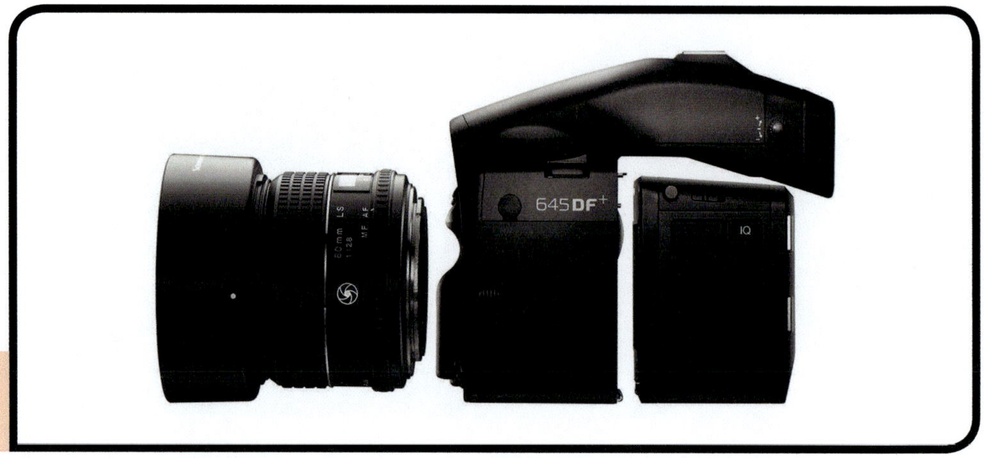

Figure 1.3 Medium-format camera front view

and relay evidence to investigators. This may be a great asset to the forensic photographer, but it does come at a financial cost.

Mirrorless Camera Systems

Relatively new to the market are mirrorless cameras, sometimes known as micro four-thirds cameras. These cameras offer similar controls, as well as removable lenses and accessories while remaining smaller and lighter than their DSLR counterparts. They typically have larger sensors than point-and-shoot cameras, making the images these cameras produce far better in quality. They are called mirrorless because they lack a mirror directing the image to the viewfinder; rather, the photographer composes the image using an electronic viewfinder (EVF) or LCD screen on the back of the camera. The disadvantage of an EVF is it uses power, which can shorten the life of the battery. It is highly recommended to obtain additional batteries and keep them charged or on a charger while using a mirrorless camera.

Comparable to DSLR camera systems, mirrorless cameras use interchangeable lenses and, with the exception of Olympus and Pentax who use the standard micro four-thirds lens mount, will require the appropriate lens to mount to the camera body. There are lens adapters available for many mirrorless camera systems that allow mounting of DSLR lenses. This is convenient if the user has an existing system and wants to retain their current series of lenses. Be aware that some lenses mounted upon mirrorless camera systems may prevent features like autofocus and automatic aperture selection, requiring the photographer to set those manually.

Mirrorless cameras feature a range of sensor sizes from full frame to almost as small as point-and-shoot digital cameras. Cameras with smaller sensors may have a smaller crop factor. Basically, this is when a small section of the image on the outside of the image viewed within the viewfinder of the viewing screen is not imaged. Larger sensors tend to perform better in low light, as well as have less noise, especially when shooting with a high ISO. Also similar to DSLR cameras, there are several accessories available to mirrorless cameras like external flash units, remote controls, and battery grips.

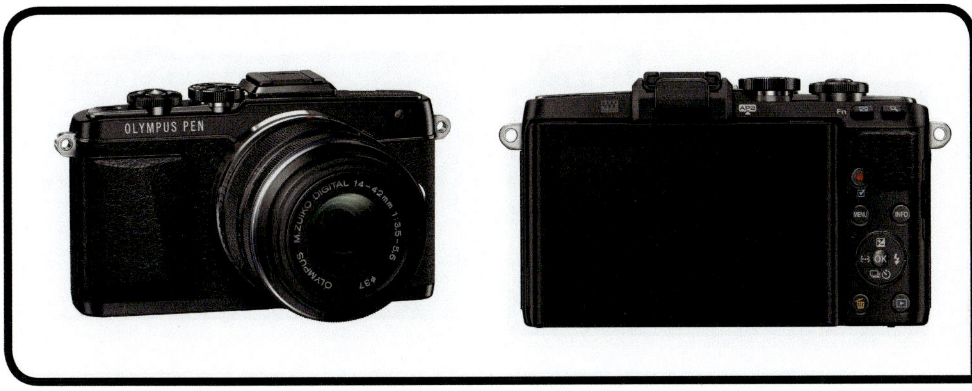

Figures 1.4 – 1.5 The front and rear of a mirrorless camera with attached lens

Point-and-Shoot Cameras

Perhaps the least expensive and quite possibly most commonly seen type of true camera is the point-and-shoot digital camera. A point-and-shoot camera is a type of camera where the lens is not removable and has other features that are found on more advanced cameras. They are designed to capture images quickly without much skill from a user. Typically they contain a fixed built-in zoom lens and flash. Point-and-shoot cameras contain many of the automatic settings and occasionally a manual setting for the user to make specific camera adjustments, something that is normally unavailable with smartphone cameras.

Point-and-shoot cameras tend to have smaller sensors, when compared to other types of camera systems. Image quality not only is dependent upon the pixel count, but lens quality, sensor size, and camera features, which set it apart from the smartphone. More often than not, it is the typical novice's camera choice to take fun photos at events such as vacations, parties, and social gatherings. Depending upon the type of work you do a point-and-shoot camera still may be suitable for your needs however it may lack some of the control necessary for forensic photography. This is not to say that they don't have a place in the field; similar to the camera phone, they are rather easy to use and can make a great first responder or backup camera as it will fit easily inside any crime scene kit.

Point-and-shoot cameras can range from entry level, with very little in the way of advanced features or control, to advanced point-and-shoot cameras that offer a greater feature set and more manual control. When looking to purchase a point-and-shoot camera there are a few features that one must consider.

Image quality is best acquired with a large image sensor that additionally provides better performance in low light environments. Typically sensors from 1 to 1 2/3 inches are available in the higher-level point-and-shoot cameras.

Choosing a point-and-shoot camera with a big latitude of shutter speeds and ISO enables the user to operate in a greater variety of scenes and situations along with the flexibility to create a high quality image in a wider range of conditions.

Smartphones

Smartphones are now the number one selling digital camera, and are currently the leading camera type for the popular online social media photo community. The quality of an image

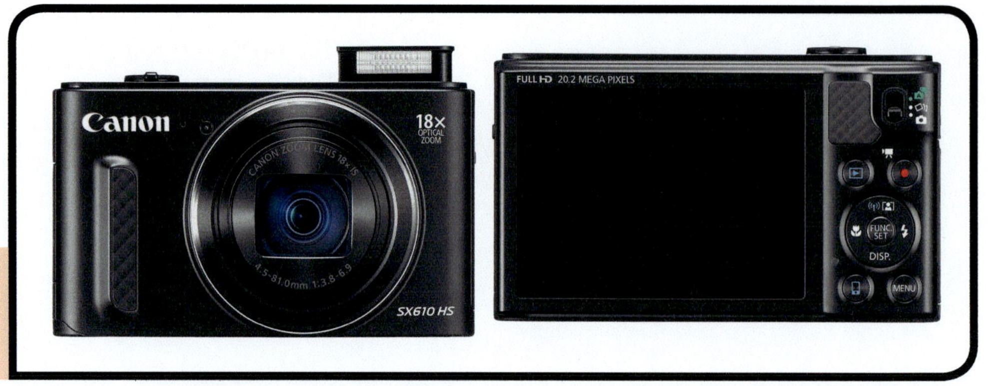

Figures 1.6 – 1.7 Front and rear of a point-and-shoot camera

created using many cell phones is now equivalent to that of point-and-shoot cameras. An added benefit is nearly everyone carries some type of camera phone. When it is necessary to photograph evidence and there is no other alternative, it is certainly better to take a picture, no matter the quality, then not to have any picture.

A camera phone certainly isn't a replacement for a high-quality digital camera, even if it has a higher resolution; remember, resolution is not the only factor in determining image quality. If the proper techniques are followed it is possible to achieve acceptable results. Camera phones vary in their capabilities. Some contain adjustments such as f-stop, shutter speed, ISO (International Organization of Standardization), and color balance (all explained in more detail in Chapter 2). Additionally, some have presets for a variety of shooting conditions like sports, portraiture, close-up, and nighttime. Each variable leads to a specific capability and can be used in forensic evidence imaging.

There are a few considerations, first and foremost, if you are using a personal device for work purposes. Are there any policies in place regarding its use? If not, perhaps there should be. Also, those images are subject to certain legal restrictions as well as copyright protection, and it becomes your responsibility to protect them. After being taken on the phone, those images should be transferred to a more secure storage space, and this may be a challenge depending upon your particular phone. That being said, these challenges can certainly be worked out, and if need be, a camera phone can be a viable alternative to a digital camera in certain situations.

There are also several applications, or apps for short, available for smartphones that allow the user greater control over their camera settings. Some apps to consider are Pro HDR, Manual, Photoshop Touch, Lightroom Mobile, and VSCO Cam, and it is recommended that you look into these alternatives if they are available for your phone.

Scanning Back/Large-Format Cameras

Large-format camera systems come in 4 × 5, 8 × 10, and other sizes and are not considered typical forensic camera systems. These large-format cameras are best used for still life, portraits, and in landscape settings or environments. They tend to be very bulky and photographers utilize much of their time setting up and properly determining exposures to acquire a great image. Often forensic photographers are new to the photographic field and the large-format camera contains numerous obstacles and technical complexities. Many books explaining the large-format camera and how to use it are available at numerous bookstores and at website vendors. Notable large-format books include Ansel Adams' *The Camera* and *Using the View Camera* by Steve Simmons, and there is also the website www.largeformatphotography.info.

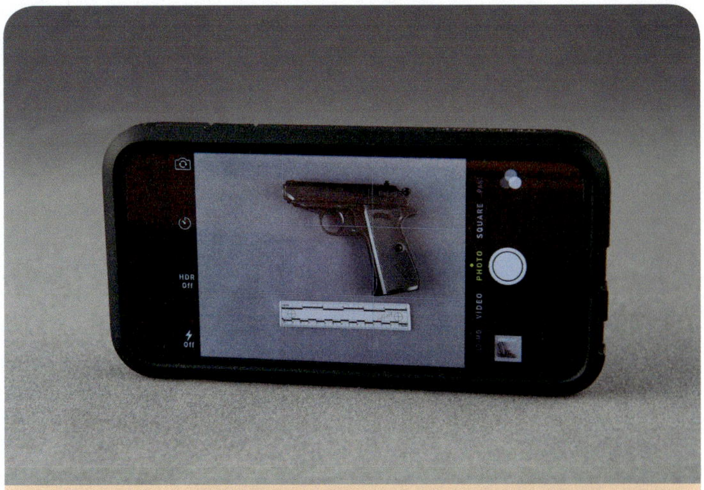

Figure 1.8 A smartphone using the camera application

Many of the large-format digital backs currently are single shot or similar to that of a typical digital camera; however, the duration of the imaging process is much longer to take a basic image. Exposure times routinely are from 10 to 30 seconds upwards to several minutes or hours. Similar to DSLR and mirrorless camera systems, large-format cameras have the ability to use interchangeable lenses. These individual lenses attach to a lens board and are fully manual. Additionally, the longer focal length needed for large-format cameras creates shallow depth of field because the apertures are capable of being closed down to *f*64 or sometimes higher. As a rule, forensic photographers wish to obtain as much depth of field within an image. Depth of field is considered the range of sharp images or focus from the closest to farthest object within the scene. Further discussion regarding depth of field will be provided in Chapter 2.

The large-format camera systems typically run from 3.5 lbs. to upwards of 12 lbs. which also adds to the burden of using this system in a forensic department. Close quarters in a laboratory or in the field setting while having the requirement to maneuver throughout a crime scene with ease and safety makes this camera system essentially obsolete for forensic photographers. The inability to capture images quickly and efficiently does not make this type of system convenient or logical for a forensic photographer.

Recommendations

Choosing the proper camera for forensic documentation can be a daunting task; therefore here are a few recommendations. Currently the preferred camera for just about all types of forensic photography is the DSLR since it allows the greatest flexibility when it comes to lenses and accessories.

In a forensic, legal, or public safety setting, budget is usually your limiting factor, and it's possible to build a system with even the smallest budgets. A great camera system should consist at a minimum of a DSLR camera body, a normal lens (55mm), wide-angle lens (16–28mm), close-up macro lens, polarizing and colored filters, external flash, flash extension cable(s), cable release, flashlight,

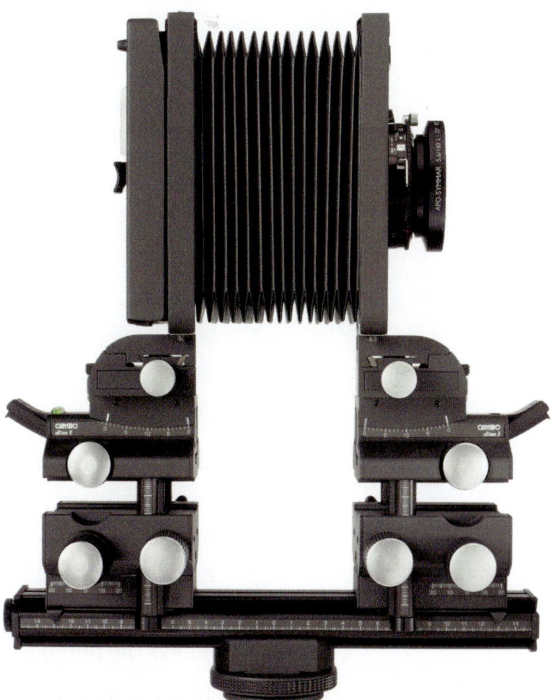
Figure 1.9 Large-format 4 x 5 camera side view

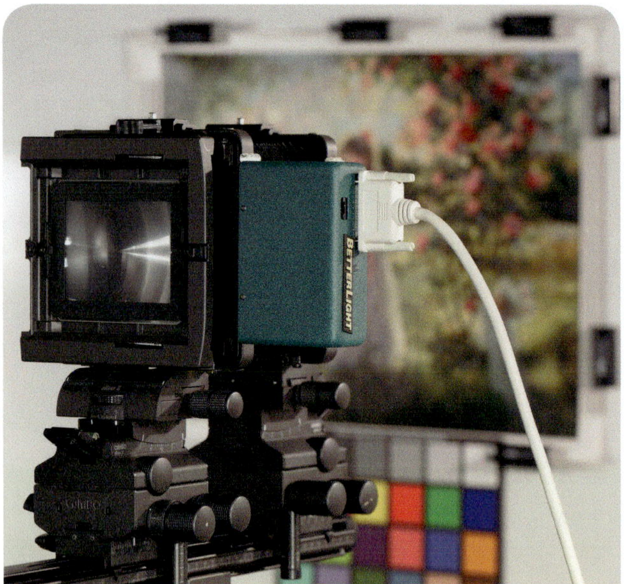

Figure 1.10 A typical 4 x 5 digital scanning back

extra batteries, multiple media cards, and a sturdy tripod. A list of recommended equipment for a forensic photographer is provided at the end of this chapter.

Lenses

A camera lens (photographic lens or objective) is a vital component of the camera system for image formation. Lenses attach to cameras in two distinct ways: the bayonet or C mount method. The bayonet style is most commonly used with DSLR still cameras because this style aligns the mechanical and electrical components up with the camera body to ensure proper communication between the camera and lens. Most manufacturers such as Canon, Contax, Nikon, Pentax, and Sony use the bayonet method to mount the lens on the camera; however, be aware that each manufacturer's lens is most likely not compatible with other manufacturer's camera bodies.

A lens has a focal length that corresponds to a specific angle of view. The focal length of the lens also represents the image magnification or decrease in image size created by the lens. The focal length of the lens is annotated in millimeters and describes the angle of view of the lens relative to the coverage of the circle of good definition produced to cover the imaging sensor.

For example, if a sensor were 24mm × 35mm, the diagonal of the image sensor would require the circle of light entering the lens to image on the sensor to be approximately 43mm. Therefore the normal lens for this example, a 35mm DSLR sensor, would be approximately a 50mm lens. This normal lens will also create an angle of view that is similar to the human eye.

When a shorter focal length lens is attached to the same camera, for example a 20mm lens, this would create a wider angle of view and is considered a wide-angle lens. Conversely, when a longer focal length lens is attached to the same camera, for example a 200mm lens, it would create a narrower angle of view and provide a zoom or telephoto effect of the scene.

Lens apertures control the amount of light that enters through the lens, which will affect image exposure. Apertures are adjustable from the large fully open position, allowing more light transmission, to a very small opening allowing less light transmission. The camera usually controls the aperture through its communication with the lens. If the lens is a manual lens or not compatible with the camera, some lenses have a manual aperture ring that allows the photographer to choose the aperture for the situation.

The aperture's primary position within the lens is fully open until the image is taken. This permits the photographer the opportunity to compose and focus on a specific area or object within the evidence scene. When the shutter is activated the aperture blades close to the

Table 1.1 Table of features, advantages and disadvantage for DSLR, Mirrorless, Medium Format Cameras

Camera Type	Top Features	Advantages	Disadvantages
DSLR	Electronic & Mechanical Shutter Options	Fast Mechanical Shutter Without a Delay	Heavier Camera Body and Lenses
	New Full-Frame Crop Factor	Multiple Lenses Available	Larger or Bulkier Camera
	High Megapixel Resolution	High-Quality Sensor	Many Menu Items and Features
	CMOS Sensors	Manual Controls	Mid-Price Range
	Dust Reduction	External Flash Controls	
	Multiple Memory Card Types		
	Large Viewfinder		
	Eyepiece Diopter Adjustment		
	Full-Size Viewing Screen		
	Large ISO Range		
	Multiple Exposure Modes		
	Mirror Lockup		
	Multiple Metering Options		
	Multiple File Type Selections		
	Multiple Whites Balance Options + Custom		
	Built in Flash & Hot Shoe		
	Video Recording on Some Models		
Meduim Format	Extremely High Resolution	Large Sensor	High Price Range
	Multiple Memory Card Types	Fast Mechanical Shutter Without a Delay	Heavier Camera Body and Lenses
	RAW, TIFF, and JPEG files	Multiple Lenses Available	Larger or Bulkier Camera
	Large ISO Range	High-Quality Optics	Many Menu Items and Features
	Fast Shutter Speeds	Manual Controls	Slower Autofocus
	TTL, Multi Segment, Center, & Spot Metering	External Flash Controls	
	Hot Shoe and External Flash Sync	Flash Sync at Any Speed	

(Continued)

Table 1.1 Continued

Camera Type	Top Features	Advantages	Disadvantages
	Flash at All Shutter Speeds	Manufacturer Shooting Software	
	Auto and Manual Shooting Modes		
	Large Display and Some Touchscreen		
	Wifi, USB, Mini, HDMI, and Audio Connectivity		
	Multiple Exposure Modes		
	Multiple Whites Balance Options + Custom		
	Eyepiece Diopter Adjustment		
	Video Recording on Some Models		
Mirrorless	Interchangeable Lenses	Smaller Manageable Size Economical Price Range	
	Various Sized Mid-Sized Sensors	Multiple Lens Choices	Newer Camera Type
	Various Crop Factors	Some DSLR Lenses Fit Mirrorless Cameras	High Power Usage for Display
	Large Sensor Size	Newer Autofocus Technology	Lagging Live View
	Multiple File Type Selections	Video Recording	Lesser Performance in Low-Light
	Multiple Memory Card Types	Smaller and Lighter to Use	
	Auto & Manual Focus	Exposure Viewed on Display	
	Touch Screen Display	White Balance Viewed on Display	
	Large ISO Range		
	Large Shutter Speed Range		
	Multiple Exposure Modes		
	Multiple Whites Balance Options + Custom		
	Hot Shoe		
	Video Recording on Some Models		

(*Continued*)

Camera Type	Top Features	Advantages	Disadvantages
Point & Shoot	Average to Large Sensor Size	Ease of Use	Limited Manual Controls
	Multiple File Type Selections	Low to Average Price Range	Limited Apertures
	Limited Focal Length Lens	LCD Screen for Viewfinder	Limited Shutter Speeds
	Large Shutter Speed Range	Small Size & Weight	Limited Focal Length Lens
	Multi Point, Center Weighted, Spot Metering		
	Multiple Exposure Modes		
	Multiple Whites Balance Options		
	Camera Flash		
	Multiple Memory Card Types		
	LCD Viewfinder		
	Video Recording		
Smartphone	Large LCD Display	Affordable	Cost to Send Images
	Internal SDXC Memory Card	Readily Available	Limited Manual Controls
	Low to Very Good Quality Sensor	Popular with Many Individuals	Limited Apertures
	Single or Limited Range Aperture	Quick and Ease of Use	Limited Shutter Speeds
	On Camera Flash		Limited Focal Length Lens
	Touchscreen		
	Zoom Options		
	Video Recording		
Scanning Back	Extremely High Resolution Sensor	Large Sensor	
	Large Sensor Size	Fast Mechanical Shutter Without a Delay	High Price Range
	RAW Format File	Multiple Lenses Available	Heavier Camera Body and Lenses
	Over 1 Sec./Image Capture	High-Quality Optics	Larger or Dulkier Camera Many Menu Items and Features

(*Continued*)

Camera Type	Top Features	Advantages	Disadvantages
	CF Card or Tethered to Computer	Manual Controls	
	Single Shot Mode	External Flash Controls	
	Medium—Large ISO Range	Flash Sync at Any Speed	
	LCD Display	Manufacturer Shooting Software	
	Computer Camera Operation Software		

selected aperture setting to allow for the proper amount of light to access the imaging sensor with regard to the shutter speed creating a correctly exposed image.

The lens aperture has a secondary effect on the image formation. The aperture also affects the range of focus or depth of field of the image. Depth of field is relevant for a forensic photographer because it can isolate a specific area of interest within an area of evidence with a shallow depth of field, or with a large depth of field the entire scene will maintain focus and items can be recognized in the entire image. More information on the use of apertures to control depth-of-field effects is given in Chapter 2.

Lenses for Forensic Applications

Determining the correct type of lens or lenses to purchase and use begins with addressing where the lens will be used and what type of images will be recorded for the final forensic evaluation. Many times one lens will not be able to cover all aspects of the forensic photographer's need. Obtaining lenses that provide specific outcomes would be the best option.

Normal Lens

The normal lens will provide images with an angle of view closest to that of the human eye and will have nearly no distortion. It is best for overall scene coverage and area coverage. The 50mm lens would be considered a normal lens for a 35mm DSLR camera. Many lenses are zoom lenses that will contain a 50mm focal length. A forensic photographer may consider obtaining a fixed 50mm lens. This will permit the photographer to document the scene without the ability to change the focal length and have consistent angle of view images.

Wide-Angle Lens

As previously mentioned, a wide-angle focal length lens is one that reduces the image's size and covers a larger area within the scene. Typically a lens less than 50mm is considered

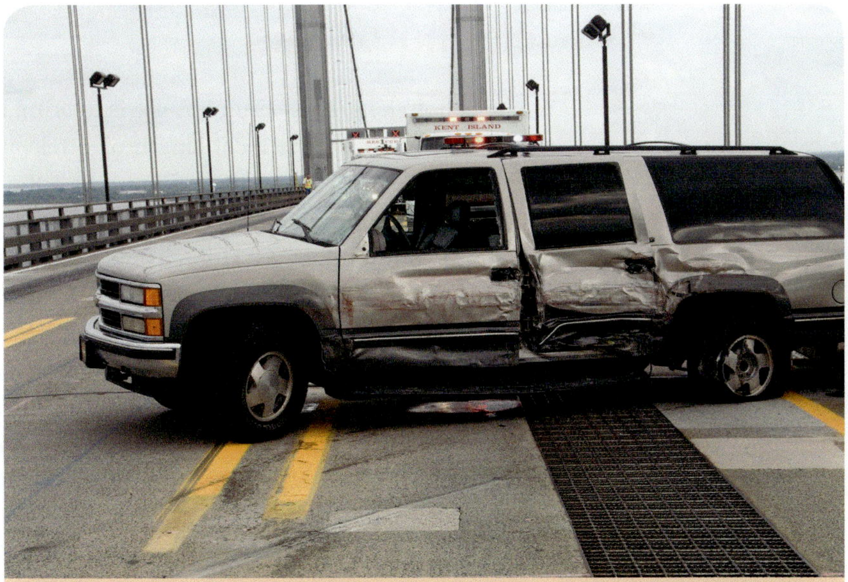

Figure 1.11 Image using a normal focal length lens

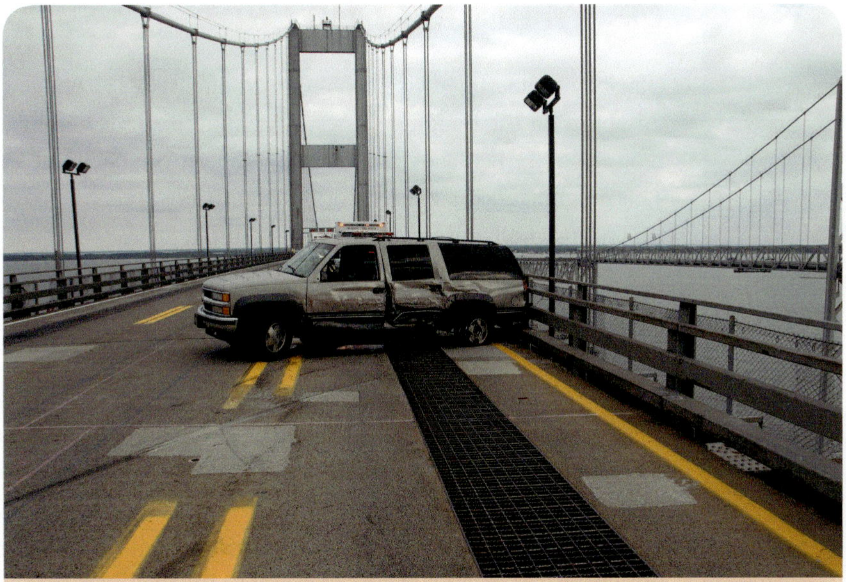

Figure 1.12 Image using a wide angle

a wide-angle lens. A forensic photographer would have available a zoom wide-angle lens that varies from 17mm to 35mm. This allows the photographer the ability to adjust to the evidence requirement and allow for some adjustments with the zoom. This lens is typically used in confined spaces such as small rooms or areas where there is a short or narrow area to capture images. Additionally, it can be used to take overall images of a large area; however, objects within the scene will be rather small and lack detail.

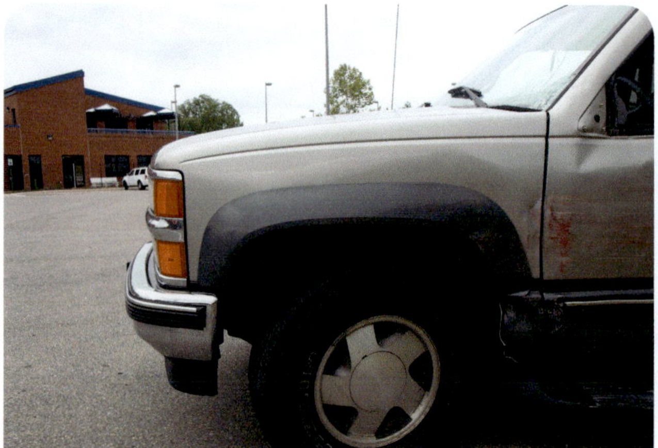

Figure 1.13 Image using a telephoto lens

Telephoto Lens

The telephoto lens' most common use is to bring objects at a distance closer. The focal length of a telephoto or telephoto zoom lens ranges from 70mm to 200mm but can go well beyond as a super telephoto lens into the 400mm or 800mm range. The telephoto lens also creates the effect that objects far apart appear as if they are closer together. As the focal length of the telephoto lens becomes larger, this effect becomes greater. One additional effect created by the telephoto lens is that the depth of field is much more shallow, meaning that the objects not within the primary focal plane are blurry. This may help in some instances to single out a specific object within a scene, but many times the forensic photographer wants to have as much of the scene in focus and as true and accurate to the original scene.

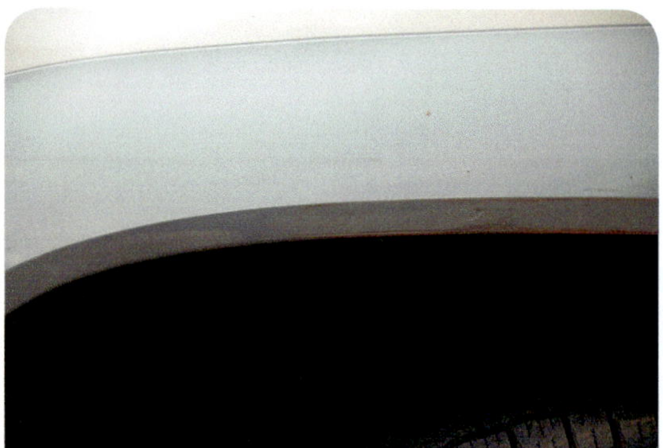

Figure 1.14 Image using a close-up lens

Macro or Close-Up Lens

Officially a macro lens is capable of producing a 1:1 image ratio of an object on the imaging sensor. True macro lenses will have a 1:1 magnification factor or larger annotated on the barrel of the lens. This magnification capability of the macro lens is very helpful in documenting small and specific objects within a scene.

In addition to the magnification factor of the lens, macro lenses are color corrected and also corrected for spherical aberration. This means that the lens will not create a curvature at the edges of the image and be sharp in focus continuously on the focal plane. For example, if one was to take a 1:1 or life-size image of a postage stamp, the stamp will be sharp in focus from edge to edge and not have any curvature or bending of lines at the edges of the stamp or frame of the image. One of the most important components to consider when purchasing or using a macro lens is that the lens quality is superior and will compose an excellent image with highly visible details.

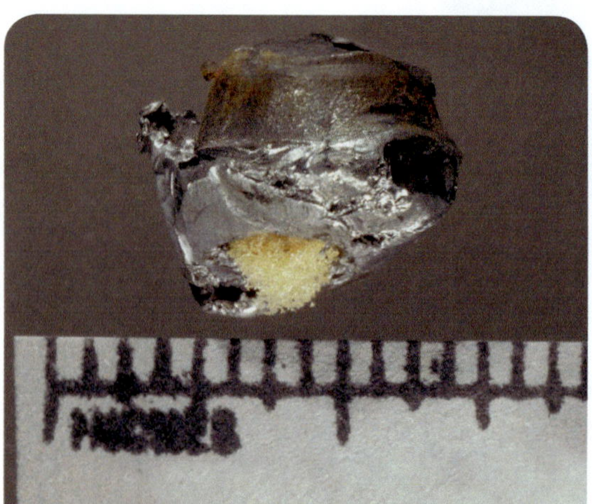

Figure 1.15 Image using a macro lens

A macro or close-up lens is available with different focal lengths. The shorter focal length lens enables the photographer to get closer to the subject to obtain a 1:1 or higher image. This may be useful in close quarters or tight spaces where there is very little room to maneuver. Macro lenses with longer focal lengths permit the photographer to capture 1:1 or higher images at a further distance from the subject. This may be useful in situations when documenting evidence on a live subject or human patient. It allows the photographer to maintain a distance from the subject so the subject's "zone of comfort" is not encroached upon. The ability to keep a slightly farther working distance from a patient will occasionally relax the patient to the extent that you as the photographer can gain the trust of the patient and have more time to capture additional images by using more photographic techniques to enhance images.

The Tripod

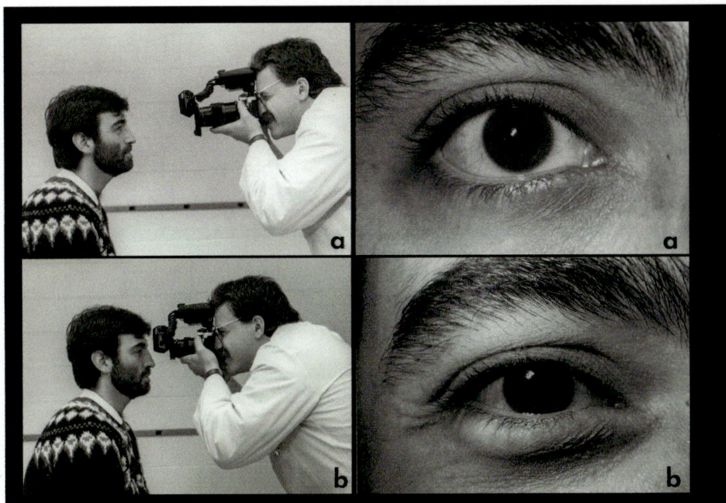

Figure 1.16 Image comparing the focal length of two lenses showing the difference between a shorter focal length lens and longer focal length lens comfort distance to patients

The tripod's primary use is to stabilize and support your camera for longer periods of time. A tripod will reduce or eliminate camera vibration and shake. They are very useful when longer exposure times are required such as when taking images in low light conditions. Situations occur during evidence documentation during poor light conditions such as in an evening, nighttime, dark overcast or rainy day, and painting with light, which will require a longer exposure time with a smaller aperture to maintain a large depth of field and greater sharpness especially when using low ISO settings to maximize the quality of an image.

Tripods allow the photographer the ability to keep the camera in a single location while preparing and framing elements of the scene. Using this method an image can be taken and reviewed without moving the camera framing and the scene can be readjusted to document specific evidence. This is particularly helpful when painting with light. The method of how to paint with light will be explained in Chapter 4, but essentially it is adding light to a scene during a long exposure to illuminate the entire scene obtaining a good exposure.

Close-up and macro photography require positioning the camera system at a location that will eliminate exterior distractions from the image detail. The tripod is very useful to keep the camera in a single stable location and maintain the exact distance to keep image magnification. It also allows the photographer to get close enough to the subject and take detailed images without camera shake.

Tripods are made out of various materials and have a wide price range. Materials consist of aluminum, carbon fiber, and then the classic wood, which is the best material for vibration reduction. Metal tripods are reasonable in price and very strong, but can be rather heavy. Some metals like titanium, magnesium, and aluminum will produce a lighter tripod. Tripods composed of carbon fiber provide high strength and less weight; however, the carbon fiber process is expensive and thus at a higher cost. A side effect of carbon fiber is that during extremely cold conditions the material has a tendency to shatter. Tripods can also be made up of a combination of materials that will provide the characteristics of all materials used.

The weight of a tripod can vary from extremely light carbon fiber to heavy metal or wood. Lightweight tripods are very convenient for traveling and transporting to remote locations. But they do have their drawbacks because they provide less stability to your camera system or items that it would hold. Heavier tripods are more stable and sturdy, eliminating vibration to provide a sharp image. A tripod needs to withstand nature's elements such as rain, snow, wind, and hazards that would bump and possibly move the tripod out of its original setup. When setting up your tripod, you must have your camera system evenly balanced. Make sure the tripod is not leaning to one direction or once the camera system is placed into the head, the additional weight may cause it to tilt and fall in that direction. Also make sure all the leg clamps and locking mechanisms are tight to keep the tripod from shifting while in use.

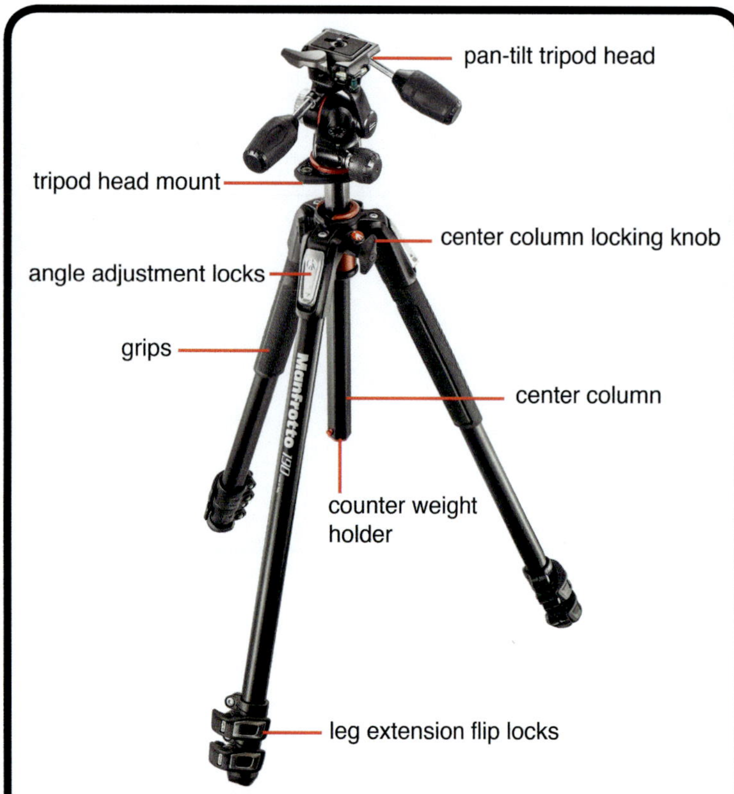

Figure 1.17 Diagram describing the parts of a tripod

The tripod can also be used for additional photographic accessories. Heavy camera gear, a telephoto lens, external flash units, reflectors, diffusers, and other items can be mounted on a tripod. Again, this is very useful when you are working alone in a difficult environment.

There are multiple variations of tripods and most are based on their intended use. They consist of small portable pocket or tabletop-sized, medium duty for small- or medium-format cameras, and heavy duty that would be used with a medium- or large-format camera system in primarily a studio or controlled setting.

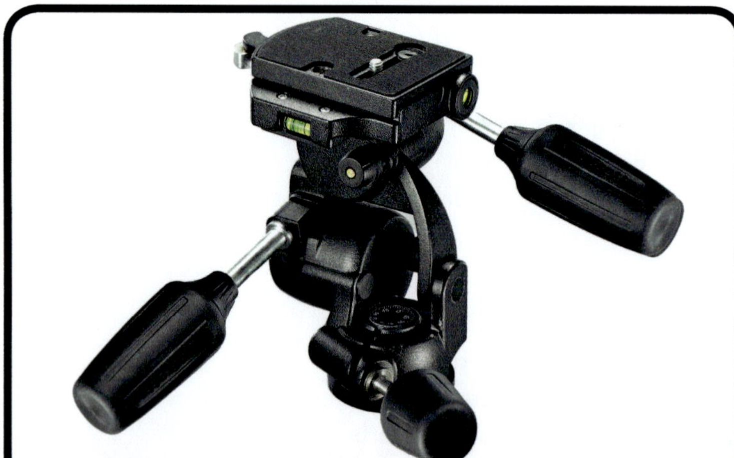

Figure 1.18 Image of a pan- and tilt-style tripod head

Tripod Head

The tripod head is a critical component of the tripod system. It is attached directly to the tripod and firmly holds the camera system to the tripod. The tripod head has controls that permit the photographer to move the camera in various directions to set up the camera and frame the image scene. Tripod heads are available in various sizes and you must make sure that it is rated correctly for the camera system you are using. Refer to the manufacturer's specifications to correctly match the tripod head to your equipment.

The most common types of tripod heads are the pan-tilt head, ball head, and gimbal head. The pan-tilt head will contain a handle that controls horizontal, side-to-side movement and a handle to control vertical, up-and-down movement. Occasionally a single handle can control both vertical and horizontal movement of the tripod head. The pan-tilt tripod head is the most common type of tripod head available.

The ball head has one control handle that will loosen or tighten the grip on the ball (sphere) of the tripod to move vertically, horizontally, and rotate the camera system very smoothly. This tripod head is very fluid and can be moved in multiple rotating directions simultaneously. One disadvantage is that it is difficult to move this tripod in a straight horizontal or vertical direction to take multiple images for a panoramic scene.

A gimbal tripod head is a specialized head for long and heavy 300mm+ lenses. A gimbal head places the weight of the camera and lens system below their pivot point where gravity pulls the setup into a level position. The best comparison is to a see-saw. The camera system is equally balanced so as the photographer applies pressure, the camera and lens smoothly moves in the correct direction with little effort. This is best suited for fast-action photography such as in nature or at sporting events. The gimbal head is very easy to use and move in any direction. Additionally, it does not require tightening of the head each time the camera system is moved.

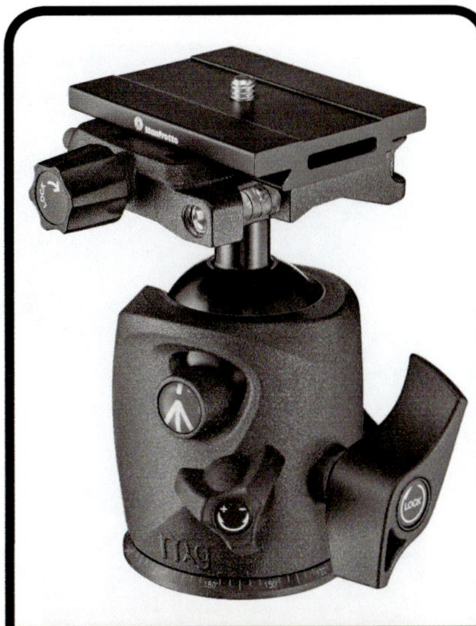

Figure 1.19 Image of a ball-style tripod head

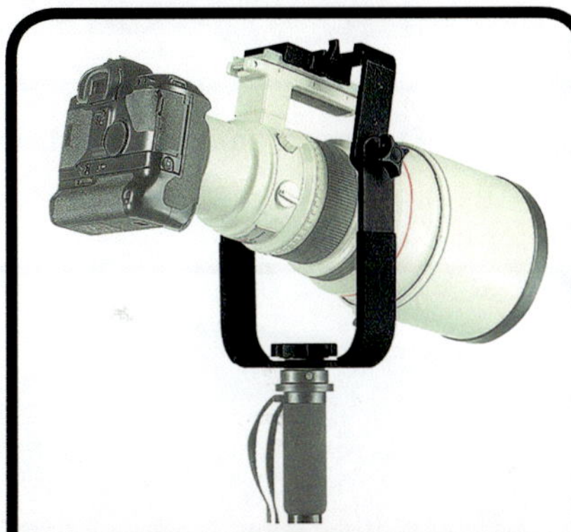

Figure 1.20 Image of a gimbal-style tripod head

External Flash Unit

The on-camera flash is a necessary item for any forensic photographer to have in their possession and available for just about any situation. Please note, we are not talking about the small pop-up flash that comes with and is attached to the DSLR. The on-camera flash is an additional flash unit that is placed on the hot shoe or used wirelessly when the DSLR trigger is activated to take an image. The flash is able to provide supplemental light to darker areas to be able to document details of evidence, balance exposures as a fill flash during high contrast daylight conditions, or stopping motion of fast moving objects. The ability to add light to specific areas is an effective way to bring out details of evidence in an image.

The power of the flash unit is provided as a guide number. The guide number is a standardized number that represents how powerful the flash output is. The higher the guide number, the more powerful the flash unit.

An on-camera flash many times is used directly on the camera itself; however, this may not be the most effective method to use this type of flash. There are accessories available to be able to use these flash units "off-camera." This gives the photographer more versatility of the flash unit and lights the subject at various angles or in different locations for more lighting options. Chapter 4 provides a greater description of lighting options and how the process effects the subject.

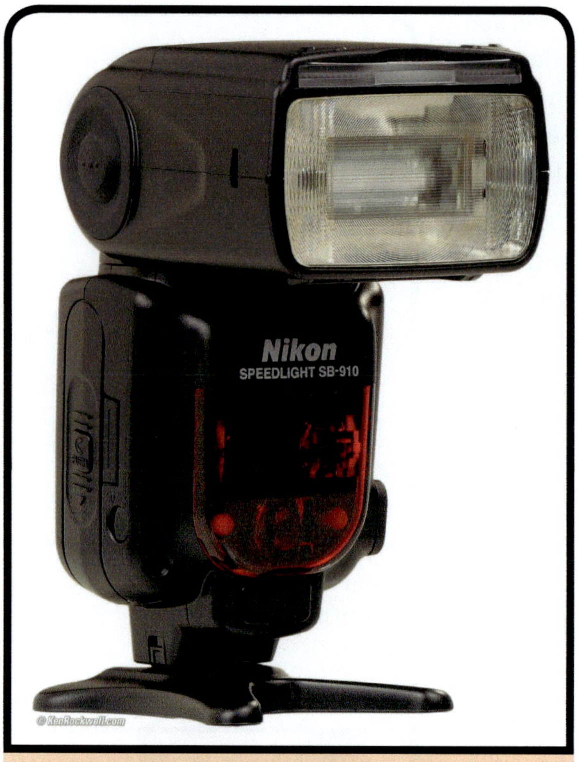

Figure 1.21 Image of an external flash unit

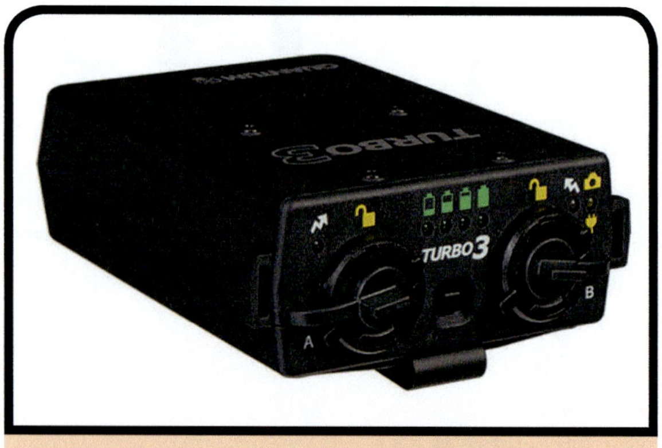

Figure 1.22 Image of a quantum external battery pack

The flash unit can be used "off-camera" through a wired connection to the hot shoe of the camera and flash unit. This sync cord, the wired connection, must be compatible to both the camera and flash unit. A bracket that attaches to the camera body will move the flash unit off the main camera hot shoe. This gives the photographer more versatility of the flash angle, off to the side, or above as well, while not having to handhold the flash unit.

A newer method for flash units is by way of wireless technology. Using a transmitter and receiver for a radio frequency, infrared, or optical method would trigger the flash unit. The wireless system permits the photographer to use more than a single flash unit and locate them at variety of locations and farther distances from the camera. A single master flash can control individual or multiple flash units by the photographer. They can adjust each individual flash unit without leaving the camera system by using the master flash groupings and numbering of individual flash units. This is very useful in a large scene where multiple flash units are spread out over a vast area. After an image is taken and reviewed, individual flash units can be adjusted by the master flash without the need of the photographer to walk through the scene adjusting the individual flash units.

Auxiliary Battery Units

External camera flash units are usually powered by a group of AA batteries. Many photographers purchase rechargeable batteries so they have a continuous supply available to always have power for the flash activation. The internal batteries are easily changed during an assignment, but recharging stations or multiple packages of new batteries are needed to fulfill an entire assignment. The internal batteries and flash units are not as powerful as an external battery unit. They do not recycle the flash unit quickly, the time it takes to power the flash unit back to full power. An external auxiliary power unit that attaches to the flash unit by a dedicated power cable will provide a continuous flow of power and will recycle the flash unit quickly for continuous shooting. The auxiliary power units are usually reasonably small and will fit into a pocket or clip to a belt or strap. Additionally, the auxiliary power packs when fully charged can last a long period of time, sometimes for an entire assignment or an entire day of photography.

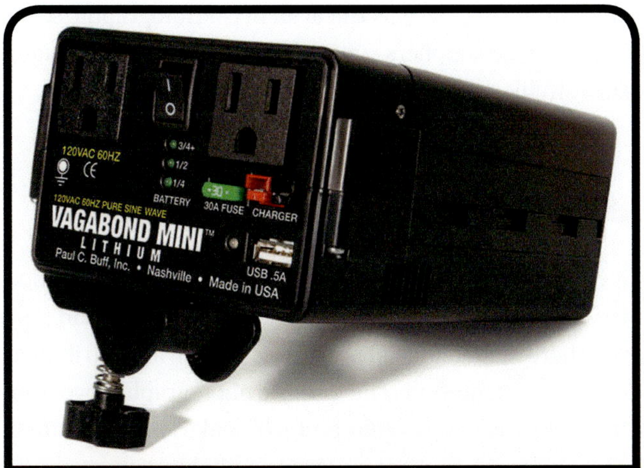

Figure 1.23 Image of a vagabond external battery pack

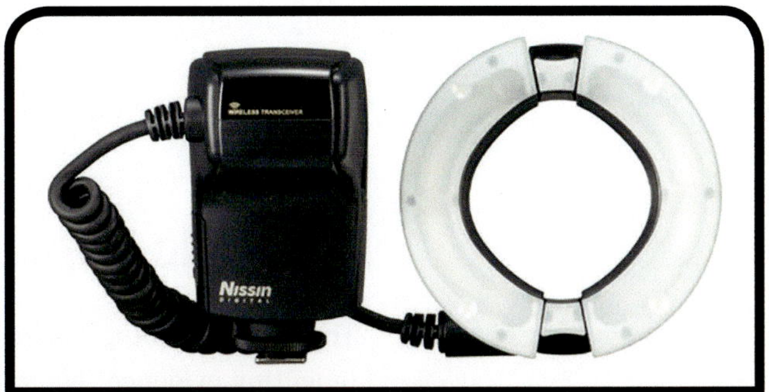

Figure 1.24 Image of a ring-light flash unit

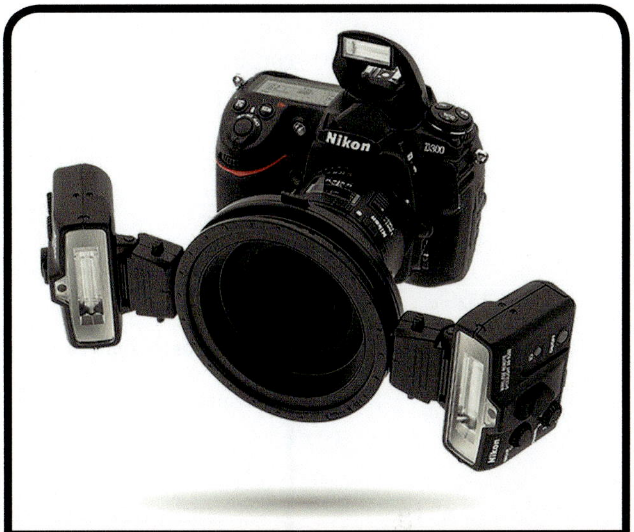

Figure 1.25 Image of a wireless twin-light flash unit system

Ring-Light and Macro Lighting

A specific on-camera flash unit is called a ring-light. The ring light is usually a series of small lights in a circular or rectangular pattern that are attached directly at the front side of the lens. This provides a well-suited shadowless light on the axis of the lens. The use of a ring-light is perfect for close-up and macro photographic photography. Since the ring-light flash unit is directly at the face of the lens and on its axis, it illuminates the object directly in front of the lens and eliminates any shadows that would have been caused by the camera or on-camera flash unit. A similar type of lens flash unit is a twin light system. This system has two small light units placed on a circular ring. The small light units are able to rotate around the lens and can be tilted to provide a direction to the light emitted from the small light flash. This can give different lighting styles and offer dimension to the object.

Scales

Scales are necessary when documenting evidence that will be used in a comparison, such as footwear and other types of impression, fingerprints, and blood spatter. A scale may also be necessary when the photograph is used to show the location of an item relative to something else, such as the distance of a weapon to a victim. The appropriate scale should be approximately the same size as the evidence

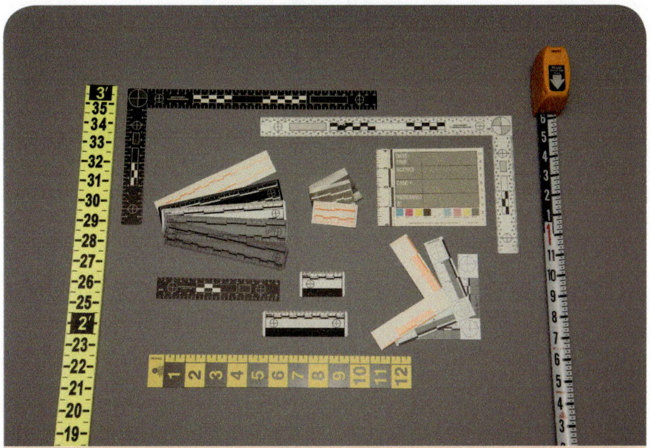

Figure 1.26 Scales are available in various shapes and sizes to suit the subject being photographed

being documented, and on the same plane or surface as the evidence. Photographic scales may be purchased from many of the forensic suppliers such as Safariland (formerly Lightning Powder), Arrowhead Forensics, Sirchie, Evidenet, and Lynn Peavy.

Forensic Photographic Accessories

The forensic photographer will have a primary set of gear that will be available when documenting evidence. The main pieces of equipment such as the camera, lenses, and flash units are always available; however, there are additional accessories that will contribute to the success of photographic evidence documentation. The forensic photographer over time will find that they will use certain accessories more often and will make sure those items are available. Table 1.2 is a list of accessories that many forensic photographers should consider when obtaining and developing a forensic photography equipment kit. Many are useful both in the lab and on location so it is important to purchase equipment that can handle various conditions in the laboratory or out in the field during a variety of weather conditions.

Table 1.2 Table of recommended photographic accessories

Camera (35mm or Medium Format)	High-quality camera to create detailed images of evidence
Normal Lens	Provides images with an angle of view that is the closest representative to the human eye and will have nearly no distortion. It is best for overall scene coverage and area coverage. The 50mm lens would be considered a normal lens for a 35mm DSLR camera
Wide Angle Lens	17–35mm, this lens is typically is used in confined spaces such as small rooms or areas where there is a short or narrow area to capture images. Additionally it can be used to take overall images of a large area; however, objects within the scene will be rather small and lack detail
Telephoto Lens	70–200mm, the telephoto lens's most common use is to make objects at a distance look closer
Macro or Close–Up Lens	1:1 magnification or larger capability of the macro lens is very helpful in documenting small and specific objects within a scene
Esternal Flash	An on or off camera flash unit that will supply additional light to the scene. Can be triggered with a hot shoe, wireless or wired
Memory Cards	Additional memory cards. Might need more than one type depending on if you have more than one camera system and the type of memory card they require
Owners' Manuals	Camera, flash, and any electronic items. Electronic items have many features available to the forensic photographer and the manual is an easy way to quickly and successfully configure the system to accurately document evidence

(Continued)

Camera (35mm or Medium Format)	**High-quality camera to create detailed images of evidence**
Tripod	Used to reduce camera shake and steady camera during long exposures. Great to use during capturing images with available light, painting with light close-up and macro photography
Shutter Release	Used to activate the camera and reduce camera shake. Can be a wired or wireless camera shutter/trigger release
Wireless Remote	Control flash units without being tethered by a sync cord
Filters	Polarizing, Red 82b, Orange, Yellow, Blue
Additional Batteries	Rechargeable batteries for all equipment that is battery powered: camera, electronic flash, lights, etc.
Marking Devices	Chalk, markers, pens, pencils
Measuring Devices	Rulers, tape measures, and scales to determine size and location of evidence
Gray Card	18% gray card to assist with exposures and color calibration
Notebook and Index Cards	Used to keep notes and sketches when documenting evidence and recording images
Flashlight	Illuminate areas of the scene and can be a safety accessory if necessary
Tool Kit	A small variety of screwdrivers and accessories to repair equipment
Camera and Lens Cleaning Kit	Lens cleaner, cloth, brush, and blower
Clamps	Clamps to hold items or keep items out of the way of evidence without destroying the area. Construction clamps or clothespins
Plastic Bags	A variety of ziploc or non-ziploc plastic bags to keep items contained or out of the weather conditions

Chapter 2 Basic Photography Principles

It is important to have a basic understanding of the principles of photography because they will have an effect of image formation.

Light

The essence of photography is all about light and this is the primary ingredient for image documentation. Photography is the act of creating images on an imaging sensor by capturing the reflected light off an object or scene. Image capture includes both visible and invisible spectrums. Using light effectively is one of the most essential requirements to sufficiently document details within a scene or object as a recorded image. This understanding of light behavior and how to manage or alter light in a way to highlight evidence details is an asset of a forensic photographer.

The production of light from a source will have specific characteristics. It will contain a physical size, brightness, direction, and a color output (color temperature). All of these characteristics will determine the appearance of the object as the captured image. The modification of light by objects within the scene produces the contract to be captured on the imaging sensor. Light is modified in a way where it is reflected, transmitted, or absorbed in various degrees from the scene. The true reflected light captured is unique for that specific time. The light captured will contain the forensic details and specific information of the evidence.

Light will originate from a point or diffuse source, which affects the characteristics of the light. The point light source is considered a direct lighting style. Lighting styles are covered in more detail in Chapter 4. The diffuse light source is non-directional and usually travels through a semi-opaque material, for example clouds, or reflected off a surface such as a wall or ceiling.

A light also is defined by its brightness and size. Sometimes the brightness or size is adjustable and this is a great advantage to the forensic photographer. Artificial lights, such as an electronic flash unit, will have an adjustment to regulate the quantity of output. Additionally, artificial lights will have adaptors that will alter the size or nature of the light being emitted from the source. Some of these are soft boxes, snoots, umbrellas, reflectors, grids, barn doors, and gels (color, diffusion, or neutral density).

Exposure

Exposure is the total amount of light that hits the sensor of a camera. It is controlled by the amount of light entering the camera and the duration or how long the light hits the sensor. Exposure is ultimately responsible for the formation of the image. Essentially, light and its effect on exposure creates the picture. Too much exposure (light) and the picture will be too bright, washed out, or overexposed, and conversely too little exposure (light) and the picture will be dark or underexposed. There are several ways to control exposure in the camera; each of those controls besides allowing more or less light to hit the sensor also has its own unique effect on the image. However, before evaluating exposure, it is important to know how the camera determines what the correct exposure is.

Light Metering

Inside most cameras is a device called the light meter. The light meter is responsible for reading the amount of light entering the camera and determining, or making suggestions for what settings should be used for that exposure situation. While modern light meters do a good job of determining exposure, they do not know whether or not the scene they are pointing at is inherently light or dark or something different.

Light meters assume the scene is neutral grey, or between dark and light. Therefore sometimes, especially with scenes that should appear light or dark, the meter in the camera may not provide the optimal exposure. For example, if photographing a snowy scene, perhaps a mountain or snow-covered forest, the meter inside the camera doesn't know that the subject is nearly white (snow), and that the resulting image should probably be bright and not grey. Since the light meter assumes grey, this snowy scene may appear darker in the image than was in reality of the scene. The light meter underexposed the image.

This may not be a bad thing for forensic photography, since overexposing light subjects can lead to loss of image detail, and the purpose of forensic photography is preserving that detail. However, it's important to know how your camera interprets the scene and the subject of the photograph. Knowing this, it is possible to correct the exposure needed to capture details of the evidence.

There are two types of light meters: a reflected light meter and an incident light meter. The reflected light meter reads light that is reflected off the subject. A camera light meter uses a reflected light meter to determine the average exposure for the scene interpreted as 18% gray. The incident light meter reads light falling onto the subject and scene. Some light meters are portable and are called handheld light meters since they are not built into cameras, but rather are a separate device entirely. Independent handheld light meters are built to measure specific methods or can measure all methods. Some manufacturers that measure all the lighting methods include Sekonic®, Gossen®, Kenko®, Voitlander®, and others.

Light meters provide results based on three factors or calculations: ISO, shutter speed, and f-stop or aperture. Many times the results given by the meter will be sufficient for picture taking; however, there will be some instances where changing the values may be required dependent upon the subject and details needed to be captured. Adjusting the exposure variables is discussed in detail further on in this chapter.

For the purposes of forensic photography, it's probably not necessary to use more than the meter beyond the one inside the camera, especially using digital photography, where the results of the exposure are immediately viewable. It may be a good idea to have an external handheld light meter available and knowledge of how to use it in a working environment such as within a studio setting or on location. Understanding the principles behind how a handheld light meter works and the ability to adjust the variables will give the forensic photographer the capability to enhance the way evidence is photographed.

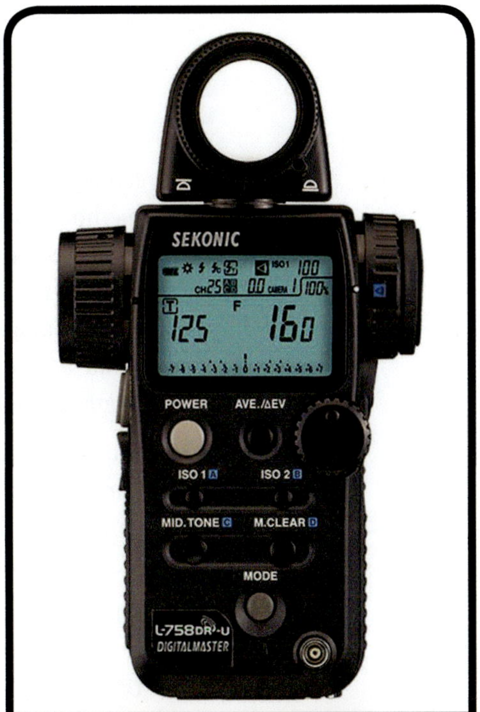

Figure 2.1 Image of a handheld light meter

Shutter Speed

The shutter controls the duration of the exposure. The shutter is usually built inside the camera; however, some cameras have a mechanical shutter contained in the lens, or can be an electronic shutter.

Two types of the mechanical shutters are the leaf shutter and the focal-plane shutter. The leaf shutter is similar to the aperture with metal blades arranged in a circular fashion that completely close and open for the selected period of time chosen by the shutter speed, whereas the aperture maintains a consistent opening for light to travel through for the specified amount of time and will not close down completely.

Focal-plane shutters are the primary shutter used in DSLR cameras. The name focal-plane shutter comes because this type of shutter is situated immediately in front of the focal plane or imaging sensor of the camera. The most common type of focal-plane shutter is the two-curtain type where two fabric or metal curtains travel either horizontally or vertically across the camera's imaging sensor. The first curtain opens after the appropriate delay set by the shutter speed, while the second curtain follows the same path and closes behind it. In most cases these curtains will travel at the same speed but, as previously explained, the gap or delay in the second curtain will be dependent upon the shutter-speed setting. This determines the duration of light used to create the exposure on the imaging sensor. The focal-plane design permits the ability to obtain accurate high shutter speeds, up to 1/8000 second.

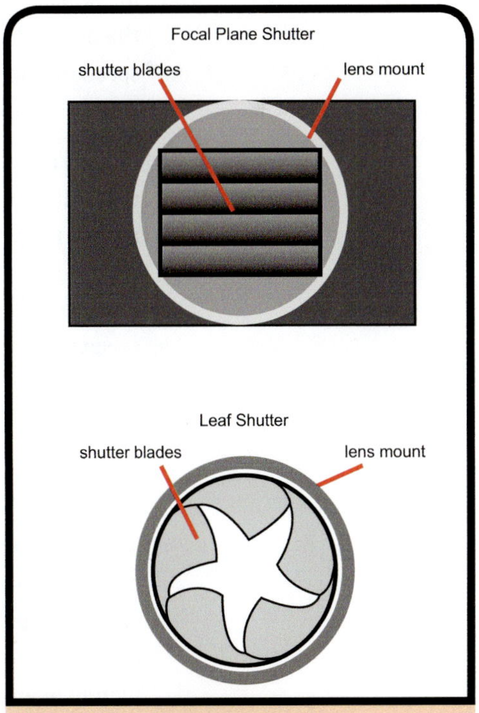

Graphic 2.1 Graphic of camera focal plane and leaf shutter

The electronic shutter is a process where the camera powers the digital sensor on for a selected amount of time to capture the image and then turns off after the exposure process is complete. Because there is no mechanical function, electronic shutter speeds can be extremely fast.

A global shutter turns the entire sensor on and off at once, while a rolling shutter activates one row of pixels at a time across its width.

There are two types of electronic sensors commonly found in digital cameras and they are based upon the sensor, CMOS (complementary metal-oxide-semiconductor), or CCD (charge coupled device). The design of the sensor determines what type of electronic sensor method is performed. CMOS sensors read pixel information from the top left of the sensor to the bottom right and, because of this process, images of objects that are moving quickly have a "warped or jello" artifact. This is considered a rolling shutter and may create poor quality images. Similar to a film camera, CCD sensors record images by capturing the entire frame at one time. A few camera systems contain both a mechanical shutter and an electronic shutter, therefore they are called hybrid shutters.

A benefit of the electronic shutter is its ability to capture images silently. The lack of moving parts within the camera created by the mechanical shutter permits quiet exposures. This can be very useful in situations when documenting in a surveillance situation or in a wildlife setting where you do not want to distract from the scene and situation.

Shutter speeds vary greatly from a fraction of a second and up to minutes for the darkest of subjects. The longer the shutter remains open, the more light hits the sensor and the greater the exposure. The difference between shutter speeds is usually multiples of two, double or half the exposure. Doubling or halving the light and exposure is called a full stop.

Shutter-speed selection also affects the camera's ability to stop or freeze motion. A fast moving subject will appear blurry if the shutter is open too long during the exposure. The faster the object, the faster the shutter will need to be. A fast moving car would require a shutter speed of approximately 1/1000 seconds. People biking, running, or walking would require slower speeds of 1/500, 1/250, or 1/125 respectively.

Motion may also be an issue when the subject is still, if the photographer is holding the camera. If the shutter speed is slow enough, longer than 1/60th of a second usually, the photographer may not be steady enough to prevent camera shake from causing blur in the image. A good rule of thumb is to use a shutter speed faster than one over the focal length of the lens for handheld photography. For example if you are shooting with a 60 lens, the slowest shutter speed you should use is 1/60th of a second. Lenses with longer focal lengths will magnify the motion, therefore faster shutter speeds are necessary.

Aperture

The opening in the lens that controls the light entering the camera is called the aperture. The aperture is controlled by an iris, which is composed of several blades that increase and decrease the diameter of the opening to control the light. Apertures are located in the camera's lens and control the amount of light transmitted by the lens that will enter the camera used to expose on the imaging sensor. In most cases, the lens aperture stays completely open until the shutter is depressed. This permits more light to enter the camera to make it easier to view, compose, and focus on the scene and objects. When the shutter is activated, the aperture blades close down to the selected aperture setting, with the appropriate shutter speed, so a proper exposure is achieved. Automatic lenses will perform in

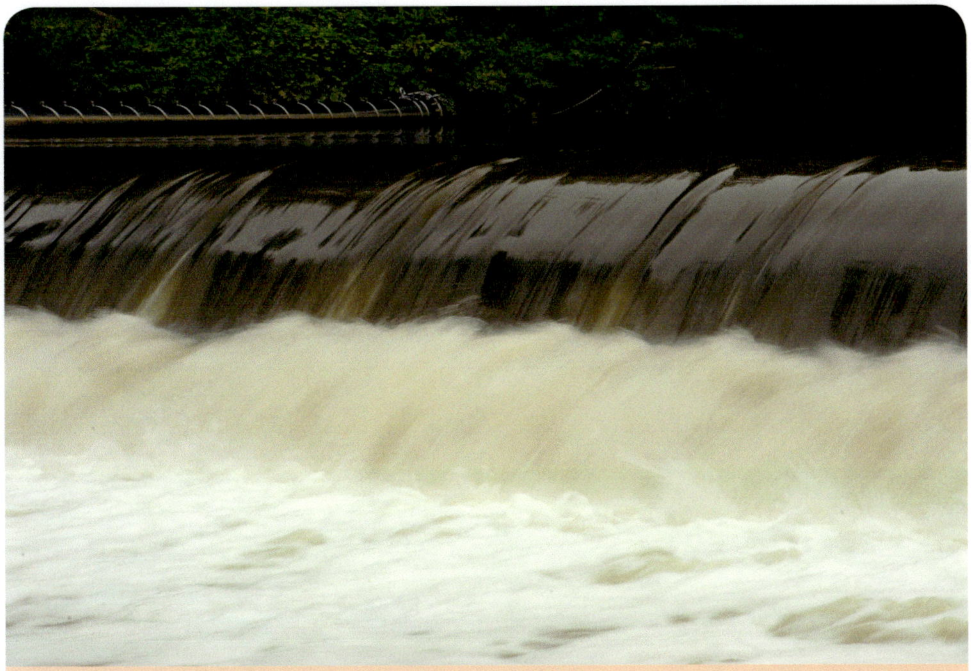

Figure 2.2 Image of slow shutter speed motion

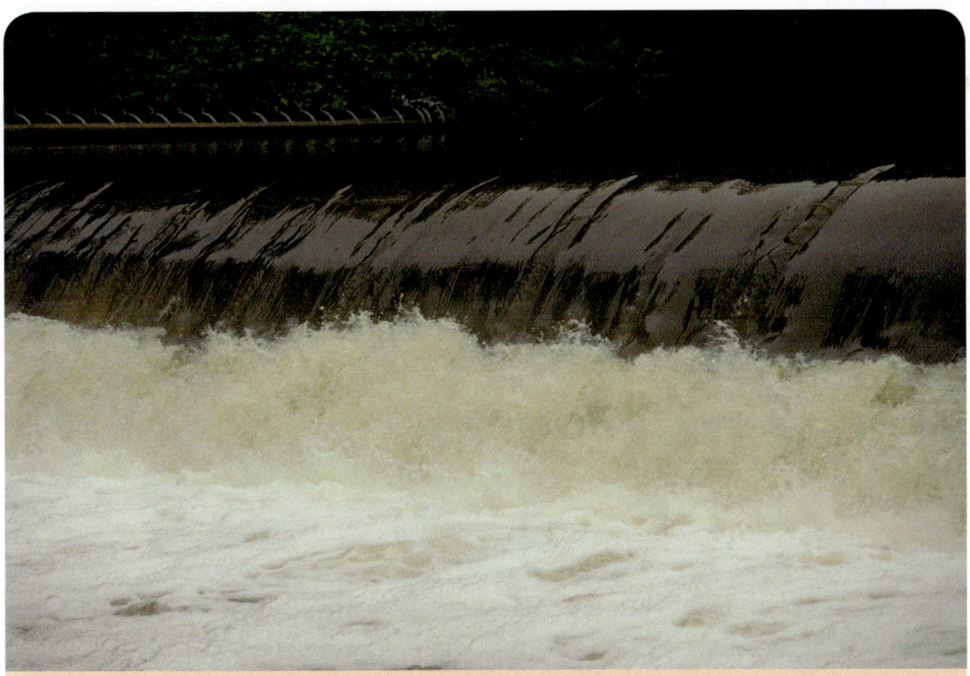

Figure 2.3 Image of medium shutter speed motion

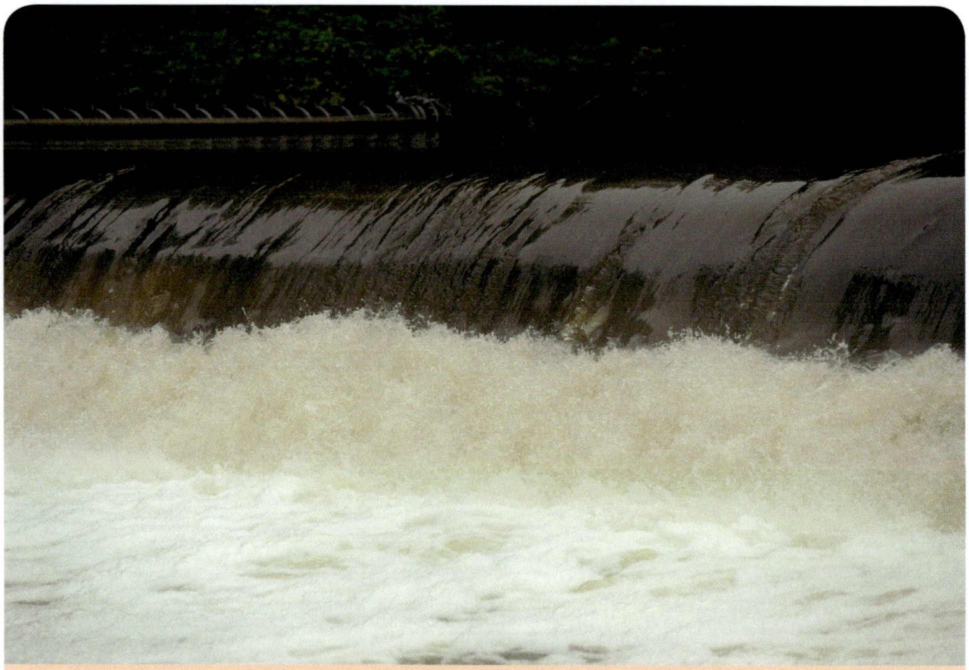

Figure 2.4 Image of fast shutter speed stop motion

this manner; however, manual lenses will close the aperture opening when the lens aperture is selected by the photographer prior to taking the image.

The aperture is specified by a number called the f-stop (also referred to as the f-number, or just f), which is the ratio of the focal length of the lens to the aperture diameter. Since they are determined by that ratio, f-stops make it a little more complicated to determine the difference between one stop of light. For example, the following f-stops are each one stop apart, double or half the amount of light depending upon the direction (*f*/2.0, *f*/2.8, *f*/4.0, *f*/5.6, *f*/8.0, *f*/11, *f*/16, *f*/22). The larger numbers allow less light to pass through the lens.

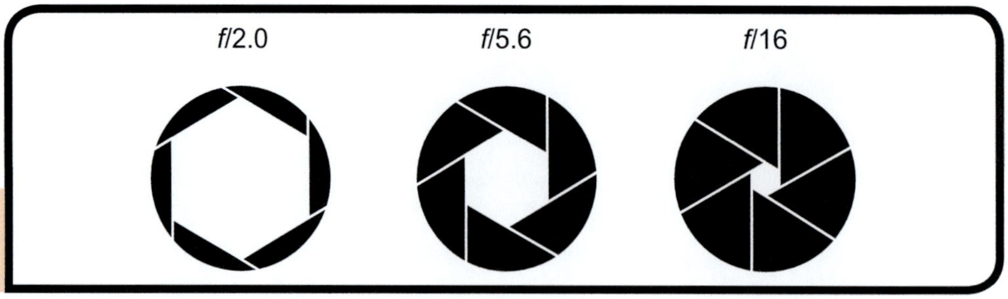

Graphic 2.2 Graphic of lens aperture

The aperture also controls depth of field of an image. Depth of field is the distance between the nearest and farthest objects in the scene that will appear in focus. Depth of field increases as the aperture is decreased, or the f-stop is increased (larger number). Unfortunately, as the aperture is decreased so is the amount of light entering the camera. A smaller aperture means a larger f-stop, greater depth of field but less light entering the lens.

The shutter and aperture work in combination to control the amount of light that exposes or reaches the sensor in a camera. As previously mentioned the light meter inside the camera will suggest settings for both of these. It is possible to take photographs at different settings, while still getting the same amount of exposure. This is called a reciprocal exposure. Reciprocal exposures are a combination of f-stops and shutter speeds that will create the same exposure when metered. In order to do this the shutter speed and aperture must be changed together to retain the same exposure. If a change to one setting causes a decrease in exposure, the other must be changed to increase the exposure the same amount. For example if the light meter's reading is 1/60th of a second at *f*/8.0 and the photographer wants to shoot at *f*/11, there should be a decrease of 1 stop (half the amount of light). The shutter speed's exposure must be increased by 1 stop to compensate for the loss of light. The resulting shutter speed should be 1/30th second since it's twice the length of 1/60th second. This is possible using certain exposure mode settings on most cameras.

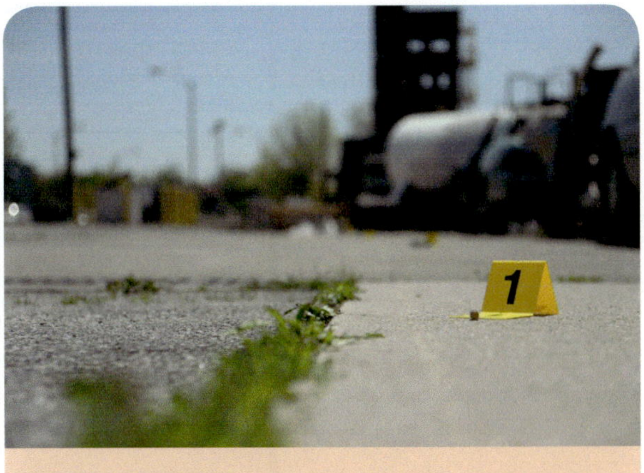

Figure 2.5 Image demonstrating shallow depth of field

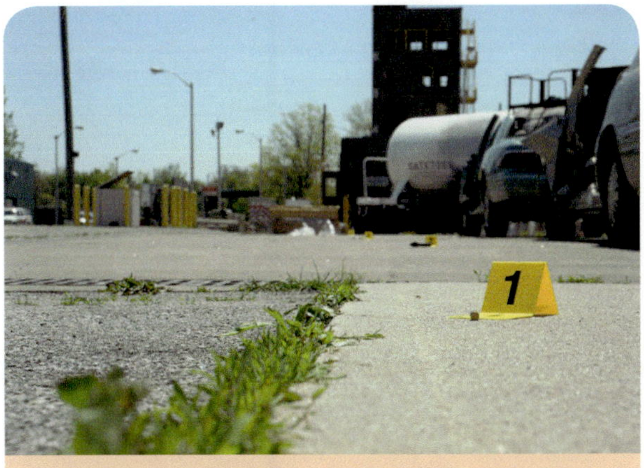

Figure 2.6 Image demonstrating medium depth of field

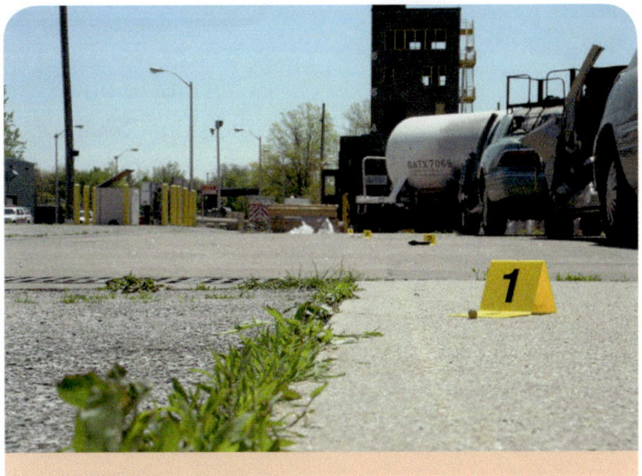

Figure 2.7 Image demonstrating large depth of field

Exposure Compensation or Exposure Value (EV)

Exposure compensation on cameras adjusts the camera's automatic exposure setting as metered by the camera. The exposure compensation feature will increase or decrease the actual exposure of the final image. If you choose an exposure value in the positive range, EV +1, +2, etc., the camera will compensate the metered scene and add more light to the imaging sensor and "brighten" the image. If an exposure value in the negative range is selected, EV −1, −2, etc., the camera will compensate the metered scene and decrease the amount of light allowed onto the imaging sensor during the exposure.

The exposure value (EV) settings are only usable when using automatic camera modes such as program, aperture, or shutter priority, which are described next. The camera system will adjust the shutter speed, lens aperture setting, and ISO settings or a combination to achieve the selected exposure value selected by the photographer.

Exposure Bracketing

Bracketing is a method of taking multiple images of a scene or object using different exposures ranging from overexposed

Table 2.1 Table of common *f*-stop numbers and shutter speeds

f-stop numbers	Shutter Speeds	
f/1.4	30 seconds	Very Slow Shutter Speed. Blurred objects in motion. Requires the use of a tripod
f/2.8	15 seconds	
f/4	8 seconds	
f/5.6	4 seconds	
f/8	2 seconds	
f/11		
f/16	1 seconed	Slow Shutter Speeds. Slightly blurred objects in motion. Requires the use of a tripod
f/22	1/2 second	
f/32	1/4 second	
	1/8 second	
	1/15 second	
	1/30 second	Medium-Fast Shutter Speed. Stops average speed motion. Able to handhold the camera
	1/60 second	
	1/125 second	
	1/250 second	
	1/500 second	Fast-Very Fast Shutter Speeds. Stops motion at fast speeds. Handhold for stopping motion
	1/1000 second	
	1/2000 second	
	1/4000 second	
	1/8000 second	

to normal to underexposed. This process is done with difficult subject matter or lighting conditions, because at times the internal camera light meter may be fooled or unable to determine an accurate normal exposure. Exposure bracketing is usually completed in increments of 1/3 exposure values. A routine bracketing of five images will contain exposures consisting of –2/3, –1/3, normal, +1/3 and +2/3 exposures.

Newer DSLR cameras have a bracketing feature that will automatically create the bracketed exposures based upon the criteria set by the photographer. It could be a series of three to five or more images and the exposure variation could be changed from 1/3 to ½ or others dependent upon the manufacturer.

A forensic photographer would utilize bracketing at a difficult scene or lighted subject because the camera might have been fooled by the lighting situation and calculated a

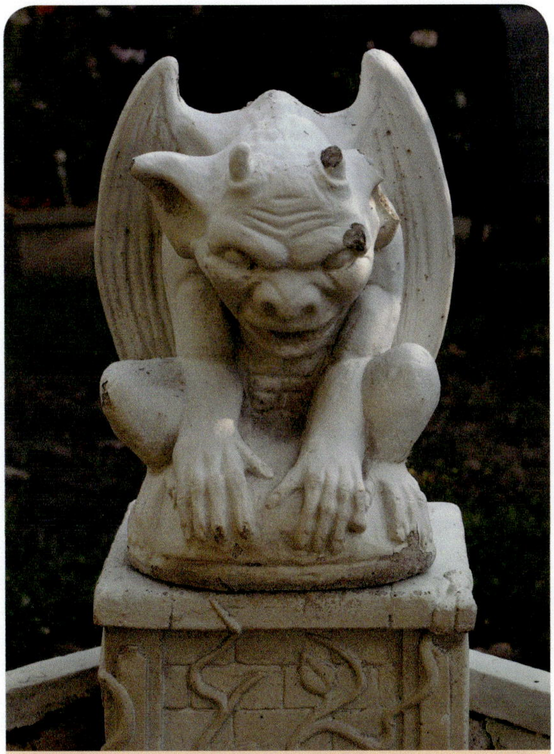

Figure 2.8 Image demonstrating N-1 EV

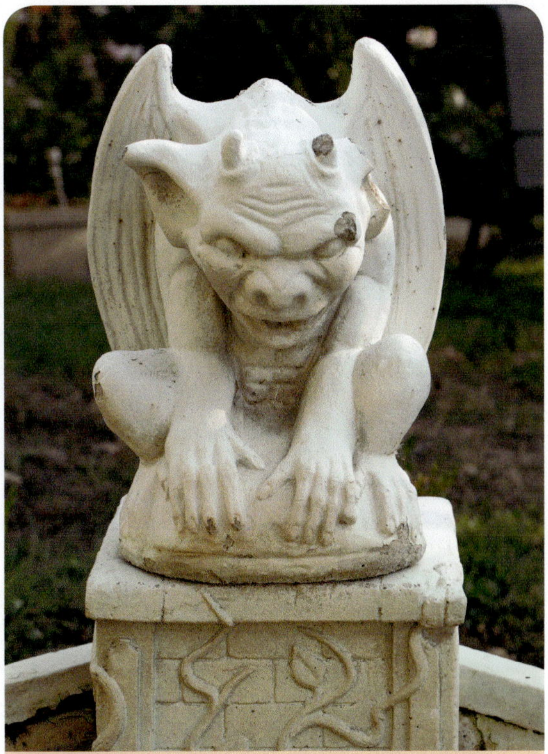

Figure 2.9 Image demonstrating normal EV

normal image exposure that in reality is either underexposed (too dark) or overexposed (too bright). In this situation the normal exposure would not accurately document evidence details within the object. By bracketing and taking multiple images, various exposure differences where evidence is correctly documented for further investigation can be effectively achieved.

For example, when there is a situation where there is a lot of light or the subject is bright or white, such as a beach or snow landscape, the camera meter will meter the scene as an 18% gray and underexpose the scene. The camera will close the aperture or use a faster shutter speed to create the "normal" exposure. The result will be that the evidence within the scene could be underexposed. Bracketing exposures of the scene by taking extra images would properly expose the variety of objects within the scene.

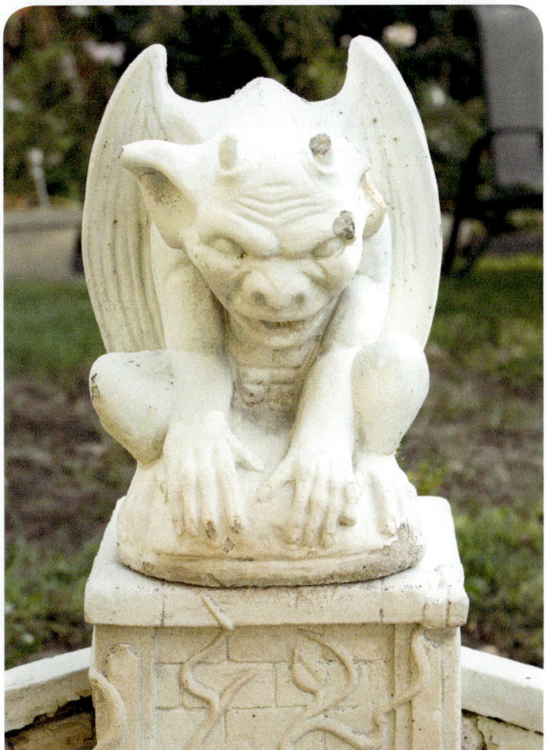

Figure 2.10 Image demonstrating N+1 EV

Exposure Modes

There are several ways to control how a camera operates the shutter speed and apertures called exposure modes. The exposure modes are commonly found located on a dial on top of the camera, or can be changed in the camera's menus. Exposure modes allow the

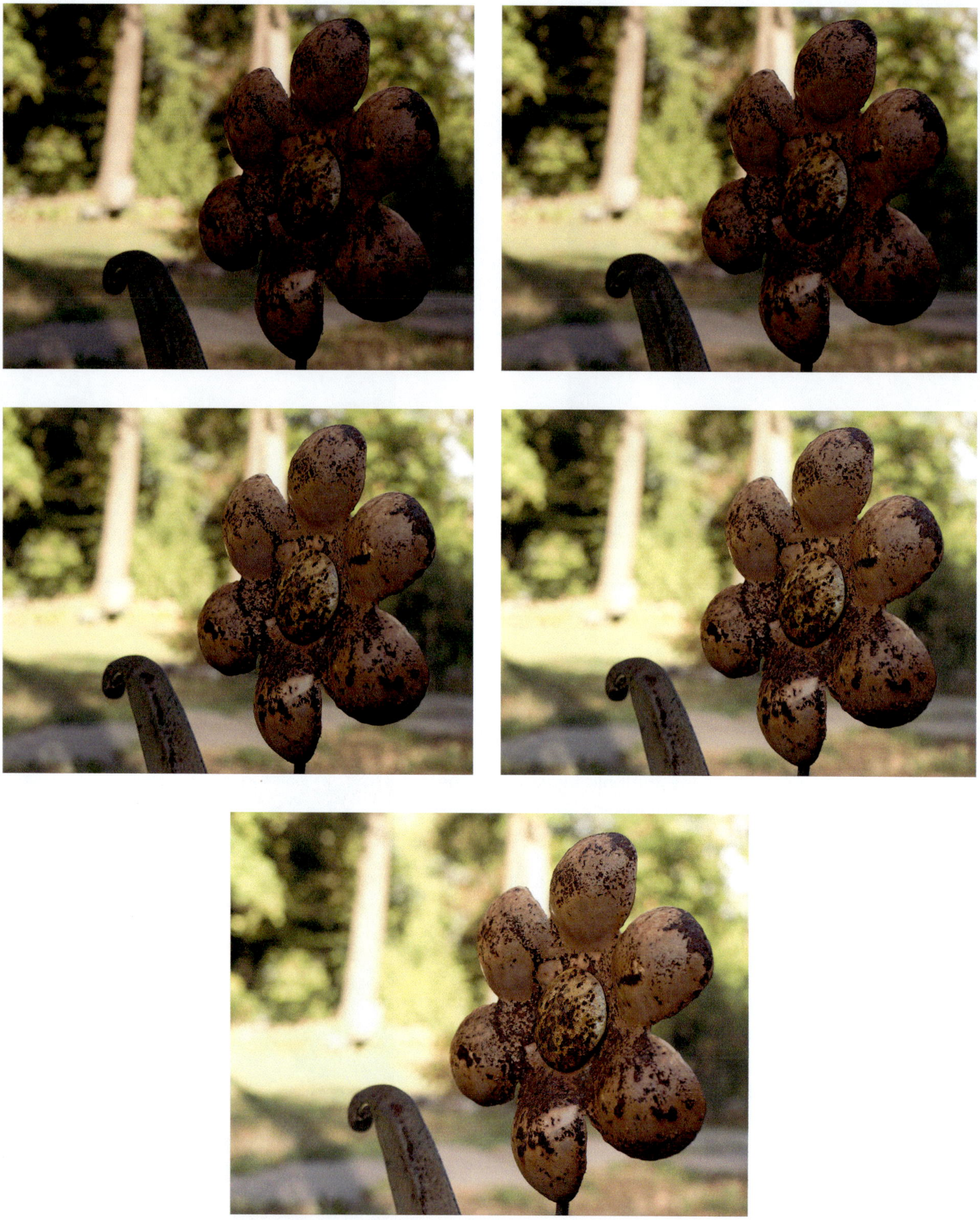

Figure 2.11 Images demonstrating bracket series of a neutral object

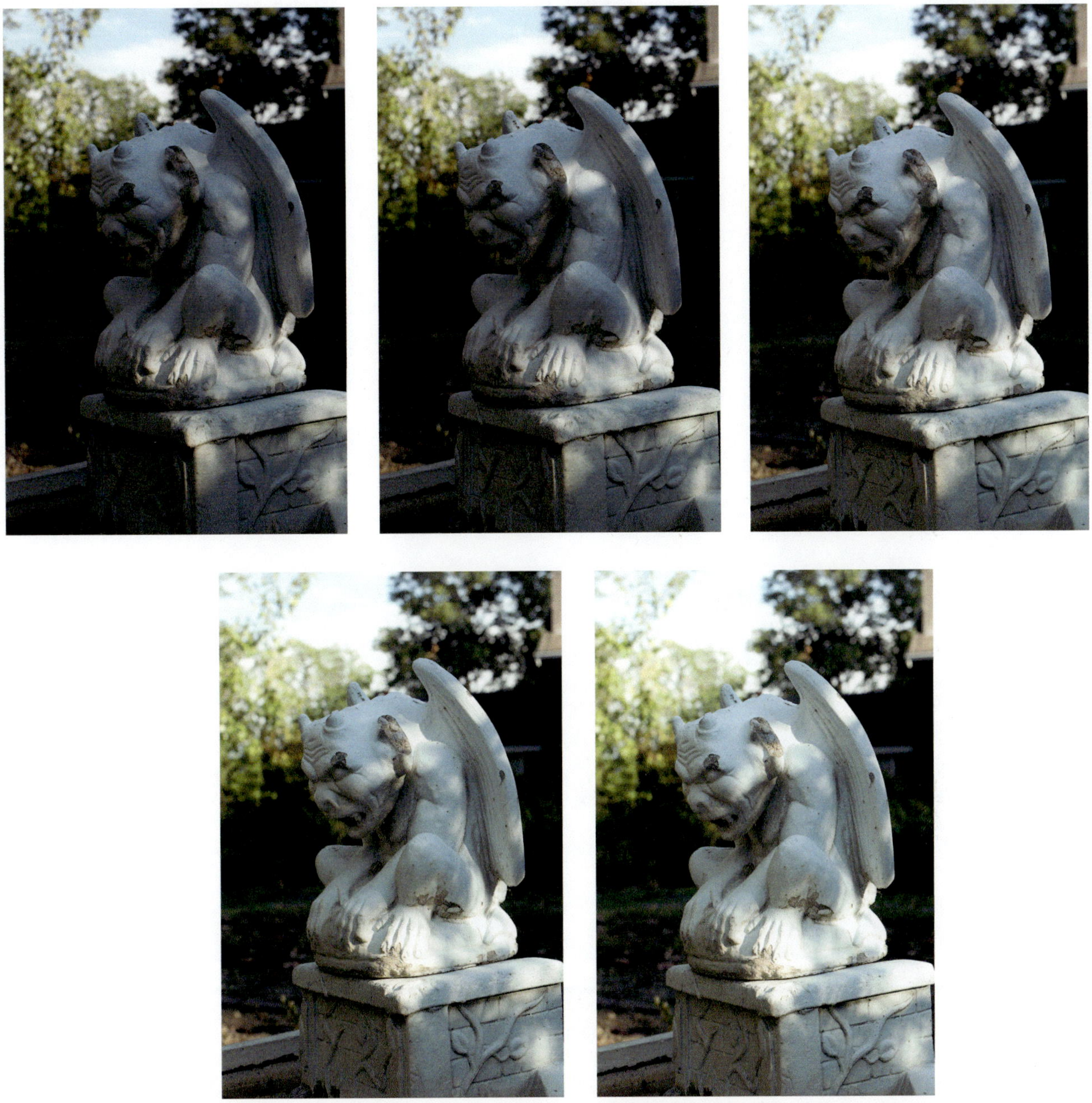

Figure 2.12 Images demonstrating bracket series of a white object with shadow contrast

photographer to take control over how the exposures are made. Some modes offer more control than others and each has its pros and cons. The most commonly found exposure modes are: auto, (P) program, (A) aperture priority, (S) or (T) shutter or time priority and (M) manual.

The most common mode used by novice photographers is the "green square," or auto mode. In auto mode, the camera makes all the decisions about exposure with very little control

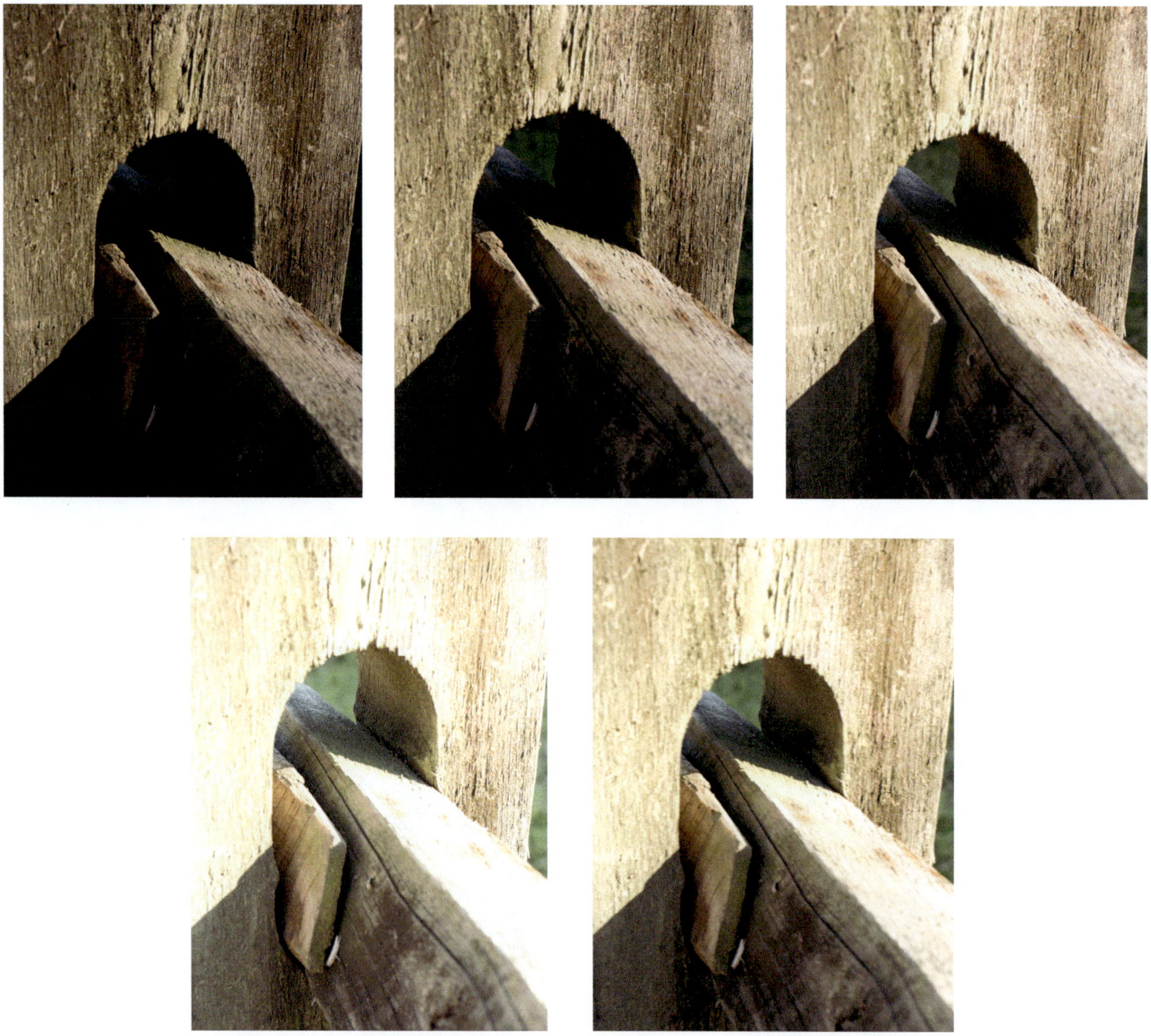

Figure 2.13 Images demonstrating bracket series of dark and bright areas

by the photographer. In many instances auto mode will get the shot; however, giving all control to the camera may not be the best choice. When set to auto mode there are many features of the camera that may not be available to the photographer. For instance, auto mode may not allow the use of the camera's exposure compensation, white balance, and ISO settings. Don't worry if you're not familiar with these concepts—they will be discussed later. In addition, auto mode takes control of that annoying little pop-up flash whether you choose to use it or not.

The P mode, which stands for program auto, is similar to auto mode as the camera automatically sets the exposure settings that will expose the image correctly. P mode is sometimes and incorrectly referred to as perfect mode. However, unlike auto mode there are several advanced settings available to the photographer as well. The above-mentioned features not available in auto mode may be set by the photographer. If the camera is equipped with a pop-up flash, in P mode control of that flash is returned to the photographer. The only drawback to this is in P mode the camera will not activate the flash, no matter how dark the subject is, so it's the photographer's responsibility to do so if needed.

On most cameras P mode allows the photographer to adjust the shutter speed and f-stop setting while retaining the proper exposure. This is called program shift and is done by rotating the cameras main control dial. Each camera manufacturer may have other methods to adjust the shutter and f-stop and you may have to refer to the owner's manual. The camera allows for the shuffling of all the settings that will produce a correctly exposed image; however, due to the amount of light in the scene not all shutter speeds will be available.

Be aware of the shutter-speed settings while using program mode, as the camera may use a shutter speed slower than you are able to hold the camera steady, resulting in blurry images. If this happens, you can increase the ISO, which will allow you to photograph at a faster shutter speed, or use a tripod to steady the camera.

A or Av is the abbreviation for aperture priority mode. Similar to program auto mode the photographer has control over several of the advanced settings such as white balance, exposure compensation, RAW image format, and ISO settings. In aperture priority mode, the photographer sets the desired aperture value or f-stop and the camera sets the shutter speed for the proper exposure. This is a particularly handy mode if you desire a certain depth of field setting. Similar to program auto mode, don't be alarmed if you cannot use a specific f-stop setting, as the amount of light within the scene may not permit an image to be taken. Conversely, if the scene is too bright, the shutter-speed display may read "HI" meaning there is too much light to get the correct exposure. When this occurs, you must change the f-stop or the ISO to compensate for the extreme light value to create an exposure. Similarly, in dark lighting conditions the shutter speed display may read "LO" meaning there is not enough light for the proper exposure; to correct this either increase the f-stop or ISO to create an exposure.

S or Tv (time value) is the abbreviation for shutter priority mode. As it sounds this mode allows the photographer to choose the shutter-speed value, while the camera sets the f-stop. Just like aperture priority mode, all the other advanced functions are available to the photographer. Again, due to the lighting of the scene don't be alarmed if you cannot use a specific shutter speed. If the scene is too bright, the aperture display may read "HI" meaning there is too much light for the proper exposure, so either increase the speed of the shutter speed or decrease the ISO. In a dark scene the aperture display may read "LO" meaning there is not enough light for the proper exposure; to correct this, decrease the shutter speed or increase the ISO.

M is the abbreviation for manual mode. In manual mode the photographer sets both the shutter speed and f-stop manually. This gives the photographer the total control over the exposure of the image. In manual mode, it is possible to completely over or under expose the image, resulting in a loss of detail. While using manual the photographer must read the light meter inside the camera to know the correct exposure. Additionally all camera settings are available to the photographer to permit the ability to fine-tune the captured image.

Table 2.2 Table of exposure modes and descriptions

Camera Exposure Mode		Description of Modes Features
P	*Program Auto*	The camera is fully automatic and determines the best shutter speed and aperture to obtain the best exposure. Ideal for point and shoot situations where minimal thought process is required.
S or Tv	*Shutter Priority Auto*	Photographer chooses the shutter speed and the camera determines the best aperture to create a normal exposure. Great for objects in motion with fast shutter speeds or on a tripod with very slow shutter speeds.
A or Av	*Aperture Priority Auto*	Photographer chooses the aperture and the camera determines the best shutter speed to create a normal exposure. Great for small apertures when imaging landscapes or needing a large depth of field using a tripod or large apertures to obtain a shallow depth of field to blur unnecessary information.
M	*Manual*	The photographer chooses the shutter speed and aperture to obtain the desired exposure, correctly imaging the subject.

Table 2.3 Table of common ISO numbers and description

ISO	
50	Records a large range of light with minimal noise
100	
200	
400	Records an average range of light with low amounts of noise
800	
1600	Images a smaller range of light and has a high amount of noise
3200	
6400	

ISO (International Organization of Standardization)

ISO (International Organization of Standardization) is the sensitivity rating of the cameras sensor. You may recognize the abbreviation from film, as it was used to rate the sensitivity of film. The higher the number the more sensitive to light the film was, and therefore it was more desirable to use in low-light situations. The same is true for the ISO settings on digital cameras; however, an increase in ISO will also increase the noise present in a digital image. Noise in digital images appears as off-color pixels, typically red and green. Even though cameras are getting much better at controlling noise, it is recommended that changing the ISO be a last resort for the forensic photographer since increased noise means decreased detail in an image.

White Balance

White balance (also called color balance) is a very important setting on a digital camera. It allows the photographer to adjust the camera for different sources of light. White balance is essential because each source of light has its own color temperature. Color temperature is a characteristic of a light source's spectrum. Color temperature is measured in degrees Kelvin (K), where the higher the degree the bluer the light.

The camera must be set for the proper color temperature of the light source or a colorcast will occur in the image. A photograph taken under tungsten light using the outdoor setting will appear too orange. Similarly, a photograph taken outdoors using the tungsten setting will appear too blue.

There are several presets on digital cameras for white balance. Here is a list of the most common presets, many of which are self-explanatory:

AWB (auto white balance): The auto setting chooses the best white balance according to the light source. Auto mode may not always provide consistent results and therefore it is not recommended. It is possible to get better results using the other modes.

Tungsten: This mode is used for photographing using tungsten halogen or incandescent light bulbs and for shooting indoors without a flash.

Flash: This mode is used for photographing using a flash, or strobe lighting. It is also recommended for shooting indoors while using the flash.

Camera Color Temperature Presets

	Sodium vapor lights	2700 K
	Incandescent	3000 K
	Warm white fluorescent	3000 K
	White fluorescent	37000 K
	Cool white fluorescent	4200 K
	Day white fluorescent	5000 K
	Direct sunlight	5200 K
	Flash	5400 K
	Cloudy	6000 K
	Daylight fluorescent	6500 K
	High temperature mercury vapor	7200 K
	Shade	8000 K

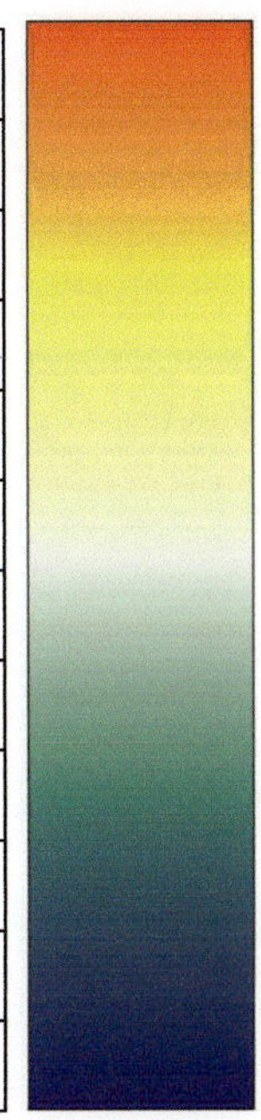

Table 2.4 Table of common camera symbols for white balance settings and color temperatures

Daylight: This mode is for use outdoors while under direct sunlight.

Cloudy: This mode is for use outdoors when there is no direct sunlight, or under cloudy conditions. It may be helpful to use a flash to add contrast to your subjects while shooting on a cloudy day.

Shade: This mode is for use outdoors when there is direct sunlight but you are photographing in the shade. It may also be helpful to use a flash to fill in the shade.

The flash, daylight, cloudy, and shade settings are relatively close in color temperature, so unless color reproduction is important to your task it may not be necessary to switch between them.

Fluorescent: This setting is for use while shooting indoor under fluorescent lighting. Many digital cameras have more than one fluorescent setting since there are different types of fluorescent lights. Simple trial and error may help you identify which setting works best.

Kelvin color temperature setting: This setting is used when you know the color temperature of the lighting conditions of the scene. It may be helpful for shooting under similar conditions often, or when color reproduction is critical. Finding out the color temperature of a light source may require a color temperature meter, or trial and error.

Custom color balance: This setting allows the camera to read the color temperature of the light by placing a neutral gray card in front of the lens and activating the custom setting. The use of this feature varies depending upon the camera; check the camera's manual for specific instructions. Similar to the Kelvin mode, this setting is useful for shooting under unchanging conditions, like a studio, where lights remain consistent throughout the entire photographic session. Typically once set, the custom color balance can be saved in the camera and will not need to be reset each time it is used.

The basic principles of photography as explained are the cornerstone to complete and accurate forensic imaging. It is best to regularly use your photographic equipment even if it is not a forensic scene. Repetition and practice will keep your photographic processes sharp and you will be able to use your equipment effectively when you are called upon for a forensic requirement. Practice using supplementary and extra equipment in situations; this will give you the opportunity to be familiar with your equipment when a similar situation occurs on location.

Chapter 3 Digital Photography

The digital photography era began when an electronic imaging sensor replaced film within the camera. The sensor is a device that captures light and converts it into an image. Sensors are made up of millions of photoelectric devices, which convert light into an electrical signal and ultimately the image. Currently there are two types of sensors, the CCD (charge coupled device) and the CMOS (complementary metal-oxide-semiconductor) sensors.

The sensor's electronic signals are processed and sent to the camera's storage media such as a compact flash (CF) or secure digital (SD) card. Images stored on the camera can be saved in a variety of file types, dependent upon the photographer's choice. Examples of common file types are the RAW file, Nikon .nef, Kodak .dcr, Canon .cr2, and a multitude of others, many dependent upon the camera manufacturer. Additionally, many digital cameras are capable of processing and storing images in standard image file formats such as TIFF or JPEG files.

Resolution

Digital imaging resolution must be thoroughly understood by photographers to be able to effectively determine correct capturing of images with regards to their final usage. Camera resolution is typically advertised in megapixels. Mega means millions, and therefore megapixels describes how many millions of pixels are within the image. This can be determined by multiplying the image's height (in pixels) by its width (in pixels). For example, an image that is 4,256 (pixels) by 2,832 (pixels) contains 12,052,992 pixels, or 12 megapixels.

A standard print requires a specific quantity of pixels to print an effective image. The following chart is a good start for determining a specific print size based on the resolution of the camera. A generally accepted resolution for prints is 300 pixels per inch; therefore it is possible to determine an approximate print size by dividing the camera's resolution by 300.

Image size (pixels)	Print size (in)
900 × 1500	3 × 5
1200 × 1800	4 × 6
1500 × 2100	5 × 7
2400 × 2400	8 × 8
2400 × 3000	8 × 10
2550 × 3300	8.5 × 11
2700 × 4800	9 × 16
3300 × 4200	11 × 14
3300 × 4800	11 × 16

When evaluating the chart above, notice as the pixel dimensions increase, the relative print size increases as well. This is because as the resolution increases, so does the size of the imaging sensor's resolution, the more detail the imaging sensor is capable of capturing. The more pixels or resolution a camera is able to capture, the larger you are able to print the image and achieve more detail within the image and print.

When determining the proper resolution, you should determine your specific needs and final usage. More resolution is not necessarily the best choice; however, capturing an image with a large amount of resolution will gather the greatest amount of image detail. Resolution limitations may include the storage media size and how much information must be gathered within the area to be documented. Many times documentation of evidence includes vast areas, such as an aircraft accident where information could be scattered over miles. If you have limited storage media or are unable to upload captured imagery to a computer or hard drive, one must determine the best-quality resolution required to gather important information while making sure all evidence is captured within the investigation site.

Resolution starting from image capture through final image products is a factor at each step of the photography process. The digital camera you use to record the scene, the monitor you use to view those images, and the printer or output device you use all have a maximum resolution that determines how much information they are able to capture, display, or print. Understanding how resolution affects each of these devices will help in determining which tools are best for you and how to use them.

File Types, Compression

Prior to photographing anything, the photographer must make a decision as to how the images captured will be saved. Digital cameras have the ability to save images in various formats, and there are benefits and drawbacks to each one. The following are the three most common file types recorded by digital cameras.

JPEG (Joint Photographic Experts Group)

The JPEG (Joint Photographic Experts Group) or JPG file format is a standardized image file format that is compatible between computer platforms, digital camera, image-sharing sites, and photo print labs. A JPEG file is readable by just about any program that supports images. The JPEG file is probably the most common image file format encountered. A JPEG file will likely be the smallest file (take up the least amount of memory) relative to the other choices. This is because a JPEG file uses a process called compression to reduce the size of the image.

The purpose of compression is to reduce the size of a file by reducing the redundancy of the information. Image compression works by combining the values of similar pixels to reduce the amount of memory necessary to store an image. JPEG compression is a lossy compression technique, meaning some of the information compressed cannot be recovered. Typically this loss of information is not noticeable, and there is no visible degradation of the image quality. However, if too much compression is used there can be a noticeable loss of image quality. Digital cameras, as well as image processing software, allow the user to choose the amount of compression applied to an image. It is best to choose the least amount of compression necessary.

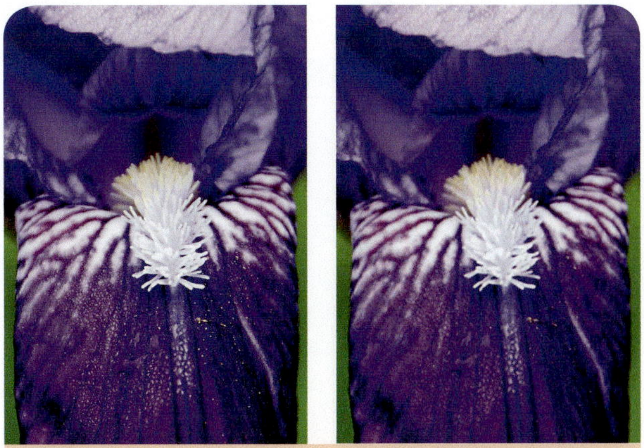

Figure 3.1 The image on the left has been compressed multiple times and the result of compression degradation is the image on the right

Image compression is not necessarily a bad thing; the process allows photographers to store large amounts of information in a relatively small file size. Image compression does, however, discard data, even if it's not noticeable it's happening. Therefore it is recommended that the JPEG file format only be used for documentation of evidence, when a picture is taken to show the appearance of evidence.

RAW File Format

The RAW file is an image that contains unprocessed data from the camera sensor. Typically the highest quality image available from a digital camera is the RAW file. Processing starts at the computer when the file is opened. This type of processing allows the photographer to change many settings after the image has been acquired with no change to the original captured image data (e.g., color balance). RAW files are manufacturer specific and may require unique software from that manufacturer to open or they may require image processing programs like Adobe Photoshop. RAW is a preferred file format for evidence comparison quality photography (footwear, fingerprints, blood spatter).

Many digital cameras allow file saving in both the RAW and JPEG file formats simultaneously. This means for every picture taken, the camera will save two files, one RAW and one JPEG. This way you will capture both the highest-quality file possible from the camera, as well as have a smaller, more compatible JPEG file. The JPEG files can then be transmitted to other investigators, attorneys, or interested parties without the need for specific software to open them. Also if prints are required, the JPEG files can be brought to any photo-processing site, such as the local chain pharmacy, for easy printing.

TIFF (Tagged-Image File Format)

A TIFF (Tagged-Image File Format) file is an uncompressed, standardized file format. The TIFF is cross-compatible between all computer platforms and is supported by all photo and graphics editing software. TIFF files are also able to provide a transparency in addition to the supporting many color profiles (RGB, CMYK, Lab, Indexed Color, and Grayscale). Similar to the PSD format file, TIFF format files are able to maintain Photoshop layers when saving the file. This again is helpful at a later time when it may be necessary to readjust the image or return the image to its original state.

Since TIFF files are un-compressed, high-resolution image file sizes are rather large. The TIFF file format's use is great for archiving the image to maintain the quality and details of the image. TIFF files should be used to store any image that has undergone image processing, as re-saving a compressed file format increases the loss due to compression.

The following file formats are typically not offered as an option on digital cameras; however, they may be used for saving files from image processing software.

PSD File (Photoshop)

The PSD (Photoshop) format is the default format used when using Adobe Photoshop. This format permits compatibility within the Adobe family of software products. It allows users to save the file while keeping all the features of the image. This is very useful for saving images that have been adjusted or used in a variety of ways such as layers, paths, masks, and effects, to be able to open them at a later time to be able to see what has been done or revert back to the original image.

Even though the PSD file is a great way to store files to be able to maintain the Adobe software features, they are large in size and users that may not have Adobe compatible software will not be able to open and view the images.

PNG (Portable Network Graphics)

A PNG file (Portable Network Graphics) format is useful because it maintains the image without reducing image quality. The PNG file permits a background transparency with minimal jagged edges. It is an excellent format designed to use for presentation or website imagery. It is similar to a GIF but provides a greater amount of detail. The PNG file is saved with a highly effective 256 colors maximum and also can provide 8 bit transparency. When used on a presentation or website, it is recommended to size the image appropriately.

PNG is a recently introduced format, so not everyone is familiar with it. But PNG has been approved as a standard since 1996. It is an image format specifically designed for the web. PNG is, in all aspects, the superior version of the GIF. Just like the GIF format, the PNG is saved with 256 colors maximum but it saves the color information more efficiently. It also supports an 8 bit transparency.

GIF (Graphics Interchange Format)

The GIF (Graphics Interchange Format) file may be a highly recognized file format when using images or graphics on the internet because of its transfer speed on website pages. The GIF file is a highly compressed file and should be avoided in forensic use. GIF files have a very small file size and are of a low quality, having a very limited color range, which is why they are primarily used on websites and the internet.

RAW	Best for comparison quality images, fingerprints, footwear, blood spatter
JPEG	Documentation quality images, sharing and sending images among colleagues
PSD	Saving working files on your computer so you can return and edit later
PNG	Preserving transparency for images on the web
TIFF	Uncompressed standardized file format, processed images requiring maximum quality
GIF	Typically used for artwork images on the web, such as charts and graphs

Chart 3.1 Chart demonstrating file formats and their best usage

Dynamic Range

The photographic dynamic range describes the ratio between the brightest highlight (whitest white) and darkest area of light intensities (blackest black) within an image scene. The dynamic range is dependent upon each phase of the imaging chain, from the capture device (such as a camera or scanner), processing of the image, then to a display device (such as a print or computer display). Each device has an individual dynamic range. Prints cannot be brighter than the white paper that the image is printed on and computer displays have a maximum intensity from the pixel brightness of the display. Additionally the human eye has its own dynamic range. Movement of images between capture, display, and output devices becomes challenging to accurately present specific details within the documented scene.

Crop Factor and Focal Length Multiplier

Some camera systems have an imaging sensor that will contain a crop factor. This crop factor is the imaging sensor's diagonal size compared to a full-frame 35mm sensor. It is called a crop factor because, when using a lens, the imaging sensor crops out the outer section of the imaging area around the perimeter.

When considering the crop factor of a lens, a wider-angle lens is required to be used to compensate for what is not recordable on the sensor. A cropped sensor is forced to use a wider-angle lens to create the same angle of view as a larger sensor.

Let's first look at and understand the angle of view and what changes occur with a change in the focal length of the lens. The angle of view is the total viewing area of the subject or scene that the imaging sensor records and is described as an angle. Wide angle of views capture greater areas of the scene and small angles smaller areas of the scene. A wide angle of view will be obtained with a shorter focal length lens and a long focal length lens will provide a narrow angle of view. The angle of view will be the image captured on the sensor of the area, or how much of the scene. Maintaining the same camera location, a narrow angle of view lens (telephoto) will capture a smaller area creating a subject that appears larger. A wide angle of view (wide angle lens) will capture a larger area creating a subject that will appear smaller.

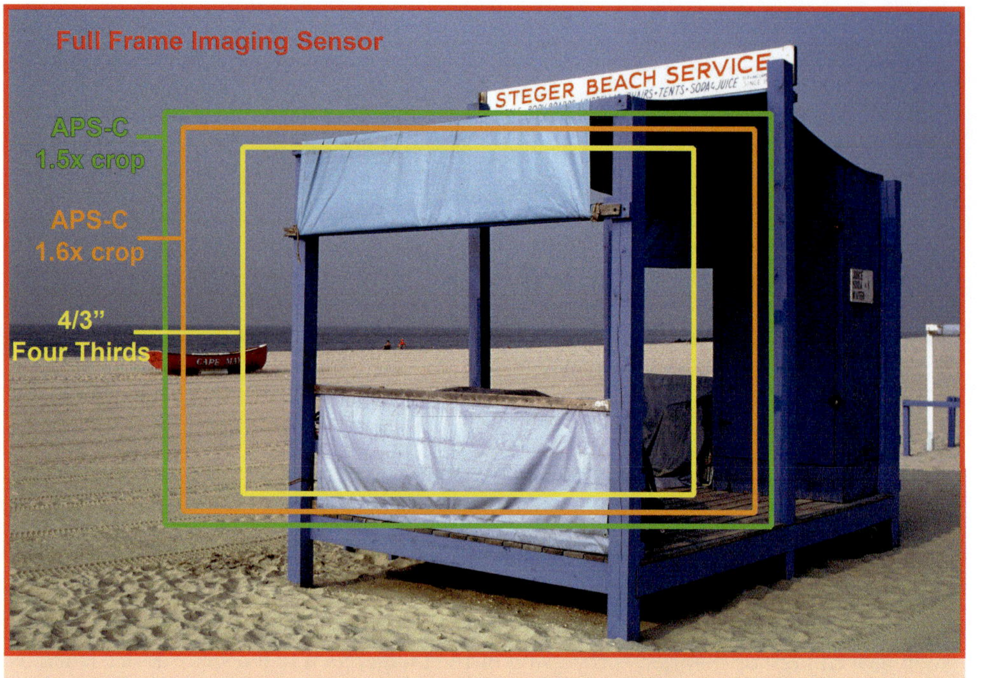

Figure 3.2 Image depicting a full-frame sensor compared to the areas of a variety of crop factors

The focal length multiplier is the mathematical relationship of the camera lens and its related crop factor. When a sensor has a focal length multiplier of 1.6X, the crop factor of a 50mm lens would create the field of view equal to that of an 80 mm lens. This is calculated by multiplying the 50mm lens times the 1.6 multiplier (50mm × 1.6 = 80mm) if it would be on a full frame 35mm sensor. The focal length of the lens is not changed due to the focal length multiplier. Only the crop of the image, thus the angle of view, is changed by the crop of the imaging sensor.

To calculate the effective focal length of a lens, the focal length multiplier of the camera must be used, which would be provided by the manufacturer. The three most common multipliers are 1.5, 1.6, and 2.0.

A DSLR that contains a full-frame sensor does not have a multiplier and therefore the sensor is the same as a 35mm film. The actual multiplier is one. Each lens has the same effective

Chart 3.2 Chart showing 50mm lens extrapolated to the focal length for different crop factor multipliers

50mm Interchangeable Lens	
Multiplier	Effective Focal Length
1.5	75mm
1.6	80mm
2	100mm

focal length as stated on the lens. A 50mm lens provides the angle of view as a normal 50mm lens without any cropping.

Some camera systems have markings or a boxed area within the viewfinder that will represent the area that will be imaged on the imaging sensor. What you see in the viewfinder sometimes is slightly smaller than what is actually imaged on the sensor. The manufacturer will provide the actual percentage in the owner's manual. The most common is a 90% less viewing area compared to the actual image.

White Balance and Color Temperature

Digital photography provides the photographer with the opportunity to adjust the color temperature, also referred to as white balance, of an image directly within the camera (see Chapter 2). In forensic photography, it is necessary to accurately document the scene. One of the most fundamental needs is to capture true color characteristics of the evidence.

The primary colors that form white light are red, green, and blue. A combination of each will create the color temperature of the light of the photographer's environment. The higher the color temperature, there is more blue light creating bluish tones; conversely when the color temperature is low, there is a higher amount of red light creating reddish-orange tones.

The color temperature of light is measured on the Kelvin scale. The Kelvin scale at a low temperature creates the reddish-orange hues. At higher Kelvin temperatures, the colors change to bluish cooler tones. The higher the degree in Kelvin 6500 degrees has a bluish tint to the light. The chart of Kelvin temperatures for various lighting conditions is an estimate of the source and what the degree in Kelvin may be. In outdoor conditions, the angle of the sun and condition of the sky (clouds, haze, dust particles, etc.) can increase or decrease the color temperature. Indoor conditions such as lamp bulbs, voltage, type of reflectors, etc. also may affect the color temperature of light.

When you take an image and have the camera set to a daylight value, there are times when sections of the image may have a reddish-orange hue. The color variance is created by the difference in color temperatures between daylight (a bluish color) and incandescent light (the reddish-orange color). Since the camera is set to compensate or make the blue neutral (white) the incandescent light stands out as the reddish-orange color.

Conversely, when the camera system's color balance is set to an incandescent value, there may be times when sections of the image will have a bluish hue. Again, there becomes a color variance created by the color temperature of the incandescent camera setting and the daylight of the light within the image scene.

The human eye and our brain processing quickly adapts to changes in the color temperature of light as we go about our daily routine. This processing neutralizes colors and adapts the variety of color temperatures to a neutral or white. The difference between the human eye and brain and camera systems is that the camera system's sensor has a specific white balance or color temperature setting per each image.

Chart 3.3 Chart of light source and their equivalent in degrees Kelvin

Source	Degrees K
Match Flame	1700
Candle Flame	1850
40-Watt Incandescent Tungsten Lamp	2650
75-Watt Incandescent Tungsten Lamp	2820
100-Watt Incandescent Tungsten Lamp	2865
500-Watt Incandescent Tungsten Lamp	2960
Professional Tungsten Photo Lamp	3200
Color Photography Studio Tungsten Lamp	3350
Photoflood or Reflector Flood Lamp	3400
Daylight Blue Photoflood Lamp	4800
Daylight	
Sunlight is the light of the sun only where daylight combines sunlight and skylight	
Sunlight: Sunrise or Sunset	2000
Sunlight: One Hour After Sunrise	3500
Sunlight: Early Morning or Late Afternoon	4300
Direct Mid-Summer Sunlight	5800
Overcast Sky	6000
Daylight Fluorescent Lamp (see note below)	6300
Average Summer Sunlight (plus blue skylight)	6500
Light Summer Shade	7100
Average Summer Shade	8000
Summer Skylight (varies)	9500–30,000

The best way to understand and visualize how each white balance setting on the camera effects an image and the lighting condition is to cycle through each white balance setting and evaluate what effect it has in that lighting condition. By referencing the color temperature and camera preset charts above, you are able to determine the scene's color temperature and what white balance setting creates the most neutral or white–white of the image, creating a correctly color-balanced, natural-looking image. It is important to continue evaluating white balance and color temperatures in each new environment as well as different times of the day or if conditions change. Photograph outdoors in full sun, on a cloudy day, in the shade, in the morning and in the evening and cycle through each white balance setting. Once complete, continue to an indoor location and photograph scenes with incandescent, the variety of florescent lights and other lights that may be common when you are on location. Again cycle through all the camera white balance settings and evaluate how each white balance setting effects the image and light.

Light sources have their own unique color, or "color temperature," which varies from red to blue. Red-hue light sources include candles, sunsets, and tungsten bulbs, and appear "warm" in images, whereas clear blue skies give off a "cool" blue light.

A camera system's auto white balance (AWB) tries to determine the best white balance for the scene for each image that is taken. Many times the AWB setting will create fluctuations between images because it may sense multiple light sources and choose different color temperatures for individual images; therefore it is not recommended for use.

Camera systems also have the ability to set the white balance manually. First the camera will have a preset of color temperatures that are a specific number in degrees Kelvin for each light source like florescent, tungsten, daylight, cloudy, and shade. In addition to the presets, a photographer can set the degrees Kelvin specific to the degree from 2,000 degrees (candles) to 10,000 degrees (skylight).

Photographic Filters

Filters as a mechanical device on a lens or flash are an effective method to modify light by transmission, absorption, and interference. Camera lens filters must be of the highest quality as they are in line with the optics of camera image formation. Filters are primarily made of glass, plastics, polyester, gelatin, or cellulose acetate.

Color Space and Color Profiles

The digital image is acquired by light entering the camera system and the imaging sensors' electronic signals are turned into numerical data. The captured light is a reflection of additive colors red, green, and blue light. The quantity of each creates the individual color and specific numerical data. At the other end, we have a final product of a printed image. This printed image is made up of subtractive color inks cyan, magenta, yellow, and black. Printed image inks absorb color light and the color is seen by the color that is not absorbed.

Color spaces are composed of three primary color models. The first one we will discuss is the RGB color model. The RGB color model recognizes three primary additive colors, red, green, and blue. The mixture of these three colors will create all other available colors. The additive RGB color model is developed where the addition of all three colors of light will produce white light.

The creation of various colors is dependent upon the mixture of each individual RGB color light source and how it is blended to create specific colors. This color model is used in computer monitors, television sets, and at movie theaters. An example of color creation, red and green overlap creates yellow, blue and green create cyan, and red and blue create

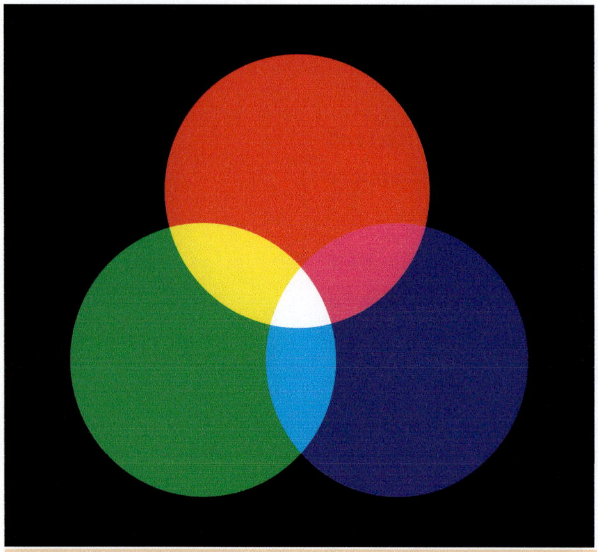

Graphic 3.1 RGB light demonstration to create white light

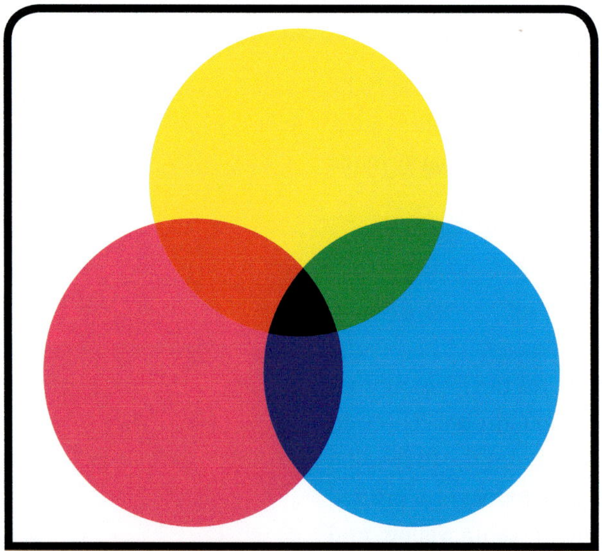

Graphic 3.2 CMYK demonstrating paint pigments to create printed colors

magenta. The RGB color model applies only to devices that use light as the imaging source, such as computer monitors and television sets.

The CMYK color model recognizes four subtractive colors, cyan, magenta, yellow, and key (black). The primary inks used in the CMYK color model are cyan, magenta, and yellow, which are used in color printing processes. The CMYK inks absorb color light and are also considered subtractive colors. The absorption subtractive process absorbs specific colors: cyan is the opposite of red, meaning that cyan acts like a filter that absorbs red. The amount of cyan applied to a paper will control how much red will show. Magenta is the opposite of green, and yellow is the opposite of blue. Since CMYK ink application will vary it has the ability to create numerous colors. The CMYK subtractive color model applies to printed items.

CIELAB and CIE XYZ are similar color models that replicate human eyesight. These color models incorporate a massive number of colors so they are excellent models to use when converting from one color model to another such as from RGB to CMYK or vice versa. CIELAB can be used while image processing; however, it is not commonplace and is more difficult to understand and use, unlike the RGB and CMYK color models.

Color Space

A color space is a mathematical method where certain colors are recorded, described, and/or displayed. Color spaces describe a set of physical colors and the corresponding names or numbers that have been created to describe them. A PMS color—a part of the Pantone system color space descriptors—is an example of an analog model, where the highly structured mathematical descriptions were used for color mixing can be found in Adobe RGB 1998. sRGB files are also an example of a type of color space useful for use preparing images for web or monitor viewing. There are three values used in an RGB system or four values found in CMYK systems.

When choosing a color space, scientific photographers can establish a detailed mapping function used for capturing color, processing color, and how the color at output will look. This is established within the mathematical color space or an image's color gamut. A gamut of a color will be part of what defines an image. For example, Adobe RGB 1998 and sRGB are two different color spaces that are both based on the RGB color model. The Adobe RGB 1998 space will display more colors with a wider gamut. sRGB is a smaller color space and will compress or suppress more color information. The most common reference standards for color space, recording, and display are the CIELAB or CIEXYZ color spaces. These systems were designed to mimic the colors that the average human can see. When selecting what color space to select for a camera, use the widest gamut available located in the camera's preferences. This will lead to files with the most information.

The RGB and CMYK color spaces are vast. Many of the most common color spaces are Adobe RGB (1998), sRGB, and Prophoto RGB. A color space and color profile terms can be used interchangeably. The profile describes the specific color space. Each color space contains its own individual set of colors. When changing from one color space to another, any colors that are not within the new color space will be eliminated and not transferred to the new color space and are called "out of gamut."

Color Profile

The numerical model of the color space is the color profile. Input devices, computer systems, printers, and output devices require access to profiles to evaluate the image colors and interpret the colors to accurately process them.

Photographers usually only work with a few color profiles and they are dependent on their work environments. The photographic environment, processing device, and output device primarily determine the color profiles or spaces.

Adobe RGB (1998) was created by Adobe in the late 1990s, when Photoshop implemented full color management and as Adobe Photoshop became the professional software of choice, Adobe RGB became the universal standard. Most DSLR cameras offer Adobe RGB as a color space and it is recommended since it has a higher color gamut than the sRGB color space.

The sRGB color profile space is one of the smaller color spaces and is more commonly used with older monitor color spaces and unmanaged monitors. Currently, sRGB images are the most appropriate choice for web images because most web browsers have no color management profiles. sRGB is not a wide color space and is least common as a working space for professionals.

Monitors, projectors, desktop printers, or other output devices contain "device-dependent" color profiles or spaces. These device-dependent color profiles are usually provided by the manufacturer and process the incoming image to accurately output the image.

Color Management

Individual imaging devices record images, which are displayed or printed by other methods by another device or manufacturer. The difference in the image's color as the secondary device views it may be slightly different from the original recorded image. Color management of the image is a challenging process between devices by each device's color space. The processing of the image by each device converts the image's color information so the appearance of color will be maintained through each piece of equipment used by using algorithms and mathematical models. Using color profile standards that are usable across all imaging platforms coordinates the languages of the algorithms and equations.

Color profiles have been created and managed by the International Color Consortium (ICC) for users working with images on computers that have different operating systems. They assign an image profile to allow its image attributes to remain the same regardless of the device.

Color management is a tedious and complex process where collegiate courses and books have been written to assist to develop proper methods. The first step in this process is to calibrate your monitors and assign a color profile that will reduce any variances from the original image. The color profile can be assigned by the imaging device during capture or at a later time when processing the image. By choosing a larger color space, the color variance or loss can be observed to reduce clipping, loss of color, and information.

Color gamut is the process where color management translates the image colors across platforms to maintain its integrity. Gamut mapping uses rendering techniques to convert difficult colors within ICC specifications by making decisions to manage the losses or gain of color within the image file so they are usable by devices and users to create any accurately colored image.

There are four types of rendering used by the color language: absolute colorimetric, relative colorimetric, perceptual, and saturation intents. The user has the ability to choose which rendering technique will provide the best image color and this can sometime be a personal preference.

LYNDA.com® is a useful web resource that can assist with understanding and developing a color-management process. XRite® uses a consumer-friendly calibrated color target tool to improve color management and reproduction called the ProPassport, which is added to the imaging scene. Other items such as a color checker or a basic black and white target can be used. Placing these items in a scene may be difficult due to the nature of the scene, the magnification of the image, or the imaging equipment. A target assists in providing the proper color reproduction for forensic imagery.

Metadata

Images provide a large amount of details to investigators; however, there is additional information embedded within the image file that assists in providing image information detail. Image files contain segments of data that identify and support the information within the visual image. Each file type will have data segments; however, they do not all have the same kind or quantity of digital information. The various metadata fields and information available are description and caption information, photographer's information, IPTC, camera data and image data, video or audio data, DICOM, XMP, EXIF, history, and many others that can be imported or created by the photographer or individual using the image file.

Metadata Descriptions

Description and Caption Information

This permits the photographer or user to input information such as: document title, author, description, rating, description writer, keywords, copyright, and URL.

Photographer's Information

This permits the photographer to input information such as: title, address, contact information, phone numbers, email(s), and websites.

IPTC extension information can be used as a chain of custody to add information on individuals who have viewed or used the image and for what purpose.

Camera Data and Image Data

Camera data and image data contains the camera and image creation information such as: make, model, date/time, exposure mode, shutter speed, aperture value, ISO, lens used, focal length, flash and if flash was fired, metering mode, pixel dimension, resolution, color space, and file source.

Video or Audio Data

Video or audio data contain the camera and image creation information such as: frame rate, video width and height, aspect ratio, tape name, scene, shot/take, log comments, timecode, track number, sample rate, audio sample type, loop, beats, and tempo.

DICOM (Digital Imaging and Communications in Medicine)

DICOM permits the photographer or user to input information such as: patient name, ID, date of birth, sex (male or female), study ID and date, physician, series description, image width/height, and frames.

IPTC (IIM and Core and Extension)

IPTC is a method for captioning digital images where many photo-editing programs will be easily read. This is an advantage for a forensic photographer so they can caption images directly within the image file and it will be available to any investigator or viewer of the image.

XMP

XMP is a metadata format that Adobe created that is similar to that of the IPTC and EXIF metadata. It is the primary metadata format for Adobe applications and will contain an extensive amount of image data.

Many times the image file information will include the XMP file which is attached to the original file and provides a larger amount of fields to support much more descriptive details. This is the newer data format used by IPTC core and extension for storing and accessing image metadata. Additionally, the XMP metadata will recognize if cropping or resizing of the original image has altered the image to include the software that was used for editing. The photographer or investigator is also able to embed details that support the investigation by creating custom fields.

EXIF

Similar to the XMP metadata, the EXIF (exchangeable image file) format provides information that identifies information about the camera and the settings used to capture the image. The EXIF will include camera make and model, shutter speed, aperture, lens settings, date and time, color space, pixel dimensions, and other information that will provide detail of the image. GPS (Global Positioning System) information from some camera models and smartphones will exist within the EXIF metadata.

History

Metadata history records information about any changes or adjustments that have been completed on the original image. The history will record the editing of the image file to include saving or converting; however, it does not divulge what type of editing has occurred. Numerous edits within the history may create a concern that the image has been manipulated in some manner and further investigation or discovery of the original may be necessary.

Metadata is useful for imputing specific information regarding the forensic location, subject matter, and evidence at the scene. Case file numbers and keywords can be added so the images captured can be easily recognized for a particular case. The images can be filed and sorted by keywords to differentiate between subject matter and specific areas or details within the case. Examiners and investigators can place notes within the metadata for others to see and identify details within the subject and image. There are many possibilities and uses for metadata within the forensic field that add much more detail where investigators can use and understand when reviewing evidence imagery.

Management and Storage of Images

It is important to care for your images once they have been captured and recorded on the camera storage media. Properly transferring and downloading images to a computer or other storage device is also a critical part of securing imagery. If you do not back up your imagery correctly, there is a good possibility that images or a large collection of images can be lost forever. Images can be downloaded from the camera media by a variety of methods. You can remove the media and use a card reader, connect a cord directly from the camera to the computer or storage device, and some manufacturers permit wireless transfer from the camera system. All these methods are viable; however, prior to deleting or formatting the camera media card, ensure that all the images have been correctly transferred and are usable.

Formatting camera cards create a data-free card that is ready for new images. If you do not format cards on a routine basis and just delete or erase images, you are actually not removing images. There is still data and information remaining on the card and new images are written over existing data on the card. Additionally, media-card manufacturers recommend formatting cards with the camera format feature and not with a computer.

An important part of transferring and archiving images is how or what to properly name images or a collection of images. There is no set standard but it is recommended that your facility have a standard method so the imagery can be easily recognized and retrieved when necessary. Date, item number, or case number can be used in the naming of image collections and files. It may also be useful to use a combination of each to differentiate images taken of the same case, but at different locations or dates so they can easily be placed into the group to show a relationship within the case and used by investigators. These collections of images should be stored in folders labeled similarly to the images by case, date, location, or any other identifiable information.

More important than just storing imagery is to effectively archive digital photos. This requires a specific workflow and a standard operating procedure that will store and archive all images. Each captured image should be kept in two separate locations in case of accidental corruption of working files, lost files, computer or storage crash, fire, flood, or natural disaster. Archive storage is a safe storage where at least one set of your images is stored at an off-site location. The archival media could be to another hard drive, memory stick, DVD, offsite storage, or secure cloud storage. Ultimately once you format your camera media all images are located in two separate locations, one working set and one archived set as a backup.

Understanding storage devices will keep your files safe and usable for a long period of time. Some care needs to be taken when using CD, DVD, and Blu-ray discs to increase the longevity of the stored media. Select and use a high-quality brand that uses gold as a reflective layer; be careful when handling discs not to touch the surface and hold them by the outer edges so the surface doesn't scratch or become dirty. It is best to keep discs in a cool, dark, dry location to avoid heat and moisture. It is recommended to keep discs in jewel cases and not in paper or vinyl sleeves. When you must write on the disc to annotate content information, use non solvent-based felt-tip permanent markers that are dedicated for writing on CD, DVD, or Blu-ray labels.

When writing to discs, it is best to choose the slower writing speeds to eliminate errors and maintain quality.

RAID Storage

RAID (redundant array of independent disks) in simple terms is a group of hard drives acting as a single super hard drive. RAID storage media is designed for different purposes and is configured to do different things such as high-end performance or safe storage. RAID systems are most commonly found in network storage to support a massive amount of storage, backup, and information access between computer workstations and basic devices.

The most common and familiar are the RAID 0, RAID 1, and RAID 5 drives. RAID 0 is considered a performance RAID and uses striping, where the multiple drives are all treated as a single drive and the information is divided into pieces and written across the multiple drives creating the enhanced performance level. It is like taking the information and expanding it into a larger area by writing the information on all drives. The great part about RAID 0 drives is the ability to handle super large files such as video and HD files; however, if one of the hard drives fails, all information is lost.

RAID 1 systems is used to write and duplicate information on multiple disks, creating a copy of a single hard drive onto another hard drive. The RAID 1 is used primarily for storage of media and information dependability. In the event one hard drive fails, the second or backup hard drive is available to retrieve information. Performance is reduced with a RAID 1 and RAID 1 systems are somewhat costly because you must purchase two of the same size discs. If you require 1 terabyte (TB) of storage the RAID 1 must have at least two 1TB hard drives to maintain the backup storage.

RAID 2 is similar to the RAID 0; however, the information data is broken down into smaller bits and uses supporting hard drives for backup and error protection to be able to access backup information if original data is lost. Because the RAID 2 must have a large number of disks, they are very expensive and rarely used.

RAID 3 is also similar to the RAID 0 because it stripes information over multiple hard drives; however, it uses one single hard drive as the backup drive. Since all the drives are working at the same time, accesses to the drives is limited to one read or write session at a time. These drives are not usually found in basic office spaces. The RAID 3 does provide the backup that is not available with the RAID 0 and is well suited for speed and large files.

RAID 4 is similar to the RAID 3 where it strips and backs up information; however, it is done at a larger data level. The hard drives become more independent and users are able to read data and information while other events are being accessed from the drives. The backup disk is also written when users write information to the RAID 4. A minimum number of hard drives required for a RAID 4 is three.

RAID 5 is the best combination of all RAID drives and provides both high performance and the backup needed for most facility applications. It stripes and backs up information between multiple hard drives instead of a single disk. Because the information is written and backed up across all hard drives multiple users are able to write simultaneously. Because of the RAID 5 design, if you lose a hard drive, information is still available because the backup information is on a different disc. Three discs are the minimum.

RAID 6 is very similar to a RAID 5; however, it utilizes two hard drives for backup. It is designed where if one drive fails during data retrieval, the RAID keeps working without notice. With a RAID 6 you will need a minimum of four hard drives.

There are a system of RAID levels beyond the basic 0 to 6 that include multiple RAID such as RAID 1 + 0 and 0 + 1. This supports the ability to have a RAID 0 with high performance mirrored with a RAID 1 so information is uniformly backed up on the RAID 1.

RAID is a reliable storage system for large amounts of information such as HD videos, large images, and support information. It should not be considered a substitute for an archival location to store information. There is always the possibility for a total RAID failure, virus, or deletion/overwriting of information.

Backup software automatically backs up imagery, folders, and additional data to dedicated locations such as external hard drives, servers, or cloud storage. It is recommended to have this software regularly back up your information at scheduled times dependent upon how often you add images and information. You may want to consider a backup scheduled after each workday or perhaps one to two times each day to maintain a safe backup of files.

There may be some concerns when using cloud storage due to the risks involved with the level of reliability and security of the cloud storage company. Cloud storage may not be the ideal place to archive imagery and data but may be a very good location for backup files.

Image Cataloging Software

Forensic photographers take many photos at the crime scene and in the laboratory, and gather evidence at multiple locations, so they require a means to organize imagery. Cataloging them with photo-managing software can organize them in a way that they are easily recognized and accessible to retrieve at a future time. Many of the software programs contain a variety of ways to categorize images and data as well as having basic photo-editing ability.

Photo managing software's primary purpose is to provide a means to easily access a specific or a group of images quickly. The software also supports operations such as tagging which enables the user to categorize images with software presets such as location or date; however, specific tagging can be added by the photographer to add individual details such as case number or subject information. These tags can be searched by the user individually or in multiples to find specific images within a large database. Software containing many preset and customizable tagging or category options is more efficient when looking for images in a vast database.

Photo-managing software features that are most advantageous to users include how the program categorizes images, and how fast the images can be retrieved from a large database from a search-engine feature. Additionally, how the overall user interface allows a variety of organizational tools to be easily available allows for quick search ability and fine tuning to customize features and tools that you would use regularly. The photo-editing features in most photo-managing software are basic and can be used for simple procedures such as cropping or possibly adding text; however, it is better to use professional editing software when enhancing images.

Software for file management ultimately needs to be compatible with all file formats such as RAW, JPG, TIFF, PNG, or others. The ability to use a variety of file formats can support the editing features and organization of images, and save files into many file formats. In each file format created, you have the ability to tag, code, and label images to successfully find images in the database.

Image-managing software's ability to support social media and share images on many sites such as Facebook or Flickr will allow you to post supporting imagery and information to public or internal sites. The ability to share and upload large albums, galleries, or individual images is a way to view images among organizations and can also be used in connection with a cloud as another method of backing up files.

Image-management software ranges in features from a basic photo browser to a very robust digital image management system (DIMS). The following are some examples of software that may be used to manage images:

- Adobe Bridge
- Adobe Lightroom
- Phase One Media Pro

- Apple iPhoto (Macintosh platform only)
- ACDsee
- Dims
    - Linear systems
    - Mideo systems
    - VeriPic

Be sure to compare the features offered by each solution before making a decision. Also you should consider the size of your image collection (present and future), backup, security, access control, and, as always, budgetary constraints.

Chapter 4 Light and Lighting

Effectively utilizing light will create an image that will give forensic investigators the ability to analyze details of a scene and evidence. Light has a specific size and output to illuminate subjects. Most lights are adjustable or have the ability to control brightness, thereby providing the forensic photographer an ability to control how objects are illuminated. The light that illuminates an object will come from a specific direction relative to the object's surface(s). Supplemental lights can be added to the single directional light source to support and expose additional details of the scene or object. The following information will explain and demonstrate a variety of lighting methods and how the style affects characteristics of the scene and object.

Creating effective lighting for forensic documentation is more than simply adding light to a scene. It is necessary to have a technical knowledge about light, adjustments, and related behaviors. There is light, and then there is lighting. How to create effective light for forensic photography does not have to be an overly complicated challenge. Using basic equipment in conjunction with some practical strategies can lead to detailed and successful outcomes. It is possible without great skills in photographic lighting to produce adequate results but, very often, artificial lighting photographs will look more like amateurish snapshots for the uninitiated. Good lighting makes the characteristics of subjects visible and can make the nearly invisible visible. This is the ultimate goal of good lighting required for and used in scientific photography. Proper lighting and using a variety of techniques will reveal many characteristics of a subject.

Forensic imagery using artificial light must be carefully considered. Photographs for evidence need to be first and foremost about scientific data and not about an interpretation or bias. They need to exhibit neutral points of view. The forensic photographer must determine what type or types of lighting supports and delivers the best information detail to investigators. Good lighting should not be throwing light randomly onto a subject to simply capture an image. Forensic images cannot embellish, amplify, or distort characteristics of subjects. The lighting that is created must reveal the characteristics of the subject and *not* imply a bias or lead to a false perception about the subject that compromises truth and reality. Forensic pictures must be about facts and not create uncertainty.

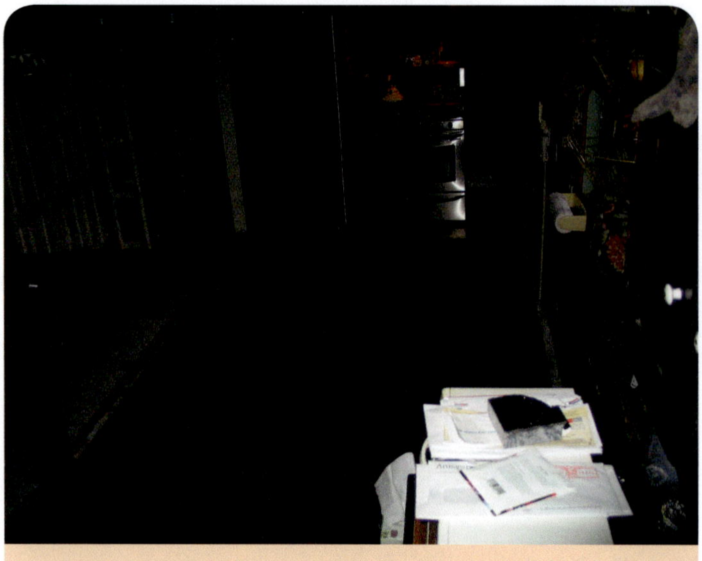

Figure 4.1 Example of poor lighting of a scene

Sometimes creating factual pictures can be more challenging than expected. How lighting is administered can be one element for changing the details of evidence. Photography is an interpretive process and lighting defines and reveals facts about an object. This outcome is based on professional decisions and knowledge used by the forensic photographer. Lighting can change the emphasis of details and make common subjects look dramatic. It can distort relationships of evidence within the scene or make the subject appear normally as a viewer might expect it to be.

The primary light source and how the qualities of the lighting complement the scene are used to create and emphasize details of the scene and object. The details and the importance can be diminished or accentuated simply by where and how a light is shined onto and at a subject. Effective lighting is a process that starts with an analysis of the scene and objects of interest, then determines what is needed to be recorded and why.

The scene and subject will always play a pivotal role in determining the use of effective lighting strategies. Scenes and subjects may contain a variety of challenges. Objects can be solid such as vehicle tires or shiny like a knife or bullet casings, transparent like a glass window or water. Scenes may be somewhat flat and cover large areas or are three-dimensional and have many cavernous areas that are a challenge to illuminate. A scene's characteristics will determine how and which lighting style to use. Due to the quantity of variables, a forensic photographer may be required to use multiple lighting techniques within the same scene or situation to highlight numerous details for analysis.

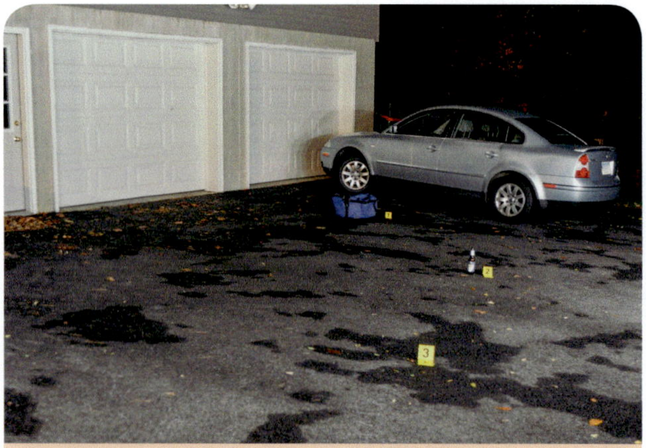

Figure 4.2.1 Example of effective lighting of a scene

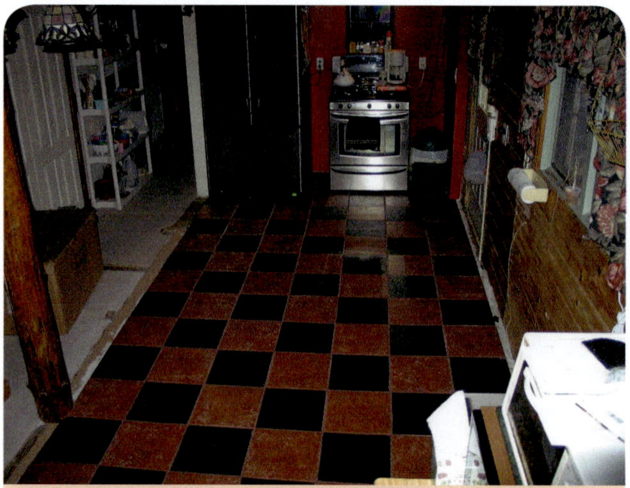

Figure 4.2.2 Example of location of objects lit within a scene

Fundamental methods for lighting consist in the most basic form of the use of a main light and a fill light, since our world in its natural state consists of only one point light source—the sun. There is a subliminal expectation by viewers to see only one shadow. The main light creates the shadow and the fill light will brighten the shadow area to be able to see details.

A light's quality describes how the light enhances, or fails to enhance, details of the subject. The lighting style, whether it is a harsh direct light or soft diffuse light, will present different appearances and effects on the subject. Direct light creates a very harsh directional light and sharp, hard shadows within the subject matter. This harsh light can come from the sun or most commonly the on-camera flash. The size of the light will have a direct relationship to the harshness of the light.

When making lighting decisions, it is important to consider what you are trying to emphasize within the scene and how the light interacts with the evidence. Color, texture, shape, topography, cracks, or any other characteristics of the evidence that are relevant must be distinct and measureable. Lighting can come from above and is called reflected light, or light can come from below a translucent or transparent object and be called transmitted light. Some situations will require both transmitted and reflected light components to show surface and internal characteristics of the evidence.

Lighting Styles and Effects

Available Light

There are situations when the use of an external light source or flash unit is not available or not practical to use and the only light source is available light within the scene. During these times, you may need to rely on best practices you have learned in low-light situations. One tip to consider is to use a sturdy tripod for long exposures. If you are without a tripod, you must increase your ISO to allow a handheld camera shutter speed. It is also useful to use a fast lens and/or prime lens that has a large aperture near *f*/2.8 to allow as much light as possible onto the imaging sensor. Some lenses and cameras have a built-in image stabilization feature that will adjust for image blur during hand-holding of the camera.

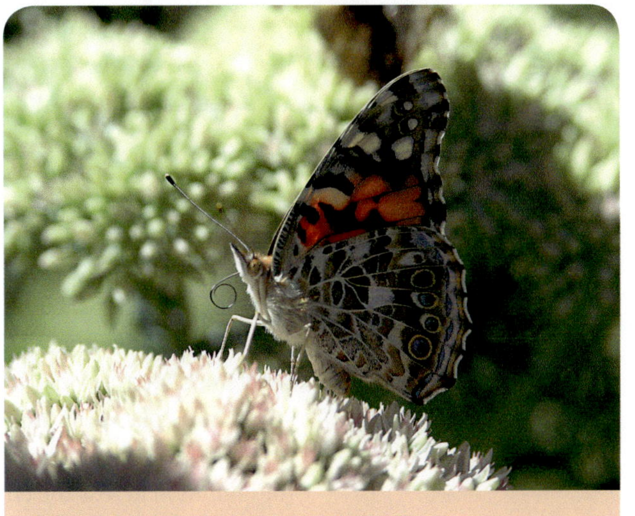

Figure 4.3 Image example of available light

When capturing an image, make the light your friend. Situate yourself in a position where the light will illuminate your subject. Signage, streetlights, reflected lights, and window lights are useful to capture the subject matter. Wide-open apertures will create a low depth of field, so in this situation maximize the depth of field by focusing on the primary subject in the scene. Later within this chapter we will discuss the painting with light method during low-light situations and how this process will increase the depth of field of the image.

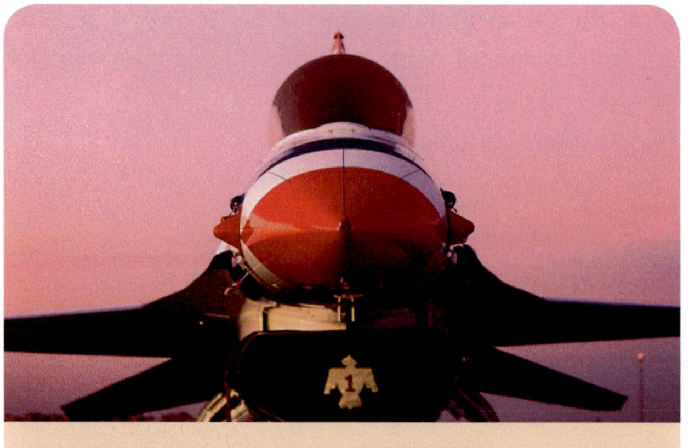

Figure 4.4 Image example of available light

Frontal or Direct Lighting

Frontal lighting is created with the light behind or near the photographer's camera and lens that makes pictures look as though the light came from the camera's lens itself or on axis with the camera, similar to that of an on-camera flash. The light on the subject is reflected directly back into the lens imaging surface. Frontal lighting is used to minimize shadows within the evidence and created a very flat textureless image. This lighting style creates high contrast; however, it does not show the dimensional shape or texture of the subject. One item that a photographer must take into consideration when using frontal lighting is not to create a hot spot or an over-exposed area within the scene. Diffusing the main front light, which will be explained further as lighting method, moving the light source further away from the subject, and using a larger focal length lens can eliminate this.

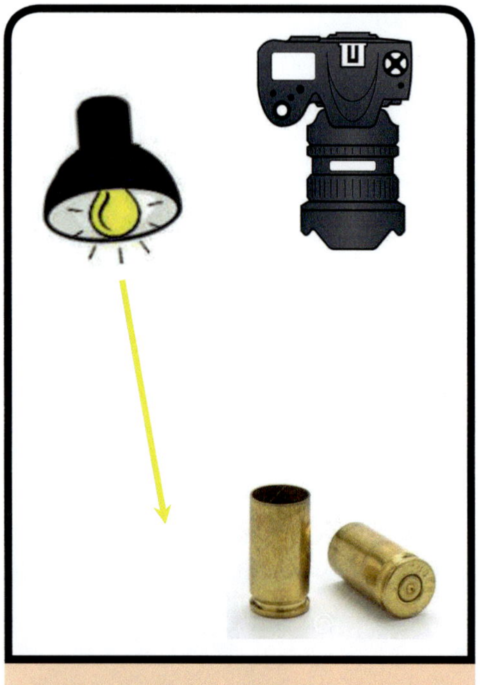

Figure 4.5 Frontal lighting diagram

Bounce Lighting

Bounce lighting uses a technique where the flash or external light source is reflected off an object or surface to create a softer and directional illumination of the subject. A direct flash or light is rather harsh and flattens the subject matter. Bounce lighting is a soft lighting style that reduces harsh shadows and creates a gentle appearance. Items such as a wall or ceiling are readily available indoors. Objects such as portable reflectors, white cards, or opaque plastic diffusers can be attached to the external camera flash unit to bounce and soften the light.

When using the bounce lighting technique, the light emitted from the flash unit is reflect and this reflected light is reduced from the original output. This requires the photographer to make adjustments to his exposure setting to compensate and create a quality exposure. Elements that may require changing would be to increase the ISO, open up the aperture or have a lower f-number and decrease the camera shutter speed.

Copy (45-Degree) Lighting

Copy lighting or 45-degree lighting, uses one or more lights positioned at 45-degree angles off axis from the camera lens. The primary use for copy or 45-degree lighting is to discern an items shape and size. In the event a single light source is used, a white of reflective material can be placed on the opposite side of the main light to reduce shadows. This type of lighting is also useful for copying flat work or paper products. It creates a shadow-less even illumination across the entire imaging area. It is best to use a copy stand making the camera's imaging plane parallel with the objects surface. Lights must be evenly spaced at 45 degrees off the centerline of the lens. The illumination from the lights overlaps and creates a smooth even illumination across the entire surface.

Side (Oblique) Lighting

Side lighting consists of light that falls on a subject within the scene at approximately ninety degrees to the side of the camera. The light skims across the surface of the scene at a very low oblique angle. This lighting technique adds dimension and texture to object, bringing edges into sharper focus and enhancing the visual impact of the image. Side lighting is usually used to show detail by creating shadows on the surface of the evidence. This means that one side of a subject will be lit and the other side will be in shadow. It is most commonly used when photographing impressions, tool marks and certain types of fingerprints but can also be used to photograph dusty footwear impressions and indented writing. In terms of helping to convey a subject's shape and form this is ideal. Of the three directions, side lighting creates the strongest sense that a subject has three dimensions. An issue created with the use of side lighting is that it does not evenly illuminate your

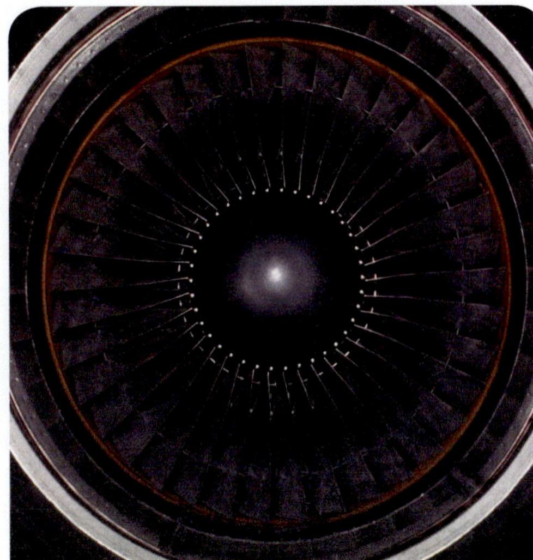

Figure 4.6.1 Image example of front lighting of an engine turbine

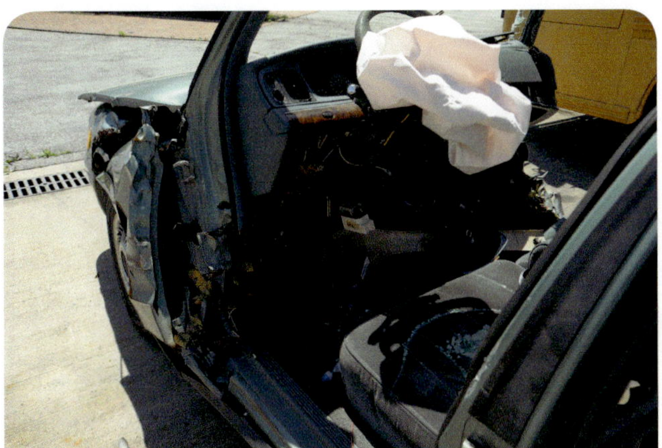

Figure 4.6.2 Image example of frontal lighting without fill flash

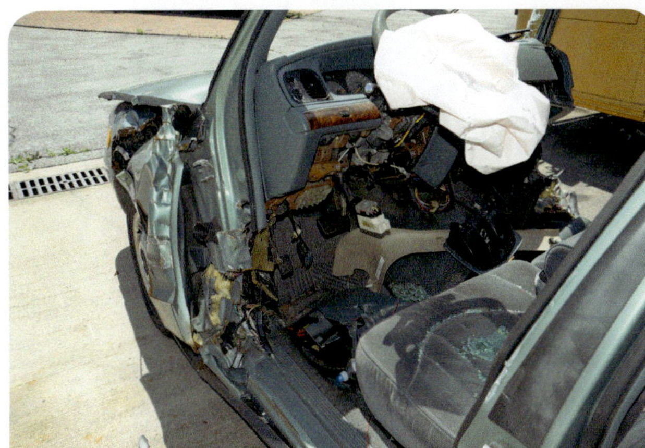

Figure 4.6.3 Image example of frontal lighting with fill flash

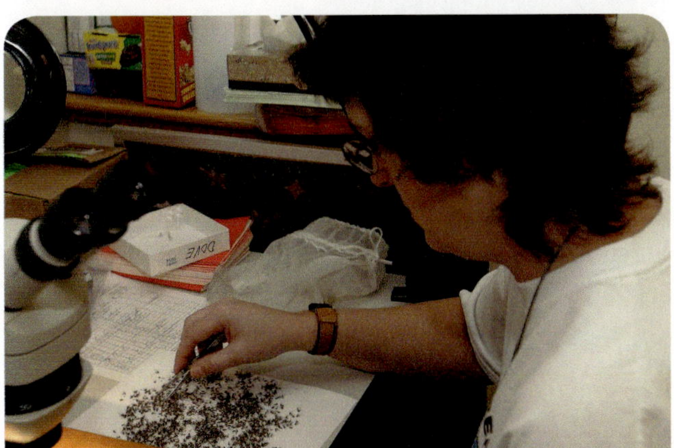

Figure 4.7 Image example of bounce lighting, mosquito counting

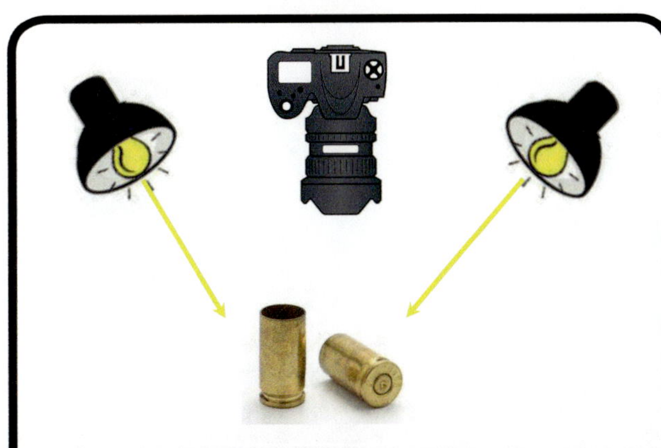

Figure 4.8 Copy lighting or 45 degree lighting diagram

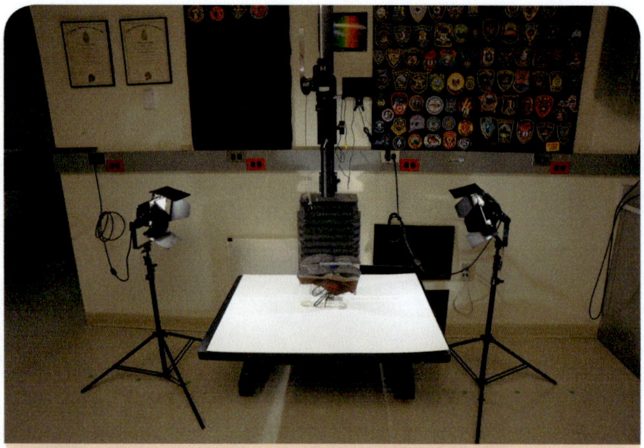

Figure 4.9.1 Image example of 45-degree lighting system

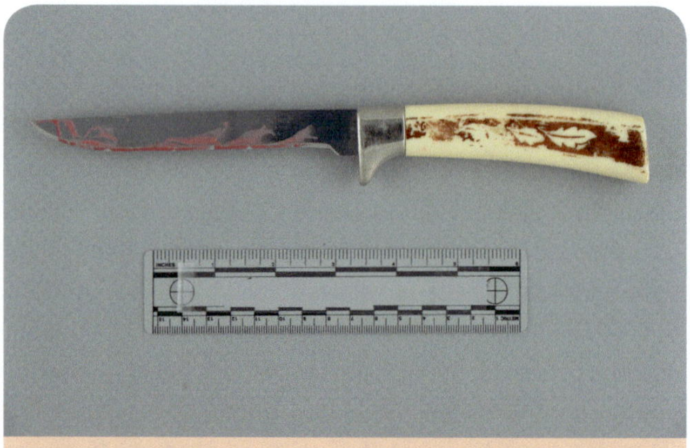

Figure 4.9.2 Image example of diffuse lighting of evidence, shot in a light tent

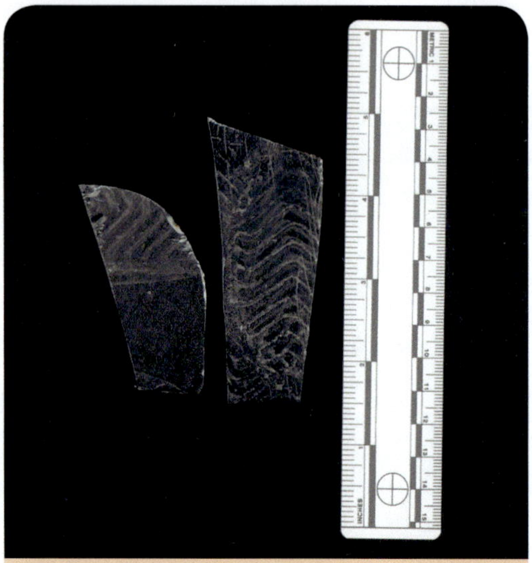

Figure 4.9.3 Image example of 45-degree lighting of evidence

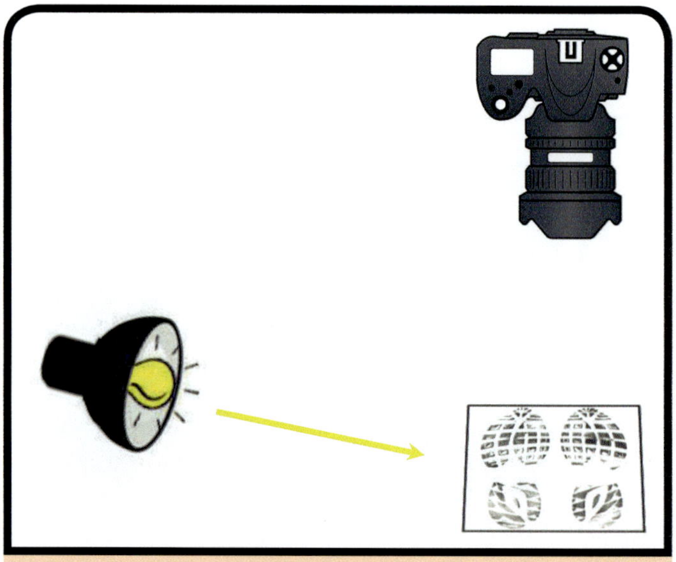

Figure 4.10 Side lighting diagram

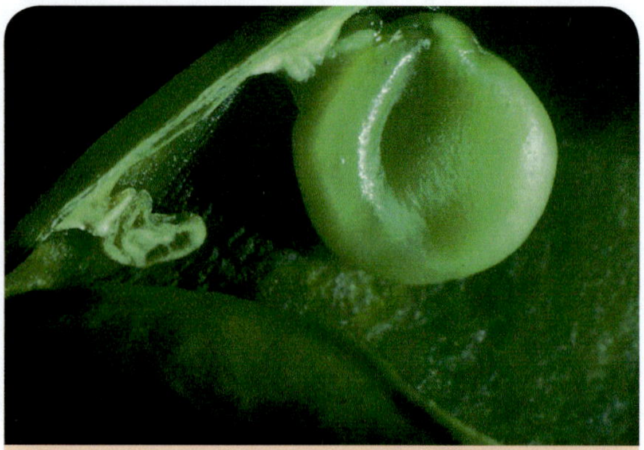

Figure 4.11.1 Image example of side lighting, pea pod

subject. One side of a subject will be lit and the other side will be in shadow. In terms of helping to convey a subject's shape and form this is ideal.

Side lighting is most effective when you want to emphasize texture, dimension, shapes, or patterns. It enhances the subject's contours and textures.

Back Lighting

Back lighting is created when the light source is behind the subject being aimed towards the camera. The photographer will expose the image for the light source behind the subject. The subject, which is in front of the light source, becomes a silhouette.

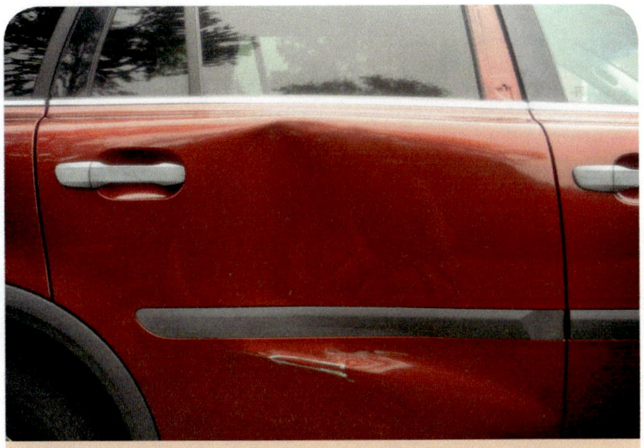

Figure 4.11.2 Image example without side lighting

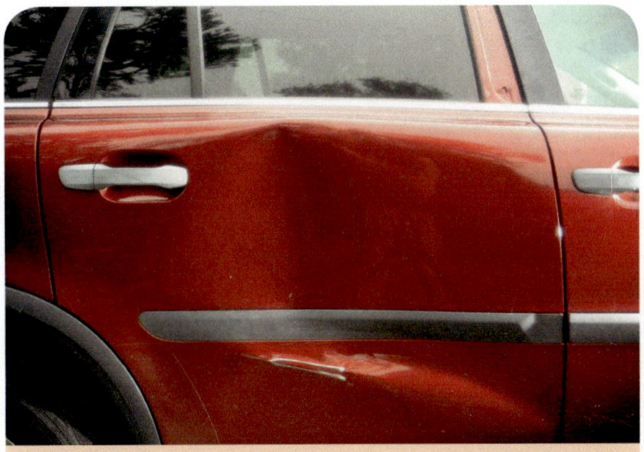

Figure 4.11.3 Image example with side lighting

Silhouettes appear flat and almost like a cardboard cutout. If the shape of your subject is strong this can be a very effective way to provide the shape of the object. Additionally depending upon exposure the image can create a halo effect around the subject.

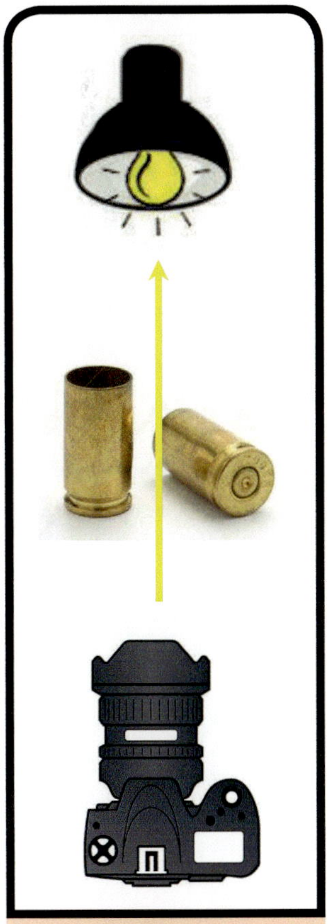

Figure 4.12 Back lighting diagram

Diffused Lighting

Diffused lighting is usually used for photographing evidence with shiny or reflective surfaces and creates a soft light that results in a smooth even light. This type of lighting uses an opaque material placed on or between the light source and the subject to soften the light. The effect is a reduction in reflections and hot spots. Material used to diffuse the light can be as common household items such as white linens or an empty water/milk bottle. There are many diffusion devices for sale that are available for forensic imaging and are easily adaptable to lights and lighting systems you may currently use.

Shining light through a milky plastic bottle is the easiest and a highly effective method to make a broadly diffused light. The plastic bottle can be easily cut at the bottom and top leaving only the cylinder bottle for use as the diffusion material. The height of the tube will be determined by the focal length of the lens. Once positioned over the subject, the lights can be positioned close to the diffusion bottle. This type of lighting behaves much like tent-style lighting and subjects will be surrounded and bathed in a diffuse 360 degree enveloping light.

Diffuse Tent Lighting

Shiny objects like highly polished metal or mirrors have entirely reflective surfaces. A shiny surface can be a very tough subject to light and photograph for sure. Lights, cameras, photographers, and anything else will be reflected back to the camera. Depending on the size or prominence of the reflections, they can be terribly distracting and certainly are not a positive element in the photograph.

Using a broad light similar to the diffuse lighting strategy will create a successful image; however, the broad light being used will reflect itself in the shiny surface of the subject. The broad light will create a highly reflective surface to be captured by the photographer. Another method to light shiny objects is by using tent lighting which is sometimes a

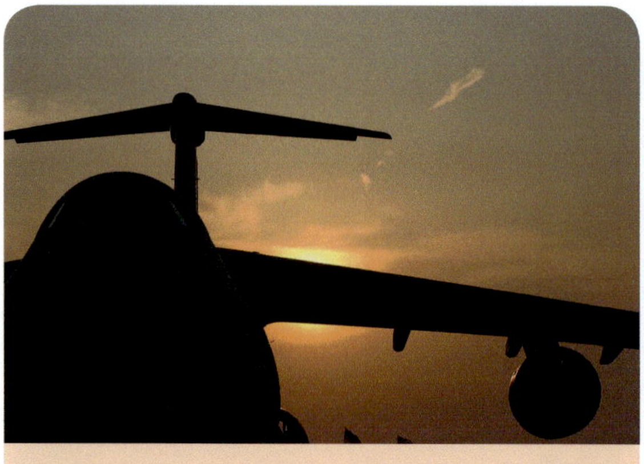

Figure 4.13.1 Image example of backlight, C5 aircraft

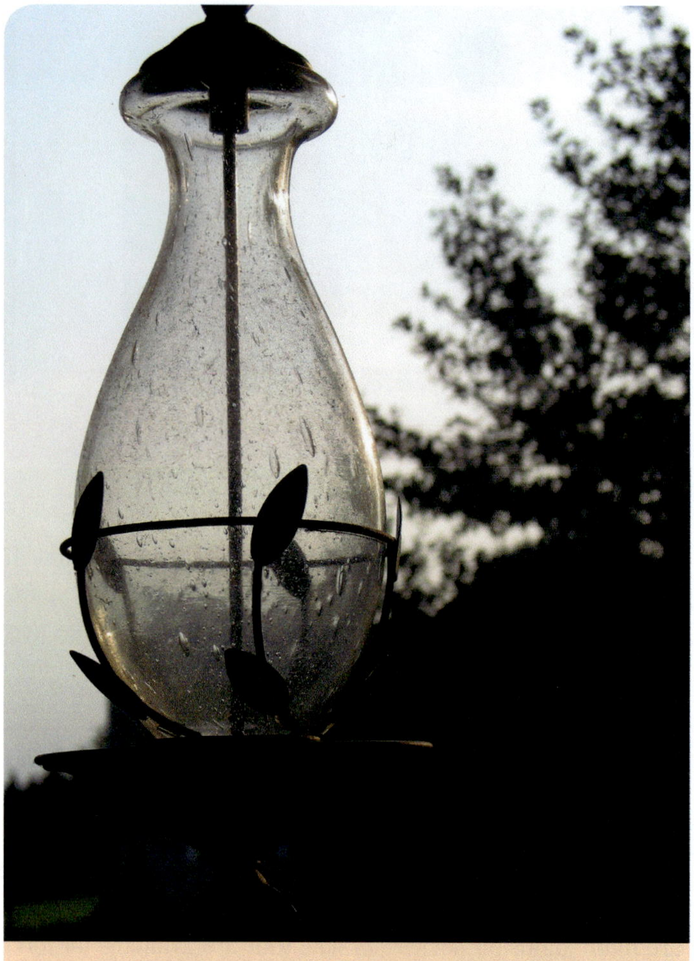

Figure 4.13.2 Image example of backlight, birdfeeder

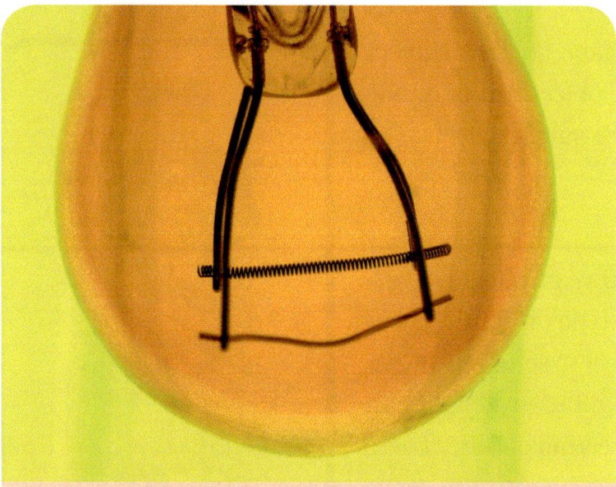

Figure 4.13.3 Image example of backlight, lightbulb

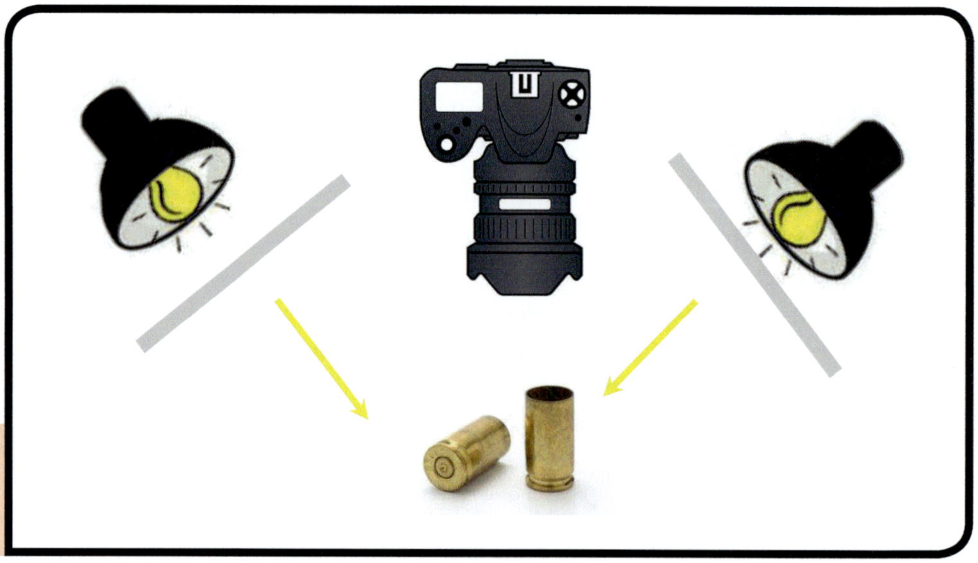

Figure 4.14 Diffuse lighting diagram

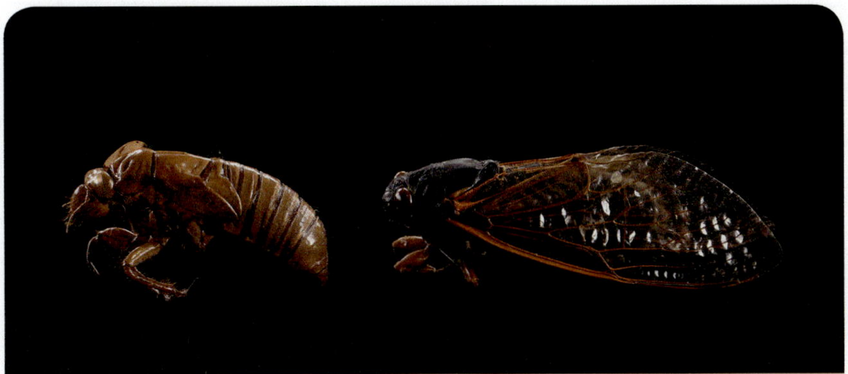

Figure 4.15.1 Image example of diffuse lighting, umbrella

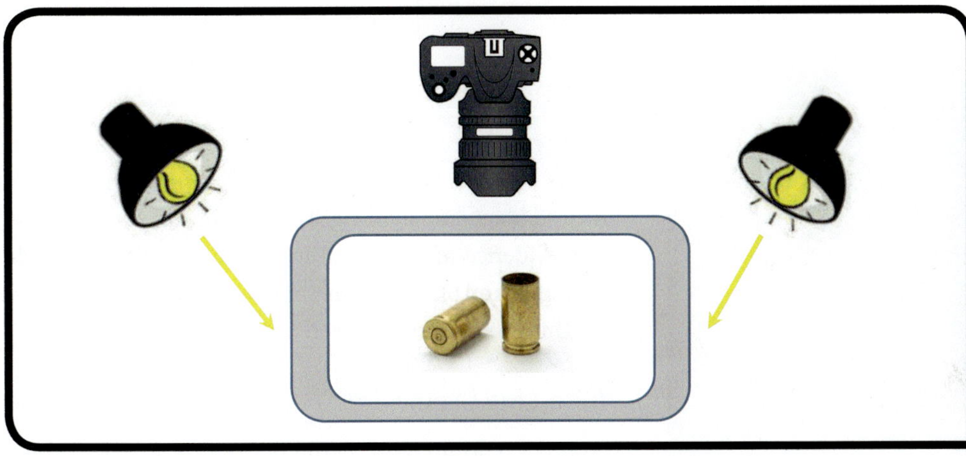

Figure 4.16 Diffuse tent lighting diagram

better approach when lighting a mirror-like surface. The tent is created out of a white semi-rigid material similar to white foam-core or cardboard. It can also be constructed with a combination of materials such as a white metal or cardboard framework, then enclosing the open area with a white linen or heavier semi-opaque plastic similar to a shower curtain. The size of the tent will be determined by the size of the evidence. A single light or multiple lights are shined through the inside of the tent. The light is bounced around inside the tent and is delicately reflected in the highly polished and reflective surfaces of the subject.

Transmitted Lighting

Transmitted lighting is produced by light shining through the subject and toward the camera and imaging surface. It creates a background that contains no shadows and projects the transparent or translucent subject of evidence onto the imaging surface. The transmitted light can be adjusted from 90 degrees to 45 degrees for the desired effect. The most common use of transmitted lighting is in photographing evidence on glass or transparent objects such as a fingerprint on a drinking glass.

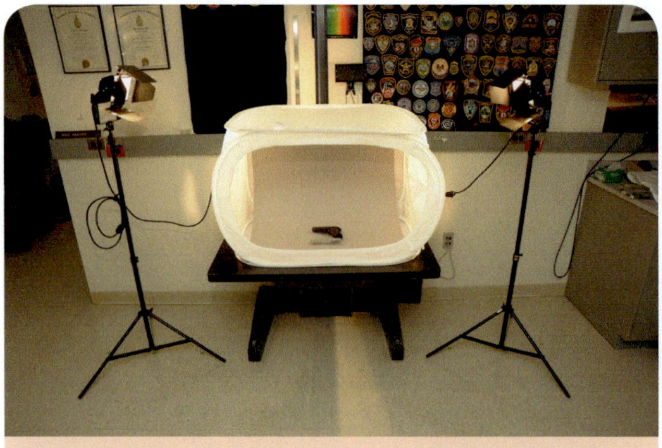

Figure 4.17.1 Image example of diffuse tent lighting system

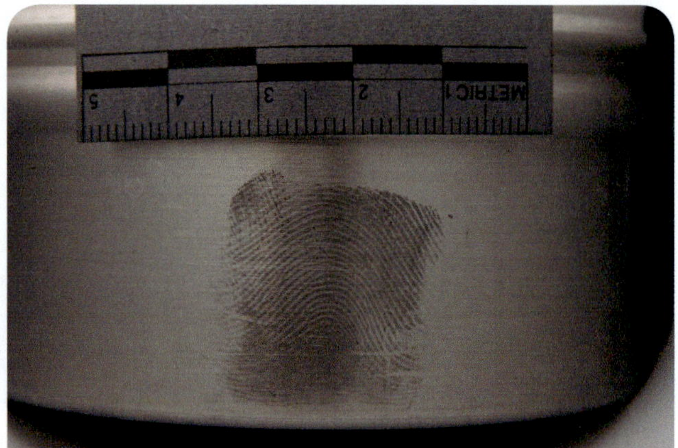

Figure 4.17.2 Image example of tent lighting fingerprint on metal

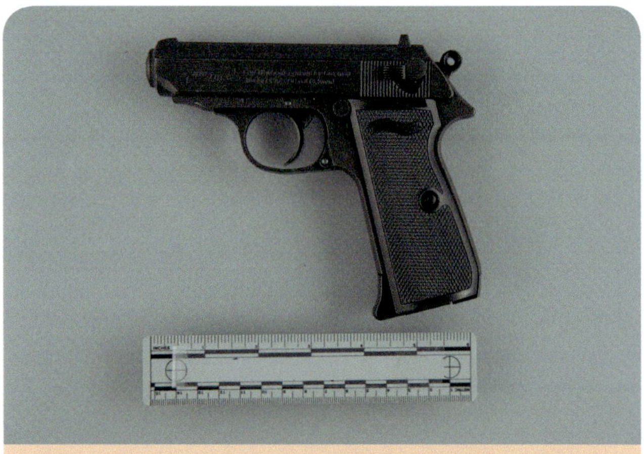

Figure 4.17.3 Image example of tent lighting of evidence

Alternative Transmitted Light

An alternative method for forensic imaging or transparent objects and specifically glassware is in the forms of white line and black line lighting. Though the effects of lighting glass evidence may be seen in all areas of the glass. The white-line and black-line methods are best describes by the way the light is seen at the edge of the glass.

White-Line Glassware

If there is a bright light on the side and/or on the surfaces of the glass subject closest to the camera, then the lighting is known as a white-line lighting. As the light passes through the glass, the glass absorbs light. Maneuvering the lights and reflections gives the photographer the ability to place different amounts of reflection on areas of interest upon the surface of the glass. This will enable the capture of fine details and help to show specifics and form of the glass. White-line glassware lighting is useful to reveal glass artifacts and edge definition. White-line lighting is produced by placing a piece of black material behind the subject then adding two lights outside the field of view. These lights are directed through the glass subject from behind it using an oblique of view to the camera lens. It is best to locate pieces of black cardboard or other black material to act as a curtain or baffle to the lights so the lights do not shine directly into the camera's lens. In this fashion, there is the creation of slits of light that comes from behind the glass subject. Light coming from this direction will become trapped within the vessel and cause the edges of the glass to glow white. With white-line lighting, fingerprints, and other particulates material can quickly become the focal point of a photograph if prominent in the composition and made highly visible by this type of lighting.

Black-Line Glassware

Transmitted light that passes through the glassware and creates no reflections on the camera-facing surfaces produces a black-line lighting pattern along the sides and edges of the glass. Black-line lighting occurs because the light is transmitting through the glass without reflection. The glass absorbs portions of the light and acts as a filter providing information like color, density, and thickness of the glass. Black-line lighting is created by initially placing a white or light gray background behind the subject. Place the glassware on a sheet of glass that is elevated above the table thereby allowing light to enter the glassware from the bottom. The last step is to shine a small spot of light directly behind the subject similar to back lighting. This will make the subject appear backlit and display dark edges. It is important to have only the diffuse or bounced backlight striking the glassware. If you would like to bring out detail within the surface of the object place a light in front or to the side of the camera. You may want to use a soft diffuse light or use an object to block any direct light from striking the glassware. Opposite to that of the white-line lighting edges, the black-line lighting appears to flatten the visual space of the glass.

White-line and black-line lighting methods of lighting glass can provide different information about the evidence and glass structure. Reflecting light through a glass or clear object containing defects or evidence on or within the glass creates a white-line appearance and may permit the photographer to record specifics of evidence. Conversely light being absorbed by the evidence and glass creating a black line will also permit the photographer to record specifics of evidence. Both methods are capable of supporting investigations and providing facts for the record.

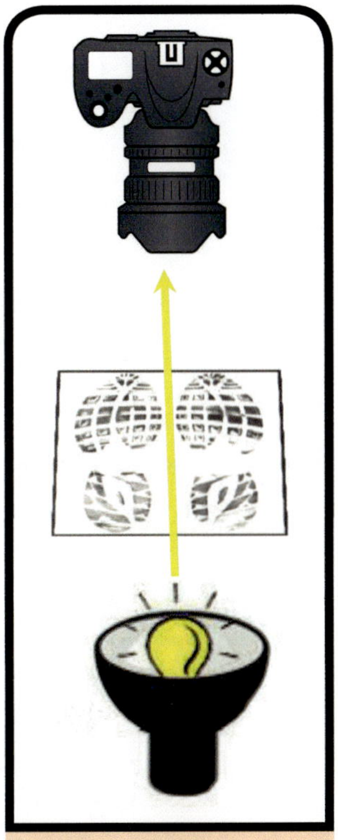

Figure 4.18 Transmitted lighting diagram

Polarizing Light and Filters

Light travels in waves that oscillate in a variety of directions. One can consider that light travels in a vertical (up-and-down) direction and horizontally (side-to-side) direction.

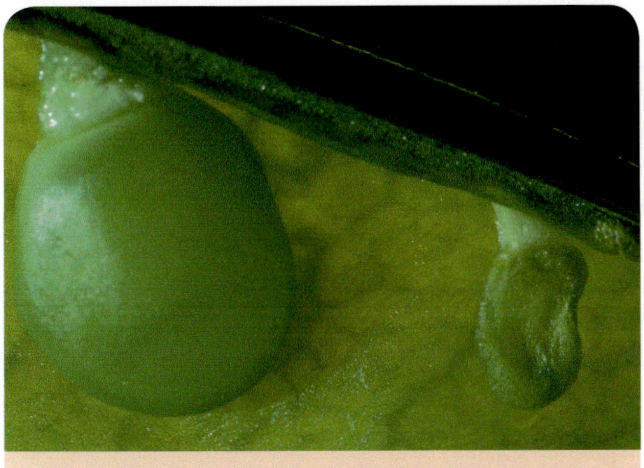

Figure 4.19.1 Image example of transmitted light, pea pod

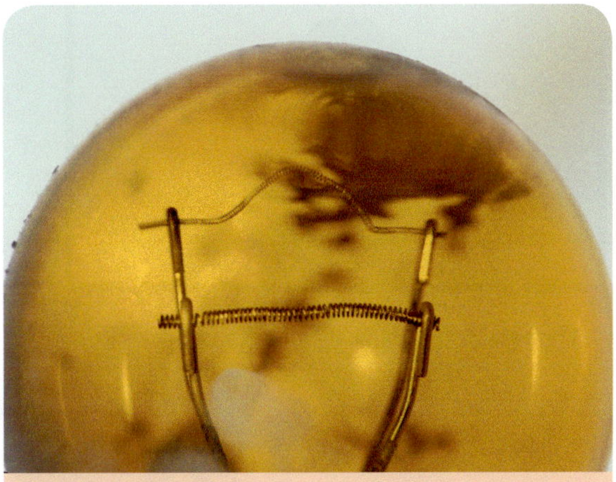

Figure 4.19.2 Image example of transmitted light, light bulb

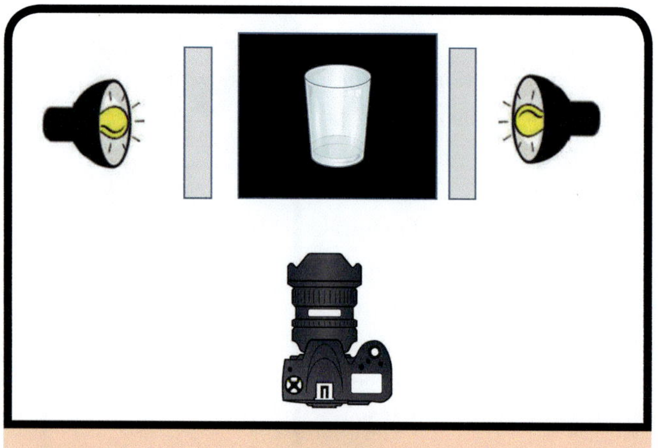

Figure 4.20 White-line lighting diagram

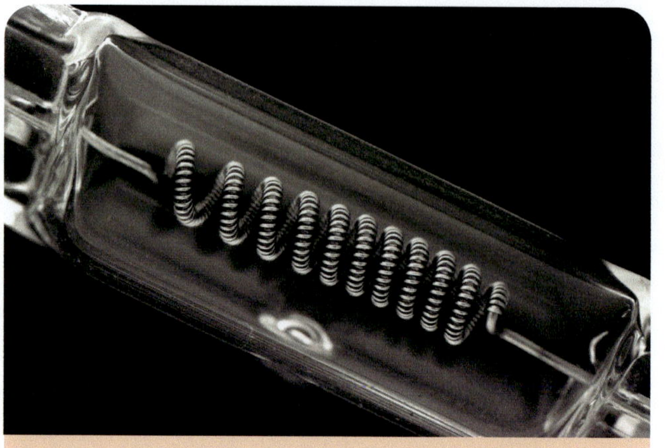

Figure 4.21 Image example of white-line, lightbulb

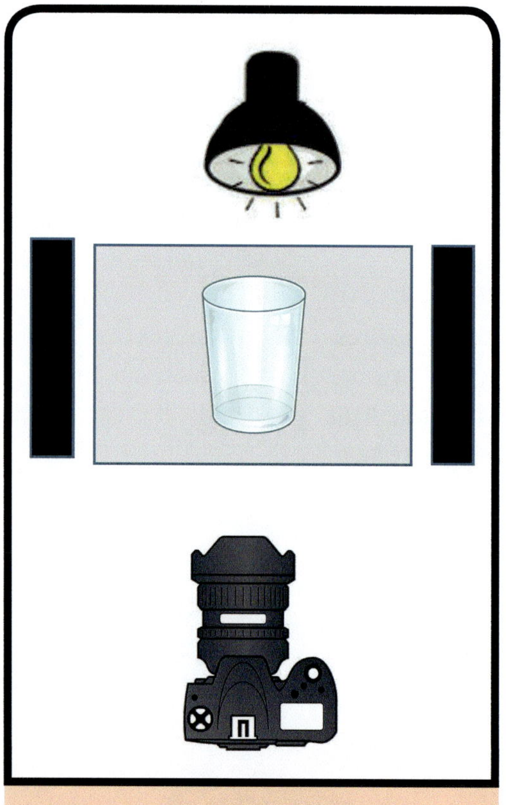

Figure 4.22 Black-line lighting diagram

A polarizing filter will modify or eliminate light from one direction and only permit light aligned in only one direction to enter the camera system. Imaging polarization is most effective on reflections and flat surfaces such as water, roads, vehicles, windows, and the sky. Make sure that you use a circular digital polarizing filter on your digital camera system. Linear polarizing filters cannot be used for auto-focusing cameras or with in-camera metering systems because they remove the polarized light before it reaches the light meter. A circular polarizer is necessary for auto-focus camera systems. Circular polarizing filters contain a linear polarizer as the first element of the filter that orients the light in one direction. The linear polarizer is then followed by a quarter-wave plate, which modifies the now linearly polarized light. This modification allows the light to travel in a circular motion and remain polarized before entering the camera and this light does not affect the meter.

Neutral Density Filters

Neutral density (ND) filters are used to lower image brightness in the red, green, and blue spectrums evenly. ND filters have no color component to them and are used to remove brightness only. ND filters typically come in variances densities. A filter of a .3 increment will effectively remove 50% or the light that goes through the filter. There are filters sold with numerous densities, including .1, .6, and .9. Microscopes routinely come with ND filters built-in. In landscape photography, ND filters are often used to allow the use of long exposure times. This is desirable for making running water smooth, for example, or other more aesthetic reasons. In microscopy, ND filters are used to make the illumination comfortable for viewing or imaging.

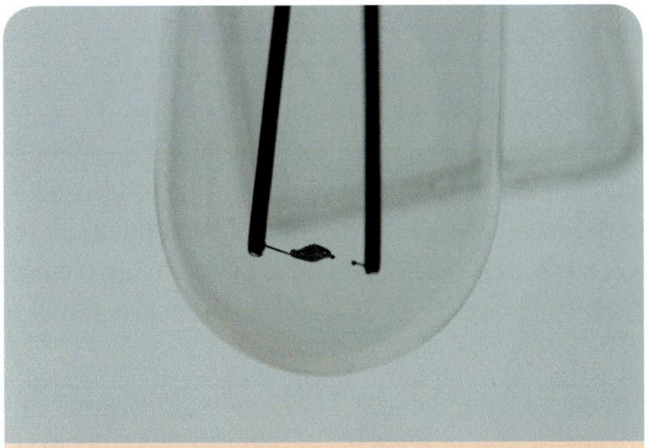

Figure 4.23 Image example of black-line lighting

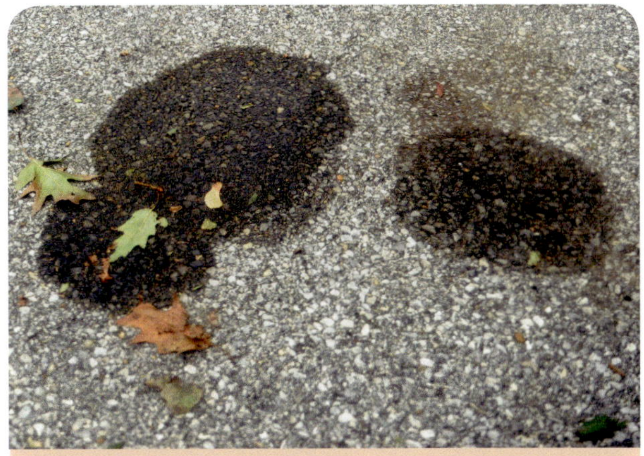

Figure 4.24.2.a Image example of oil stain without polarizing filter

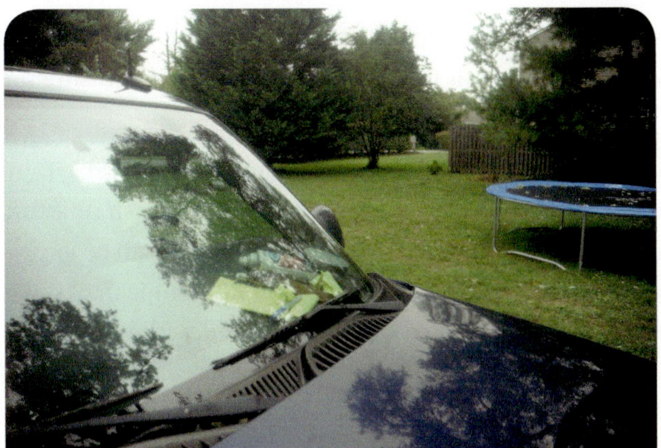

Figure 4.24.1.a Image example of windshield without polarizing filter

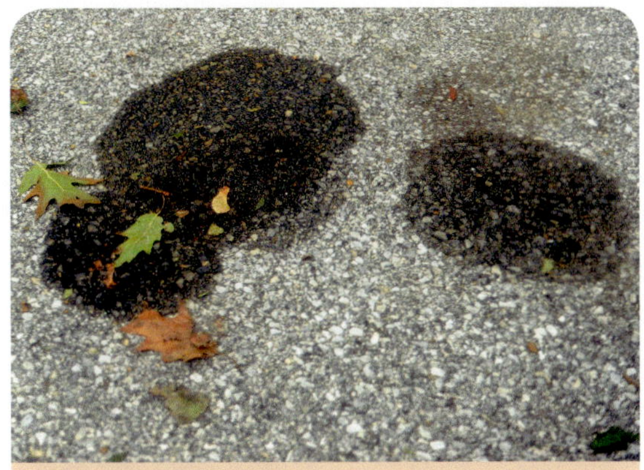

Figure 4.24.2.b Image example of oil stain with polarizing filter

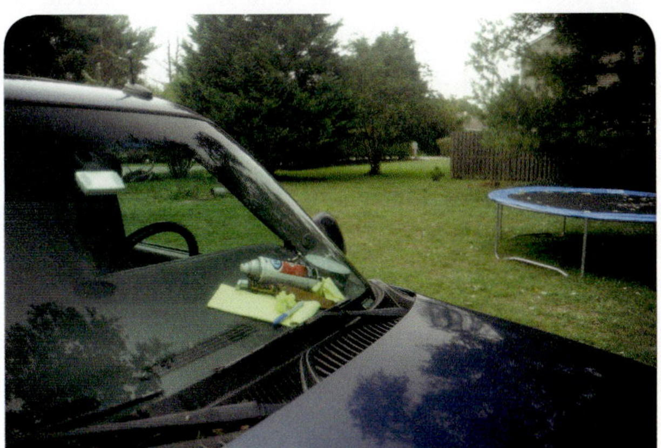

Figure 4.24.1.b Image example of windshield with polarizing filter

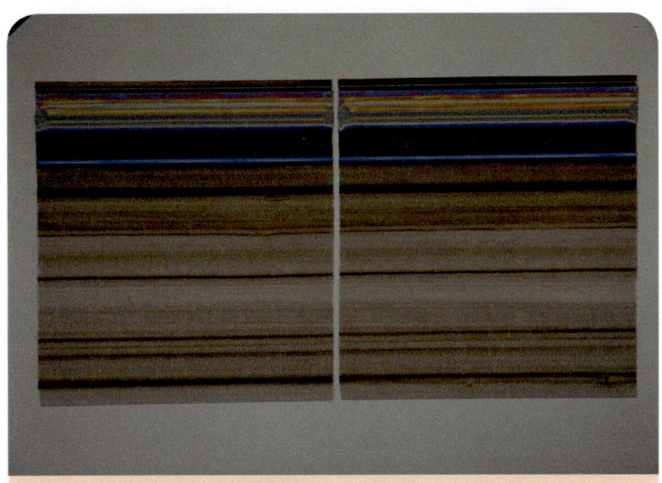

Figure 4.24.3 Image example of polarized plastic bag

Painting with Light

Forensic photography takes place at a variety of locations, weather conditions, and times of the day. Nighttime situations tend to occur often and create a challenge for any photographer. Painting with light is a solution to provide excellent images of the evidence and their location within a large scene. The process uses external light sources to illuminate the entire scene during a long shutter-speed exposure setting. Additionally, this process allows the photographer to use a low ISO setting to capture great details and a small aperture to achieve a maximum depth of field.

The process begins by securing the camera to a solid tripod and framing your scene and image. In M (manual mode) set the camera shutter speed to "B" (bulb). If this is not available, set the camera shutter speed to the longest exposure available. Adjust the ISO very low, 50 or 100 ISO, and adjust the aperture to *f*/22 or *f*/32, or the smallest you have available.

You will want to use a cable release, remote trigger, or the timer on your camera to activate the shutter. These will eliminate any camera shake that would occur by depressing the shutter release button.

The next step is to use your external flash to illuminate the entire scene and if possible minimize any secondary lights from vehicles or emergency lighting. An external flash unit that has a high guide number will provide enough illumination. These flash units can be expensive; however, they are multipurpose and can be used in everyday photographic needs. It is also recommended to obtain an external power source similar to ones described in Chapter 1 to support the amount of output and length of time required to create a successful image by painting with light.

The process for illuminating the scene with an external flash is completed by first activating the camera shutter. You will then quickly go to the subject that is the farthest distance from the camera and trigger the external flash at subjects within the scene. As you are activating the flash unit, move back and forth through the scene as well in the direction toward the camera. When triggering the flash unit, you will want to always shield the flash output from shining directly into the camera lens. As you are walking back towards the camera, the new flash exposures overlap and expose the shadow area created by the individual and new areas of the scene.

This process can be completed by a single individual or by multiple people with many external flash units. If multiple individuals are working together to illuminate the scene, try not to flash onto another individual. The result would be a "ghost" image of the individual who the flash shines upon.

A great part of digital photography is the immediacy of viewing the newly created "painted with light" image. It is recommended to practice this process prior to using it within an active investigation scene and also try to use the equipment you would normally take to an investigation site so you are familiar with how your camera and flash units work together to create an amazing "nighttime" image.

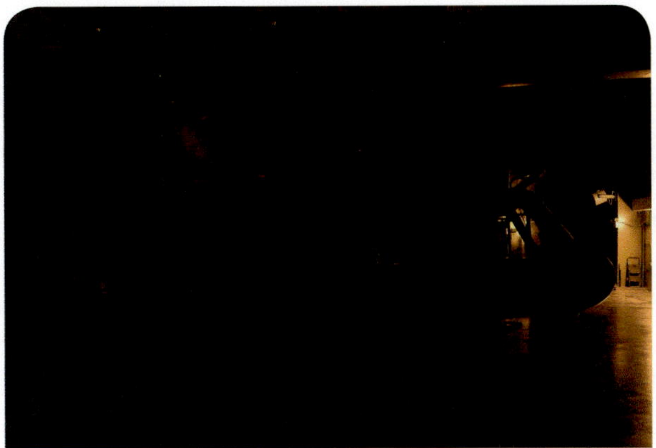

Figure 4.25.1 Image example of helicopter without painting with light (only available light)

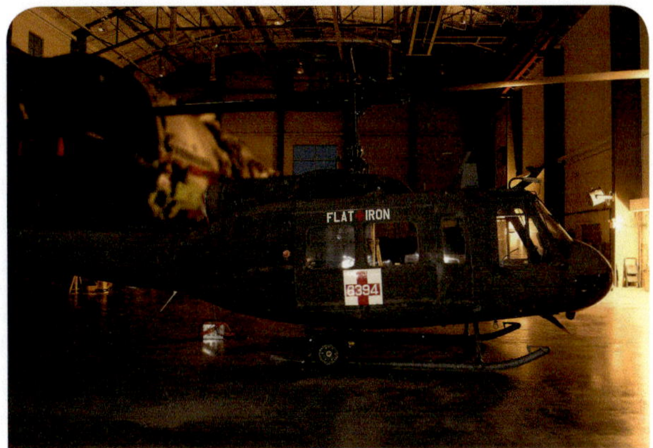

Figure 4.25.2 Image example of helicopter illuminated by painting with light

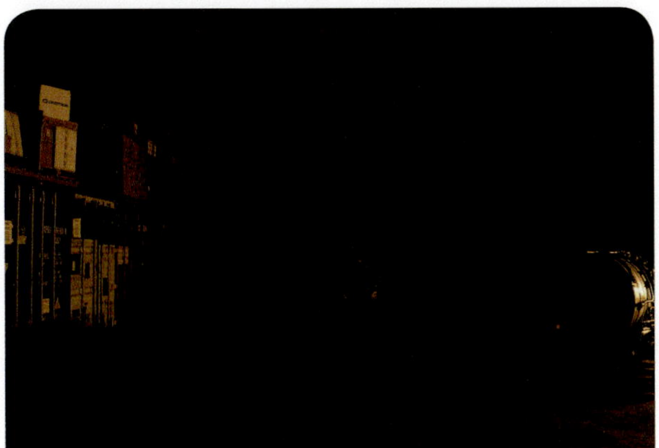

Figure 4.25.3 Image example of open bay without painting with light (only available light)

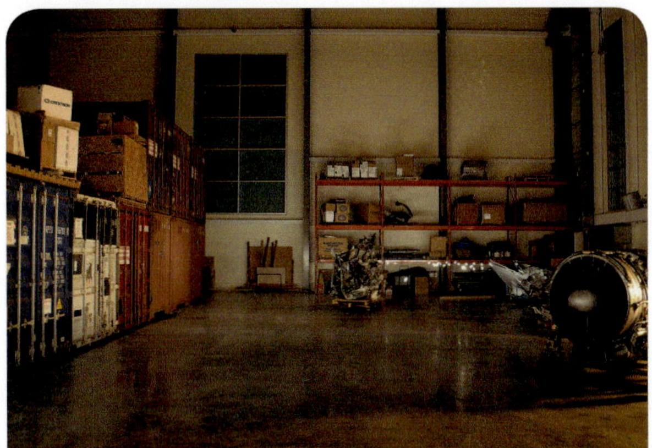

Figure 4.25.4 Image example of open bay illuminated by painting with light

Creating Effective Lighting

When deciding upon which lighting effect would be best to provide the greatest information to the investigator, one must consider a few items.

1. Analyze the scene and subject of interest.
2. Determine what is to be emphasized.
3. Choose the appropriate lighting style or multiple lighting styles in a single or multiple images.

Effective lighting is the product of knowledge, skills, and using the correct lighting technique and continuously practicing and honing your skills. Depending on the subject, effective lighting can be rather easy to achieve or extremely challenging. Start by evaluating the situation and evidence for documentation then develop a strategy to light the subject. One of the best ways to go about determining what is best is to remember KIS—"Keep It Simple." It is easy to overthink and complicate the process. Remember, the lighting enhances the subject and it should not be the main characteristic of the photograph. Many times it is very useful to use a single light source and method. In addition to a light's brightness and color temperature, the physical size of the light guide is an important characteristic for artificial light photography. Additionally, a light should be proportionally sized to an object's size. As a rule of thumb, small subjects benefit from using small lights and larger subjects may benefit from larger lights. This may not always be available, but one may want to take it into consideration when purchasing additional lights or making modifications to an existing light.

The lighting of forensic evidence does not have to be complicated. Using some practical and proven strategies makes it possible to produce highly effective and detailed images. The object of evidence and the scene will determine the quality of light and lighting style to support the evidence. The ability to control light and understand lighting style characteristics will make a forensic photographer more effective and valuable.

Chapter 5 Crime Scene Documentation

The primary focus of crime scene investigation is documentation and collection of evidence. It should go without saying that one of the best ways to document a scene is with photography. As essential as photography is for documentation, it still must be supplemented with detailed notes and sketches.

Safety at the Crime Scene

Before entering any crime scene there are some safety guidelines you should follow. These guidelines are for your own personal safety, which should be your number one priority, but are also to protect the scene from contamination:

- Wear latex gloves, facemasks, hairnets, and coverall gowns.
- Change your gloves and wash your hands often.
- Wear a facemask with a filter if there are possible aerosol or airborne pathogens.
- Properly dispose of contaminated clothing and supplies.
- Be alert for sharps and/or broken objects.
- Do not place your hands where you cannot see.
- Do not smoke, eat, or drink in the crime scene.

Crime Scenes

General Scene Documentation

Photographic documentation serves as a permanent visual record of the crime scene. This record is for investigative purposes as well as to be used as evidence in court. Since it is likely to be many months or even years before the investigation concludes, the scene will certainly not remain in the same condition. The images of the crime scene will be shared with other investigators, prosecutors, defense attorneys, and jurors. The scene photographs may very well be the only way they can view the original condition of the scene.

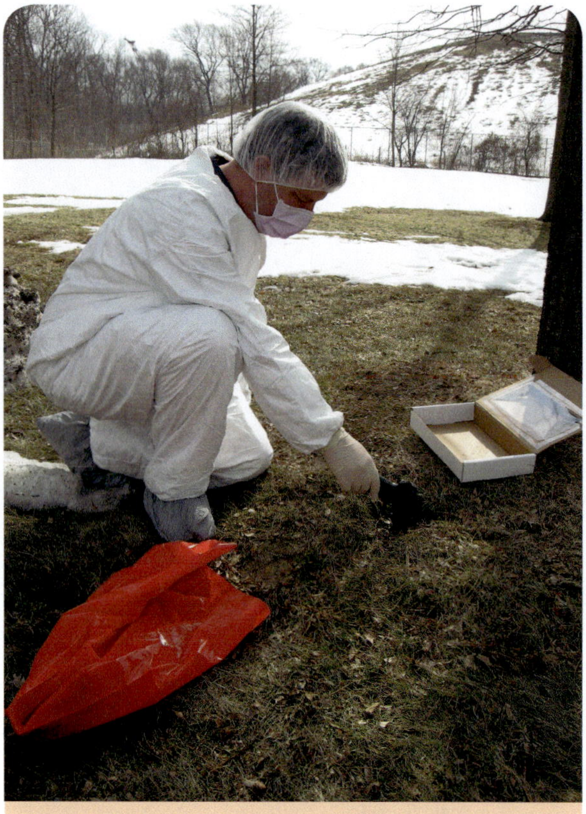

Figure 5.1 An analyst wearing the proper PPE (personal protective equipment) at a crime scene

Crime scene photographs should record the details of the scene as well as the location and appearance of the evidence in their original condition. In some cases, the photographs taken at the scene will be used as evidence for forensic comparisons such as impressions, fingerprints, and blood spatter.

Not all crime scenes are alike; however, there are some general guidelines to follow while documenting a crime scene. First of all, photographs should be supplemented with detailed notes; therefore, it is important to keep a photo log detailing notes about the subject of the photographs. This will assist you as well as other viewers in knowing the subject of your images as well as their location. With the use of digital cameras, it is no longer necessary to document the camera settings, since that information will be stored in the metadata of the images.

It will be helpful to develop a consistent routine to perform crime scene documentation. This will not only aid in the interpretation of your images by others, but also will make documenting a scene smoother and ensure critical images are not forgotten. Your routine can be as simple as the order in which you document. For example, you may choose to enter the scene, documenting the path of entry and working around the scene in a circular direction photographing into the room as you go. Consistency in your photographic methods will also make it easier for viewers of your photographs to get a clear picture of the appearance of the scene. Think of photographing a crime scene as telling a story; if the story is well organized it will be much easier to understand.

There is no right or wrong method to documenting a crime scene as long as it is entirely documented. Several approaches may be taken, for example, photographing a room from all walls facing inward, or photographing from all the corners facing inward, or photographing from the center of the room facing outward. It makes no difference what approach is taken as long as the scene is completely documented. Whatever approach is taken, care should be taken to ensure that parts of the scene that may be out of view in one photograph are covered in another. For example, floors and ceilings are often overlooked when photographing the other side of a room.

Provide several overlapping views to show the location of evidence. Compose your images so that they overlap each other slightly. Overlapping photographs ensure that the entire scene gets documented and nothing is left out. It also aids in the reconstruction of the scene afterward, and can be helpful in identifying the location of items within the scene.

Give the viewer a frame of reference in the photographs, which helps establish the location of items within the scene. It is also helpful to provide a frame of reference when transitioning from a distant photograph to a closer one. This can be accomplished by including an object in an overall image prior to photographing that same object close-up, or the

Photography Log

Case #:______________ **Date:**___/___/___ **Photographer:**__________ **Camera:**______________ **Page #:**___ **of**___

Frame:	Notes:	Subject:

Figure 5.2 An example of a photography log

contents of that object (like a cabinet or closet). Another example would be photographing the entrance to a room just prior to documenting the interior of that room. This will help convey that transition from one room to another to the viewer.

It is imperative to completely document the scene so take plenty of pictures. However, be sure to do so in an organized fashion. Taking too many pictures without consistency, or haphazardly moving from location to location, will make it more confusing for the viewer or someone interpreting the images after the fact.

A common method of effectively documenting a crime scene includes the use of the following views: long-range views, medium-range views, and close-up photographs of the evidence.

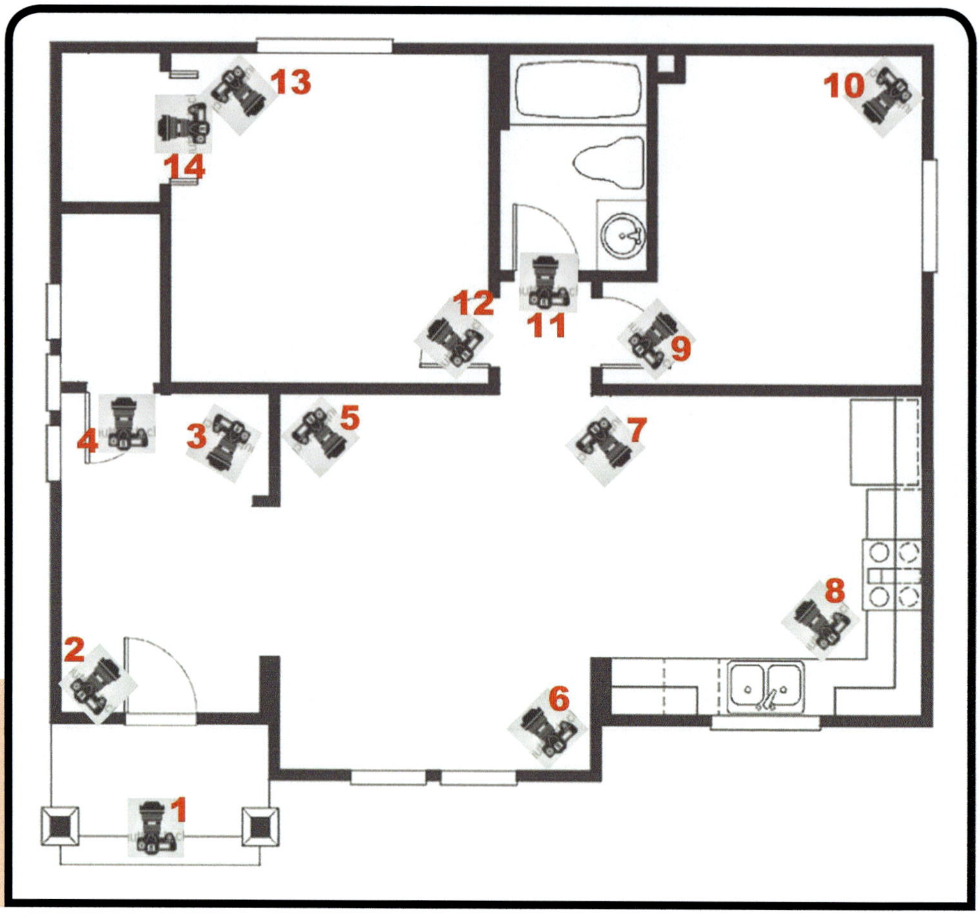

Figure 5.3 Scene photographs should be taken in such a way that they are not difficult to interpret; this illustrates a method of documenting a scene in an organized order

Together, these views are useful for documenting the overall condition of the scene, as well as providing further detail of the scene and the evidence contained within it. Transitioning from long-range views to close-up photography while maintaining a frame of reference enables the viewer to view the entire scene, and get a reference for the location of evidence as well as details of the evidence.

Long-range views, also called establishing photographs or overall photographs, provide views of the entire scene. Long-range photographs establish the location and condition of the entire scene. The purpose of long-range views is to show the location of the scene among its surroundings and to delineate the boundaries of the scene.

In outdoor scenes, long-range views should encompass the entire scene as well as its surroundings and routes of entry and exit. The views should be taken from several directions as well as overlapping one another. Long-range views may also be used to show the locations of secondary scenes as well as the paths of travel between the scenes.

Long-range views of indoor scenes should include the exterior of the building along with its immediate surroundings, as well as any entry/exit points that may have been used. If there are any known paths that could have been used by the suspects of the crime, they should be thoroughly documented as well. Document the entry way into the building as well as the immediate area inside the entry. Be sure to document all the rooms inside the building, photographing from, at a minimum, the corners of the room. The photographs should follow an organized path through the scene; it may be helpful to photograph the building as one would walk through the interior. This will result in photographs that are organized and easy for a viewer to interpret.

It is acceptable to use a wide-angle lens for long-range views, provided the images are not intended to show the relationship of items to one another, as this may distort the perspective of photographs. The result of this distortion is that the relationship of objects to one another may not appear correctly. So, it is preferable to use a normal focal length lens (which equates to approximately 50mm on a full-frame DSLR) when documenting the relationship of objects to one another, as with medium-range views.

Medium-range views are used to document the location of items within the scene in relation to one another. Medium-range photographs should be taken showing the location of evidence as well as a frame of reference from the long-range views. The purpose of medium-range views is to provide further detail of the items within the scene as well as their locations within the scene. Medium-range views should be taken of groups of evidence in close proximity to each other. Take medium-range views from multiple directions to accurately illustrate how items relate to one another in a three-dimensional space.

Close-up views are used to document individual items of evidence. The frame of view for a close-up should only include the item of evidence along with a scale and evidence label (case number, item number, or other identifier). A normal to telephoto lens or even a macro lens should be used to minimize distortion while capturing close-up views. Close-up photos should be taken from a point of view that clearly shows the object intended. Close-ups are typically shot from directly overheard; however, for three-dimensional objects this may not be the best angle.

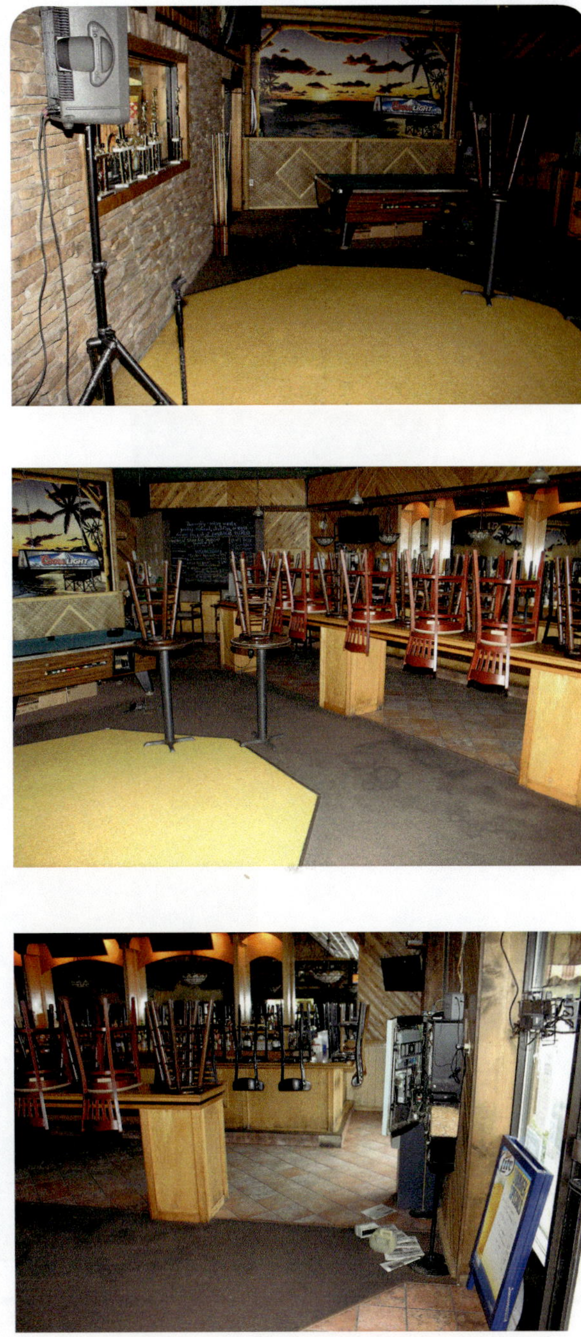

Figures 5.4–5.6 Examples of overlapping views of the interior of a business

Photographs courtesy of Police Chief Vernon L. Riddick Jr., Waterbury CT Police Department

The following timeline is a suggested order for documenting a crime scene:

1. Document the original condition of the scene
   A crime scene can be a fluid environment as items may be moved during the search for evidence. Therefore, it is important to document the original

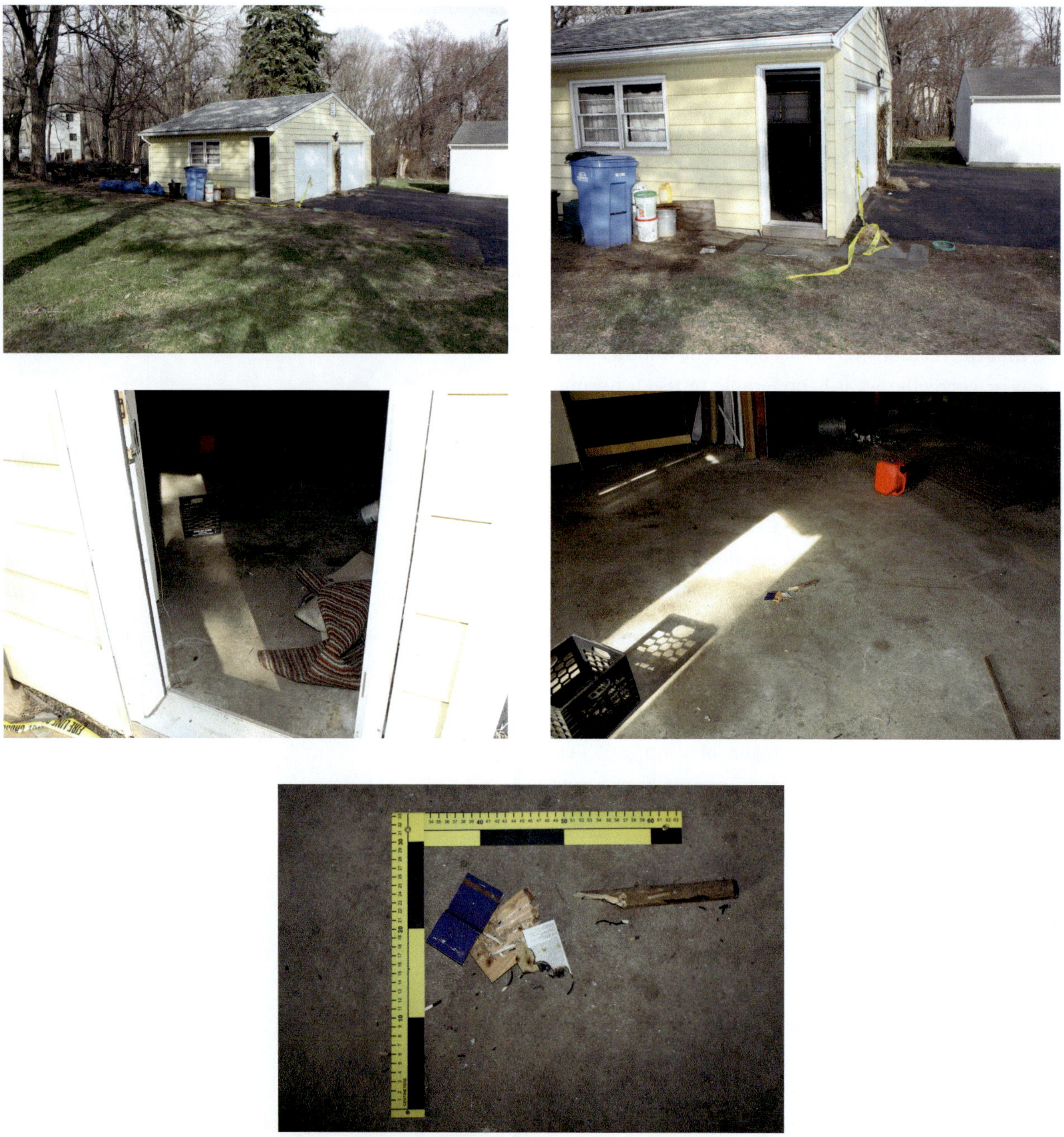

Figures 5.7–5.11 demonstrate the transition from long-range photographs to close-up views of evidence in an arson crime scene

Photographs courtesy of Police Chief Vernon L. Riddick Jr., Waterbury CT Police Department

condition of the scene upon arrival. This initial documentation can be done during the beginning stages of investigation, often called a walk-through, or just before searching through items. During this initial phase of crime scene documentation some items of evidence will be relatively obvious—a smoking gun, a body, blood spatter, etc. Be sure to document these items thoroughly. As for the rest of the scene, at this stage it is only necessary to record the overall condition of the scene. Do not get yourself bogged down taking too many photographs of potential evidence until you have determined what is important and what may be less important.

2. Process the scene
   After the initial documentation has been completed the scene is ready for processing. It is during this time that the scene investigation begins. The scene can be thoroughly searched for evidence, and since the initial documentation has been completed you need not worry about moving evidence during the search. Items of evidence should be marked and numbered for collection or further documentation.
3. Re-document the scene to show location of the evidence
   Now that the scene has been processed it should be photographed once again with the evidence still in place and marked with photo placards or labels. It is important at this stage of documentation that all the evidence is completely documented. Now is the time to ensure that the entire scene and all of the evidence are thoroughly documented in place and labeled according to their evidence numbers. Be sure to document the evidence from several different views as well as directions. Presumptive testing can then be done to determine the importance of items within the scene.
4. Document the evidence to be collected
   Take photographs of the individual items of evidence prior to packaging in order to document the appearance of each item, as well as provide greater detail of each item. The photographs should include only the item of evidence, a scale, and identifier. The composition of these images should accurately represent the item being photographed. Therefore the camera should be angled to show as much of the item as possible. For many three-dimensional objects the optimal placement of the camera may not be directly above the item. It also may be necessary to photograph more than one side of the item.

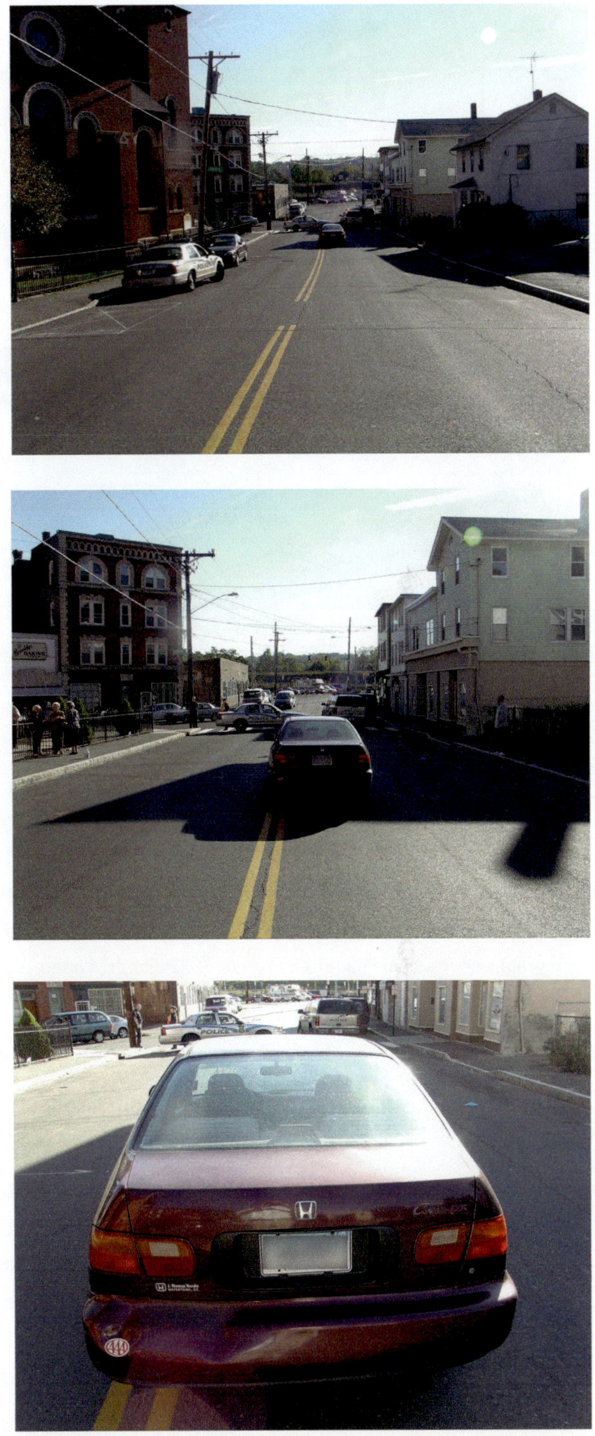

Figures 5.12–5.14 demonstrate the transition from long-range photographs to close-up views of a vehicle in a motor vehicle accident

Photographs courtesy of Police Chief Vernon L. Riddick Jr., Waterbury CT Police Department

Lighting

A portable flash is an optimal light source for documenting an indoor scene. One technique that has been found to work well is to mount the flash on the camera's

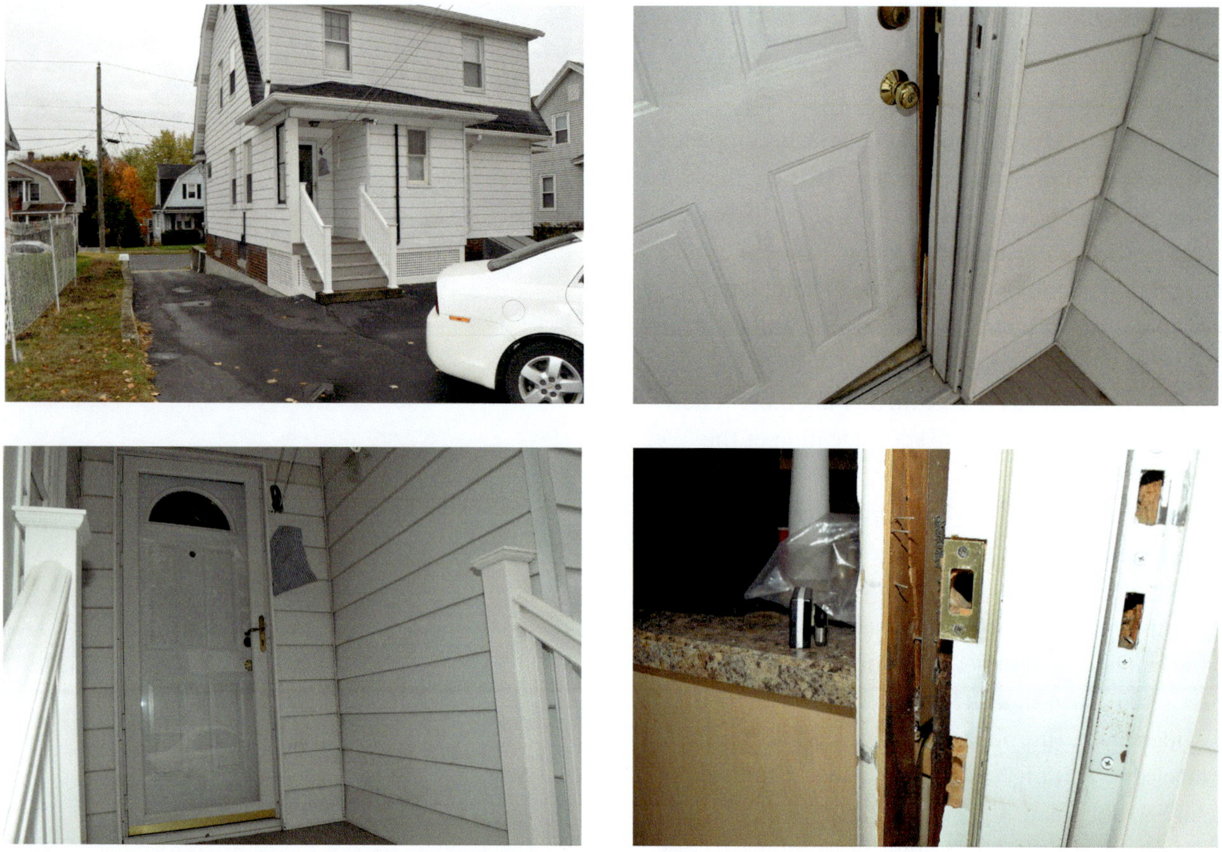

Figures 5.15–5.18 demonstrate the transition from long-range photographs to close-up views of evidence in a burglary scene
Photographs courtesy of Police Chief Vernon L. Riddick Jr., Waterbury CT Police Department

hot shoe and aim the flash at a 45-degree angle toward the ceiling. See Chapter 4 for more information about the bounce lighting technique.

This technique is well suited for homes where the ceiling is not too high and is painted white. In homes with higher than normal ceilings or in larger buildings the technique may still produce acceptable results; however, the flash may need more power and consume battery power more quickly. Be cautious using this technique in homes with colored ceilings as the resulting photographs may have a colorcast. As you transition to close-up photographs it may be necessary to remove the flash from the camera's hot shoe and use a remote trigger or cord.

It is also acceptable to use a flash outdoors as well. Using a flash in TTL (through the lens) mode, or on low power, can "fill in" shadows with light and reduce contrast on sunny days. The flash may also be used to provide needed contrast to images on cloudy days.

The following is a guide for what photographs to take at the scene of a particular type of crime.

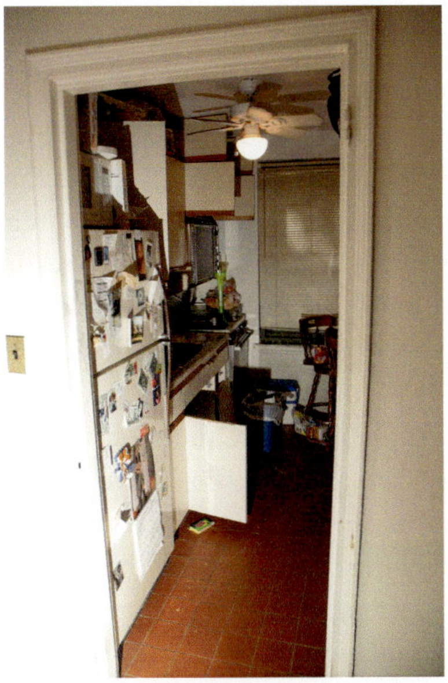

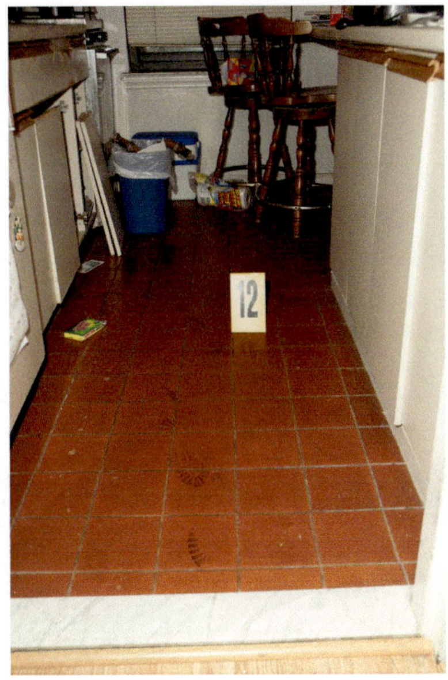

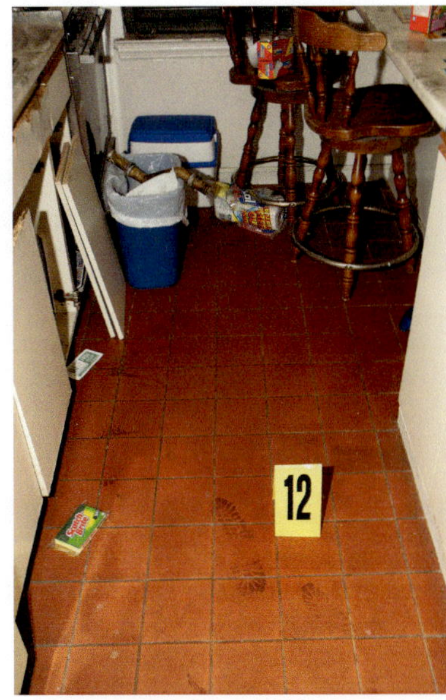

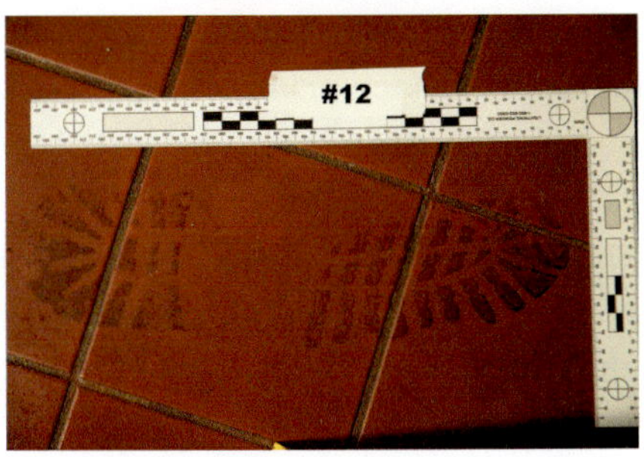

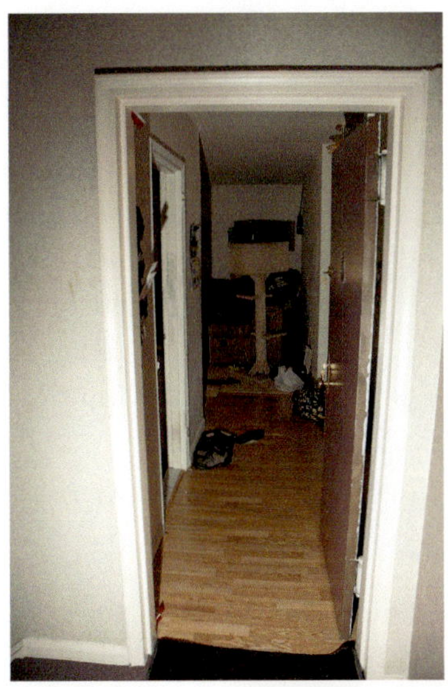

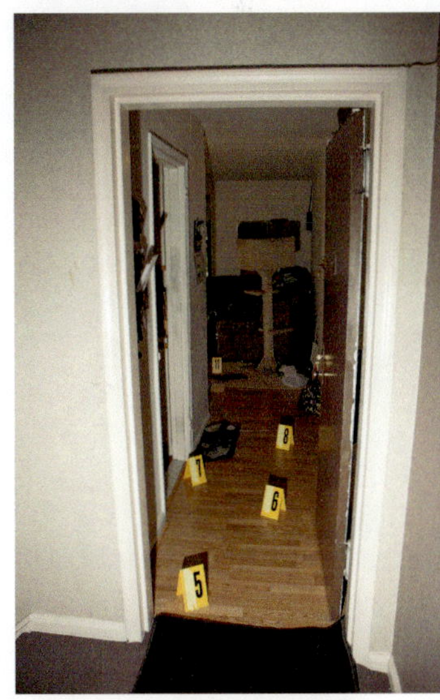

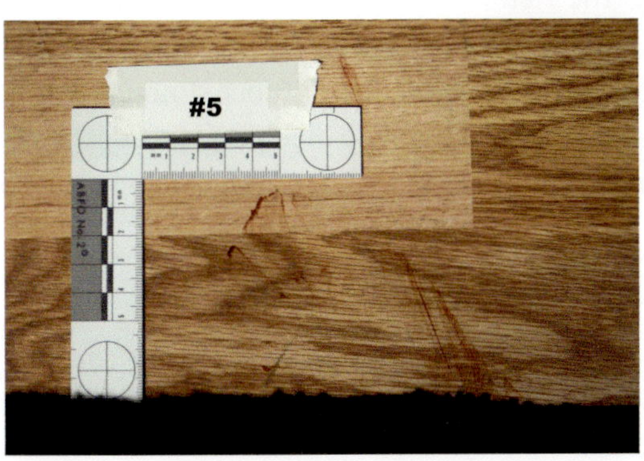

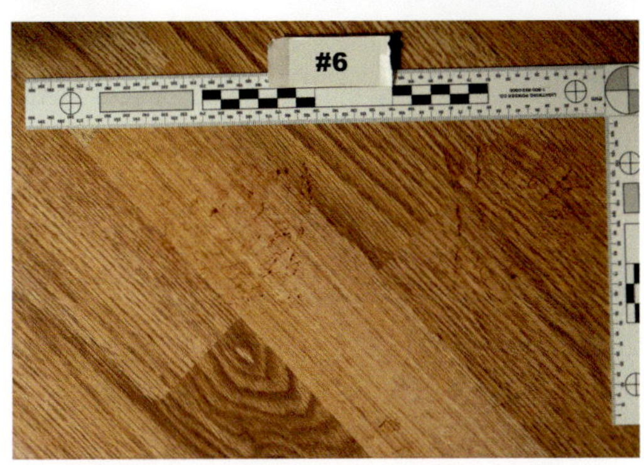

Figures 5.19–5.26 illustrate how the previously described progression of photographing a scene can help the viewers understand the location of items of evidence within the scene

Photographs courtesy of Kevin MacLaren, Westchester County Forensic Laboratory

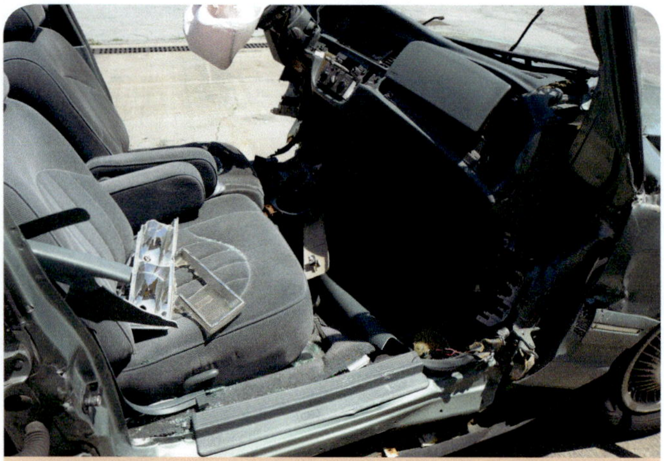

Figure 5.27 A photograph taken of the inside of a vehicle outdoors without the use of a flash

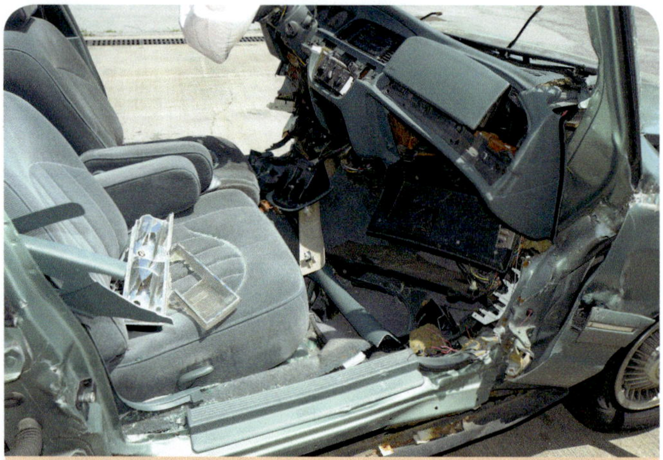

Figure 5.28 The same photograph taken with the use of a flash to fill in the shadows

Homicides

Be sure to document the location of the victim from several angles as well as any of the victim's injuries that are visible. Document as much of the victim and scene before anything is moved. If there are weapons present, document their location as it relates to the rest of the scene and take close-up photographs showing the appearance of the weapons. If there are bullet holes, damage, items missing or out of place, they too should be documented to show their location within the scene as well as close-up. Be aware of possible fingerprints and impressions; if they are found they should be documented sooner rather than later. As more personnel respond to the scene more impressions may be created, making it very difficult to determine which impressions belong to the suspect. Elimination photographs should be taken of the footwear of all personnel, including emergency medical personnel, who responded to the scene prior to the suspects impressions being documented. Photograph any known paths the suspect may have taken as well as entrance and exit points they may have used. If a suspect is in custody it may be necessary to photograph their condition upon arrest. See the section on documenting injuries later in this chapter.

Suicides

If there is any doubt as to the manner of death, then the scene should be treated as a homicide and documented as such. Thoroughly document the position of the victim from several angles. Document the presence of weapons as well as their relationship to the victim; be sure to include a scale so it is possible to show the distance. Photograph the victim's wounds, both entry and exit if they exist, and be sure to include a scale next to the wounds. Take close-up photographs of any unique characteristics of the body, clothing, or the victim's surroundings.

Arson/Fire Scenes

Photograph the fire in progress if the opportunity exists. If it is not possible to get close to the fire due to firefighting efforts or for safety reasons, then it is recommended to photograph the fire at a distance using a telephoto lens. Be sure to include photographs of the smoke and smoke patterns, as these may be helpful for determining what, if any, accelerants were used to start the fire.

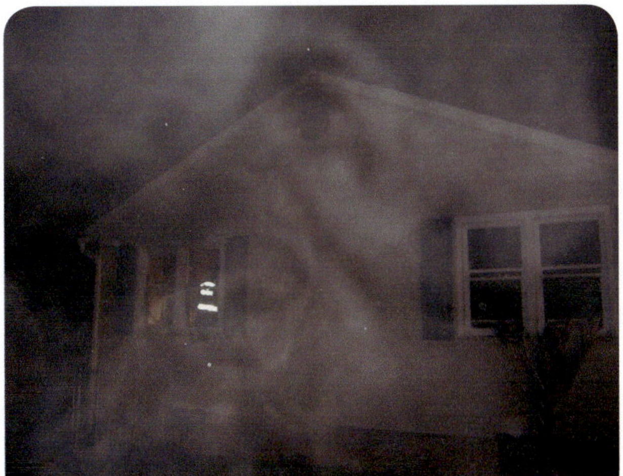

Figure 5.29 A photograph of a residence during fire using a flash. Notice how the smoke is illuminated by the flash and the visibility of the residence is affected

Photograph courtesy of Victor Zamaloff

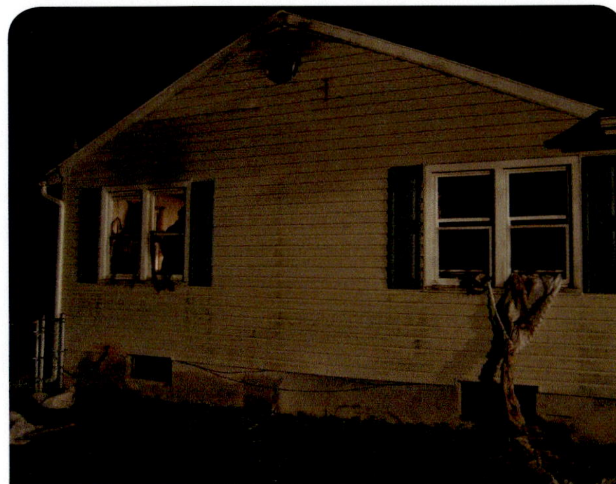

Figure 5.30 A photograph of a residence during fire without the use of a flash. Notice how the smoke is not visible, this is because of the longer shutter speed and available light illumination

Photograph courtesy of Victor Zamaloff

Photographing through smoke, steam, and fog can be difficult. Try to avoid direct flash if at all possible; aiming the flash at an angle away from the camera will cut down on the reflection of the flash off the smoke. Additionally, using a tripod and long exposure time may cut down on the reflection as well.

Photograph the surroundings including witnesses and spectators. Oftentimes an arsonist will stick around to watch his work so you may be fortunate to capture an image of the suspect that can be used as an investigative lead or in the prosecution of the crime.

Photograph the fire-suppression activities including both the automatic systems in place as well as responding fire companies.

Photograph the exterior of the structure from all angles and corners. Document the surroundings of the structure to establish its location. Document all damage to the exterior of the structure including any structural failures such as windows, roofs, or walls.

Photograph all rooms within the immediate area of the fire origin, including all walls and both sides of the doors. Include the interior of any closets or cabinets if present. Photograph all heat-producing appliances present. Document the locations and condition of the furniture as well as any protected areas left by the furniture.

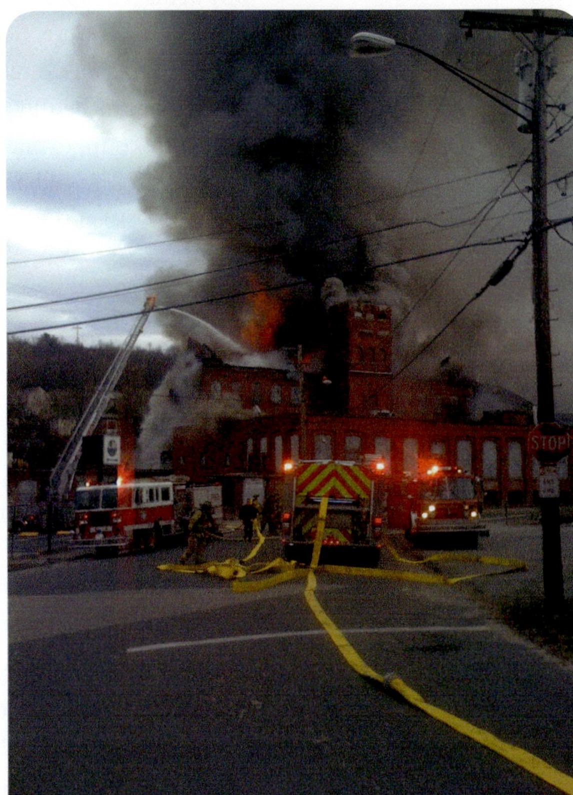

Figure 5.31 A photograph of fire suppression activities during a fire

Photograph courtesy of Police Chief Vernon L. Riddick Jr., Waterbury CT Police Department

For more information regarding fire scene documentation see the NFPA (National Fire Protection Association) document 921, "Guide for Fire and Explosion Investigators," Chapter 16.

Motor Vehicles/Accident Scenes

Document the surrounding area and structures to establish the location of the vehicle. Photograph each side of the vehicle and all four corners.

Take close-up photographs of any damage to the exterior of the vehicle. Photograph the license plates and vehicle identification number, as well as any decals and bumper stickers. Document any other unique identifying appearances.

For cases that involve the interior of the vehicle, completely document the interior including the seats (front/rear), floor area (front/rear), dashboard, gauges, and ignition area. Document the contents of the glove compartment, trunk, and any other storage compartments. Document the location and appearance of any evidence contained within the vehicle.

Burglaries

Photograph any signs of forced entry, or routes taken by the burglar, as well as the exit if they can be determined. Document any damage to the building and its contents as well as any items that appear out of place. Photograph any evidence of items missing, or where the missing items were. Be sure to document all physical evidence such as fingerprints, footwear impressions, and tool-marks. It may be helpful to talk to the owner or victim as they may be able to identify items missing or that do not belong, like something left behind by the burglar. Be sure to document any items the burglar may have touched, or perhaps left his DNA on. You would be surprised how many times a hungry thief stops for a snack before leaving the scene of a crime.

Photographing in Bad Weather/Adverse Conditions

Typically, crime scene photographers cannot choose the conditions they document in. So even if the weather or conditions of the scene are unfavorable for photography, the scene should be documented. Certainly if the scene and/or evidence can be protected until conditions improve it is advisable to do so; however, if it is safe it's not a bad idea to document the scene in its current condition.

Photographing in the rain or snow presents some serious challenges to the photographer. Firstly, it is important to protect your gear from the getting wet. This may be accomplished using several methods. An underwater camera housing designed for scuba diving will certainly protect a camera from water. Custom-made housings are available for many models of camera but may be cost prohibitive. Universal housings designed to fit a class of camera tend to be less expensive. Don't worry about lighting; housings are available for flashes as well. If you find yourself in bad weather often, or perhaps have the need to shoot underwater, there are camera systems designed for underwater use. As well, many point-and-shoot

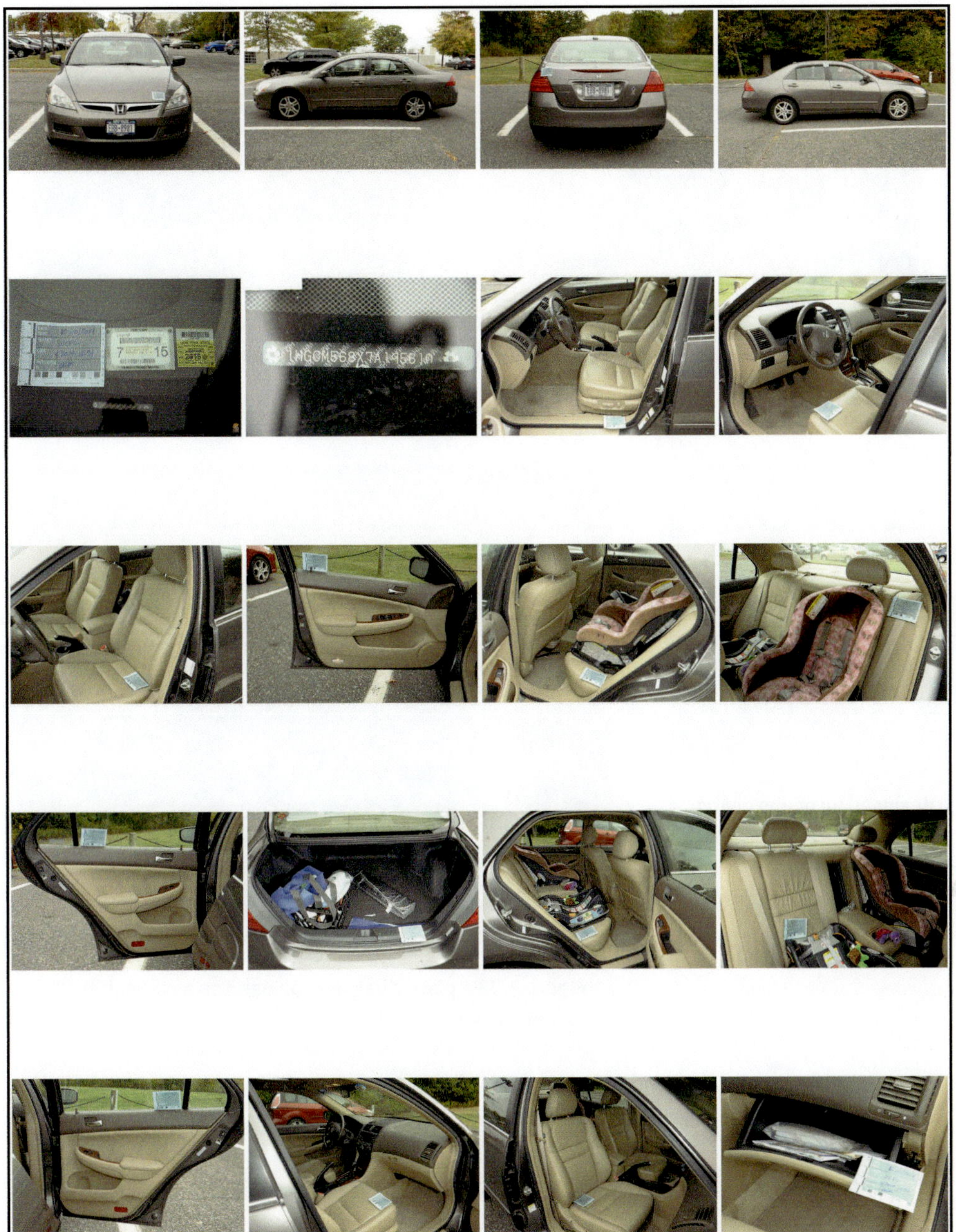

Figure 5.32 A contact sheet of photographs documenting the exterior and interior of a vehicle

cameras are designed for use in adverse conditions. These cameras are typically marked for sporting activities and go by the name "tough" or "all weather," or something similar.

A less expensive option is a rain cover, or shield, available in various sizes and materials to fit many cameras. A plastic garbage bag can make a good camera cover in a pinch; just be sure to cut a hole for the lens. If nothing else if available, a golf-size umbrella and a partner can protect the camera, and photographer as well, from the elements.

Figures 5.33–5.34 Demonstration of a technique for documenting under the seats of a vehicle

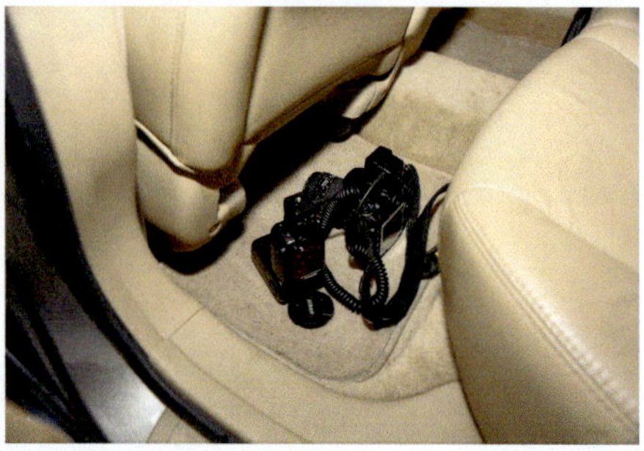

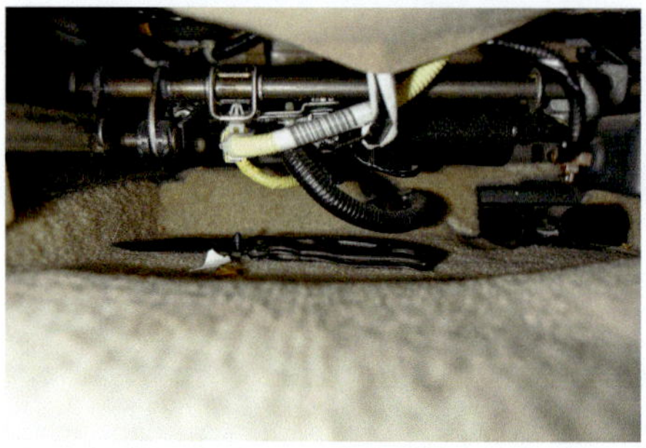

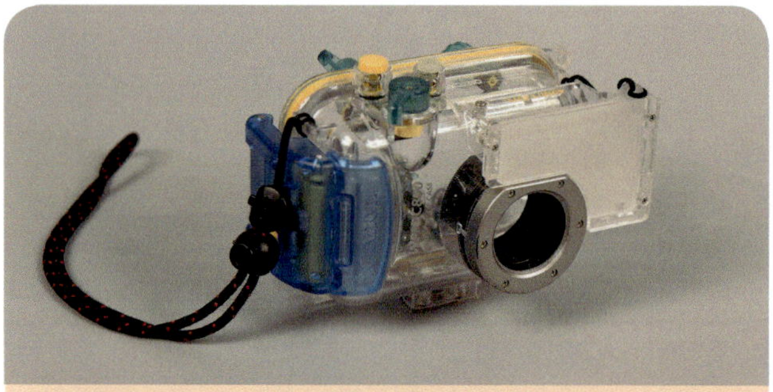

Figure 5.35 A waterproof housing designed for scuba diving will protect a camera from the elements. Several types of housings are available from custom fit for particular cameras, to universal cases that will accommodate several models of cameras

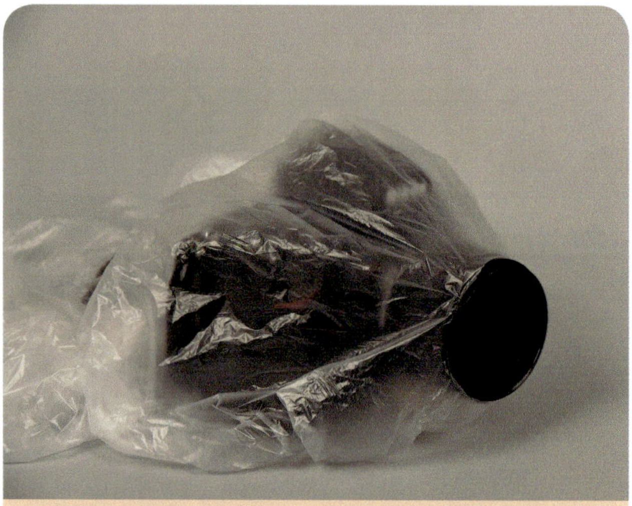

Figure 5.36 A plastic bag may be used as a makeshift camera cover

Photographing Impression Evidence (Footwear, Fabric, and Tool Marks)

Impression evidence may be classified into two categories:

- two-dimensional impressions, which are made when material is transferred as a result of contact with a surface and subsequent separation (e.g., walking on a dusty floor); or
- three-dimensional impressions, which are made when an object leaves an impression of its surface features in a softer material. (e.g., stepping in dirt, mud, or snow).

There are several sources of potential impressions left at crime scenes including footwear, tire tracks, fabric impressions, tool marks, and fingerprints. Although these items vary in size the photographic setup required to properly document them is relatively similar.

These impressions must be documented correctly since they may be used by a forensic analyst to make comparisons. Typically, these images will be printed at a 1:1 reproduction ratio, the actual size of the impression. Ensuring that the camera is set up correctly will make this scaling possible. The use of proper lighting techniques will bring out the details in the impression.

The generally accepted resolution for impression documentation is 300 pixels per inch at 1:1 or actual size. To determine the area in which the camera will reproduce at this resolution, divide both the horizontal and vertical resolutions (pixels) by 300. The result will be the area (in inches) the camera can reproduce at 300ppi. Anything larger than this result should be documented in sections.

The following equipment is necessary to properly document an impression:

- A normal to telephoto lens, approximately 50mm to 105mm. Optimally you should use a macro lens or other lens designed for close-up photographs. These lenses are typically made to higher standards than other lenses and will result in less distortion. *Do not use a wide-angle lens to document an impression; the distortion caused by a wide-angle lens will make it difficult to create a life-size print from the image.* This is true no matter the size of the impression.
- A sturdy tripod is necessary to support the camera. The tripod ensures that, once set up, the camera will stay in place. It also makes it possible to take several photographs without having to worry about recomposing the photograph for each shot. In the event that the scene contains multiple impressions the tripod setup allows you to move your gear from impression to impression without having to set up the camera again for each shot.
- Use a portable flash with sync cord or floodlight for adjusting the lighting. Multiple lighting angles are necessary to document the impression. Photographing with more than one lighting angle is important because some details in the impression may reveal themselves under different angles. One advantage to using a floodlight for impression documentation is being able to see the effects of different lighting angles on the impression. However, if you are using a portable flash, you can easily use a flashlight to preview lighting angles, then substitute the flash when taking the picture.
- A scale the approximate length of the impression is necessary and should be placed on the same plane as the impression, and close to the impression.

The proper setup for impression evidence can mean the difference between an image that provides enough detail for a forensic comparison and one that does not. Setting up for the photograph is relatively simple and should only take a few extra minutes.

Photographs of impressions should be taken at the highest-quality format possible. Typically, this is the RAW format, so set the camera accordingly.

The camera should be mounted on the tripod so that the lens is perpendicular to the impression. Making the plane of the camera's sensor parallel to the impression ensures that everything will be to the same scale.

Be sure to place a proper scale in the image, and on the same plane as the impression. The scale can be marked with a case number and item number or other identifying information. If you're shooting a 3D impression that is deep in mud or snow it may be necessary to dig a

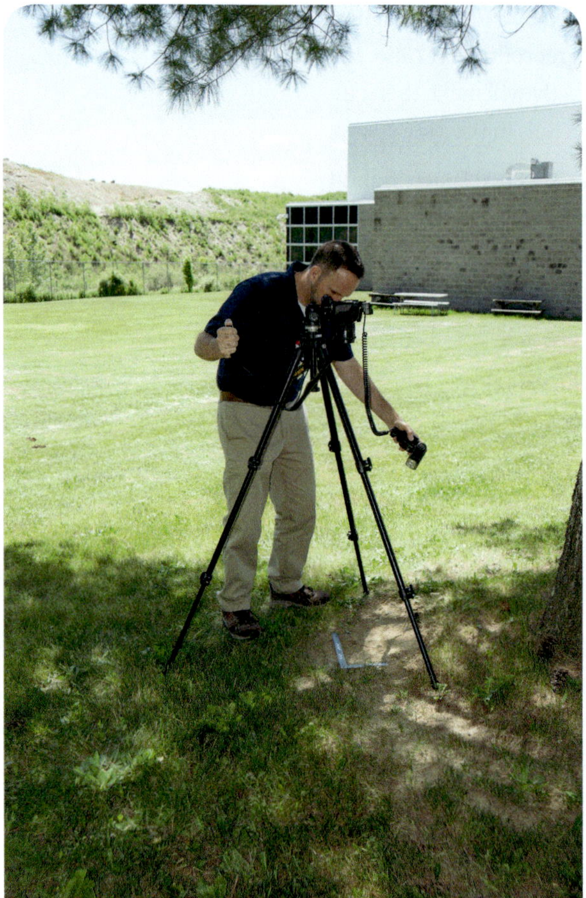

Figure 5.37 A demonstration of the proper setup for impression documentation

Photograph courtesy of Brandi Clark

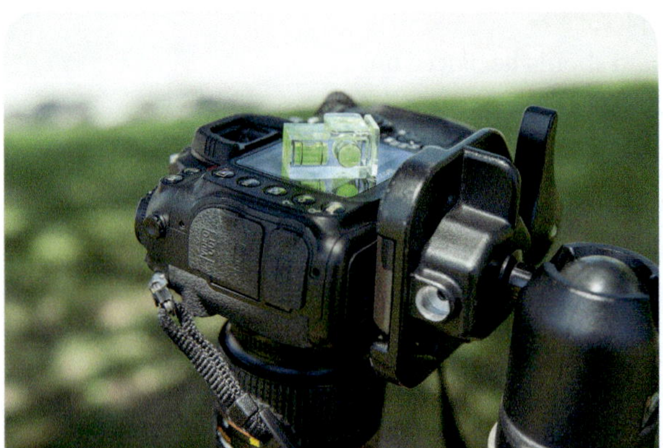

Figure 5.38 A small bubble level may be used on the back of the camera to ensure the imaging plane is level, be sure to only use this technique if the ground you are photographing is level as well

small trench for the scale near the impression. Be sure not to disturb the impression when doing so.

Compose the photograph so that the impression and scale fill the entire frame of view. This will maximize the amount of the camera resolution used and record the maximum detail possible.

Once the setup is complete take several images using different lighting angles as well as directions. It is recommended to take at least one photograph in the natural or existing light conditions. This is especially true if the impression is outdoors on a sunny day; the natural lighting may be one of your better shots. It may not be beneficial for cloudy days or indoors; however, the natural light shot can aid in demonstrating the different lighting angles used. A helpful technique for controlling light outdoors is to create a shadow in the impression by blocking the sun. Then use a flash or other light source to control the angle and direction of the light.

Photographing Tire Impressions

Establishing photographs of tire impressions are necessary for the reconstruction of crime events. These photographs should already be part of the overall documentation of the scene. If it's available, approximately 6 feet of each tire impression should be documented using the impression technique. This ensures that one rotation of the tire is fully photographed, because treads vary throughout the circumference of a tire.

Place a long-scale or tape measure parallel to the length of impression to be documented. Take a medium-range photograph of the impression. The tape measure should not be moved for the remaining steps. Document at least 6ft of the impression in approximately 2ft sections, treating each section as you would any other impression. Repeat these steps for each individual tire track identified.

Photographing Fingerprints

The National Institute of Standards and Technology (NIST) guidelines specify that a fingerprint image should be at least 1000 pixels per inch (ppi) at 1:1. To determine the area in which the camera will reproduce at this resolution, divide

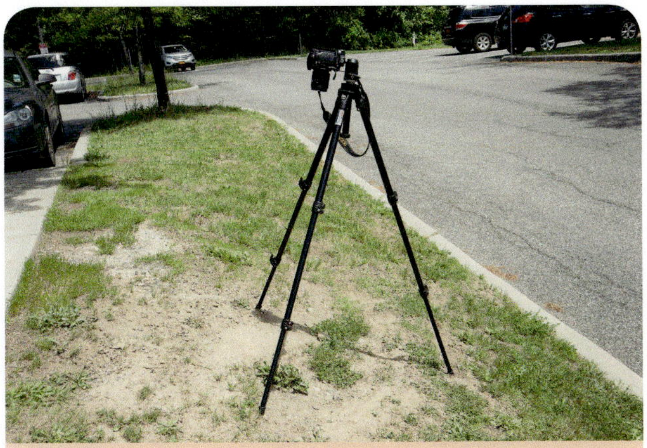

Figure 5.39 A demonstration of the proper setup for impression documentation on a sloped surface

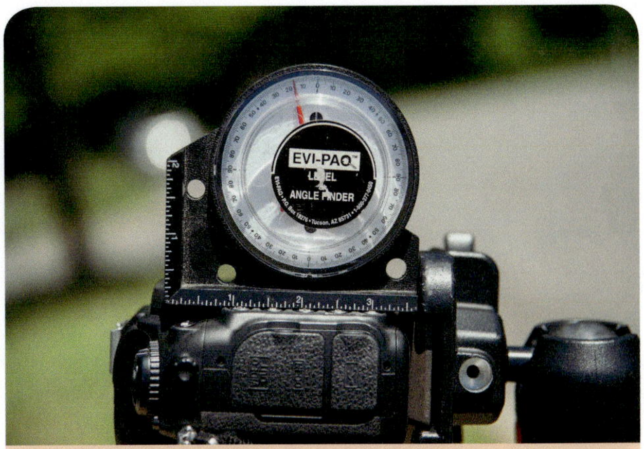

Figure 5.40 An angle finder, like this one found in a trajectory kit, may be used to ensure the imaging plane of the camera is parallel to the surface of the impression. Be sure to check the angle of both the horizontal and vertical axes of the impression

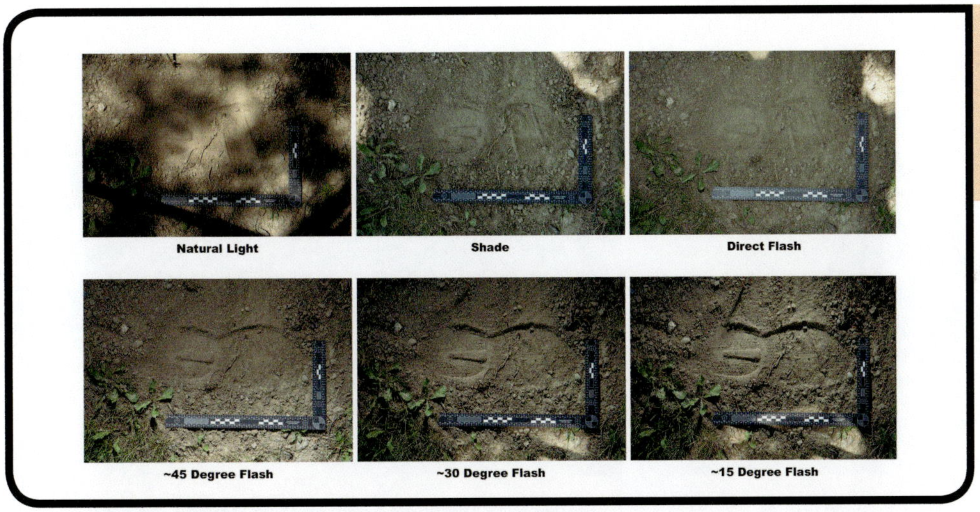

Figure 5.41 Examples of several different lighting angles and their effects on a three-dimensional impression

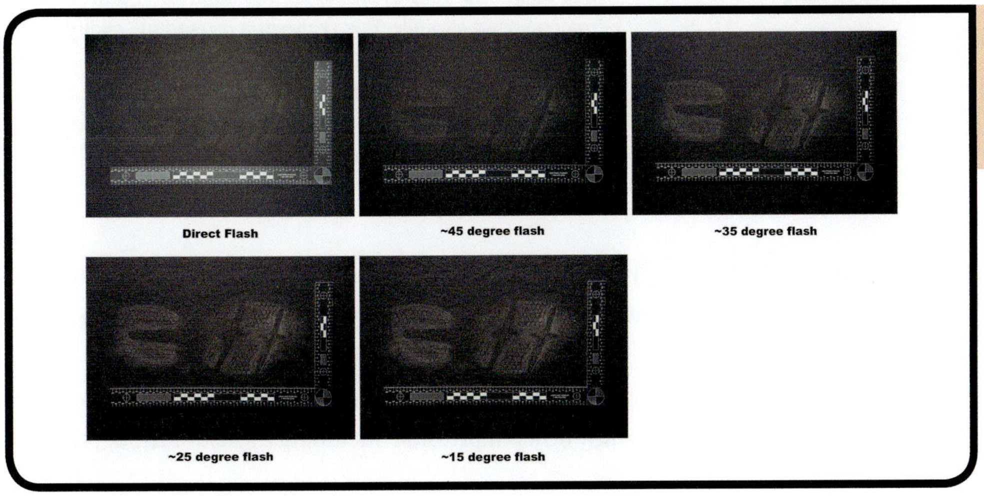

Figure 5.42 Examples of several different lighting angles and their effects on a two-dimensional impression

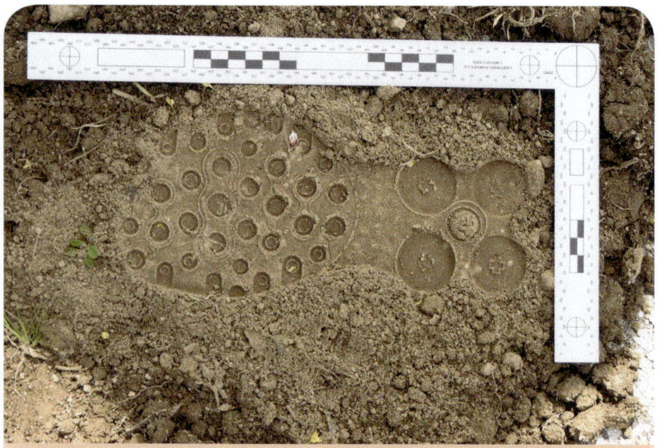

Figure 5.43 A properly documented three-dimensional impression

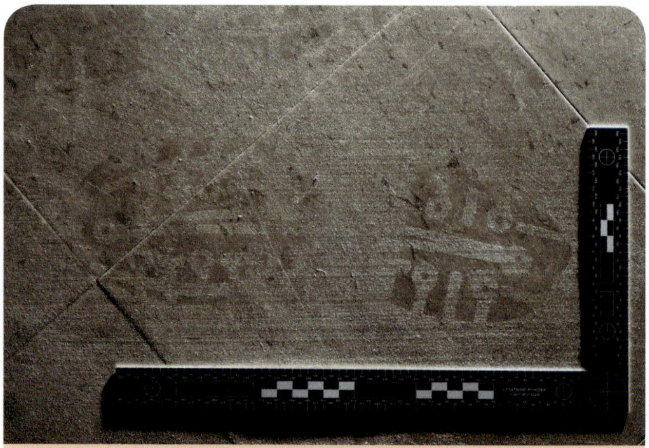

Figure 5.44 A two-dimensional impression caused by a suspect stepping in dust and removing some of that dust; this type of impression is called a negative impression

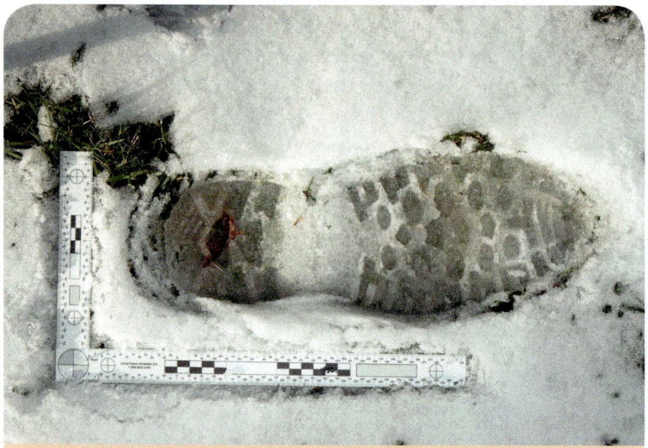

Figure 5.45 An impression in snow; the scale is sunken in the snow to ensure it is on the same plane as the impression

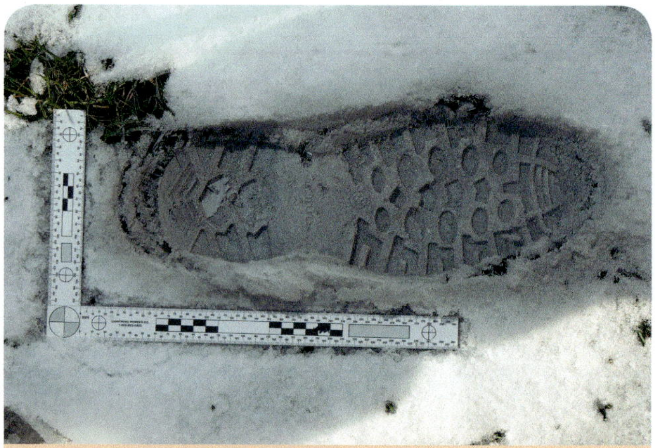

Figure 5.46 The same snow print as Figure 5.44 after it has been treated with primer spray paint (snow print wax may be used as well). This technique is used to solidify the impression prior to casting with dental stone. An added benefit to this treatment is that it may bring out additional details so it is recommended to re-photograph the impression after spraying

both the horizontal and vertical resolutions (pixels) by 1000. The result will be the area (in inches) the camera can reproduce at 1000ppi. Anything larger than this result should be documented in sections.

Fingerprint documentation presents a unique challenge because of its small size; however, fingerprints should be treated like any other impression, including the use of the appropriate

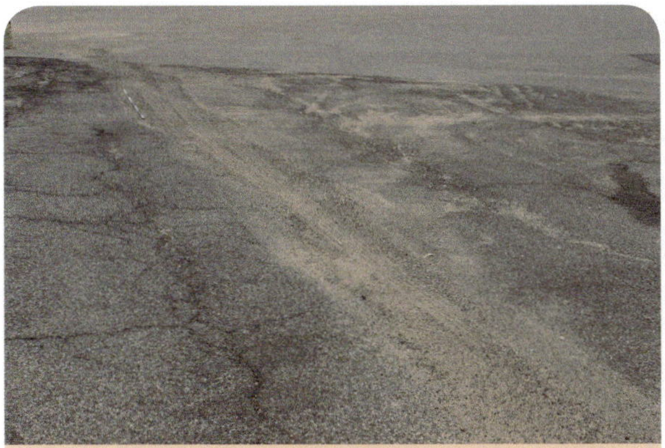

Figure 5.47 A long-range photograph of a tire track to establish its location in a scene

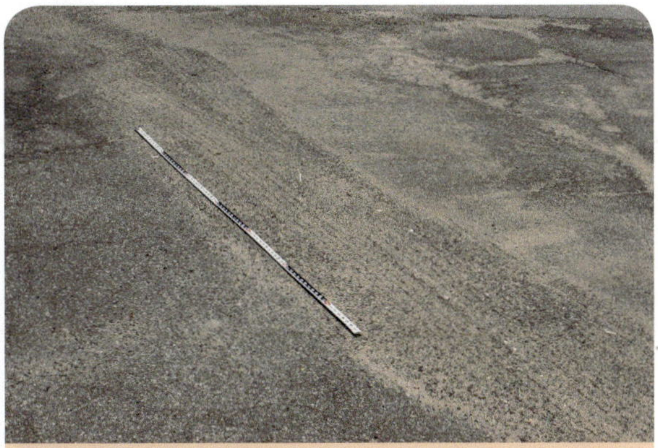

Figure 5.48 A medium-range photograph of the tire track in Figure 5.47 showing the location of the impression documentation

size scale. For fingerprint photographs the entire scale need not be in the photograph. Be sure to include at least the lines of the scale and the case identifiers.

The use of a longer focal-length macro lens will increase the working distance necessary to document fingerprints and ease some of the challenges. There are several aftermarket accessories available specifically for documenting fingerprints; however, I recommend doing your research since some of these accessories may be lower quality than a decent macro lens. If you find yourself shooting multiple fingerprints a ring flash can be a helpful tool, especially one with adjustable light angles.

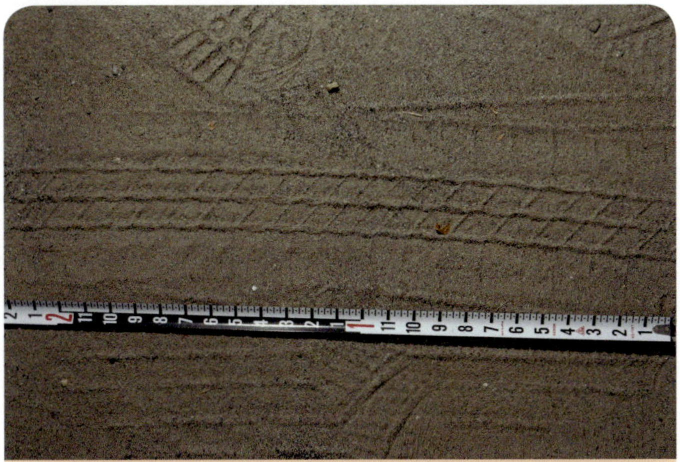

Figure 5.49 One of a series of impression photographs of the tire track. There should be approximately three to four 2-foot adjoining sections of the tire track to ensure one entire rotation is documented

The following is a simple way to document multiple fingerprints at a scene. Set the camera lens to manual focus and compose and shoot the first image. Leave the lens set to manual focus for the remaining fingerprint photographs. When approaching the next fingerprint you can quickly position the camera by gently moving the camera back and forth until the fingerprint is in focus, take the shots, and move on.

An issue that frequently comes up when documenting fingerprints is the inability of some lenses to focus close-up. This is due to the design of the lens and usually happens with the lower-quality lenses typically included with camera kits. There are two ways to deal with this issue. The first is replacing the lens with a better-quality macro lens. If that is not possible the other way of dealing with this issue is to slowly move the camera away from the fingerprint until the lens will focus. It may not be the optimal

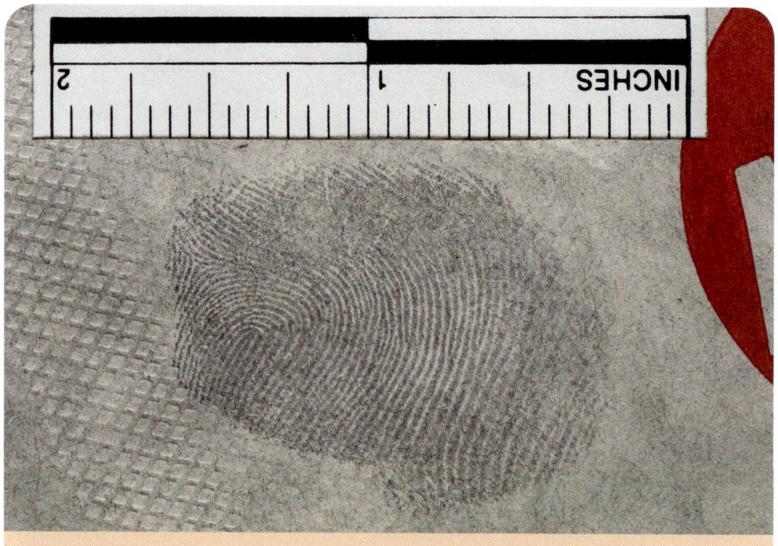

Figure 5.50 A properly composed photograph of a dusted fingerprint on a fast-food bag

situation, but a sharp image of a smaller fingerprint is certainly better that a larger blurry one.

Photographing Blood Spatter (Sectoring)

Large patterns of evidence such as blood-spatter patterns must be documented to show the entire pattern, as well as to provide the details necessary to determine the angle and

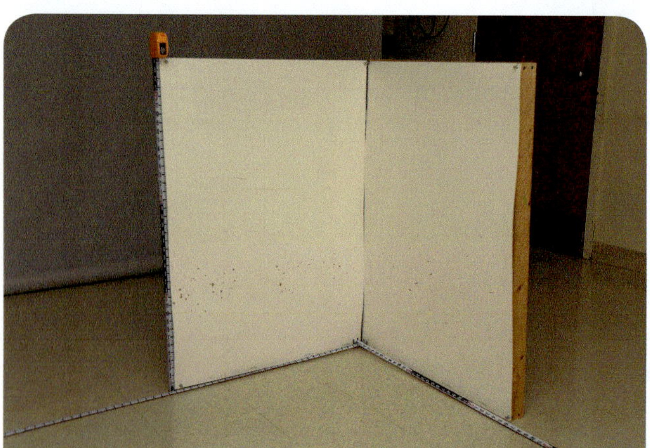

Figure 5.51 A blood-spatter pattern located in a corner documented to show location of the pattern

Figure 5.52 One "wall" of the blood-spatter pattern documented with the pattern on the same plane as the sensor

direction of the pattern. Using a technique called sectoring where the subject is divided up into smaller sections then re-documented close-up allows the photographer to record the overall look of the pattern as well as provide greater detail.

Scales, anchored to immovable objects such as the wall and floor, should be placed near the pattern. Then the entire pattern is documented in place. A wide-angle lens may be used for this part of the technique; however, it must not be used for the close-up shots.

The spatter pattern is then divided into even sectors and marked. The sectors should be approximately 1.5 to 2 feet across. Mark each sector with its own unique identifier, such as letters or numbers

It will be easier to document if the sectors are the same dimensions (rectangular) as the image. Be sure not to divide any impression evidence that is in the pattern such as handprints or fabric impressions.

The pattern should now be re-photographed to show the location of the sectors. The scales should remain in place for the remainder of the photographs.

Photograph each sector close-up leaving enough room for overlap. Be sure to keep the camera perpendicular to the evidence. Include a more precise scale in each sector.

Ideally the pattern should be shot using a tripod, as it makes completing the entire pattern much easier. It will also allow all individual sectors to be shot at the same distance, which makes scaling the photographs easier. Be sure when documenting the individual patterns that they are all shot with the film plane parallel to the subject. Do not tilt the camera up (or down) to photograph sectors above or below the height of the tripod or other support.

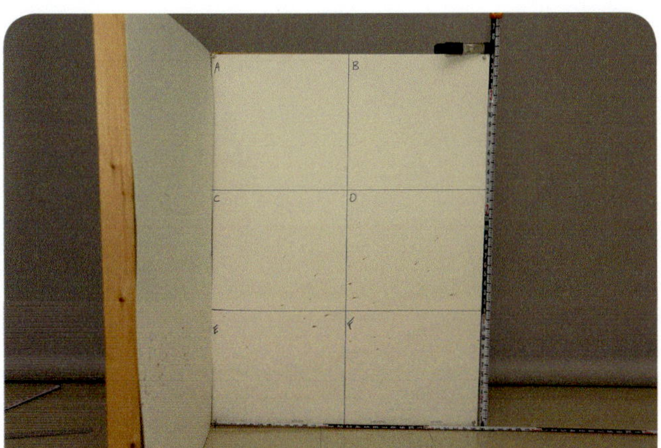

Figure 5.53 The same pattern from Figure 5.52 documented after being divided into individual sectors

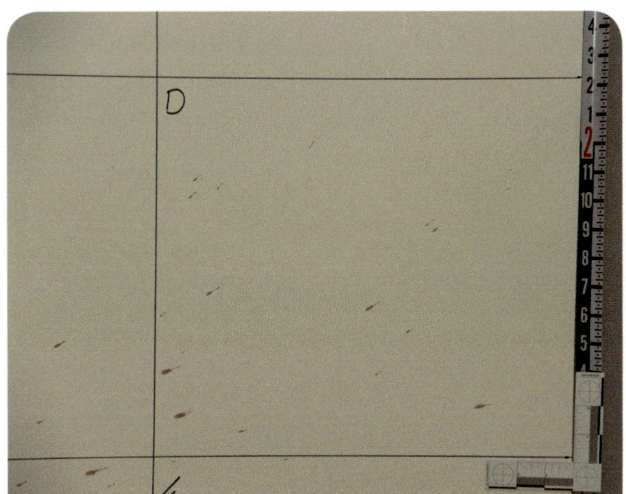

Figure 5.54 A sector of the pattern documented close-up to show greater detail

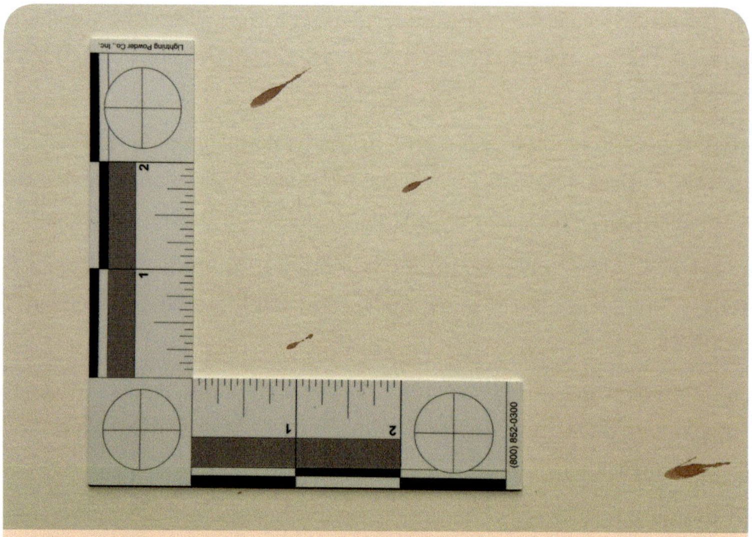

Figure 5.55 Individual stains may be documented even closer to show greater detail if necessary

Recommendations and guidelines for crime scene photography, fingerprint and footwear photography, and other topics related to imaging and photography may be found at the following sites:

- SWGIT (Scientific Working Group on Imaging Technology) webpage: www.swg-it.org/documents/current documents
- SWGFAST (Scientific Working Group on Friction Ridge Analysis Study and Technology) guidelines for digital imaging of fingerprints: www.swgfast.org/Documents.html
- NIST's (National Institute of Standards and Technology) Organization of Scientific Area Committees (OSAC) for forensic science: www.nist.gov/topics/forensic-science/organization-scientific-area-committees-osac

Chapter 6 Evidence Documentation

The purpose of evidence photo documentation is to provide a record of the appearance of physical evidence. The photographs may be used as part of the case record, as evidence in court, or by other investigators. It is crucial that photographs of evidence properly represent the appearance and condition of the evidence. It is also important that the quality of the images do not detract from the viewer's ability to visualize that appearance.

General Evidence Handling Precautions

Recent advances in forensic technology have greatly increased the sensitivity of evidence testing, especially that of DNA. Because of this sensitivity, it is not uncommon for investigators or even forensic analysts to have their own DNA show up in evidence samples. Even though it may be common, or even easily explained, this shouldn't be an excuse for sloppy evidence handling.

The following personal protective equipment should be worn when handling evidence:

- latex gloves;
- a clean or disposable lab coat;
- face mask;
- hairnet.

To reduce the risk of contamination, suspect and victim evidence should never be handled in the same area or at the same time. In addition, gloves should be changed in between handling items of evidence; any other clothing that becomes contaminated should be changed as well. Evidence should only be handled in designated areas and surfaces should be cleaned with a solution of 10% bleach in between items of evidence. Large rolls of butcher-type paper may also be used as a surface for evidence handling as they may be discarded after the evidence is put away.

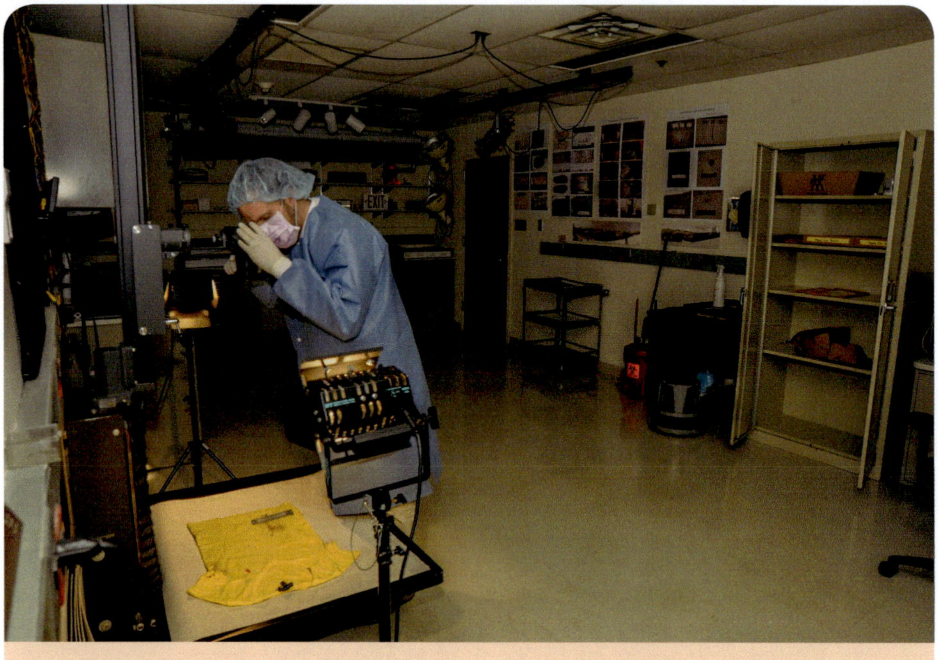

Figure 6.1 Proper PPE (personal protective equipment) being worn by a photographer while documenting evidence in the laboratory
Photo courtesy of Brandi Clark

General Evidence Documentation

Setup

Place the evidence on a new or recently cleaned distraction-free background. Examples of background material are: seamless background paper, a paper roll of background material typically used in photo studios which is available from most professional photo-supply stores; butcher paper, available from many office supply stores; or a neutral countertop. Avoid using floors, carpets, or any other surface without proper protection.

Use even illumination, which can be accomplished by using two light sources set at approximately 45 degree angles to the evidence. Be sure the lights are of equal power and distance from the evidence. This may also be accomplished using the bounce flash technique described in Chapter 4.

The camera should be placed directly overhead of the evidence or as close as possible to avoid distortion. For larger items of evidence, the photographer may require the use of a ladder or scaffolding to get to the height necessary to fit the evidence in the frame of view.

Be sure to include a case number and scale in all images.

Photograph all sides of the evidence.

Take close-up photos of any important details on the evidence such as biological staining, cuts and tears, or trace evidence adhering to the evidence.

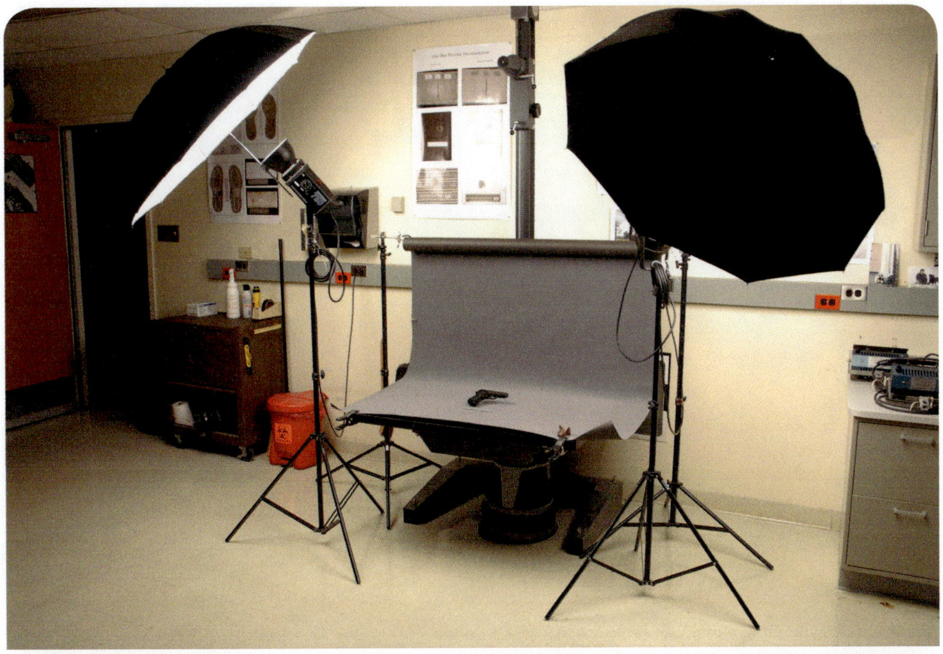

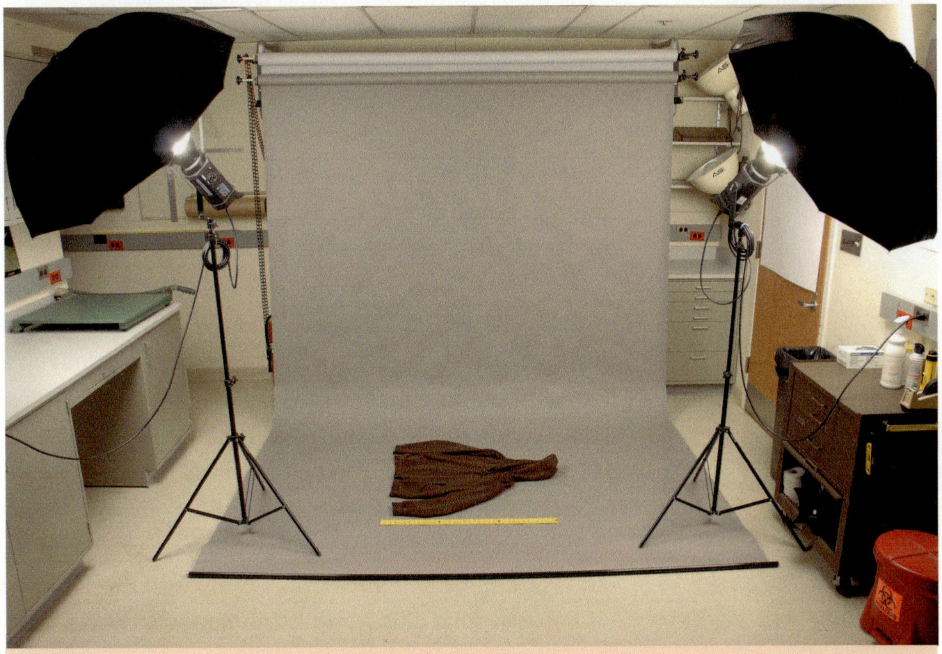

Figures 6.2 – 6.3 Examples of the setup for evidence documentation in the laboratory or photo studio

Photographing Highly Reflective Objects

Reflective objects such as firearms, knives, car paint, glass, or mirrored surfaces present a unique challenge. To make documenting reflective objects easier, diffuse the light as much

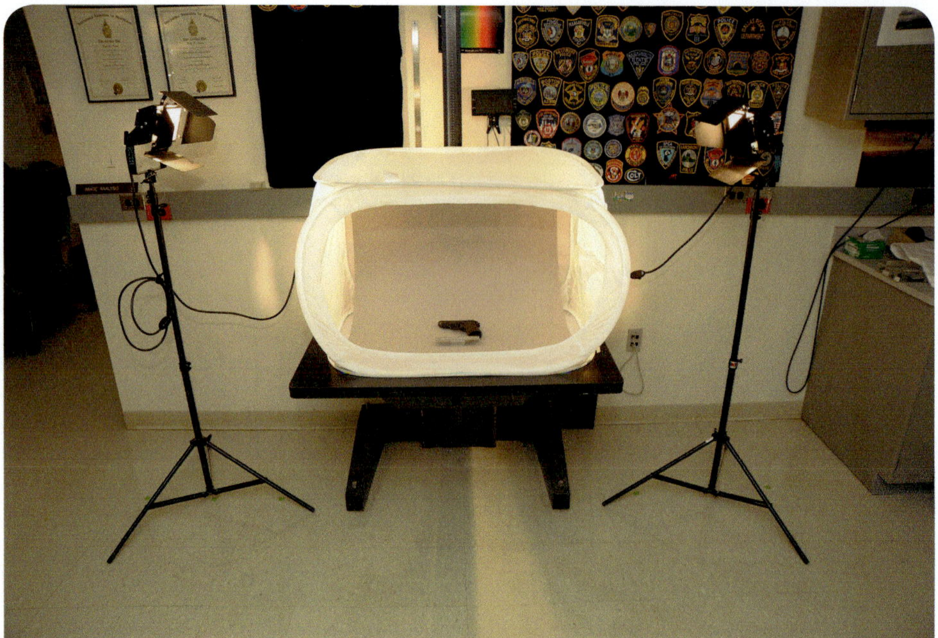

Figure 6.4 A light tent being used for the documentation of highly reflective evidence

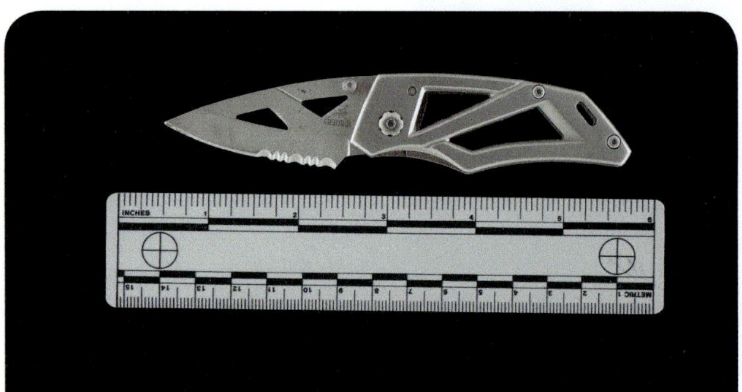

Figure 6.5 Photograph of a knife inside a light tent

as possible. Think about making the light larger, or coming from many directions. Bouncing the light may work in many situations. Simply aiming the flash at a ceiling or wall may do the trick. This works well for larger items, scenes, or rooms. However, for smaller items it may be more practical to construct a diffuser. There are commercially available diffusers for this purpose called light tents, typically available for under $100. Construction of a light tent is also relatively simple using either paper, or similar diffuse material (such as Savage Trans-lum). Construct a frame and cover with the diffusion material for a makeshift light tent. For smaller items a Styrofoam cup with the bottom cut off makes a great diffuser; this technique also works well for fingerprints on shiny surfaces.

To use the light tent or diffuser, place the subject inside the tent and light the tent from the outside. It is beneficial to use more than one light; however, it is possible to use one light if necessary. For a dual light setup, place each light on opposite sides of the tent far enough away to light the entire side of the tent without the light spilling over. For a single light setup, start by illuminating only the top of the tent, or just one side, some trial and error may be necessary to find the best lighting location. If the lights are too close to the tent some reflection may result in the subject; if this is observed move the lights farther away from the tent.

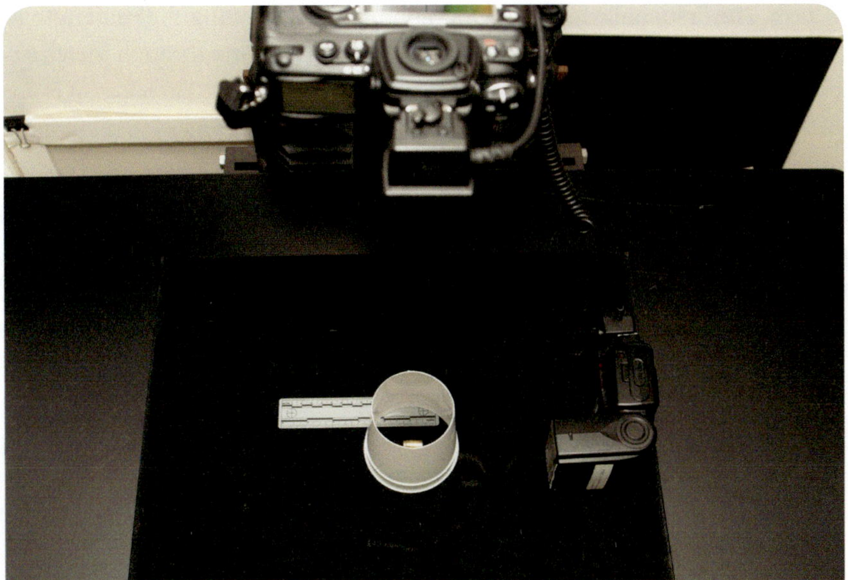

Figure 6.6 For smaller objects a rolled up piece of white paper, wax paper, or plain white cup (with bottom removed) may be used as a small light tent or diffuser. The diffuser can be lit using a portable flash or continuous light source. This technique works well both in the laboratory and on location

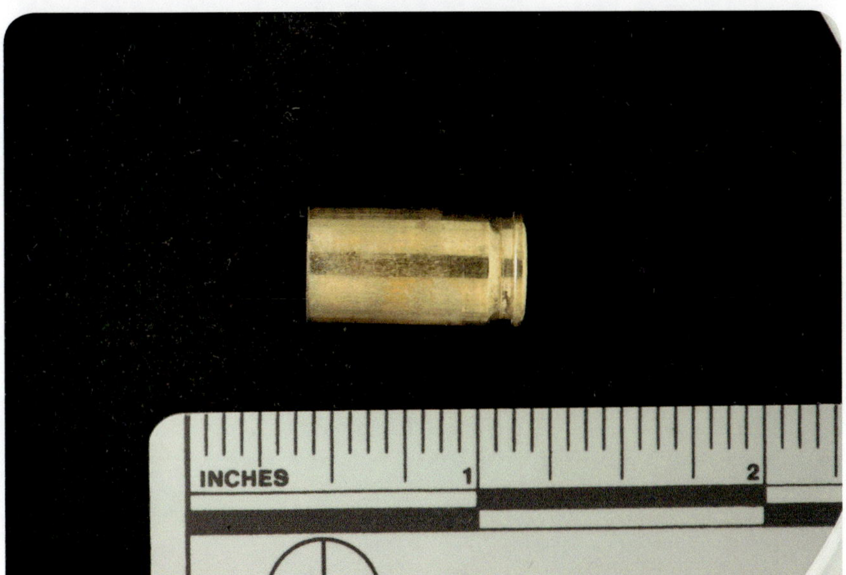

Figure 6.7 Photograph of a cartridge casing inside the cup from Figure 6.6

Photographing the Surface of Glass

It is not uncommon to encounter evidence on the surface of glass, especially footwear impressions and fingerprints. Documenting evidence on the surface of glass can be a very difficult task. The first challenge to photographing glass is getting the camera to focus on the subject. If using autofocus, the camera may end up focusing through the glass, or perhaps focusing on a reflection in the glass, often the photographer. Therefore, it is preferable to set the camera to manual focus for this task. By setting the camera to manual focus the photographer can control what the lens focuses on.

If you must or prefer to use autofocus, a trick to getting the camera to focus on glass is to momentarily place an object (like your hand or scale) in the frame just in front of the glass. Be sure the focus is set to single servo mode, then press the shutter button halfway to activate the focus. Once the subject is in focus, without releasing the shutter button, remove

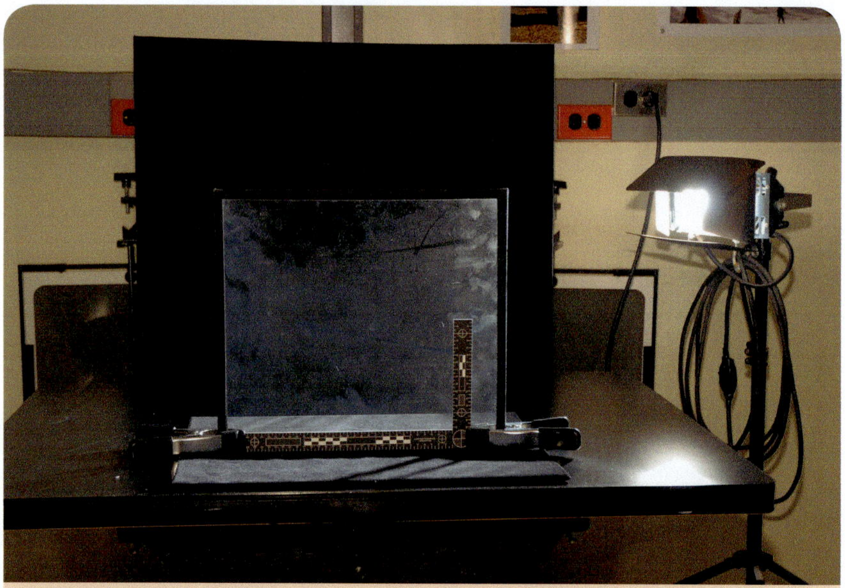

Figure 6.8 The setup for documenting the surface of glass, using the transillumination lighting technique

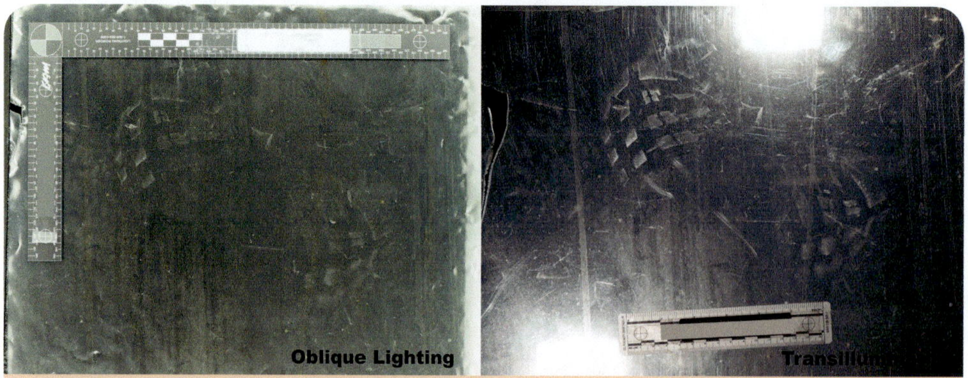

Figure 6.9 A comparison of the oblique lighting technique to the transillumination lighting technique on a footwear impression left on a piece of clear plastic

the object and press the shutter-release button completely to take the picture. The camera should not refocus unless the shutter button is released.

Lighting the surface of glass is also very difficult, as typically glare from the light source reflects back into the camera and obscures the subject, or the light travels through the glass and illuminates the area behind the glass which makes the subject difficult to see.

To light the surface of the glass, use a narrow beam of light as well as an oblique angle. Move the light source closer or farther from the glass to control the area or the glass that is illuminated.

Remove the area behind the glass by blocking the glass with a dark object such as black poster board, paper, or

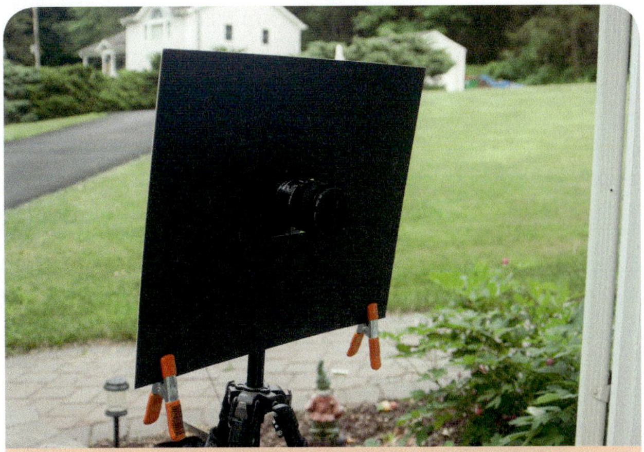

Figure 6.10 Black (or dark) cardboard may be used to mask off the camera and will help reduce the reflection when documenting evidence on glass

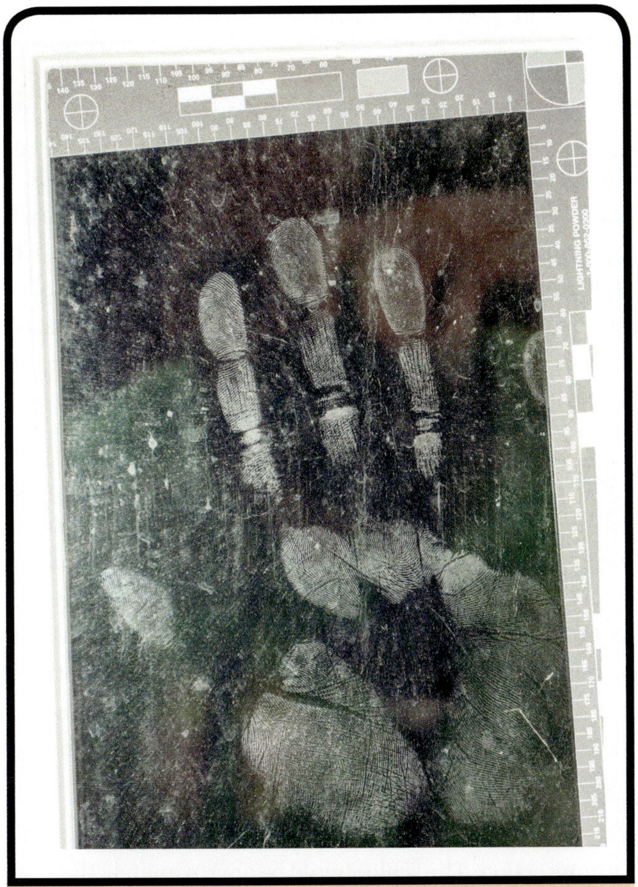

Figure 6.11 A photograph of a handprint on glass without the use of a camera mask, as in Figure 6.10

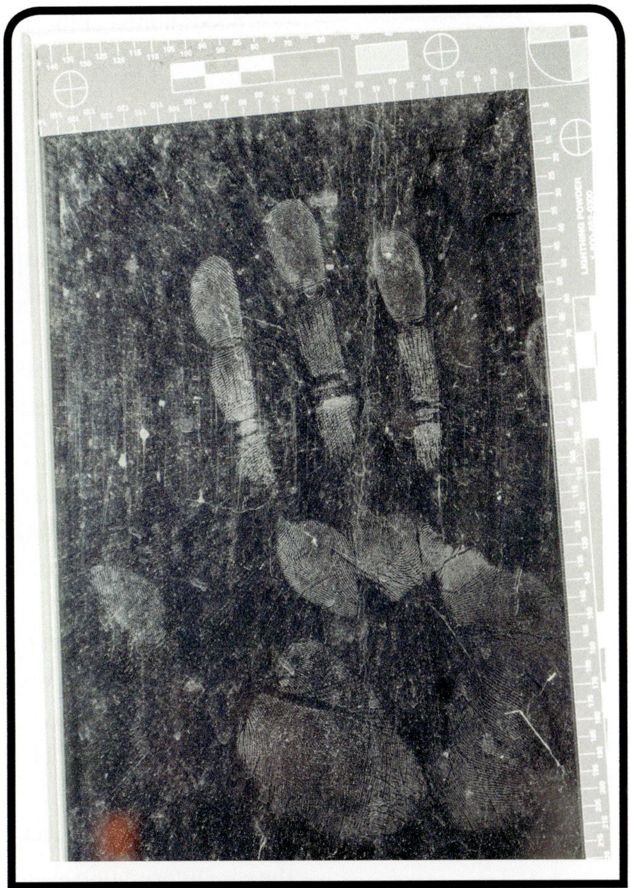

Figure 6.12 A photograph of a handprint on glass using a camera mask, as in Figure 6.10

seamless material. A dark jacket or other clothing may also work in a pinch. It will also be helpful to darken the environment around the glass if possible, this will help eliminate any reflections in the glass.

Once these steps have been taken, another issue that may arise is reflection off the glass. Essentially we have just created a mirror, so you may get a really nice photograph of yourself taking a photograph. To prevent this from happening construct a camera mask by cutting a hole, large enough for only the lens of the camera, in a dark piece of cardboard or black poster board. The board should be as large or larger than the subject. Place the mask in front of the camera, with the lens protruding through the hole; this should remove any reflections of the camera, photographer, and the area directly behind the camera.

Photographing Impressions in the Lab

When impressions are collected from a crime scene and brought back to the lab, they should be documented in a laboratory environment. This is still important even if the impression was documented at the scene, as the controlled environment of the studio or lab may provide better results that at the scene.

To set up for documenting impressions, use a copy stand or sturdy tripod to mount the camera directly above the impression as you would at the scene. The camera must be perpendicular (90 degrees) to impression so that the image of the impression will be uniformly at the same scale. Using tungsten, halogen, or other continuous lighting to evenly illuminate the impression, generally starting at approximately 45 degrees. The lighting may be adjusted to provide the contrast necessary to emphasize the impression. As a general rule shallower impressions require smaller angles of light. The lighting may also be accomplished using flash, but it may be difficult to preview the lighting. Use a flashlight or other light source to preview the effects of a lighting angle and as a guide to place the flash.

The camera should be set to its highest-quality image output, typically RAW file format and the largest native file size. Be cautious as some cameras interpolate (artificially enlarge) image data, which results in a larger image that does not contain extra detail. Check the camera's manual if you are unsure of your camera's settings. The generally accepted resolution for impression documentation is 300 pixels per inch at 1:1 or actual size. To determine the area in which the camera will reproduce at this resolution, divide both the horizontal and vertical resolutions (pixels) by 300. The result will be the area (in inches) the camera can cover at 300ppi. Anything larger than this result should be documented in sections.

Position the impression directly below the camera on a level surface and place a scale with the case information even with the impression. The scale should be approximately the same length as the impression. Be sure the impression and scale are at the same level; if not use something of the same height to get the scale even with the impression. This scale may be used later to create a 1:1 reproduction or life-size print.

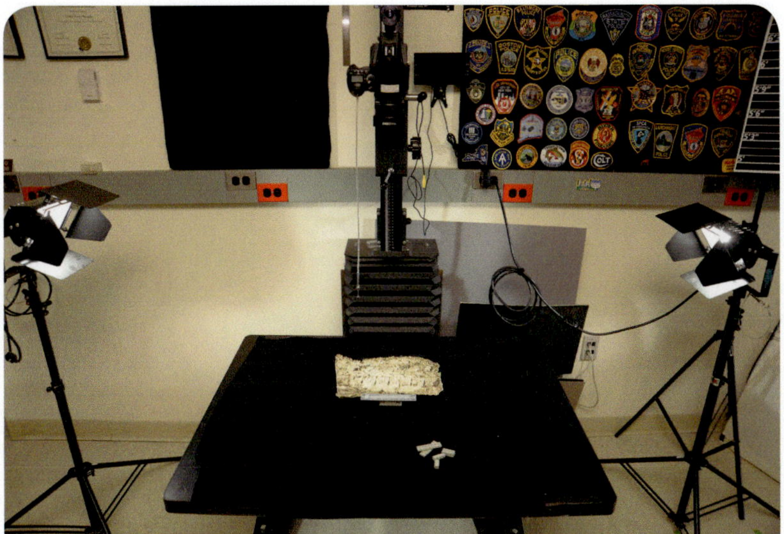

Figure 6.13 An example of a desired setup for impression documentation in the lab. The camera must be mounted perpendicular to the impression in order to scale the image

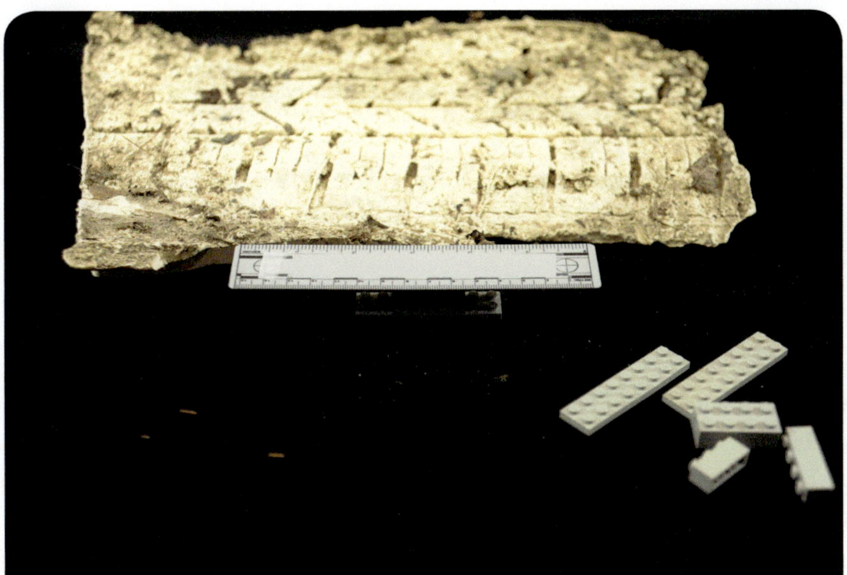

Figure 6.14 Lego© or other blocks are used for leveling the subject as well as getting the scale at the same height as the impression

Adjust the camera so that the impression fills the frame; be sure the longest dimension of the impression is horizontal in the frame. The use of a macro lens or quality normal to telephoto lens is preferred; however, a zoom lens may be used as well, provided the zoom is not set to less than approximately 50mm. A lens wider (less) than 50mm may cause a

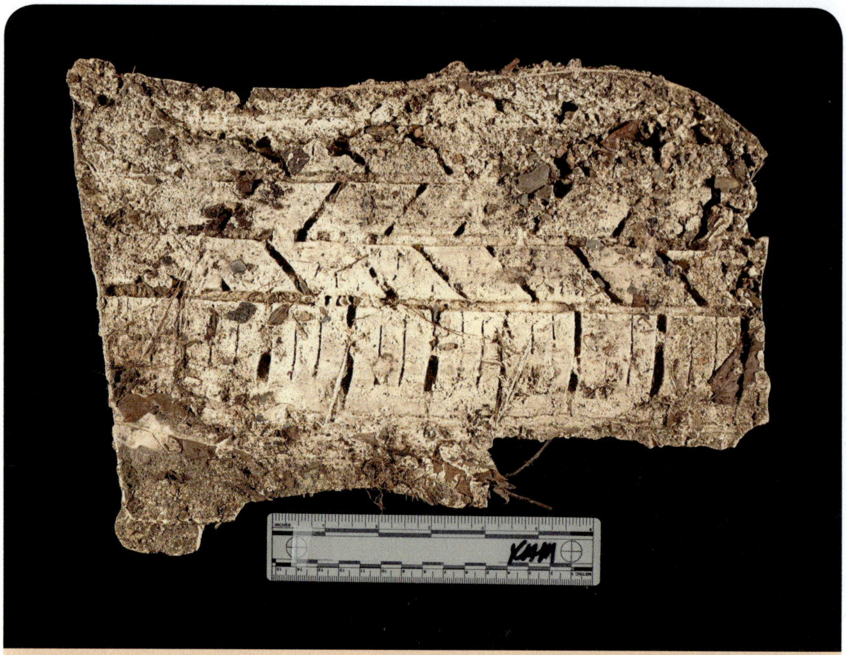

Figure 6.15 The resulting image of the dental stone cast from Figures 6.13 and 6.14

barrel-like distortion in the photograph that will make it difficult to achieve a 1:1 reproduction of the image.

Be sure the image is in focus, take a picture, check the exposure, make any adjustments necessary, and re-shoot.

Documenting Injuries to a Victim or Suspect

Document entire body, front, back, and sides on neutral background like a plain white wall if available. Document the condition and appearance of the clothing. The clothing may also be collected and documented further; however, it may be important to document how the clothing was worn on the person at the time. Document the location of any jewelry.

Take medium-range photographs of any injuries to show their location on the body. Take close-up photographs of the injuries with a scale, from several angles, as well as close-up photographs of both sides of the hands.

Photographing Bite Marks

Bite-mark photographs should be taken with an ABFO (American Board of Forensic Odontology) No. 2 scale. This is a specially designed scale for use with bite-mark photographs, available from many crime scene supply vendors. Be sure the injury is perpendicular to the camera lens; this will ensure that when a scaled photograph is produced from the images, the entire bite mark will be to the same scale. Do not use a wide-angle lens, as it will distort the scale of the bite mark. See later in the chapter for UV photography which can aid in the visualization of bite marks.

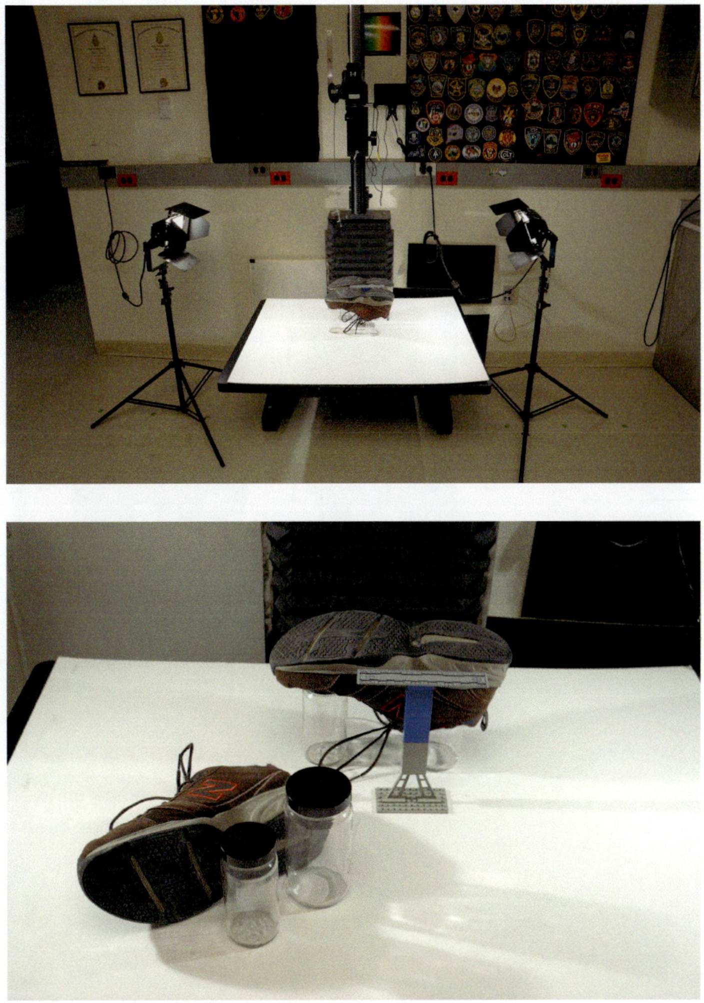

Figures 6.16–6.17 A demonstration of a technique for photographing the bottom of footwear. Lego© blocks are used to hold the scale, and jars used to level the sole of the footwear

Autopsy Photography

Sometimes it is necessary to travel to the medical examiner's office to document the body of the victim of a crime. These photographs are typically taken at the direction of the medical examiner or coroner. Avoid distractions, including people, in the background of the photographs. Generally, the following photographs should be taken. Photograph the body as it was received. These photographs should be taken from directly overhead or as close as possible to overhead. If the photographer cannot get directly over the victim, the victim may be positioned on his side and the photographs can be taken from the side. If it is possible to turn the body over, be sure to photograph the back of the body as well. Photograph any physical evidence adhering to the body before it is removed. This is especially important since the body may be washed during the autopsy. The victim's clothing will be removed prior to the autopsy and may be photographed separately on a clean surface.

Once the body is clean it can be photographed again, similar to when it was first documented. All wounds on the body should be documented; provide both medium-range and close-up photographs and be sure to include a scale.

The medical examiner may request photographs of wounds inside the body. These photographs can be taken while the organs are still in the body, or on a clean blank surface when the organ is removed. In order to be acceptable in court the image must not be prejudicial, so be sure to keep backgrounds free of excessive blood, as well as other distractions.

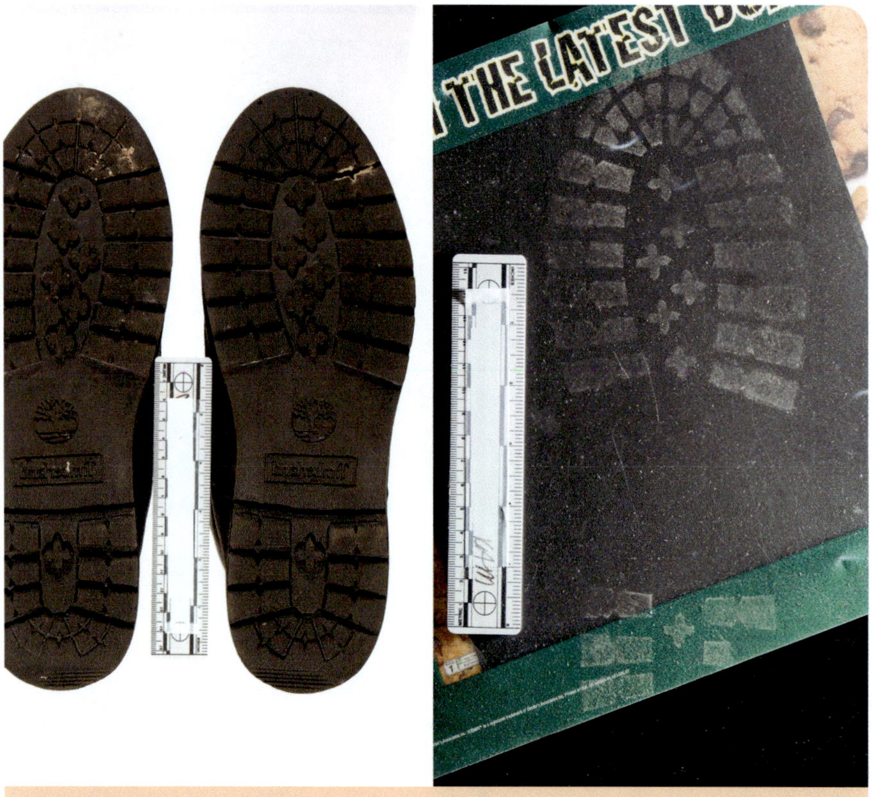

Figure 6.18 Known footwear compared to an unknown impression left at a crime scene. The image of the footwear has been flipped horizontally to match the orientation of the impression. Footwear impressions are mirror images of the footwear that left them

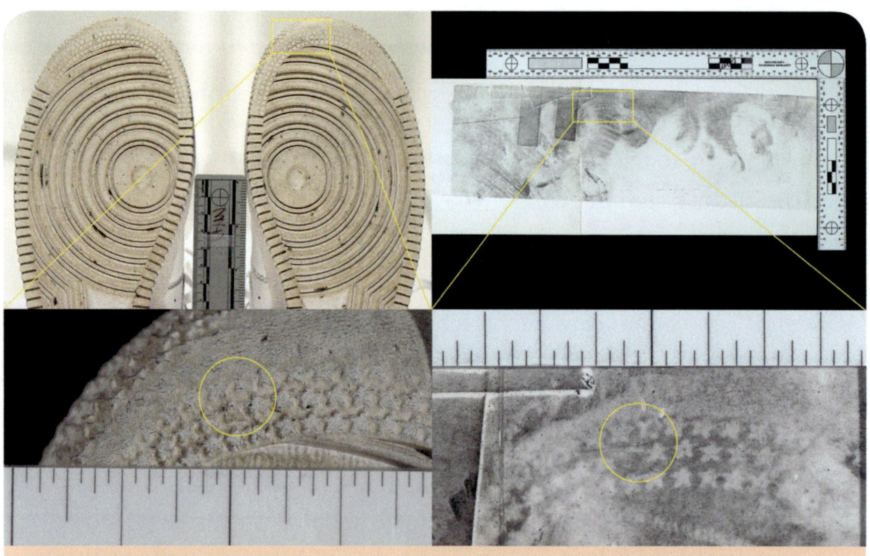

Figure 6.19 Known footwear compared to an unknown impression left at a crime scene, as well as close-up images of the area where identifying characteristics were found. Again, the image of the footwear has been flipped horizontally to match the orientation of the impression

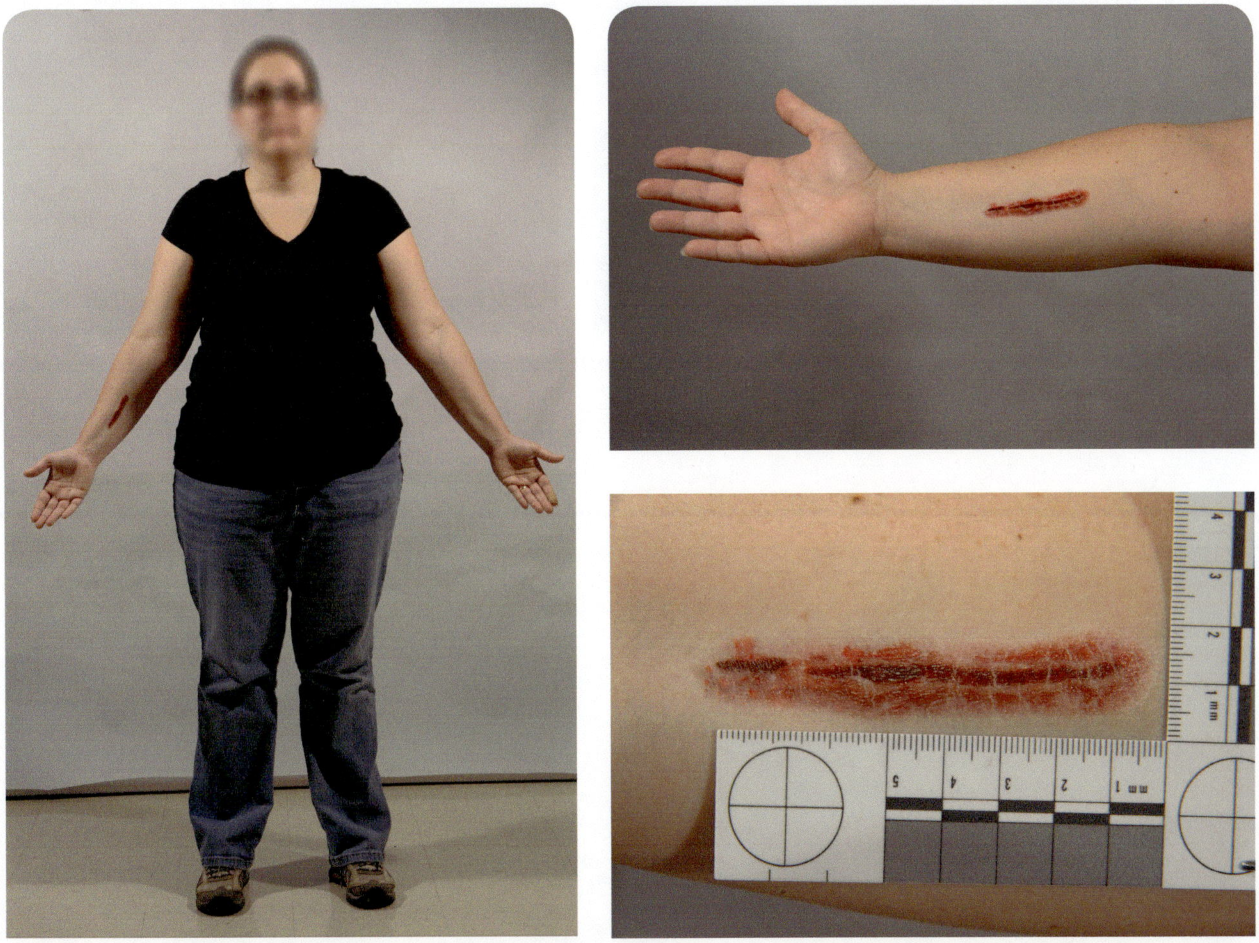

Figures 6.20–6.22 A demonstration of long, medium, and close-up photographs of an injury

Lighting for Autopsy Photography

Lighting in an autopsy room can be very tricky. The reflective metal tables typically used to perform the autopsy, the body's fluids, and the water used during the autopsy may reflect light and cause glare in the photographs. A helpful lighting angle to use in the autopsy room is bounce lighting. If the ceiling in the autopsy room is not too high or off-white in color it is possible to bounce the flash off the ceiling to diffuse the light source. This technique will sufficiently spread the light and decrease the amount of glare coming from the subjects. The technique is helpful for both overall shots as well as close up photographs of the body.

A good lighting technique for relatively small objects in the autopsy room is the use of a diffusor between the flash and subject. This technique is described in Figure 6.6.

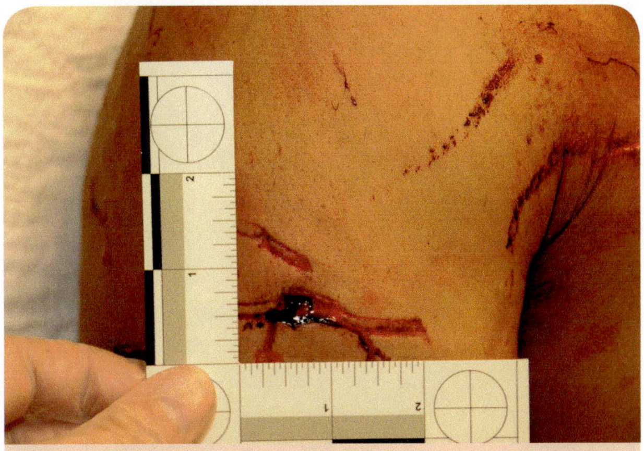

Figure 6.23 A photograph of a dog bite using a properly sized scale

Photo courtesy of Police Chief Vernon L. Riddick Jr., Waterbury CT Police Department

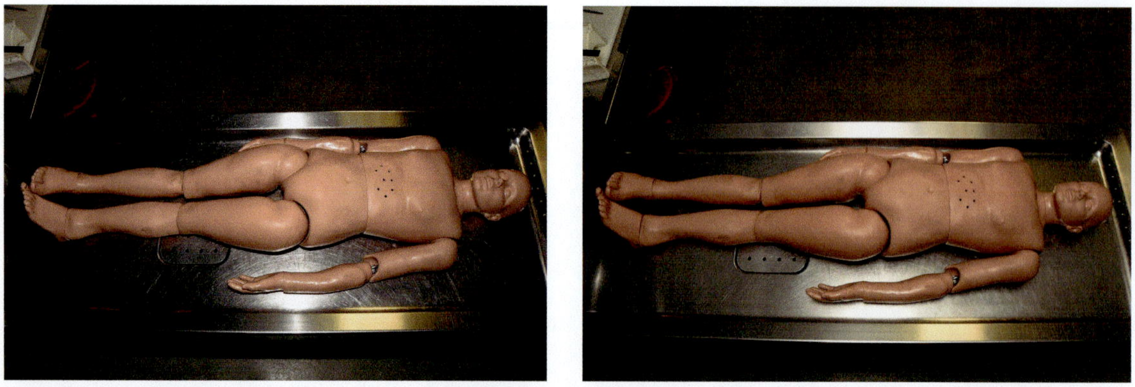

Figures 6.24–6.25 A comparison of lighting techniques in the autopsy room

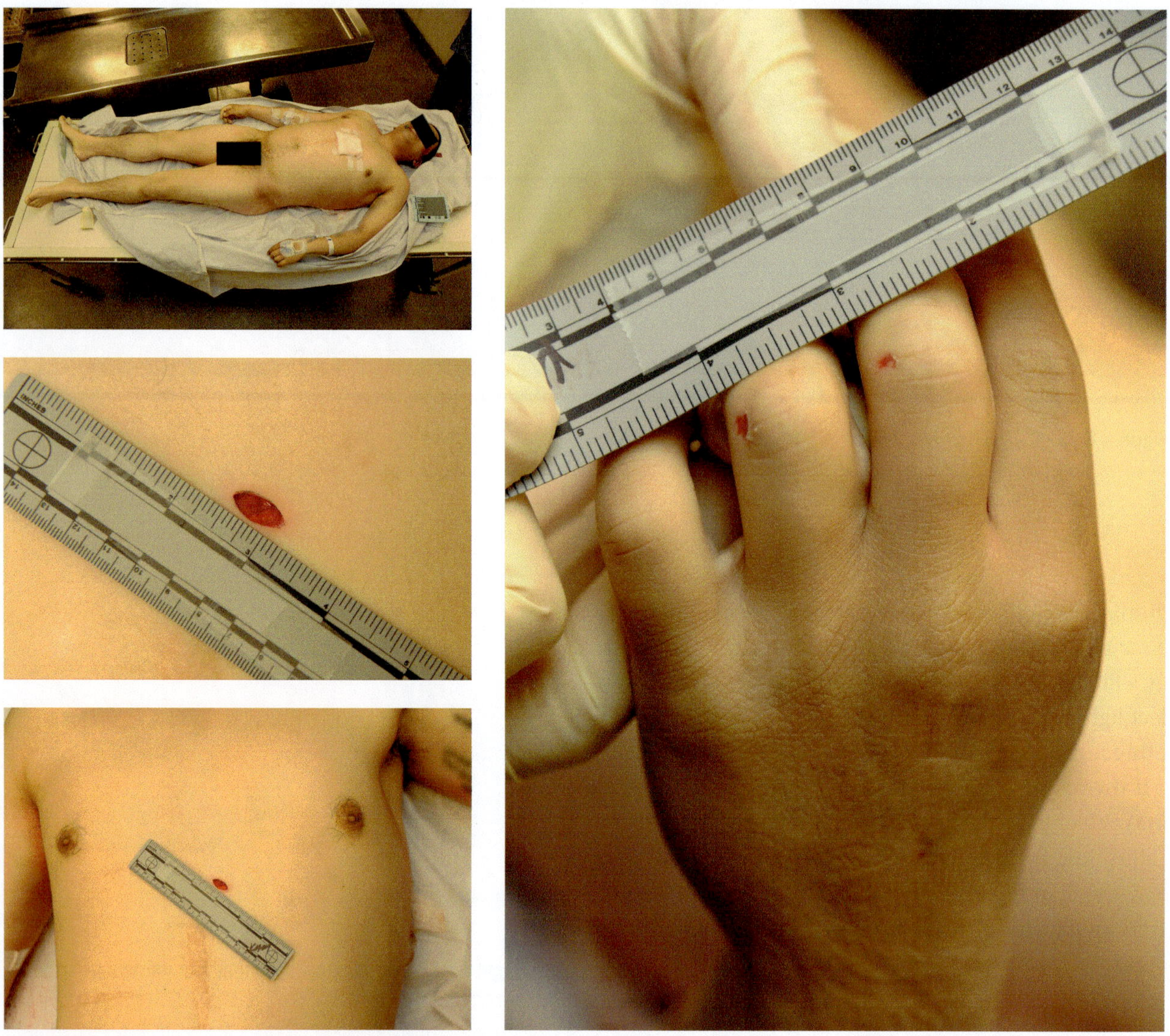

Figures 6.26–6.33 Examples of autopsy photographs showing the entire body as well as the location of injuries

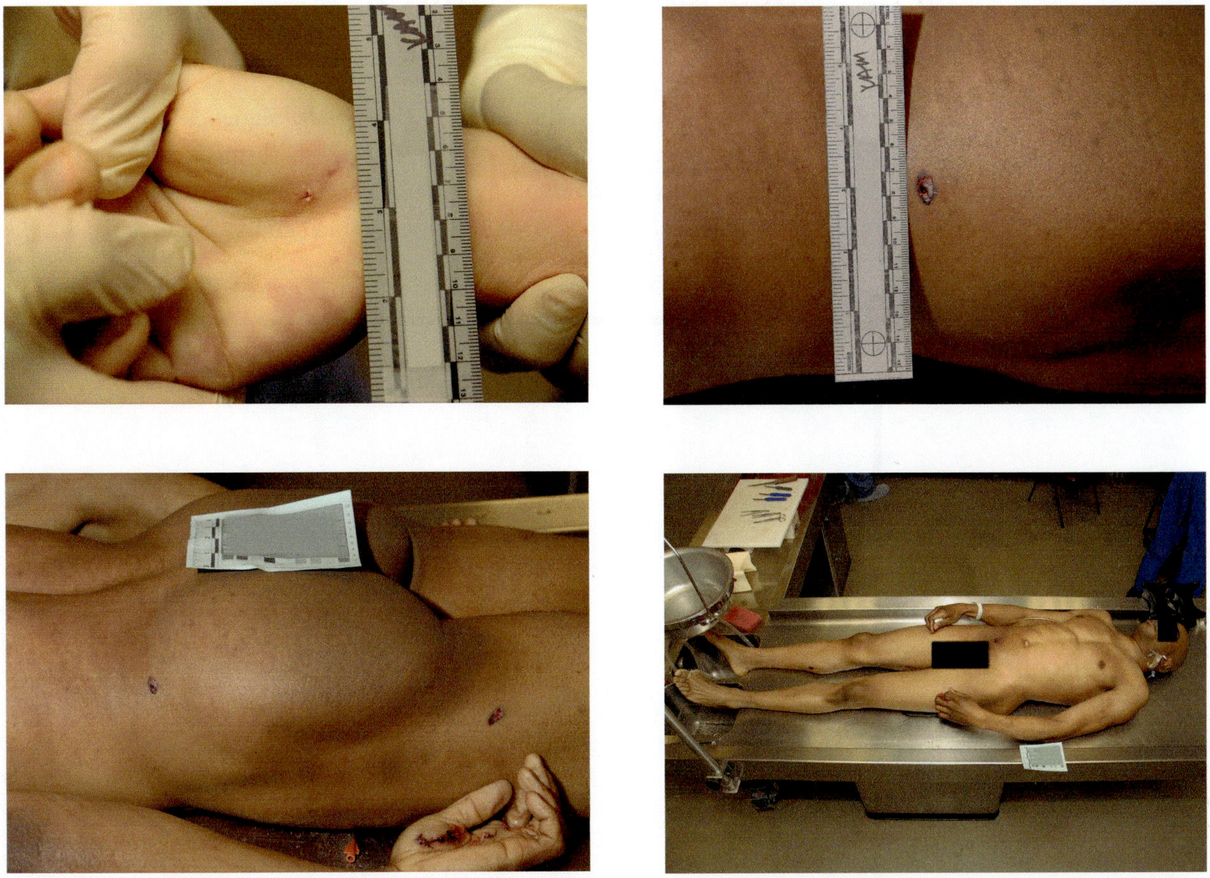

Figures 6.26–6.33 Continued

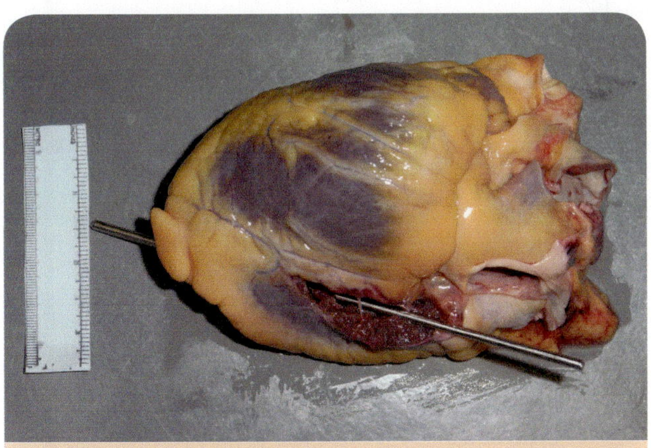

Figure 6.34 A photograph of the heart of a gunshot victim; a metal rod was placed in the heart to show the path of the bullet

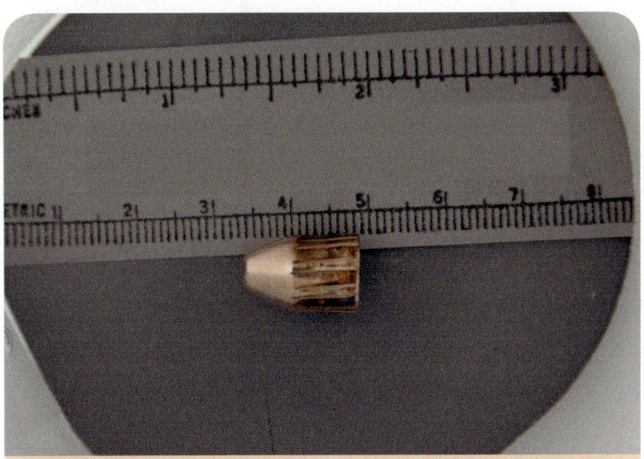

Figure 6.35 A photograph of a bullet removed from a victim using the lighting technique described in Figure 6.6

Fluorescence Photography

The Electromagnetic Spectrum

The electromagnetic spectrum is the range of all possible frequencies of electromagnetic radiation. Electromagnetic radiation is energy that travels through space in the form of waves. Visible light, X-rays, and radio waves are all examples of electromagnetic radiation. Just outside the frequencies of visible light is energy that can be used to make images that

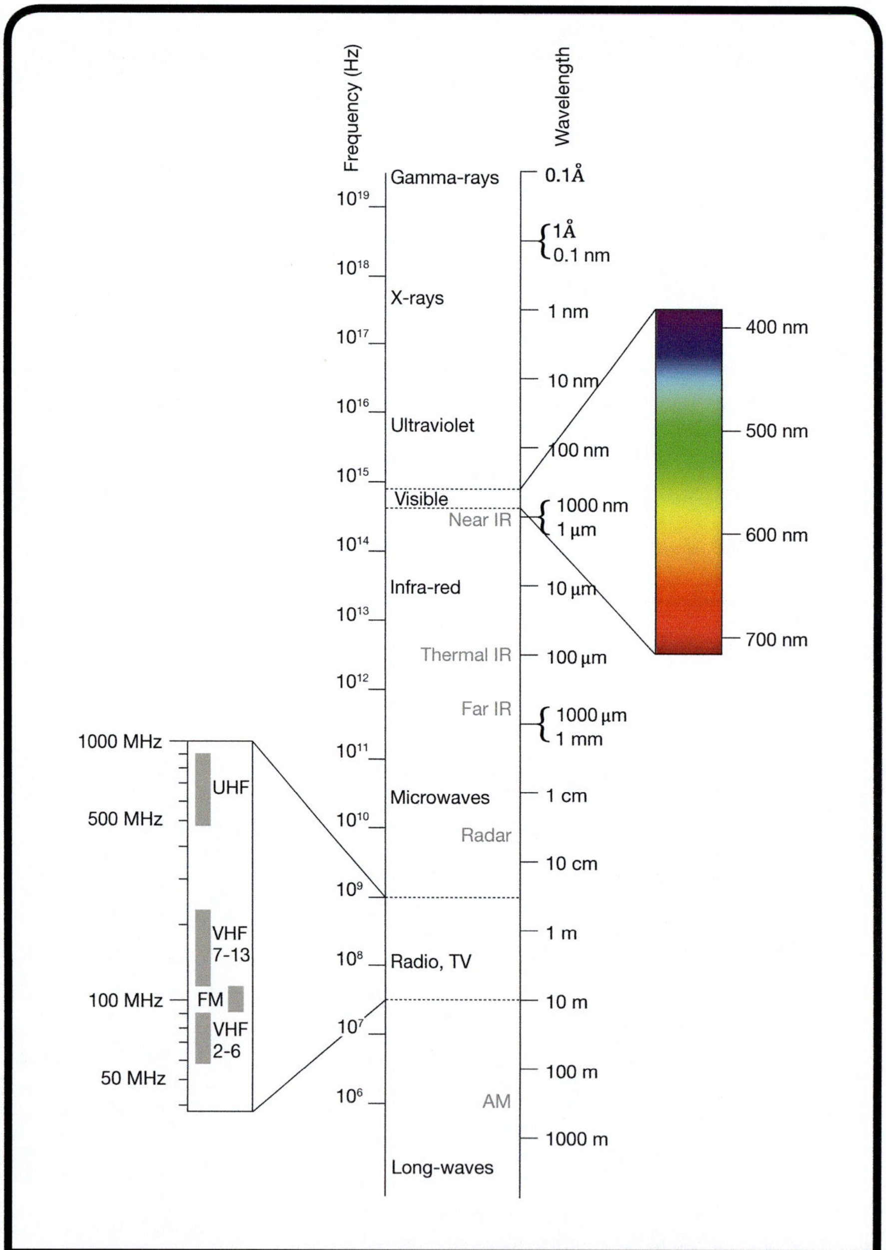

Figure 6.36 The electromagnetic spectrum includes all known wavelengths of energy, including visible light from approximately 400 to 700 nm (nanometers)

are invisible to human eyes. Photography using infrared (IR) and ultraviolet (UV) wavelengths can be used to reveal characteristics of evidence that cannot be seen with visible light.

Forensic light sources, also known as alternate light sources, crime-lights, or crime scopes, are often used in the search for evidence. They visually enhance the appearance of evidence such as latent fingerprints, bodily fluids, hairs and fibers, bruises, wound patterns, questioned documents, bone fragments, and several other types of evidence.

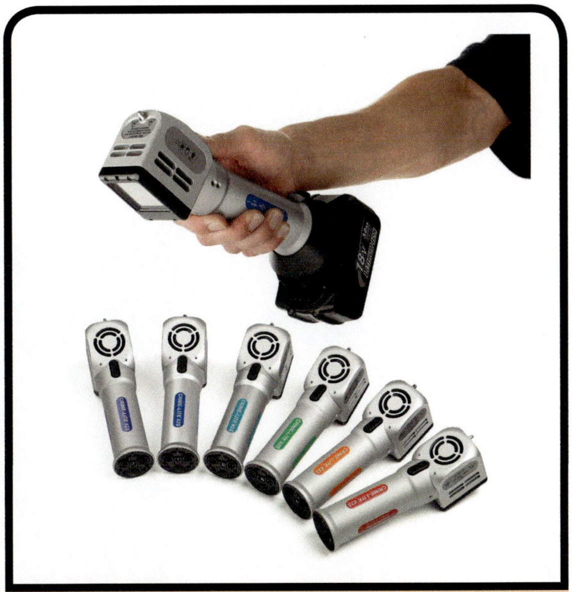

Figure 6.37 Examples of light sources for fluorescence, infrared, and ultraviolet photography

Photo courtesy of Foster and Freeman

Forensic light sources rely on the principle of fluorescence. The light source's energy causes the subject to emit light of a different wavelength. The use of the light source typically entails wearing special colored glasses or goggles that block the energy of the light source, therefore enhancing the observation of the emitted light.

Forensic light sources are available from many forensic suppliers and come in several configurations. Light sources can either be a single wavelength or several adjustable wavelengths. The type of evidence you are searching for will dictate the light source needed and wavelength/filter combination used.

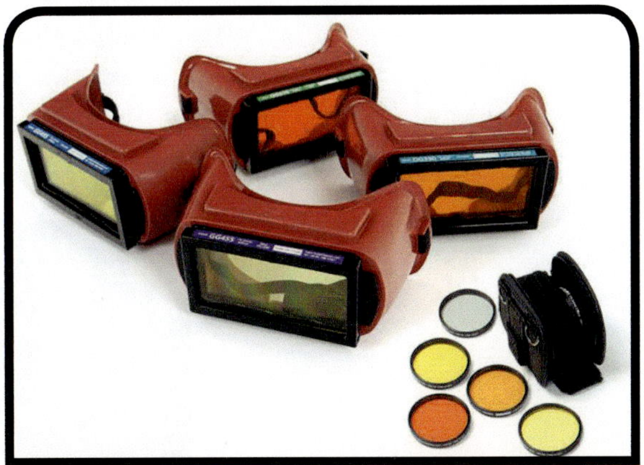

Figure 6.38 Examples of barrier filters and goggles for use with forensic light sources

Photo courtesy of Foster and Freeman

The glasses or goggles that are used with the forensic light source, often called the barrier filter, are designed to block the illumination or excitation energy of the light. Blocking the excitation energy allows the viewer to better see the fluorescence of the evidence being searched.

Since the reaction observed occurs in the visible light spectrum it can be documented with a typical camera. The only special equipment needed is a filter of similar properties to the glasses used with the light source. Many light source manufacturers will supply the corresponding filter with their system. If a filter is not available, one may be purchased from a photography supply store.

There are several options for the type of filter used, either threaded to screw onto the lens, or square filters that slide into a filter holder. Also there are Kodak Wrattten ®filters that are relatively inexpensive and available in multiple colors. You can have success by stacking several of these filters to match the barrier filter of your light source. In a pinch if there is no filter available you may hold or temporarily mount the specific glasses or goggles to the front of the lens.

The following is a list of suggested equipment for fluorescence photography:

- a tripod, to hold the camera steady for the typically long exposures;
- a fast lens (large aperture), to allow as much light as possible to reach the sensor;
- a shutter-release cable, so the camera can be triggered without shaking the setup.

Photographing the Fluorescence

The room will need to be dark to make photographic exposures but, prior to darkening the environment, mount the camera on the tripod and compose the image to include the area of interest. It is a good idea at this point to photograph the subject under "normal" lighting

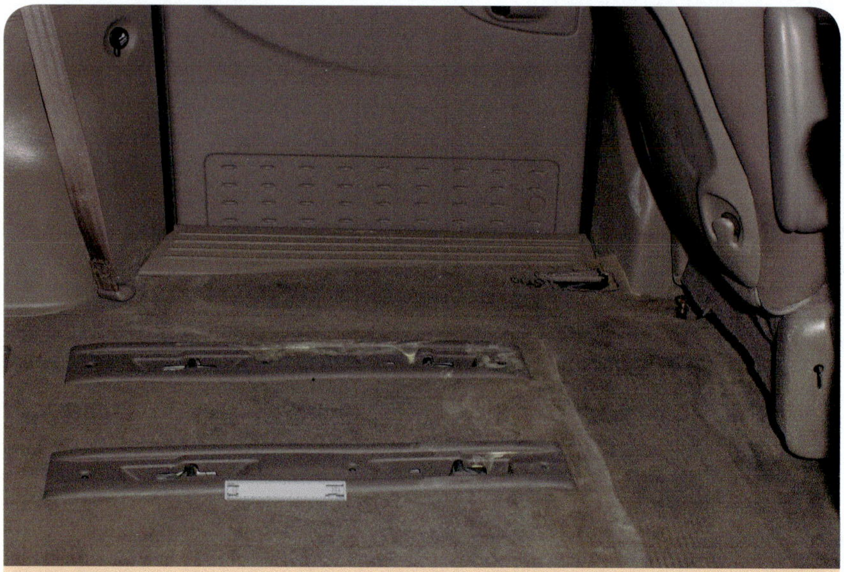

Figure 6.39 Photograph of the interior of a vehicle where the attempted cleanup of blood was suspected

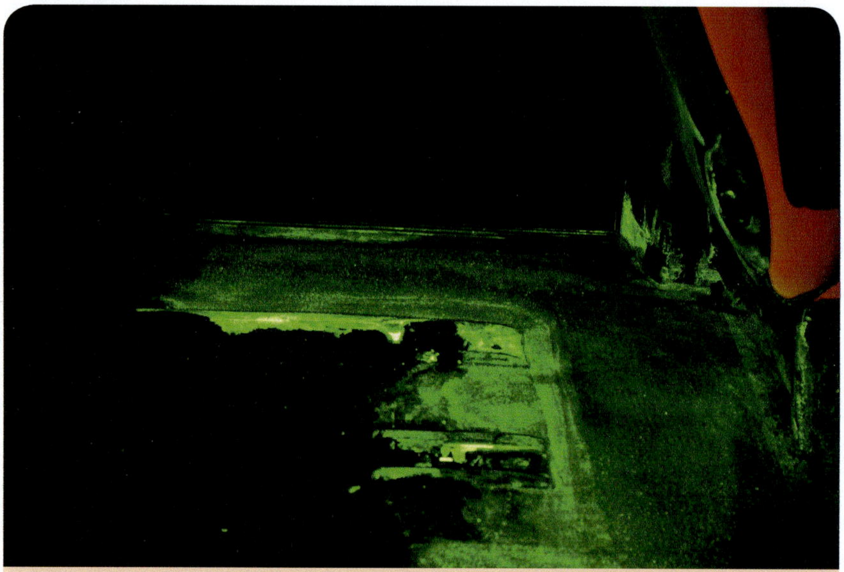

Figure 6.40 A photograph of the fluorescence of the solution used in the attempted cleanup of blood. 30 Seconds, f4.5, ISO 125, no flash

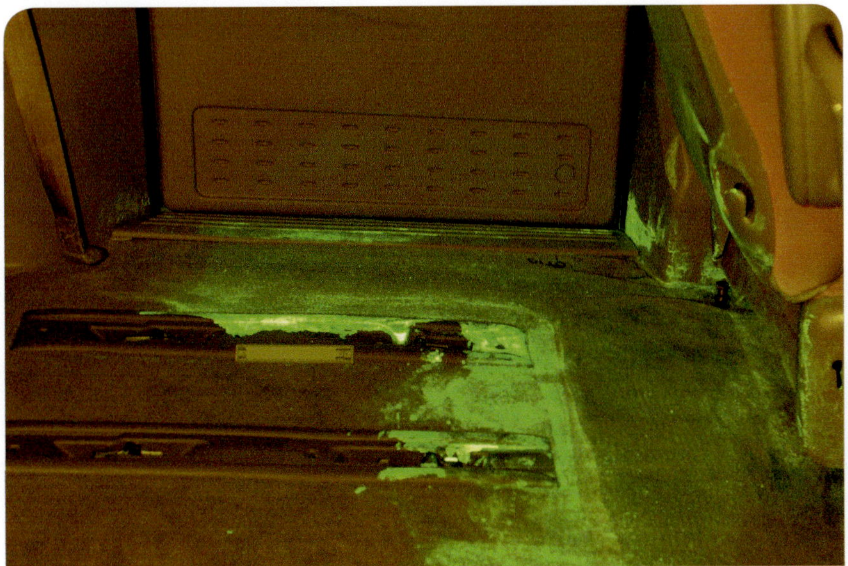

Figure 6.41 A photograph of the fluorescence of the solution used in the attempted cleanup of blood. 30 Seconds, f4.5, ISO 125, flash set to manual mode 1/16th power

conditions. It may be possible to use the camera's P (program auto) mode to get the proper exposure for the fluorescence. Allow the cameras meter to choose the exposure settings and adjust the exposure using the exposure compensation function of the camera. If using P mode is not successful, try Manual mode. Set the aperture to its lowest setting and use the meter to choose the shutter speed. To adjust the exposure using manual mode, add or subtract time from the shutter speed.

Photographing Chemiluminescence (Luminol or Bluestar®)

Bluestar® is a blood visualizing reagent, based on luminol, which produces a chemoluminescent reaction in the presence of blood. The reaction takes place with the hemoglobin in the blood and glows in the dark. The reaction is capable of taking place in as little as a 1:10,000 dilution of blood, as well as on aged samples such as in cold cases. Be aware, there are some false positives noted with the use of luminol, such as copper, bleach, and even horseradish.

Equipment

Typical camera gear is all that is necessary for the photography of luminol. A tripod is a must because of the long exposure times necessary to document the glow of the reaction.

Setup

Prior to spraying the luminol, setup the camera and compose the photograph of the area to be sprayed. This is necessary since the reaction may only last a short period of time and setting up the equipment after the reaction is observed may not allow you enough time. Mount

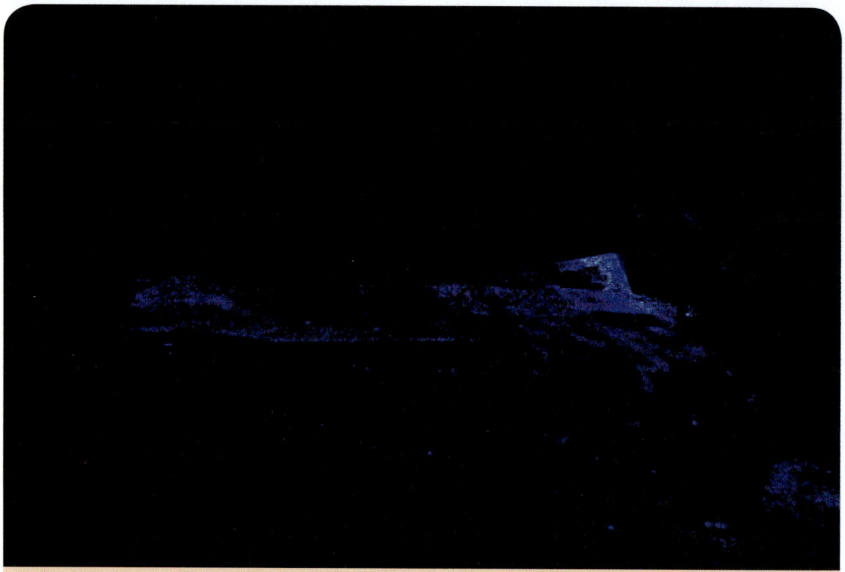

Figure 6.42 A photograph of the reaction of luminol in the suspected cleanup of blood from a vehicle. 60 seconds, f3.5, ISO 800, no flash

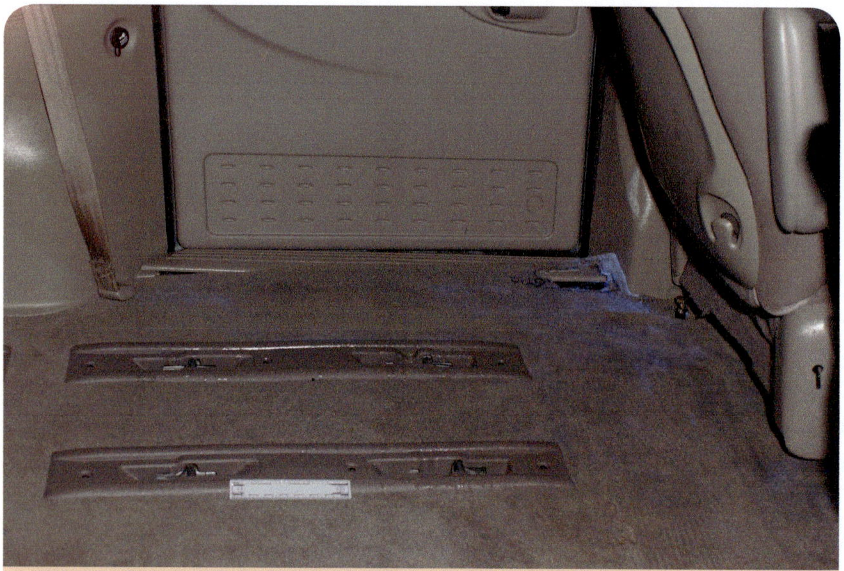

Figure 6.43 A photograph of the reaction of luminol in the suspected cleanup of blood from a vehicle. 60 seconds, f3.5, ISO 800, manual flash at 1/64th power

the camera atop a tripod and compose for the area to be treated; it is suggested to work in small areas one at a time if possible. Take a photograph of the area in the existing lighting conditions or supplement with a flash if necessary. Since the reaction will take place in the complete darkness pre-focus the camera and turn off autofocus otherwise the camera may try to focus in the dark. Set the cameras aperture to its widest setting and set the shutter speed to bulb setting (or for approximately 30 seconds to start). Set the flash to the manual setting and reduce the power to approximately 1/64th power.

When the camera is set up darken the environment and begin to spray the luminol. As soon as a reaction is visualized press the shutter button and record the reaction. Evaluate the resulting photograph and make any adjustments to the exposure as necessary. If the glow from the reaction is too dim, add to the exposure; if it is too bright, shorten the exposure. The surrounding area should be lit by the flash. If the exposure from the flash is too bright, reduce the power of the flash; if the opposite is true, increase the power of the flash. The luminol may be re-sprayed during the exposure if necessary though the reaction will become less intense with each respray.

Infrared and IR Fluorescence Photography

Infrared photography (IR) is useful for the documentation of gunshot residue on dark clothing, document examination (especially that of inks), and for visualizing writing on charred or aged documents. IR photography may also aid in the visualization of blood on dark garments, and may aid in identifying tattoos on decomposing bodies.

The IR radiation that is used for photography lies just outside the visual light spectrum, from approximately 700 to 900nm. Beyond 900nm, it is difficult to capture without specialized equipment. However, this equipment is available in the form of thermal imaging cameras, many of which are available commercially as well as for specialized applications.

All digital camera sensors are inherently sensitive to IR radiation. However, a special filter, called a hot mirror filter, is often located on the sensor to block that IR radiation. Some IR radiation may still pass through that filter and enable the camera to be used for IR photography. Typically, lower-end and point-and-shoot cameras have less effective hot mirror filters, making them ideal for IR photography. Unfortunately, there is no way of knowing what cameras will work best without testing them. A simple test to see if your camera is capable of recording IR energy is to point a television remote control at the front of the lens and press any button. If you can see light from the front of the remote, either on the live view monitor or in a picture, then the camera is capable of recording IR.

There are a few cameras specifically designed or modified for IR photography. In 2006, Fuji released the FinePix S3 Pro UVIR and the IS Pro, which is no longer commercially available. These cameras were directed toward the forensic market but were not overly successful and are no longer in production. Fujifilm has recently introduced a new camera though, the FUJIFILM® X-T1 IR (Infrared). There are also some Sony cameras with "night shot" feature which used infrared radiation to see in low light. As well, Canon makes an astrophotography version of one of their DSLR cameras, named the 60Da which has a higher sensitivity to IR energy. It may be possible to purchase one of these cameras online, but if not there are several companies that will modify an existing camera for you.

Companies currently offering camera conversion services include:

- lifepixel.com;
- digitalsilverimageing.com;
- precision camera.com.

Essentially you send them your digital camera and they remove the hot mirror filter, thereby making the camera sensitive to IR energy.

Light Sources

The optimal light source for IR photography is one that has the greatest emission of infrared energy. Using a light source with little to no IR emission will make it very difficult to make an exposure. Typically, light sources that emit a great deal of heat will also emit IR energy. Examples include the sun, tungsten, and halogen lights, incandescent light bulbs, electronic flash systems, and forensic light sources. The sun is a good source of IR energy; however, it may not be a wise decision to expose evidence to the elements, but if no other source exists it may do in a pinch. Another issue with using the sun as an energy source is its unpredictability; cloud cover, shade, and time of day may hinder the amount of IR energy available. Tungsten, halogen, and incandescent light sources are all great for use with IR photography. Their output is constant so you may predict your settings, but care should be taken as they produce a great deal of heat. It is more practical to use studio electronic flash systems with a high power output such as 3200 watts/secs or higher. Portable electronic flash units that work directly with cameras may not be powerful enough for this work unless the objects are very small. There are some forensic light sources made specifically for the output of IR, like the Crime-lite® 2 IR, 82S IR and ML2 IR light sources from Foster + Freeman and the Crime Scope from SPEX Forensics.

Filters

Once you have identified a camera that is sensitive to IR radiation you must have a way to block the visible light from reaching the sensor and making an exposure. Filters are designed to block light at certain wavelengths and results may vary depending upon which filter is chosen. There are several filters available that block visible light, or most of it, and transmit IR energy. The following is a list of currently available filters and their transmission wavelengths.

- Kodak Wratten 87 (Tiffen 87, Schott (Heliopan) RG780, Peca 904)—740nm and above;
- Kodak Wratten 87c – (Schott (Heliopan) RG850, B+W 093, Peca 910)—790nm and above;
- Kodak Wratten 87b (Peca 908)—830nm and above;
- Kodak Wratten87a (Hoya RM-90, Schott (Heliopan) RG1000, Peca 906)—930 and above;

- Kodak Wratten 89b (Schott (Heliopan) RG715, Hoya R-72, B+W 092, Peca 914)—680nm and above.

If the camera you are using has been converted, or is specifically manufactured to be sensitive to IR energy, it is recommended to have a filter designed to transmit only visible light and block others in order to take pictures of only visible light:

- Peca 916;
- Hoya UV & IR Cut Filter;
- Tiffen Hot Mirror;
- B+W UV/IF Cut 486.

Other Equipment

Depending upon the camera, radiation source, and filter combination, the exposure necessary to capture IR may be long. Also since the human eye cannot see IR energy, it is a good idea to have a stationary camera in case adjustments need to be made to the subject. It is for those reasons that a sturdy tripod or copy stand setup is recommended for IR photography. A cable release may also be useful for pressing the shutter button when it's out of reach or for reducing camera shake during exposures. If a shutter release cable is not available, the use of the self-timer function on the camera can serve the same purpose.

Setup

The setup for IR photography is relatively simple. The camera should be placed directly above or in front of the subject preferably on a sturdy mount.

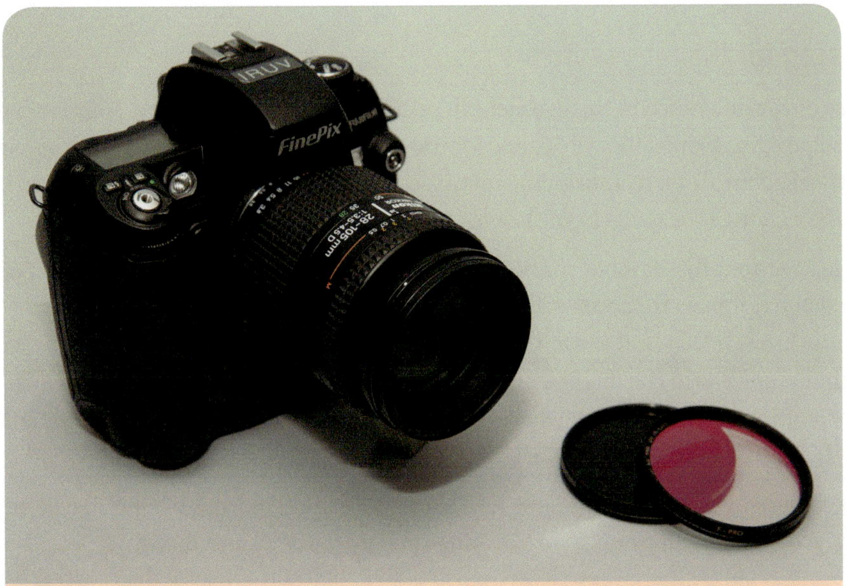

Figure 6.44 The Fuji FinePix IRUV camera, which was specifically made to be sensitive to IR and UV radiation, along with an IR transmitting and UV/IR blocking filter

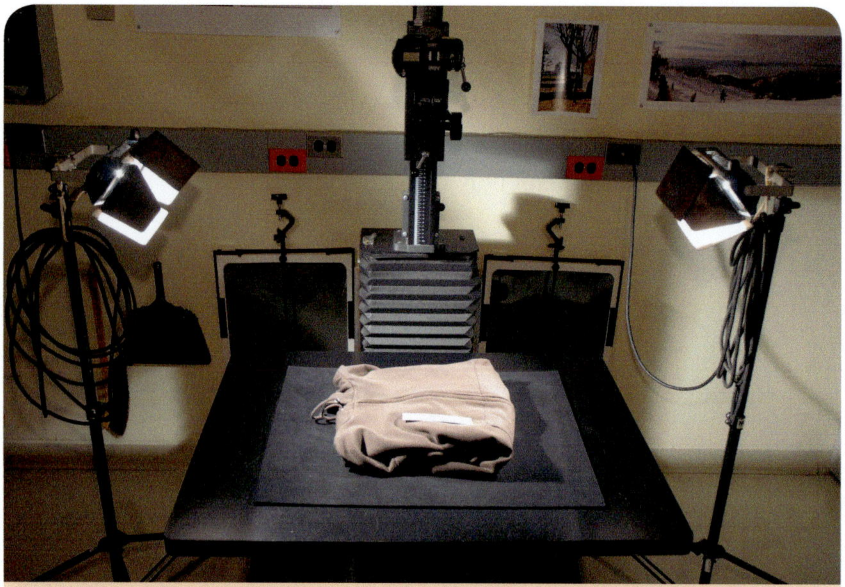

Figure 6.45 An example setup for the documentation of IR energy

Apply even direct lighting to the sample; do not bounce or diffuse the light since various materials may actually remove some portions of the invisible spectrum. The photograph should be composed without the IR filter in place; be sure to include the entire subject area and a scale and labels if necessary. An exposure may be made under visible light for the purposes of comparison.

Focusing for IR

Because of the difference in the wavelength of IR energy it will focus at a different location than visible light. Many lenses designed for use with IR have a special marking for focusing with IR called an IR focus mark, but many do not. If the lens you are using does have a mark, then change the focus from the visible light point to the IR mark.

For lenses without the IR focus mark it is recommended to use a small or narrow aperture (larger f-stop number) to increase the depth of field. Also you may determine the point on your lens through trial and error. Once you have determined the focus difference you can mark that point. Place the filter over the lens, adjust the exposure, and make a new exposure through the filter. Evaluate where the focus has shifted when using the filter and then adjust the lens focus to that location.

Set the camera to manual focus mode and place the IR filter in front of the lens; be sure not to change the focus while doing so. Now an exposure for IR can be made.

Determining Exposure

If the camera is specifically modified or designed for IR photography the exposure may be similar to that of the visible light photograph; however, that also depends upon the light

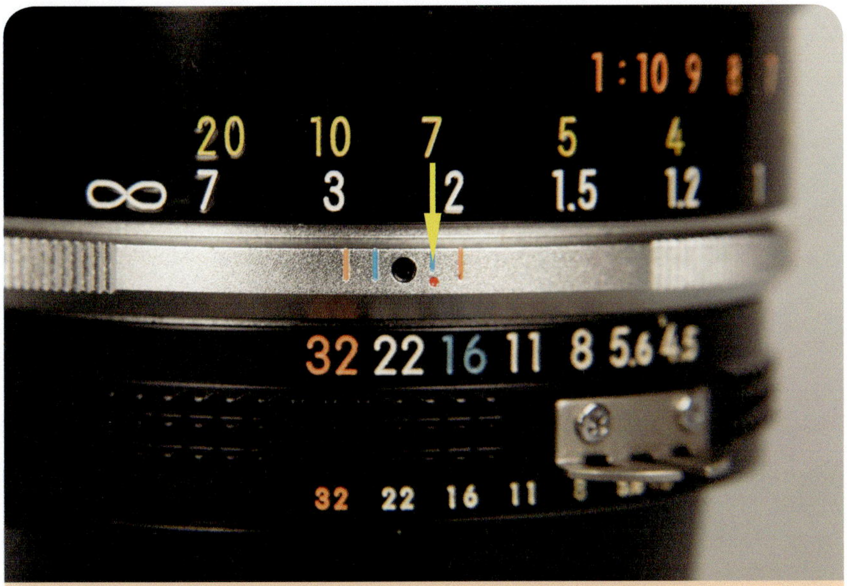

Figure 6.46 A photograph showing the IR focus mark (red dot) on a lens

source. The best way to determine exposure for the IR photograph is by trial and error. Set the camera to manual mode and begin at an exposure close to what was used for the visual light image. Preview the image and adjust your exposure accordingly. To lighten the image, increase the IR exposure by increasing the shutter speed; to darken the IR exposure, decrease the shutter speed. Reshoot and evaluate, and adjust the settings as necessary.

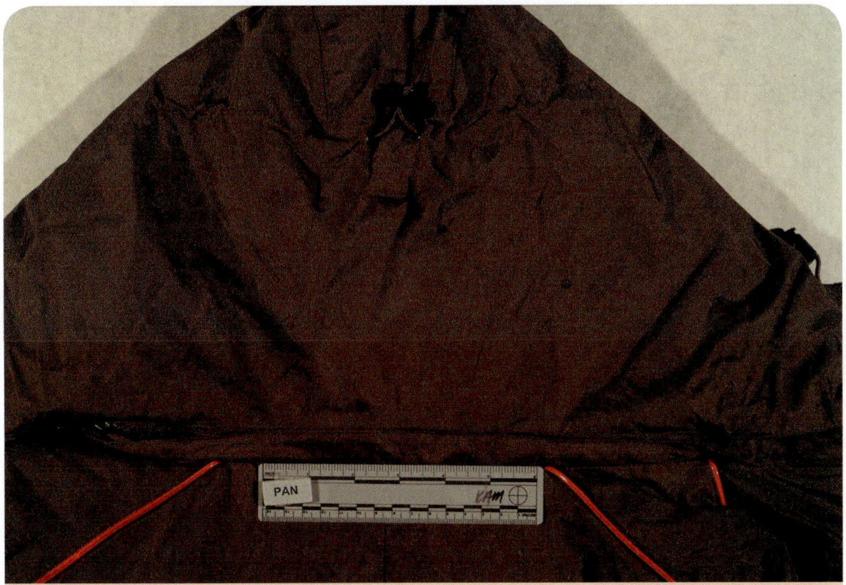

Figure 6.47 A visible light photograph of the hood of a jacket worn by the victim of a shooting

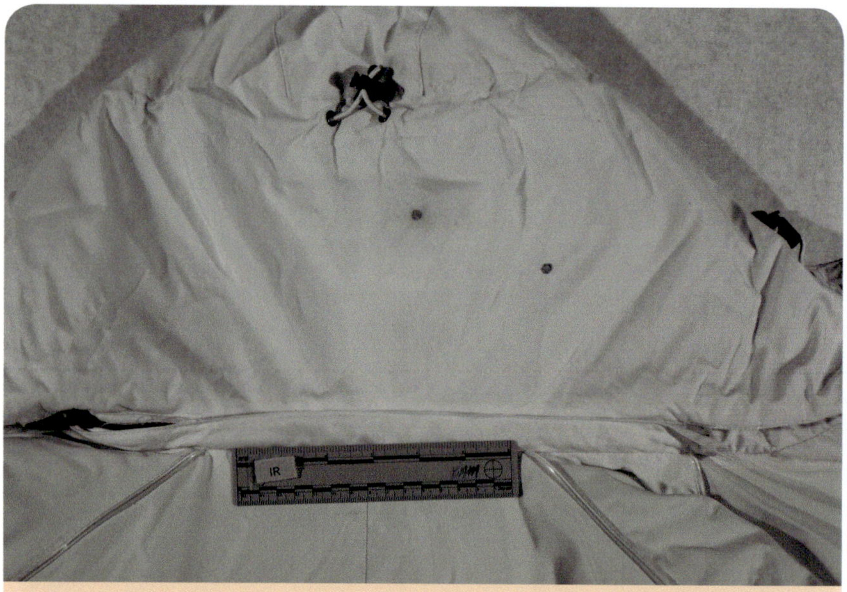

Figure 6.48 An infrared photograph of the hood of a jacket worn by the victim of a shooting showing the bullet wipe from two projectiles and a possible gunshot residue pattern around the upper left hole

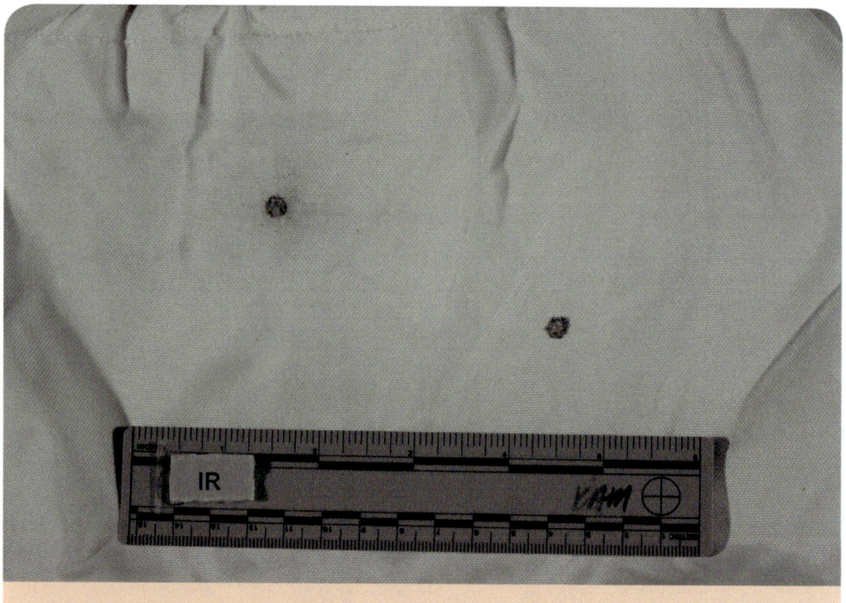

Figure 6.49 A close-up of the holes in the jacket from Figure 6.48

Infrared Fluorescence

Similar to fluorescence in the visible spectrum, IR fluorescence occurs when a subject absorbs a wavelength of light and as a result transmits energy in the IR spectrum. This

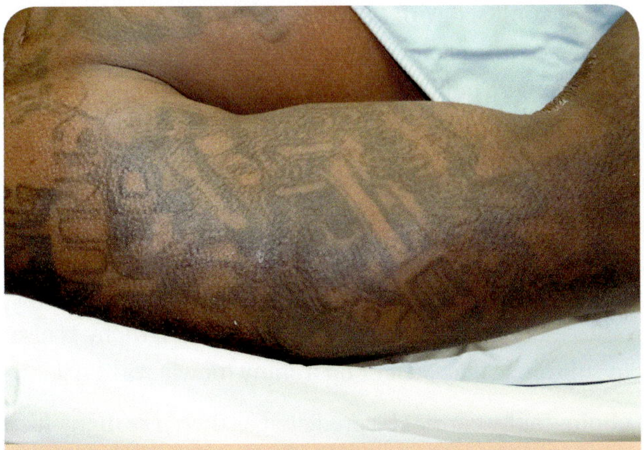

Figure 6.50 A visible light photograph of tattoos on the arm of a dark-skinned individual

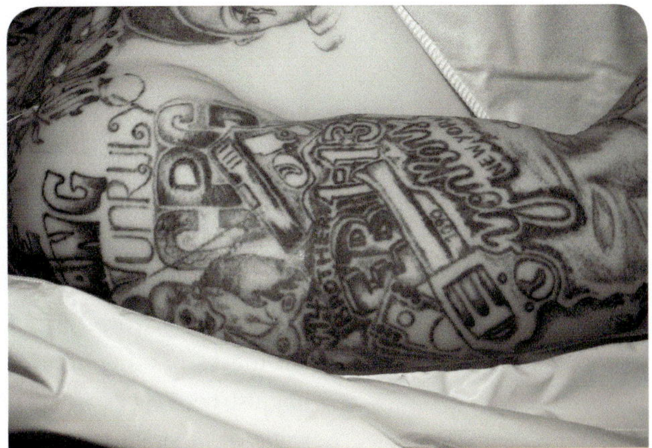

Figure 6.51 An infrared photograph of tattoos on the arm of a dark-skinned individual; the ink in the tattoos absorbs IR radiation while the skin reflects it, providing more contrast than the visible light photograph. This technique works well for tattoos on decomposed bodies

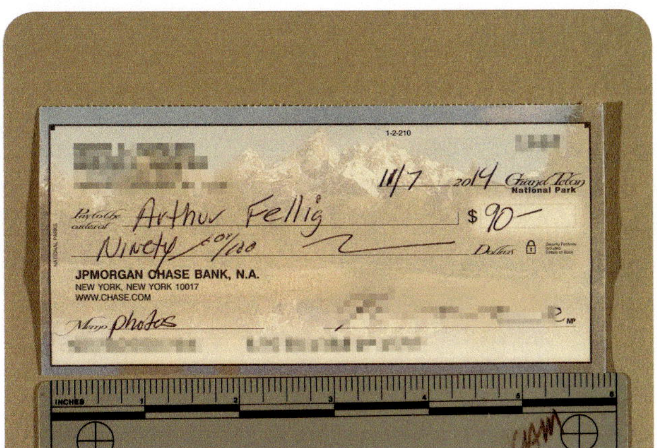

Figure 6.52 A visible light photograph of a possible forged check

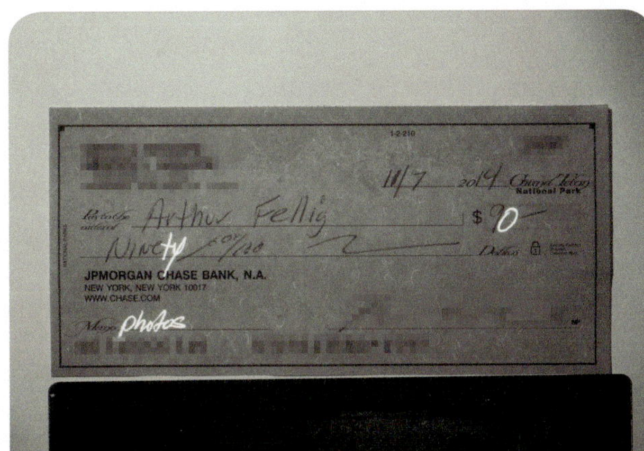

Figure 6.53 An infrared fluorescence photograph of the same check in Figure 6.28 showing where a different ink was used to change the amount of the check

usually occurs by using cyan light (approximately 450nm) as the excitation source and blocking all but IR energy from entering the lens.

This method is well suited for photographing of inks for document examination. Oftentimes inks of different manufacturers, although appearing visibly the same color, will react differently under IR fluorescence.

The setup is almost identical to the setup for IR photography; the only difference is the light source used. The excitation source should be approximately 450nm. Exposure times for this technique are often a few seconds or longer.

Reflected Ultraviolet (UV) Photography

Reflected ultraviolet photography is often confused with ultraviolet fluorescence photography, but the two are quite different. Reflected ultraviolet photography is the documentation of images using ultraviolet energy and a camera or film sensitive to ultraviolet energy, while blocking visible light and other energy such as infrared.

The use of reflected ultraviolet photography to document evidence may provide detail not visible to the naked eye. Ultraviolet photography has been successfully used to document bruises, bite marks, or other injuries to the skin, especially during the healing process. This technique has also been successful at documenting fingerprints, repainting, or overpainting on vehicles, walls, or other surfaces, even when the colors match visibly. Ultraviolet photography is also useful for low-contrast impressions in substances like dust or on a shiny (newly waxed) floor.

Typically, the results of ultraviolet photography cannot be predicted as there are many factors that can influence the results of the imaging process. Some of these factors, like the equipment necessary to make the images, may be controlled, but some, for example the subject, are not in the control of the photographer. The ultraviolet photography technique is usually a trial and error process and the results may vary.

Equipment

UV Cameras

Similar to IR photography, the best results for reflected ultraviolet photography require a camera that is specifically made or modified to be sensitive to UV radiation. Some cameras, however, may be slightly sensitive to ultraviolet radiation and it may be possible to get acceptable results using these cameras. Photographers have reported usable results with the following cameras: Nikon D70, D70s, D40, D50, D80, D300s, and possibly others.

Lenses

It may be possible to achieve results using a regular glass camera lens, but the best results will come from a lens specifically made to pass UV rays. UV lenses are made of quartz or silica; examples include the Nikon UV 105 and Jenoptik 60mm lens. Other lenses that have been used with varying degrees of success are simple lenses with fewer glass elements, as well as enlarger lenses and bellows. There are several resources online indicating what successes have been found with particular lenses:

- Coastal Optics 60 mm *f*/4 APO (to 300 nm);
- Nikon 105 mm *f*/4.5 UV-Nikkor (to 200 nm);
- Rodenstock 60 mm *f*/4 UV-Rodagon;
- Carl Zeiss 60 mm *f*/4 UV-Planar.

The following lenses were not designed for UV photography but have been known to transmit UV:

- Enlarger Lenses (Nikkor EL series);
- AF-S NIKKOR 50mm *f*/1.8G Special Edition.

Radiation Source

The optimal light source for UV photography is one with a spectrum that is high in UV energy.

Use caution when selecting a UV light source as UV energy can be harmful especially to the eye. It is recommended that the photographer and subject (if necessary) protect themselves from the UV rays. At the very least, safety glasses that block UV radiation are recommended.

Sunlight is high in UV energy; however, it may not be practical as a light source. For obvious reasons the sun's angle is not adjustable, and it differs throughout the day, while clouds and weather conditions can also affect the amount of UV radiation. These conditions make it difficult to repeat or standardize UV photography using the sun as a light source.

Electronic flash units may have some emission in UV but many are designed with filters in the head to block UV radiation. These filters are typically called warming filters, or 2A filters, and they tend to be yellowish in color. These filters may be removed, essentially converting the flash for use with UV photography. Even when converted an electronic flash may not emit enough power to light larger subjects with UV energy; therefore they may only be suitable for smaller subjects or macro photography. The Nikon SB 140UV was a flash specifically manufactured for UV photography, though it is no longer in production and may be difficult to find. The Vivitar® 285HV/285/283 are popular electronic flashes that can be easily converted for UV photography, and these flashes are more commonly available on eBay or other used equipment resellers. A web search will provide many sites with instructions for conversion.

Studio strobes have UV emission similar to electronic flashes but they tend to be higher in power and may provide enough energy for larger subjects. It will require testing to see if a particular unit will work for UV photography, and as with electronic flashes they can contain a filter that blocks UV energy. Broncolor® makes a UV flash attachment for their flash units, but the high price may be prohibitive for many public institutions. Some users have reported luck with Bowens® flash units and UV photography, or you may have success with the Calumet® travelite flash units manufactured by Bowens. A clear flash tube is also available for these flash units that does not contain a filter to remove UV energy.

There are several UV sources available commercially. Many forensic suppliers such as Serchie, Foster and Freeman, and Tritech sell light sources that are typically used in the search for evidence. These UV sources can also be used for UV photography but be aware that many have a very narrow band of emission, so choose a light source with emission below 500nm.

Caution: avoid using short wave UV energy (280nm and below) on evidence that may undergo DNA analysis.

Filters

Since most cameras used for UV photography are also sensitive to other wavelengths of light the energy entering the camera must be controlled. This is done with the use of barrier filters. For UV photography both a UV passing filter and IR blocking filter are typically needed since many of the UV passing filters also pass IR radiation. IR radiation leak is a common problem with UV photography so be cautious that the images you get are not affected by IR.

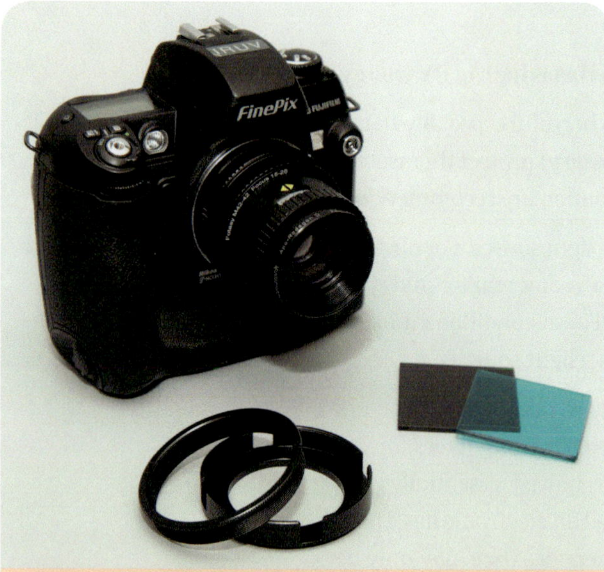

Figure 6.54 The Fuji FinePix IRUV camera which was specifically made to be sensitive to IR and UV radiation along with an UV transmitting and IR blocking filter

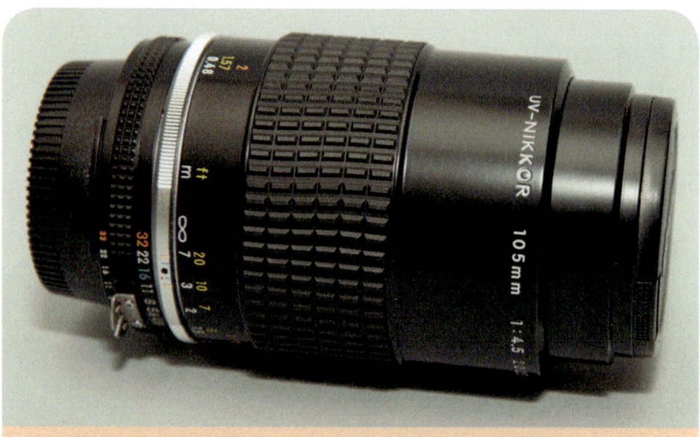

Figure 6.55 A Nikon UV-NIKKOR lens which was specifically designed to transmit UV radiation

The following is a list of some common UV passing filters:

- Kodak Wratten 18A;
- B+W 403;
- Hoya U-330,340, 360;
- PECA 900.

These filters pass some IR radiation so they should be used in conjunction with one of the following IR blocking filters:

- Schott BG-38, 39;
- B+W 489;
- Kodak Wratten 304 (infrared cut filter).

The Braader Venus filter does not require an IR blocking filter as it transmits very little IR energy,but the cost of this filter is relatively high when compared to other filters.

Film

Some photographers opt to use black and white film since it is sensitive to UV radiation but not Infrared.

Other Equipment

It is also necessary to have a tripod to hold the camera steady during what may be long exposures. It may also be beneficial to use a cable release to trigger the camera for the exposure.

Setup

Since there are many combinations of lenses, cameras, light sources, and filters that can be used for UV photography it may be necessary to test your setup. The exposure necessary to create an UV image will vary depending upon your setup and not all setups will work for every situation. For example, a moving subject such as a patient will not photograph well if they cannot remain still during the time of exposure. A relatively easy way to test your UV photography system is to photograph common flowers such as dandelions, sunflowers, or other inexpensive ones purchased from a local vendor. Under UV radiation the center of their petals will appear darker than the outside. It is believed this helps bees and butterflies locate flowers and their nectar.

Mount the camera on a tripod or some other sturdy device and compose the subject so that it fills the frame. Hand-holding the camera is difficult since the filters required will make it impossible to use the camera's viewfinder unless you are using a converted camera or other imaging device with a live preview. Be sure to include any scales or markers necessary. For a subject where motion may be an issue, such as a person, mount the camera and position the subject in such a way that they may rest comfortably while still being in the field of view.

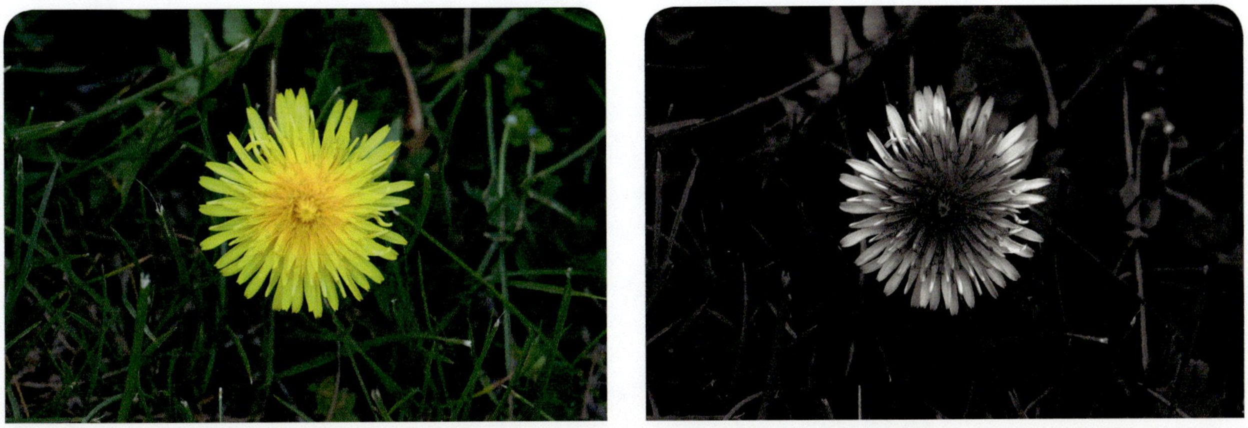

Figures 6.56–6.57 A visible light and UV image of a dandelion flower showing the darkening of the center of the flower in the UV energy spectrum

Exposure

Take an initial exposure of the subject using either the available light, or a visible light source. Apply even lighting to the subject. Do not diffuse or modify the light as bouncing or diffusing radiation may actually remove some portions of the invisible spectrum. It is most important for this reason to direct the light onto the subject directly from the source.

Place the UV filter along with the IR blocking filter if necessary in front of the camera lens. Set the camera to manual mode and adjust the exposure according to the light source. If using a flash set the shutter speed to 1/60th second and the flash to its highest power. For

Figure 6.58 A visible light photograph of fingerprints on a cabinet door

Photograph courtesy of Jordan Salkin

Figure 6.59 A UV photograph of fingerprints on a cabinet door

Photograph courtesy of Jordan Salkin

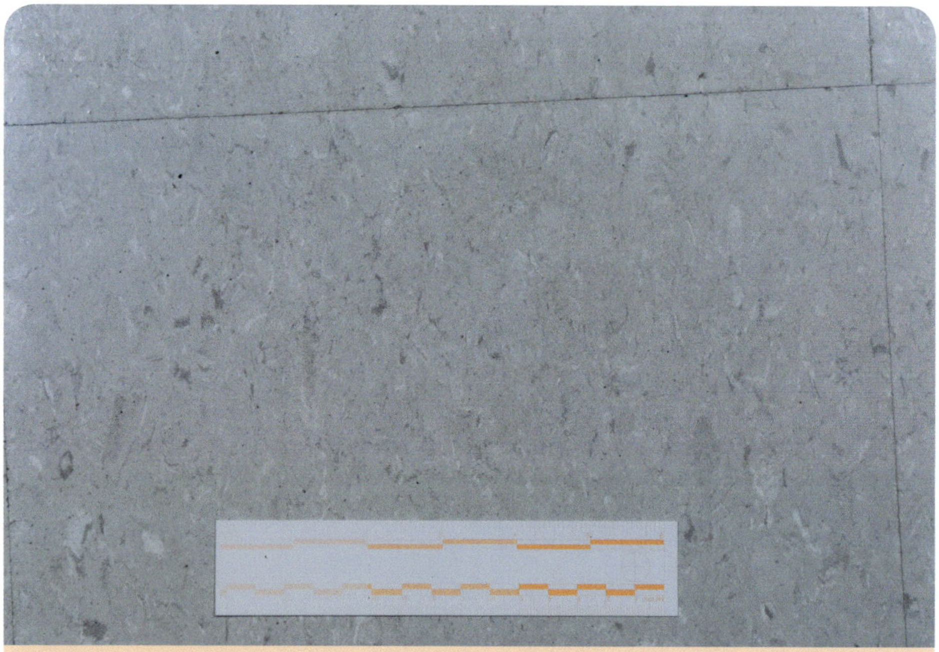

Figure 6.60 A visible light photograph of a greasy impression on a tile floor

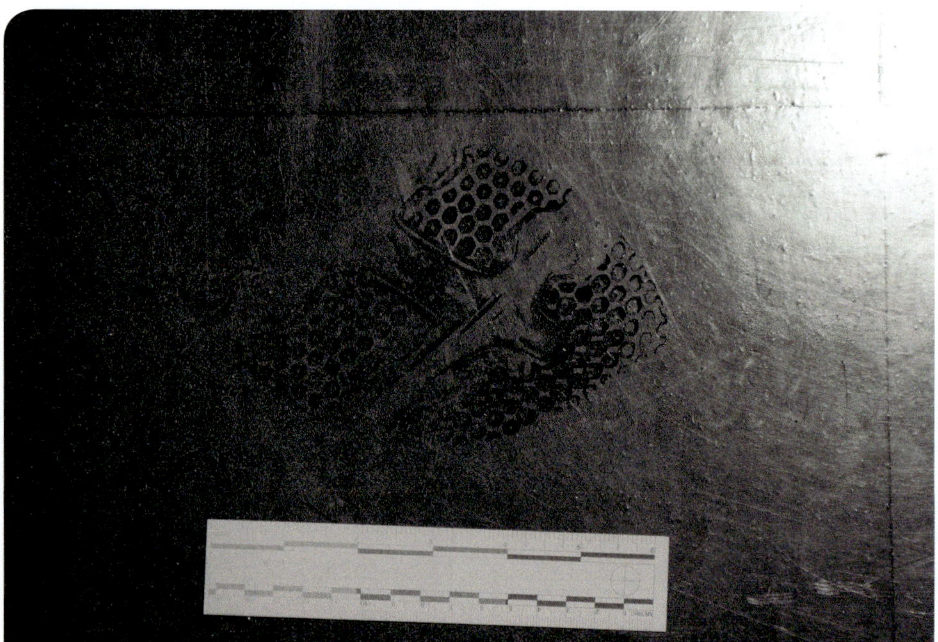

Figure 6.61 A UV light photograph of a greasy impression on a tile floor

a constant UV source, start with a relatively long exposure, approximately 30 seconds, and open the aperture to its widest setting. Exposure times will vary greatly depending upon your setup so be prepared to adjust the exposure settings. Take an initial exposure, evaluate the results and adjust accordingly.

The final images should be converted to grayscale since, like infrared, ultraviolet energy has no color value. It is a good idea to shoot using a raw file format since there may be some image processing necessary to achieve desirable results. Keep in mind the blue color channel may hold most of the UV data.

UV Resources

- Forensic Reflected Ultraviolet Imaging, *Journal of Forensic Identification* 46/63 (1), 2013
- Reflected Ultraviolet Imaging for Forensics Applications, Dr. Austin Richards, Adjunct Professor, Brooks Institute of Photography Partner, Oculus Photonics, Santa Barbara, CA Senior Research Scientist, FLIR Commercial Systems
- www.savazzi.net/photography/uv.htm
- http://photographyoftheinvisibleworld.blogspot.com/2011/01/simple-tutorial-for-reflected-uv.html

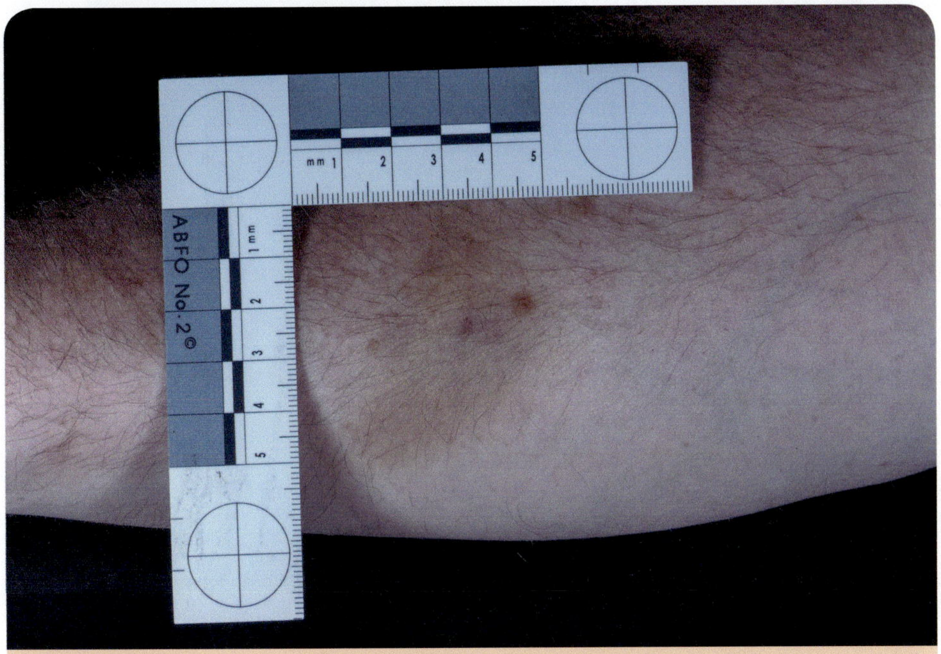

Figures 6.62–6.64 A comparison of imaging techniques used to document a bruise Figure 6.62 Visible light photograph, Figure 6.63 Infrared energy photograph, and Figure 6.64 Ultraviolet energy photograph

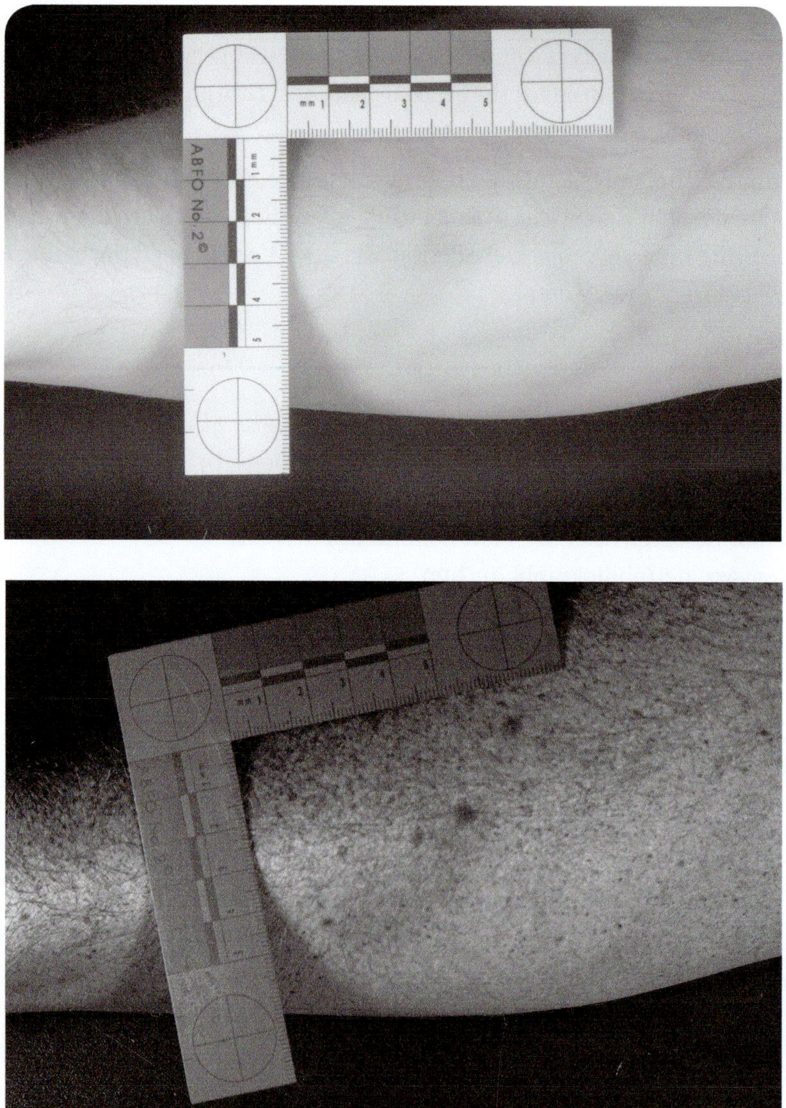

Figures 6.62–6.64 Continued

Chapter 7 Aerial Photography

It may be necessary to document details of a scene from above to provide a different point of view. Examples include documenting damage that results from natural disasters, documenting large scenes, or scenes spread out over a large area, showing paths of travel, accident scenes involving multiple vehicles, mass disasters, and plane crashes.

There are several options available to photograph a scene from above, and the techniques used will depend upon individual needs, budget, and equipment availability. In this chapter we will discuss several options for documenting a scene from the air covering a wide range of budgets and difficulties. The techniques range in cost from free (using satellite imagery and software such as Google Earth) to very costly (employing helicopters and high-end photographic equipment).

Photographing from an Aircraft

Perhaps the most common among aerial photography techniques in law enforcement is the use of aircraft. Many large departments have access to helicopters either in their own departments or nearby. Solutions will depend on specific needs and budget, or access to high-end photography equipment especially made for aerial photography. However, if you do not have access to specialty equipment, it is still possible to get quality images from an aircraft using typical crime scene photography equipment.

Equipment Recommendations

- Camera: a high-end SLR with manual control, or at the very least the ability to control shutter speed.
- Memory card: the larger the better since it is not recommended to change cards while the aircraft is in motion, especially if the doors or windows on the aircraft are open.
- Lenses: depending upon photographic needs, a VR (vibration reduction) zoom lens will allow you multiple focal lengths without having to change lenses. Be aware that the longer the lens the more potential for amplification of motion blurring. Lens filters

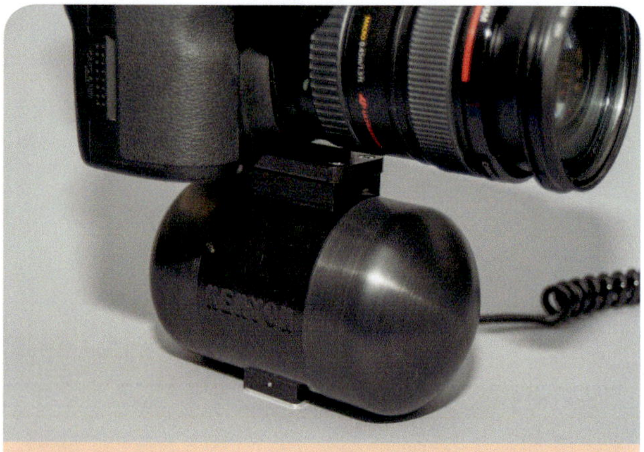

Figure 7.1 A gyroscope attached to the bottom of a camera

are useful for protection of the front element of the lens, while a polarizing filter may help reduce glare, as well as darken blue sky. It is not advisable to use a lens hood as it will cause added wind resistance if the lens is outside the aircraft; in addition it's at risk of falling off and causing damage to objects or injury to people below.

- Straps, tethers, and harnesses: be sure to secure yourself and all your equipment to the aircraft before flying. Keep necessary equipment nearby, or have an assistant available to pass you equipment during flight. You should be tethered to the aircraft either by seatbelt or harness if you are going to hang outside of the aircraft.
- Gyroscope or gimbal: a device especially made to steady a camera, may be cost prohibitive to buy but possible to rent.
- Microfiber cleaning cloth: to clean windows of the aircraft. The cloth will not scratch the fiberglass windows.
- Blackout material: to reduce reflection and glare as a result of shooting through windows.

Choosing the best aircraft for the imaging requirements

There are two main choices when it comes to identifying the aircraft and each has its benefits. The availability of certain types of aircraft may influence the ultimate choice.

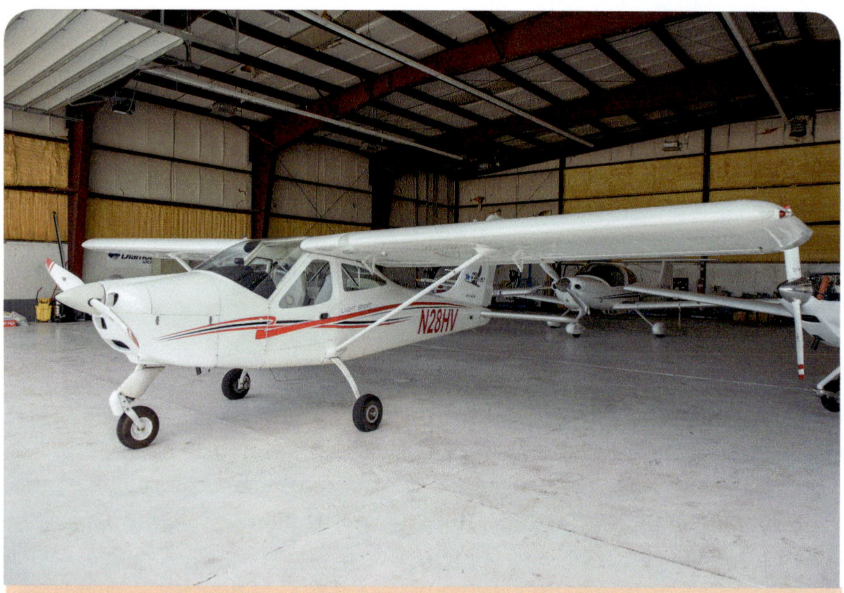

Figure 7.2 An example of an airplane with high wings
Photographer Teri Zgoda

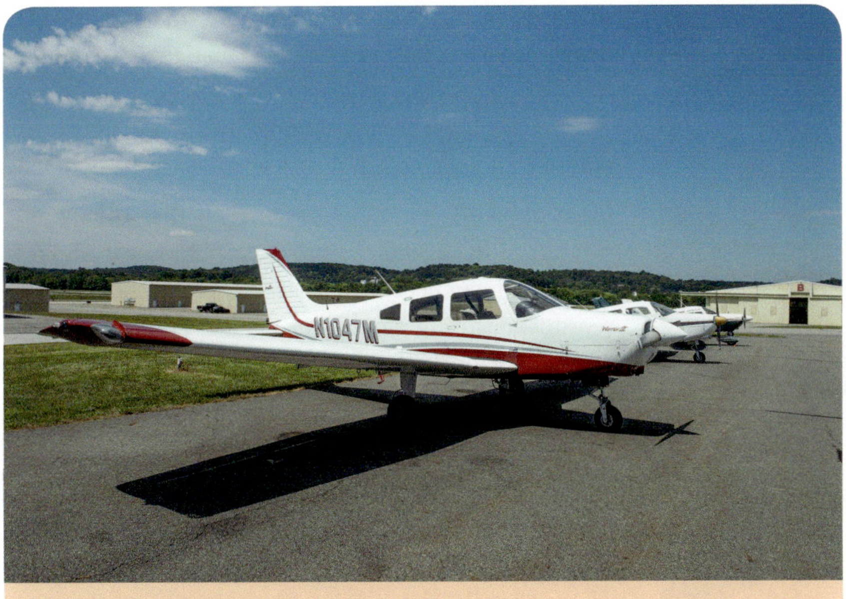

Figure 7.3 An example of an airplane with low wings
Photographer Teri Zgoda

Airplanes

Airplanes must fly above 500 feet, and 1000 feet in more populated areas, and so they are typically preferred when photographing larger areas. To remain airborn, planes must maintain a minimum airspeed and often there is little time for composing images so photography will most likely take place through the plane's window. Caution must be taken while sticking a lens out of the window, as the plane's speed and wind resistance may make it difficult or even dangerous to operate. Given the option, it is recommended to choose an airplane with high wings to avoid getting the wing in the photographs.

Helicopters

Helicopters fly at approximately 500 feet or below, and depending upon the surroundings may fly even lower. It is recommended to check with the pilot prior to takeoff. Unlike airplanes helicopters have the ability to fly slowly or hover in the same place. Depending on the flying conditions and safety, it is recommended to keep the helicopter in motion. Additionally helicopters do not have wings to get in the way of the view, and the doors may be removed prior to or opened during flight.

Aviation Safety

Safety in an aircraft is of the upmost importance. If unfamiliar with the safety procedures in and around the aircraft that you will be using, be sure to discuss them with the pilot prior to takeoff. If the pilot is landing in order to pick you up, be sure to wait for their signal before approaching the aircraft. Never walk behind a helicopter, or near the props on an airplane.

When preparing for flight keep in mind that less weight means more power, so be sure to pack only the essential items needed for the photography session. It is a good idea to

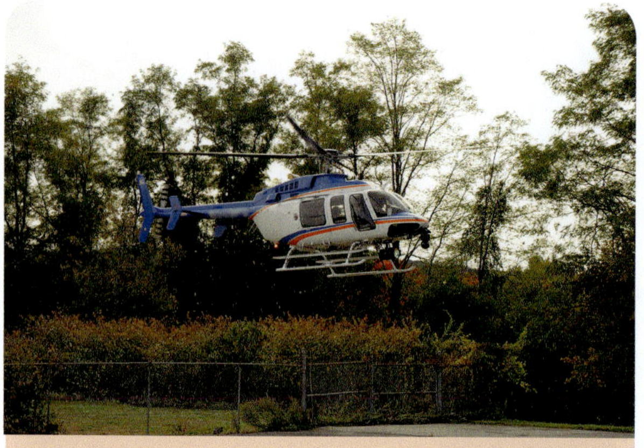

Figure 7.4 A Bell 407s, a common helicopter used in law enforcement

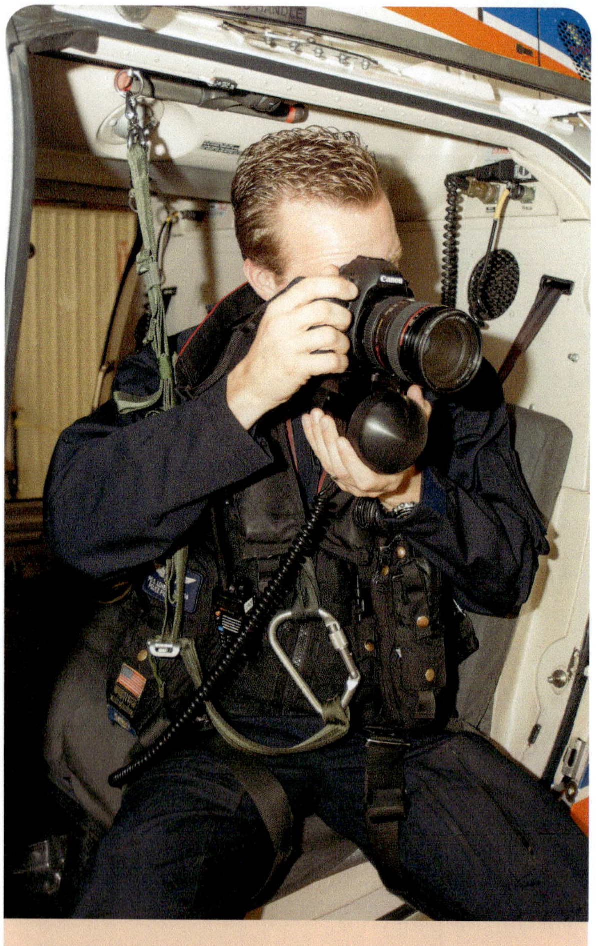

Figure 7.5 Officer Sean C. Lonergan demonstrates a method for photographing through the open door of a helicopter. The officer is tethered to the aircraft for safety

prepare a required list of photographs that are needed prior to going airborne, and even better to map them out anticipating the flight plan. This will help a pilot who is unfamiliar with the scene you are photographing. Before boarding the aircraft empty your pockets and secure any loose articles of clothing.

Once onboard you should secure all the equipment to the interior of the aircraft before departure. Loose and unsecure equipment can become a safety hazard in the air for obvious reasons. Securing equipment options can include using the aircraft's seatbelts, bungee cords, or tie downs on the equipment bag. At the very least you should have a camera strap on the camera and located over you head. Alternatively, you could use a specially designed camera rig mounted to the aircraft.

Time of Day for Flight

Depending upon the circumstances you may not be able to choose the day or time of the flight. However, given the choice, plan the flight during good weather. A cloudy or overcast day may be preferable since there will be no glare or very high contrast from the sun to interfere with image quality. When choosing a time, late morning or early evening will provide the best contrast due to the angle of the sun.

Avoiding Glare

If you must shoot through the windows, be sure to clean them prior to flight, but it's best to ask the pilot for permission first. Use a non-abrasive microfiber cloth. Avoid wearing bright clothes because your reflection may show up in the window. Some methods to reduce the appearance of reflections in the window include reducing the light in the background (interior of the aircraft), blocking the light behind you with a blackout cloth if possible, using a camera mask (as described in Chapter 6), or the use of a lens hood that attaches to the window like the LENSKIRT® Flexible Lens Hood.

Reducing Vibration

Regardless of the aircraft, vibration will be an issue and may introduce motion blur into your images. There are a few ways to reduce the effects of vibration in photographs. The easiest way to reduce vibration is by using a fast shutter speed, approximately 1/1000 second or faster if using a telephoto lens. If the lens has a VR feature be sure to turn it on; however, remain aware that it consumes power when in use and will drain batteries more quickly. The use of a gyroscope or camera gimbal attached to the camera will aid in steadying the camera and significantly reduce the effects of vibration.

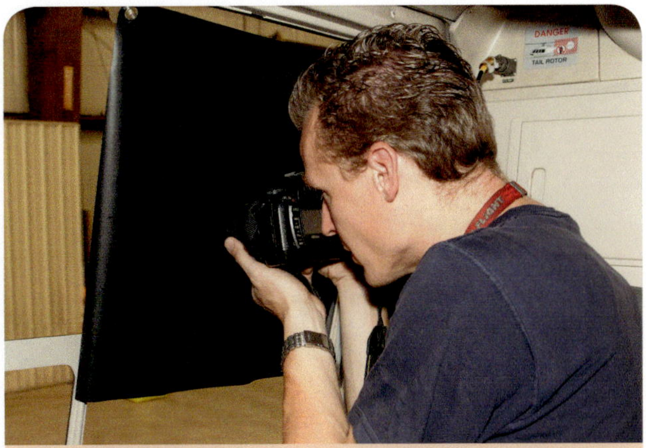

Figure 7.6 Officer Sean C. Lonergan demonstrates a technique for reducing reflection while photographing through a window. A hole is cut in the center of an opaque material, called Savage® Velvetine. The Velvetine is hung on the window, and the lens is placed through the hole

Exposure

The easiest way to ensure a fast shutter speed is selected for use is to operate the camera in shutter priority mode and then set the shutter speed to a 1/1000 second or faster when shooting with a 200mm or longer focal length lens. Do not be overly concerned with the aperture; depth of field is not an issue since the ground is relatively flat from the air.

Focus

It is recommended to use single servo autofocus because even though you will be in constant motion, the relative distance to the ground will not change significantly. For shooting from high altitudes or when using a wide-angle lens, you may use manual focus and set the lens to infinite.

Composing

Be sure your pilot is aware of the subject of interest before flight starts, and ask to be informed when you are getting close. Stay in communication with the pilot during the flight, and certainly while you are shooting. It may be necessary to circle the subject several times in order to get enough pictures and the necessary angles. If you are in an airplane, it may be necessary to bank the turns to keep the wings out of the frame; be sure to discuss this with the pilot. Helicopters are able to hover above a subject; however, depending upon the circumstances, the pilot may prefer to circle the subject as well. If it is necessary to document large areas consider using a grid pattern of the ground, ensuring there is plenty of overlap in the photographs.

Unmanned Aircraft Systems (Drones)

Unmanned aircraft systems (UASs), more commonly known as drones, are a type of radio-controlled model aircraft controlled by an operator on the ground. Thanks to advances in technology and the shrinking of electronic components, they have become extremely popular for recreation as well as commercial purposes.

Drones are small commercially available radio-controlled aircraft typically operated by a person using a transmitter usually within the line of sight of the aircraft. Drones range from very inexpensive "toys" to much costlier and more advanced systems. Drones may fly with the help of GPS (Global Positioning System), or FPV (first-person view) cameras. They

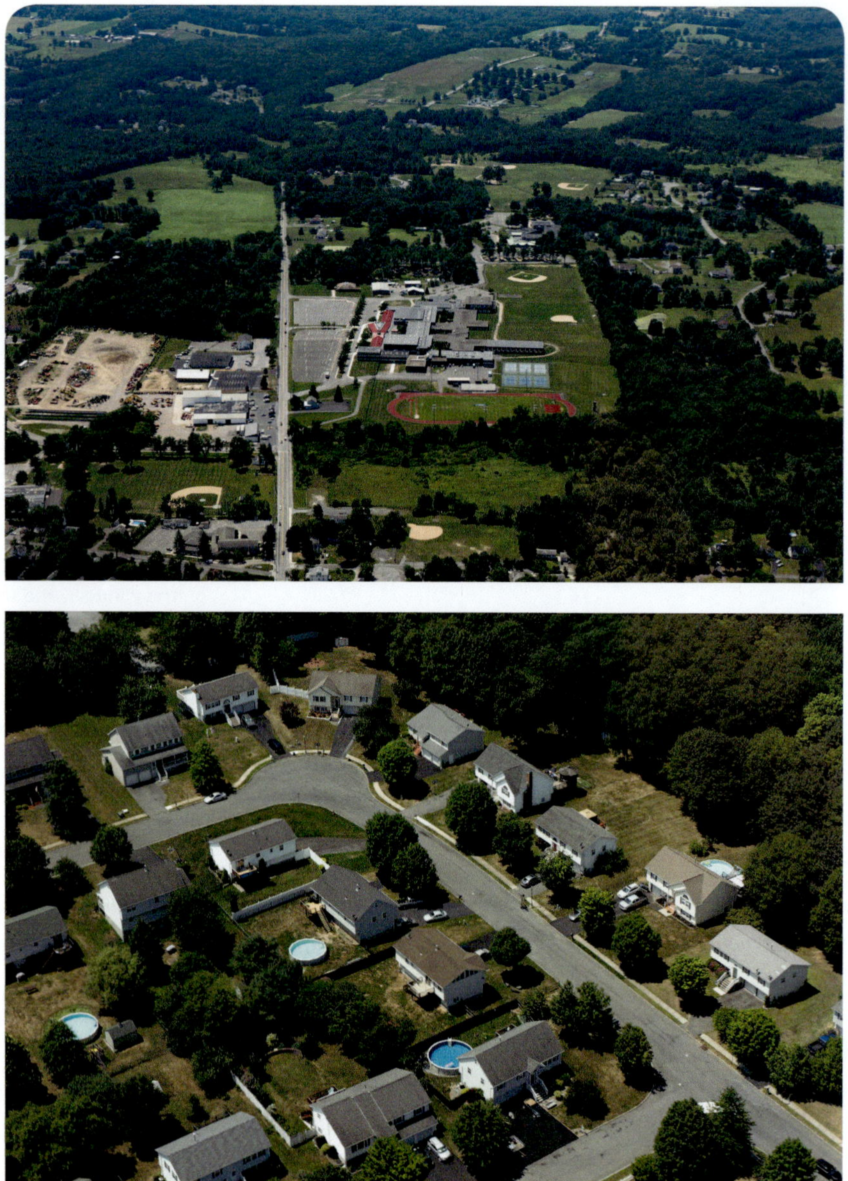

Figures 7.7–7.8 Examples of photographs taken from an airplane
Photographer Teri Zgoda

can be controlled in real time or be pre-programmed to fly a specific route. Not all drones have the same features, and there are many options in the growing market.

Multi-Rotors

The drones most commonly associated with aerial photography are called multi-rotor helicopters or just multi-rotors. The multi-rotors have several propellers mounted horizontally to give the aircraft lift. Moving the drones position forward, backward, and turning is achieved by varying the rotation of one or more of the rotors. Multi-rotors are considered

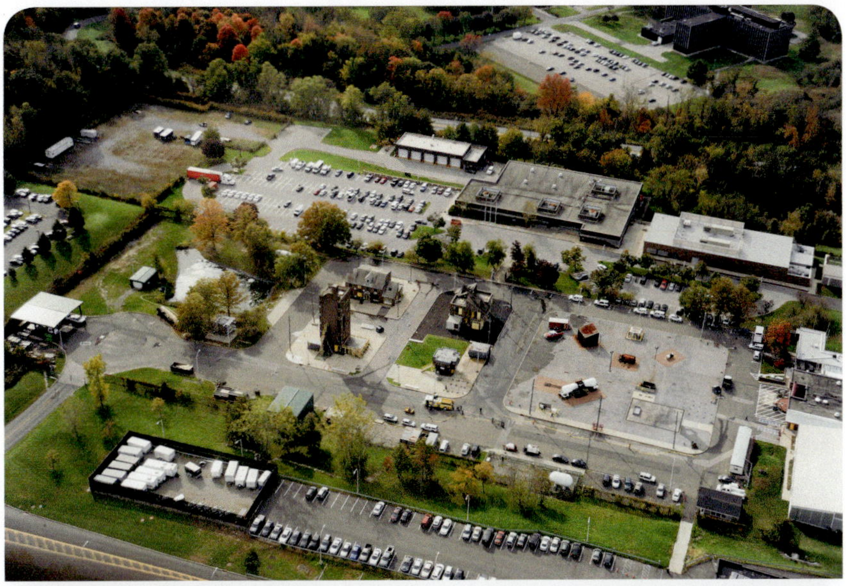
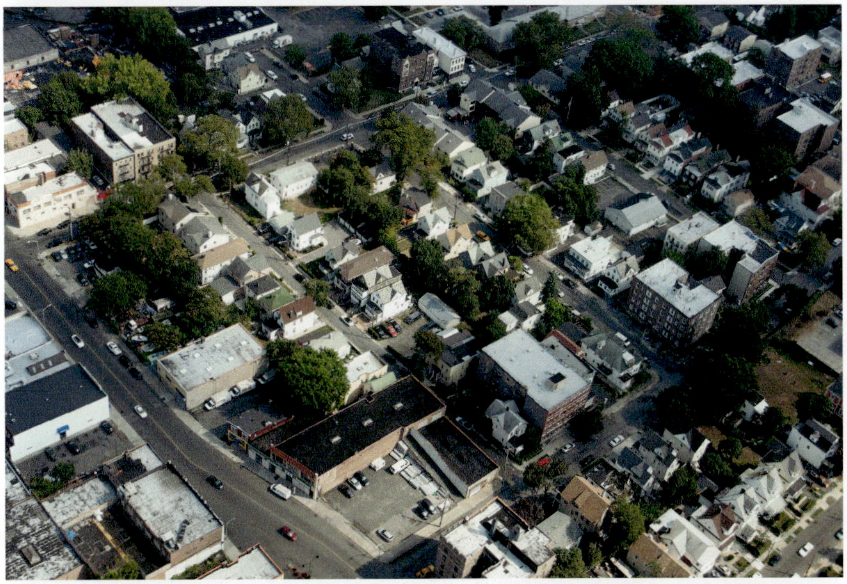
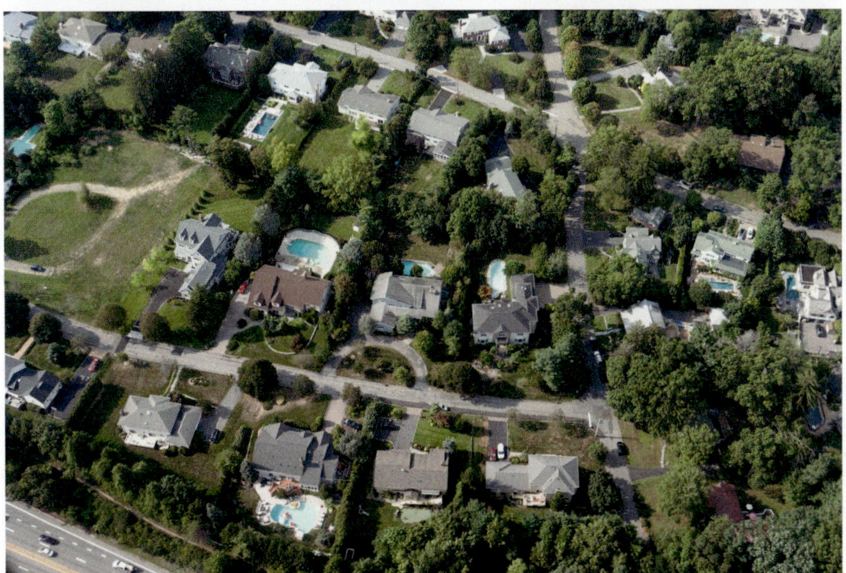

Figures 7.9–7.11 Examples of photographs taken from a helicopter

to be the most stable platform for aerial imaging since they can hover like a helicopter, and multiple rotors add to the aircraft's stability. The most common configuration of a multi-rotor is a quad copter, named for its four rotors, although it is not uncommon to encounter hexicopters (six), octocopters (eight), and other configurations of rotors as well. Rotors are usually found in even numbers as their rotation is alternated between clockwise and counter clockwise to provide for a more stable flight.

Considering the alternatives for aerial photography, multi-rotors are relatively inexpensive. One of the most popular quad copters for aerial photography is currently available in several configurations ranging from approximately $700 to $1200, and comes completely ready for use including a high-quality camera. Considering the cost of jet fuel, or chartering an aircraft, this may be considered quite the bargain.

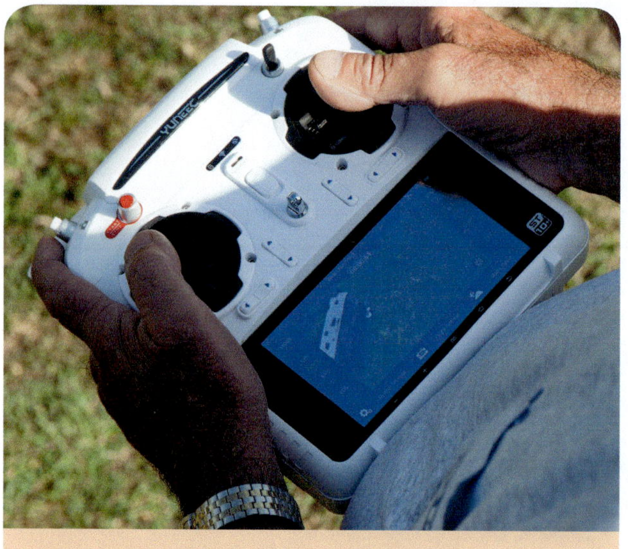

Figure 7.12 Example of a quadcopter transmitter. The LCD screen allows this model to receive video from the quad, called FPV (first person view)

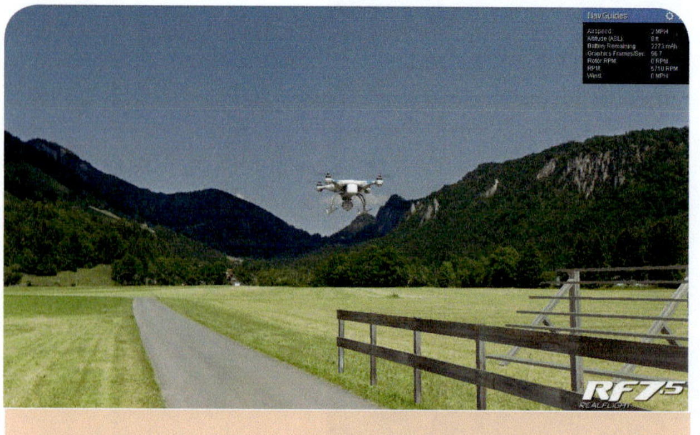

Figure 7.13 A screen shot from a flight simulator

Flying a Multi-Rotor

Flying a multi-rotor is relatively easy. There are essentially four controls for flight: throttle, yaw, pitch, and roll. The throttle controls the rate of accent of the aircraft; the more throttle you give the aircraft the faster it will climb, while less throttle will cause the aircraft to descend. The yaw controls the rotation of the aircraft clockwise or counter-clockwise and changes the direction the front of the aircraft faces. The pitch of the aircraft is the direction of travel, forward or backward, of the aircraft relative to its front. Roll is the direction of travel, left or right, of the aircraft relative to its front.

Typical controllers or transmitters have two sticks that control the aircraft's movement. Throttle and yaw are typically controlled by one stick, and pitch and roll by the other. Some multi-rotors have a feature called smart mode where the pitch and roll controls are relative to the pilot. For example, forward will always be in the direction away from the pilot regardless of what direction the aircraft is facing. In addition, some multi-rotors may be controlled via Wi-Fi using a smartphone or tablet application. These controllers typically have a shorter range than traditional radio transmitters, though that may vary by model.

There are a few ways to learn to fly a multi-rotor, and training is recommended. Even though many models fly assisted by GPS, which makes it quite easy to pilot a multi-rotor, it's always good to know how to fly unassisted in case something goes wrong. There are several inexpensive multi-rotor models available, some under $20, which fly using the same controls as larger, more expensive models. It is recommended that you practice using one of those before purchasing or flying a more expensive model. It is far better to crash a $20 toy than a $1000 investment, and many of those toys can take a crash better than their larger counterparts.

Another alternative for training is to purchase flight simulator software. Commercially available software like Real Flight™ are available for approximately $100. The software includes a controller and several model aircraft.

Drone Basics

There are basically three categories of drones: beginner, intermediate, and advanced. Beginner drones are typically compact in size; many have cameras, but they may not be suitable for aerial imaging. Beginner models typically lack more advanced features such as GPS and advanced flight modes, and they may only be suitable for indoor flight. While they may not be great for aerial photography, beginner drones can be a lot of fun and are a great way to learn to fly.

Intermediate or "prosumer" (somewhere between consumer and professional) models are larger and more robust than beginner's drones and typically are able to fly longer and carry larger payloads. Intermediate aircraft are primarily focused on aerial imaging, many of which include a built-in camera and stabilizer called a gimbal, and are designed to carry a small action camera like a GoPro®. Intermediate UAVs have more advanced feature sets, including GPS, and features like Automatic Return to Home which automatically brings the aircraft back to its takeoff spot. The very popular DJI Phantom® is considered part of this category; however, there are several other similar models available.

The advanced category of UAVs, while having similar flying features to the intermediate category, are designed to carry even heavier payloads such as a DSLR, mirrorless, and even compact digital cinema cameras. As a result, advanced aircraft tend to have even larger frames and more motors.

Drone Features

The following are some features common to drones; many are designed to make them easier to fly and as a result may improve the quality or success of aerial photographs.

RTF (Ready to Fly)

These models come mostly pre-assembled and require little to no setup in order to get flying. RTF drones include a transmitter

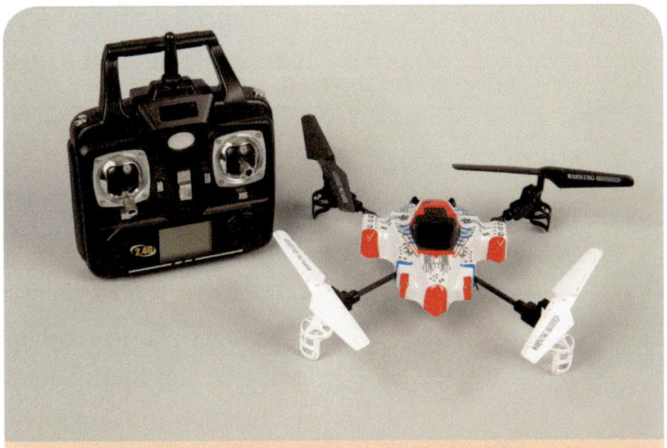

Figure 7.14 An inexpensive "toy" quadcopter can provide a great way to learn how to fly without a huge investment. Models are available for below $50

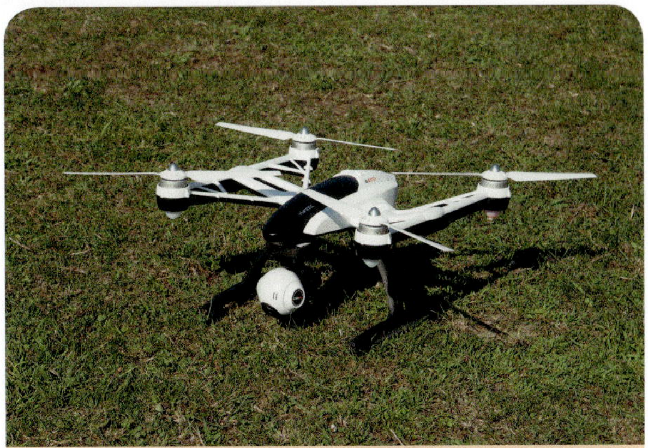

Figure 7.15 The Yuneec Q500 quadcopter is considered an intermediate or prosumer quadcopter

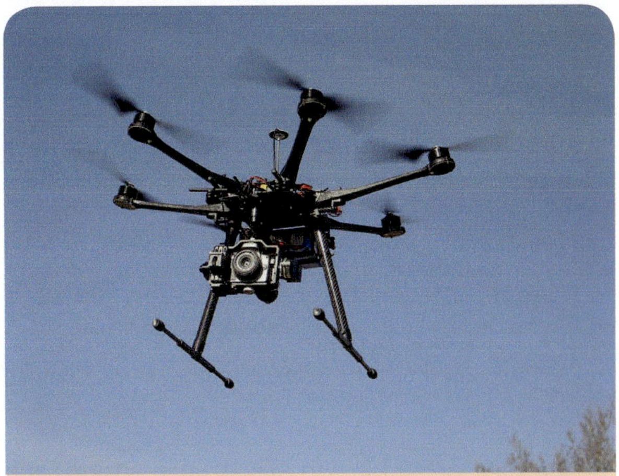

Figure 7.16 An example of an advanced drone

or controller and a battery, and many include a charger as well. An RTF drone is a great choice if you want to get flying as soon as possible.

BNF (Bind and Fly)

These models come mostly pre-assembled as well; however, you must provide a transmitter and "bind" it to the aircraft. BNF drones may include a battery and charger depending upon the model. This is a great choice if you already have a transmitter.

There are also several options for assembling you own aircraft; frames, motors, speed controllers, and flight systems are all available aftermarket. Building your own aircraft may be best left to people with some previous flight experience and a thorough knowledge of drones. There are several resources online and at hobby shops/shows if you are interested in building your own aircraft.

GPS (Global Positioning System)

GPS greatly improves the ease of flying a drone, by communicating with several satellites and aiding in the positioning of the aircraft. The GPS in a drone also allows for several other flight modes such as the return to home function.

Stick Relativity

The aircraft will always fly in the direction, relative to the pilot, that the control stick is pushed regardless of which way it is facing.

Altitude Hold

The aircraft will maintain its altitude, while the pilot has control of roll, pitch, and yaw.

Waypoint Flying

Using software or an app, the pilot sets up waypoints on a map prior to flight, and the aircraft fly's a predetermined route. This feature may be combined with camera control, to ensure the camera is always pointing in the desired direction.

Flight Boundaries or Geofence

Enables the pilot to set up a boundary that the aircraft will not leave. This is a nice feature for learning to fly, or if you want to keep the aircraft in a specific area.

Follow Me

The aircraft follows the pilot, typically using the transmitter or a smartphone application.

Drone Camera Options

There are a several camera options to consider for aerial photography using a drone. The greatest limiting factor will be the payload capability of the drone. Several intermediate drones come standard with a high definition of even greater resolution camera, so if it is your goal to get flying quickly without too much fuss, this may be the best option. However, if you have any other needs, or already have a drone, one of the following options may work for you.

An action camera, such as the GoPro®, is a small durable video and photography camera typically used by athletes and enthusiasts to record their sporting adventures. An action camera is well suited for mounting on a drone since they are typically lightweight. Don't be fooled by their size: the photo and video quality of sports cameras are very impressive. Many models now feature 4k video and 12MP photos. Several action cameras may be controlled via a remote control, or even a smartphone application, which allows the pilot to start and stop the video camera or take photographs remotely.

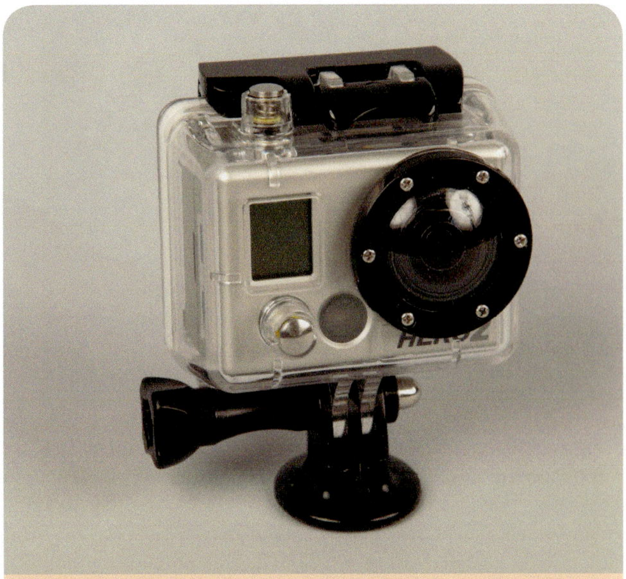

Figure 7.17 The GoPro© action camera is a popular choice for mounting to a drone

Another option that is very popular for smaller UAVs is the Mobius action camera. The Mobius camera is extremely small and light, measuring approximately 2 × 1 × 1 inches and weighing only 1.2 ounces. The camera features up to 1080p (HD) video and 3MP images and comes in a wide angle and narrower field of view version. The camera is controlled via three buttons on the body, and may be configured via PC software or by changing the camera's configuration file using a text editor. The Mobius costs around $80 depending upon the options/accessories one chooses.

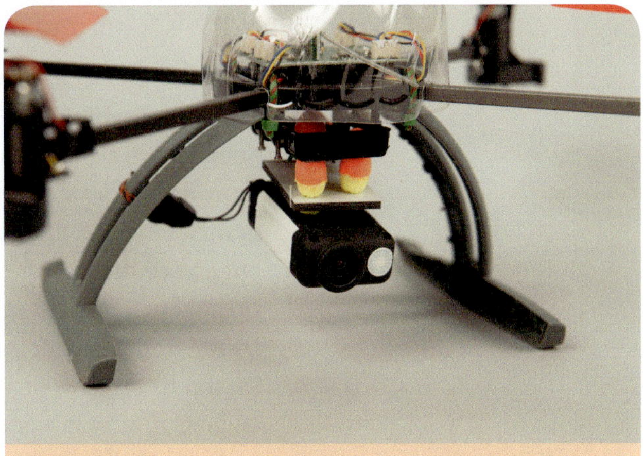

Figure 7.18 The Mobius camera mounted to an inexpensive quadcopter

For increased photo quality over action cameras or built-in cameras, larger drones will permit the mounting of point-and-shoot, mirrorless digital cameras, even larger DSLR's, or digital video cameras.

Regardless of the camera you choose, you will need a way to mount the camera to the drone. The camera mount should provide stability, vibration reduction, and even permit the positioning of the camera while in flight. The simplest way to mount a camera to a drone is with the use of an anti-vibration mount. An anti-vibration mount will separate the camera from the body of the aircraft by using rubber anti-dampening material. The vibration of the UAV may cause something called the "jello" effect on the video of some cameras. The "jello" effect is a result of the way in which some camera shutters record video. Examples of the "jello" effect may be found online.

You may also want to add a gimbal. A gimbal is a device that steadies the camera and reduces the effects of the tilt or swing of the aircraft. The camera gimbal may be combined with an anti-vibration mount. Camera gimbals are available in two types: passive, which

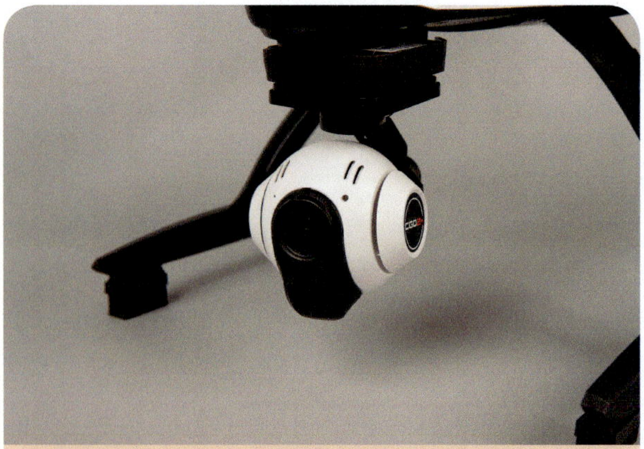

Figure 7.19 A close-up of the built-in camera on the Yuneec Q500; newer versions feature up to 4K resolution video

just attempt to keep the camera level; or active, using motors to achieve a higher level of steadiness. Gimbals can stabilize in two or three directions, called 2 or 3 axis. Another feature of some gimbals is the ability to control the camera direction remotely via a transmitter or application.

Some cameras or drones with built-in cameras support a feature called FPV (first-person view). The camera transmits video back to a receiver, allowing the pilot to see exactly what the camera sees. The receiver can be a screen built into the transmitter, an accessory screen, or a smartphone application. The video can be transmitted over Wi-Fi or analog signal and each has its own advantages and drawbacks. Be sure to check the distance of the transmission so you do not fly out of range.

Flight Safety and Federal Guidelines

Because UAVs have become so popular in such a short period of time, there have been many stories of aircraft going astray and plenty of safety concerns. Because of this, the Federal Aviation Administration (FAA) needed to speed up their adoption of guidelines pertaining to the use of UAVs. The following are some of their recommendations for recreational use of UAVs:

- Fly below 400 feet and remain clear of surrounding obstacles.
- Keep the aircraft within visual line of sight at all times.
- Remain well clear of and do not interfere with manned aircraft operations.
- Be aware of and follow the FAA regulations regarding the use of UAVs near airports or in their airspace, including not operating a drone within five miles of an airport without first contacting the control tower for permission.
- Do not fly near people or stadiums
- Do not fly an aircraft that weighs more than 55lbs.
- Do not be careless or reckless with your unmanned aircraft—you could be fined for endangering people or other aircraft.

For commercial, government, and additional information about recreational use of UAVs, visit the website http://knowbeforeyoufly.org/.

Photographing from a Drone

Once you are comfortable flying a drone it is time to think about how to capture images. Controlling a camera while in mid-air and attached to a remote control aircraft can be a challenge. Of course, if your drone has a built-in camera that can be remotely controlled via an application, the simplest way to capture images will be to line up your shot, steady the aircraft, and press the capture button on the application. However, if the drone does not have a built-in camera, you will have to find another way to capture images. Many modern digital cameras have a feature to remotely connect to the camera and control the camera; this includes several models of action cameras, point and shoots, mirrorless cameras, and even DSLRs. If

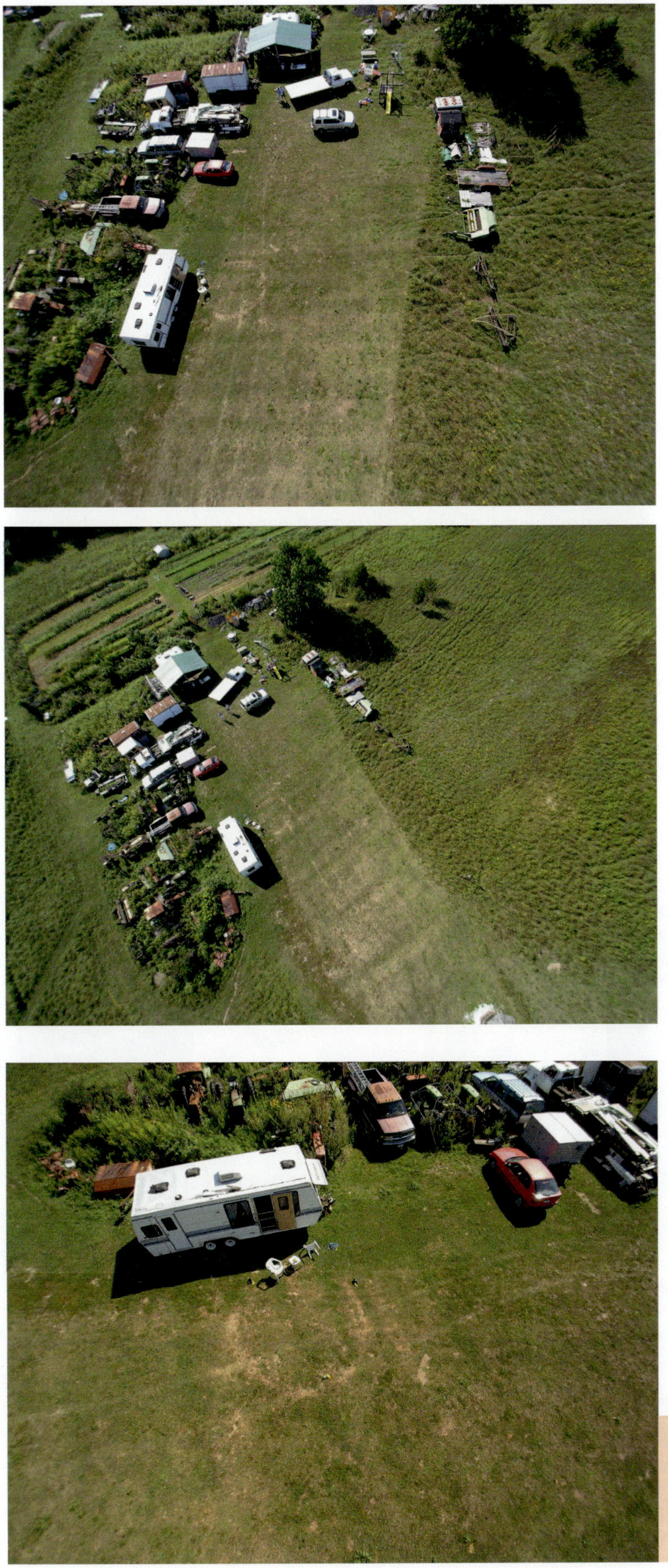

Figures 7.20–7.22 Examples of photographs taken from a UAV

Photographer Joseph P. Mancini

your camera does not have this feature, there are aftermarket accessories available that can add this function to a camera. Be aware that the signal used for this communication may share the same frequency as a UAV's transmitter and receiver. This may result in interference between the transmitter and receiver, and may cause erratic flying or a crash. Be sure to check the frequency of your UAV's transmitter and the frequency of the Wi-Fi camera before flight.

Exporting Video Frames

If you cannot use the remote function of your camera, or if the camera does not have that feature, there are still ways to capture images while in flight. If you are not concerned with the resolution of these still images, it will be possible to record video for the entire flight and export individual frames of that video to still images. There are several methods to do this and they typically require the use of video-editing software. Adobe® Photoshop, typically thought of as an image-editing software, supports the import of several formats of video. Therefore it is possible to open a video in Photoshop and save individual frames as images. If you do not have access to Photoshop, Apple® QuickTime Player Pro, a $29 upgrade from the free player, has the ability to export individual frames of video to still image formats. There are also several free programs to accomplish this as well. GOM Player is a popular free video player that supports the export of still images.

Figure 7.23 demonstrates how to save a single frame of video using Adobe Photoshop.

Figures 7.24–7.27 demonstrate how to save multiple consecutive frames using Adobe Photoshop.

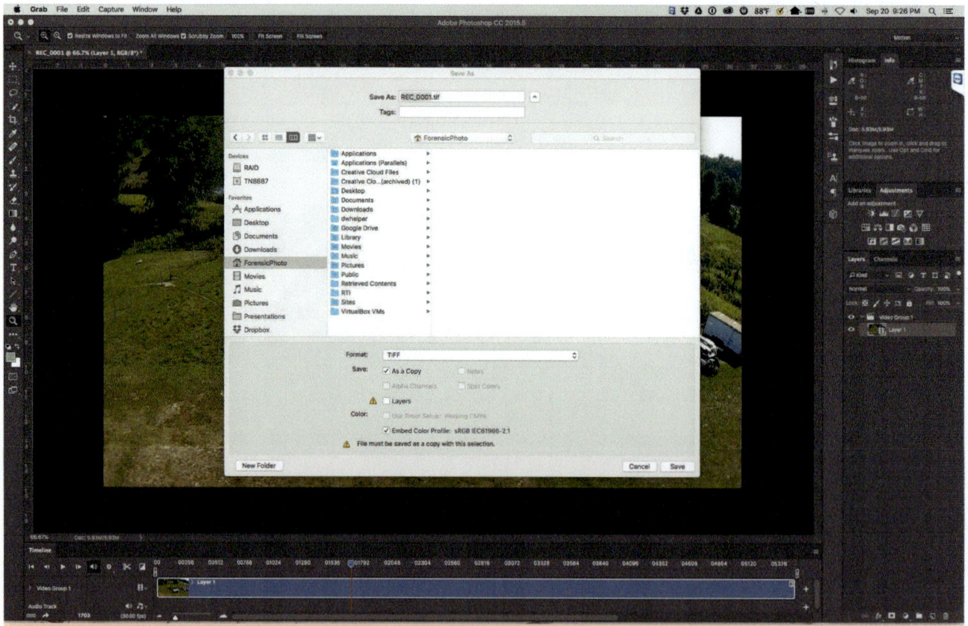

Figure 7.23 Open the video in Photoshop and choose the desired frame. Go to File > Save as, and choose the desired image format. TIFF is recommended as there will be no further compression to the images.) Uncheck the "Layers" option. Name and save the file. These steps can be repeated multiple times for additional frames

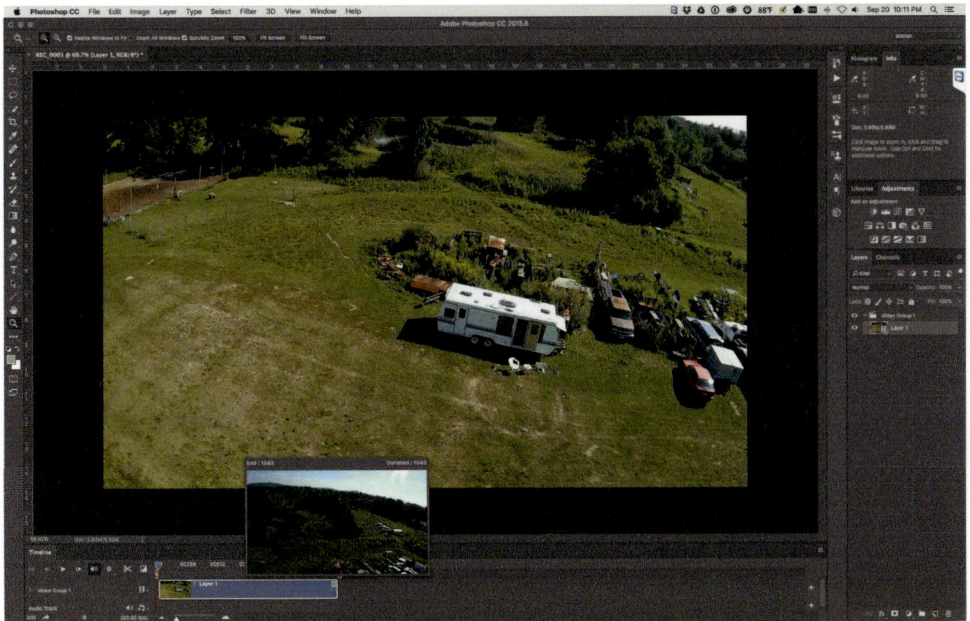

Figure 7.24 Open the video in Photoshop. Trim the video to the desired frames using the timeline. Click and drag either the beginning or end of the video in the timeline to trim

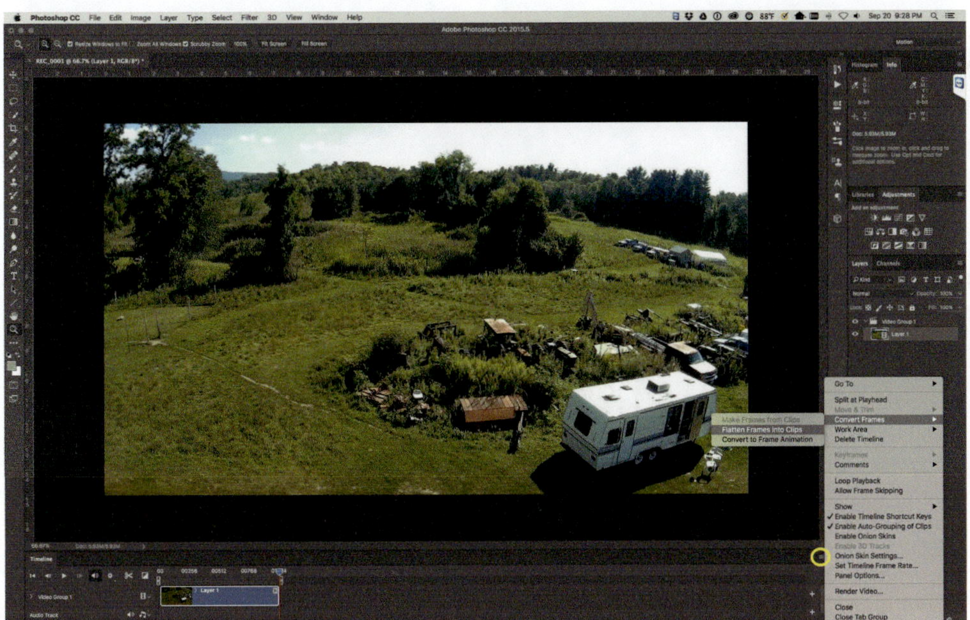

Figure 7.25 Convert the frames to layers. Click on the Timeline panel menu (located in upper-right corner of the timeline window), choose Convert Frames > Flatten Frames into Clips

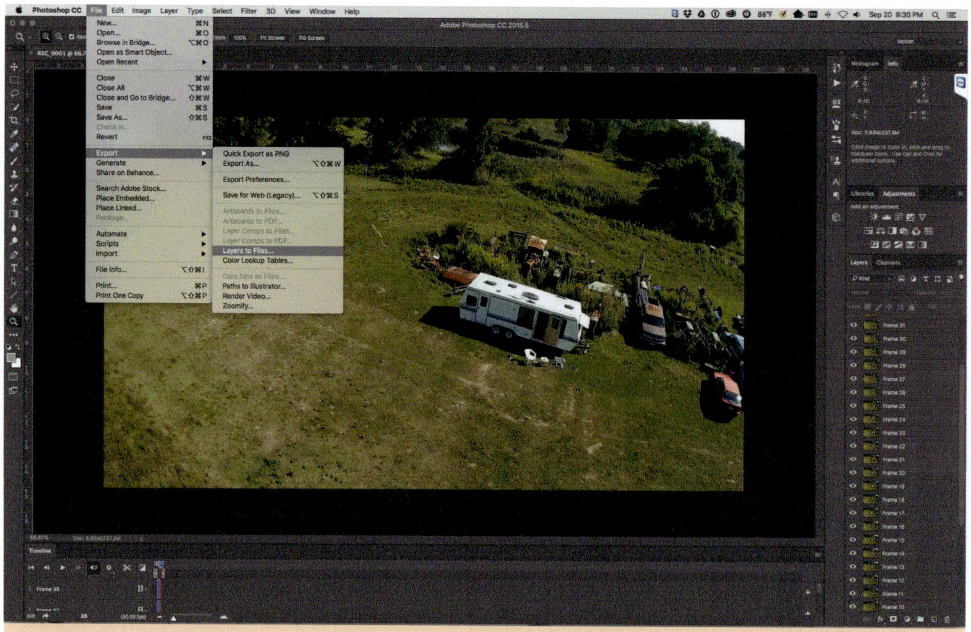

Figure 7.26 Save the layers to files. Choose File > Export > Layers to Files

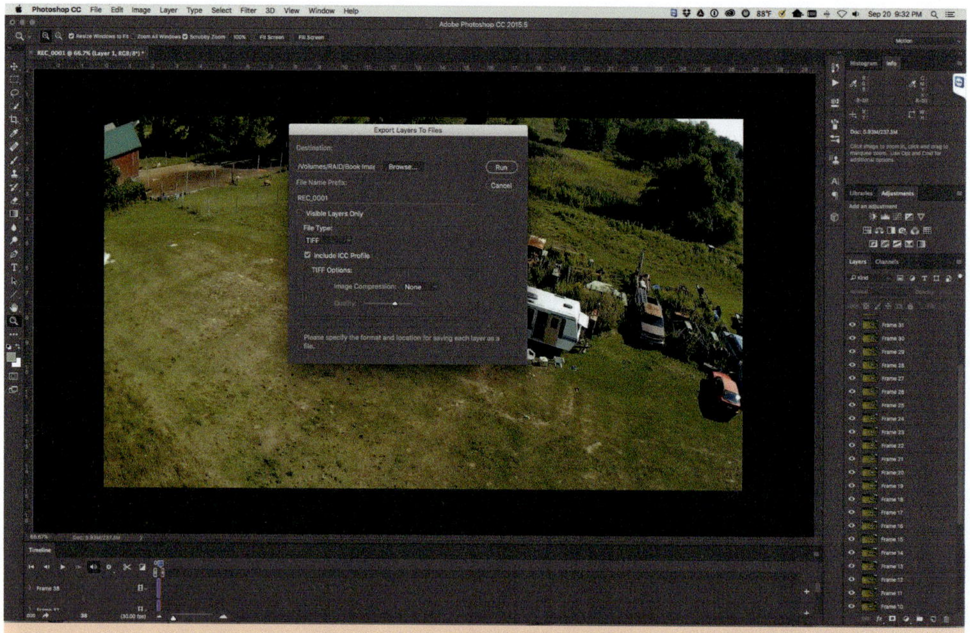

Figure 7.27 In the Export Layers to Files dialog box choose the location, name, and format of the files TIFF is recommended as there will be no further compression to the images)

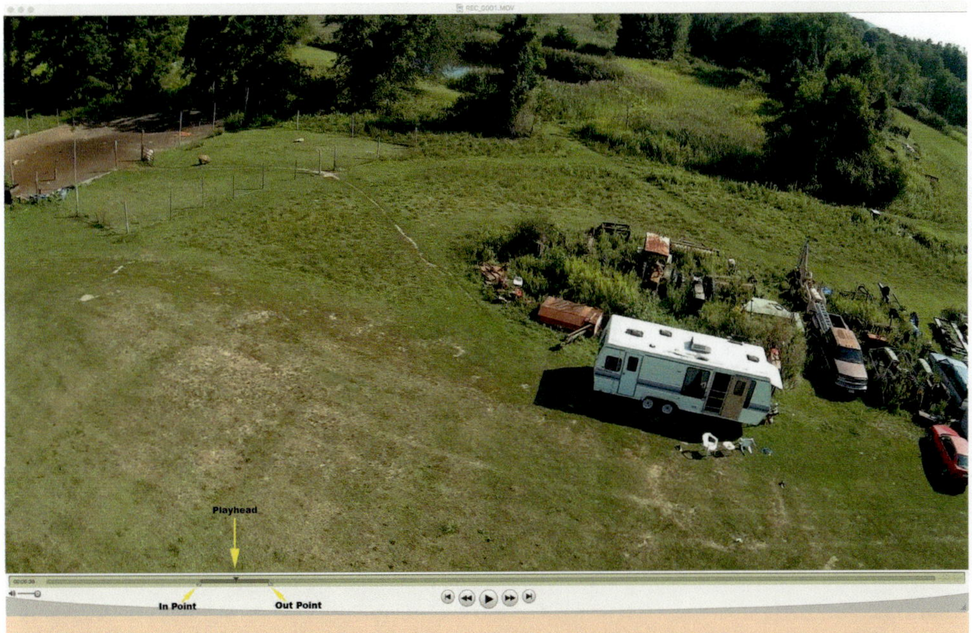

Figure 7.28 Open the video in QuickTime. Trim the video to the desired frame or frames by setting in and out points. Slide the playhead to the desired start frame and press the i key, then slide the playhead the desired end frame and press the o key. Alternatively slide the in and out points to the desired frames

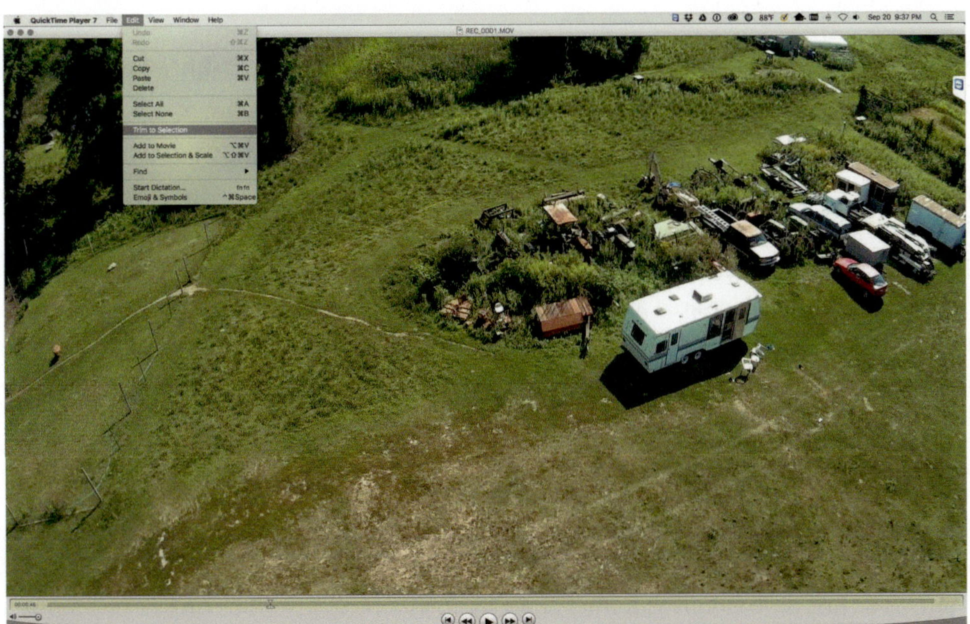

Figure 7.29 Choose Edit > Trim to Selection to trim the video

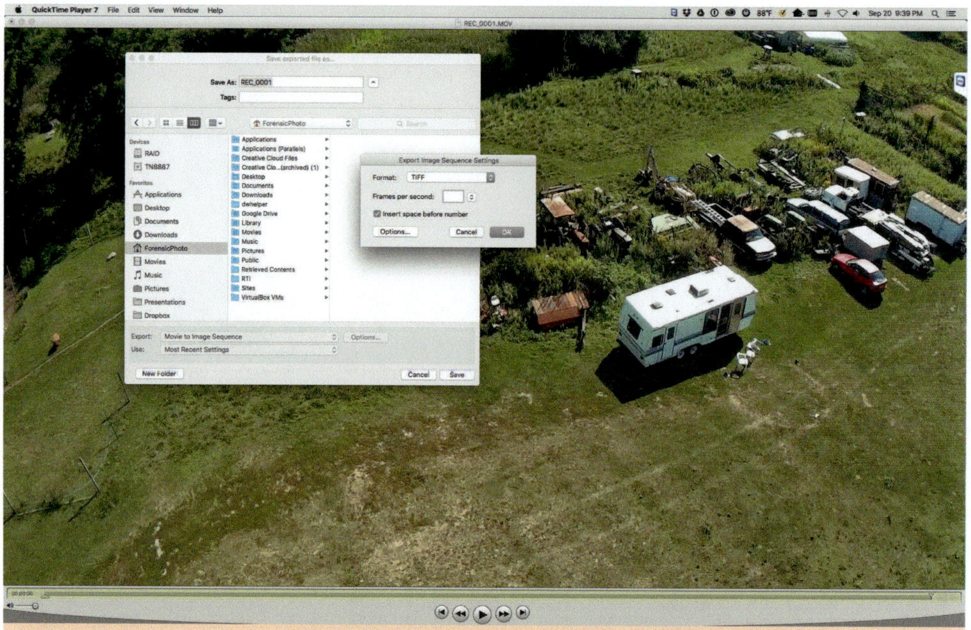

Figure 7.30 Export the frames to files. Choose File > Export. In the Export dialog box change the "Export": option to "Movie to Image Sequence." Then select options and select the image format. (TIFF is recommended as there will be no further compression to the images.) Leave the "Frames per Second" box blank to export all frames. Select "OK." Choose the location of the files and press "Save"

Figures 7.28–7.33 demonstrate how to save single or multiple consecutive frames using Apple QuickTime Pro.

If you would prefer to capture higher resolution still images from your camera, determine if your camera supports a time-lapse shooting mode. This feature allows the camera to continuously take still images at preset time intervals. Start the time-lapse before takeoff and the camera will continually take pictures during the flight. Now all that remains is to position the aircraft where desired and position the UAV for at least the length of your shutter duration. After the flight you will have plenty of still images to choose from.

Satellite Images

This chapter has presented several options for making aerial photographs. The price range of these options is wide and ranges from only a few hundred dollars to thousands. But what about if you just need a representation of an area, not necessarily photographs of a scene? As long as the time of the images is not your concern, you can capture aerial images for free using Google Earth Pro. Google Earth Pro is a free mapping and satellite imagery software available for download at www.google.com/earth/. To save aerial images using Google Earth Pro, navigate to the location you are looking to save. You can compose the area using the zoom tool and arrow keys on the right side of the screen.

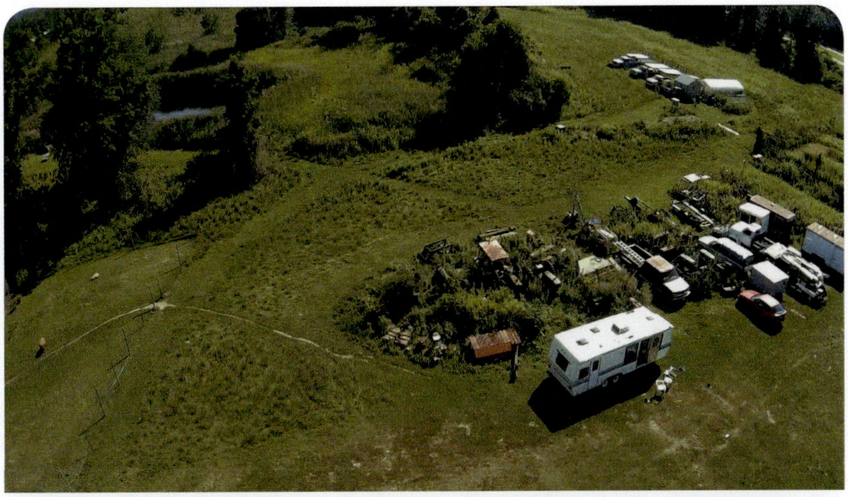

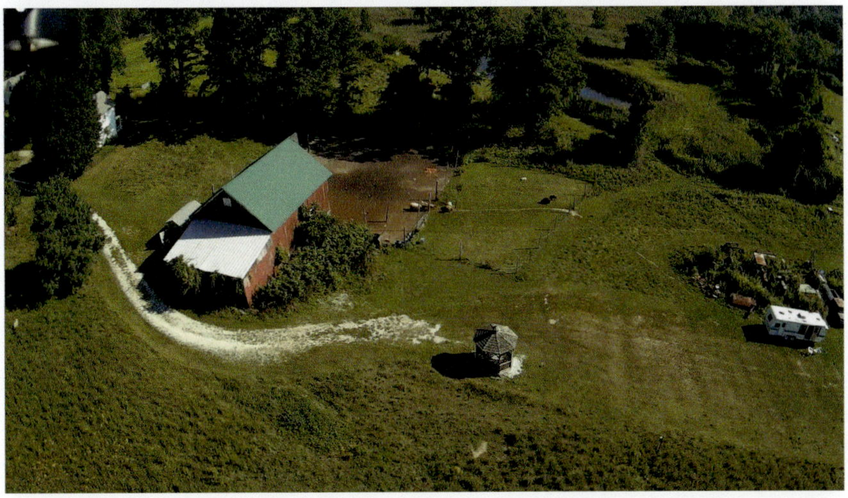

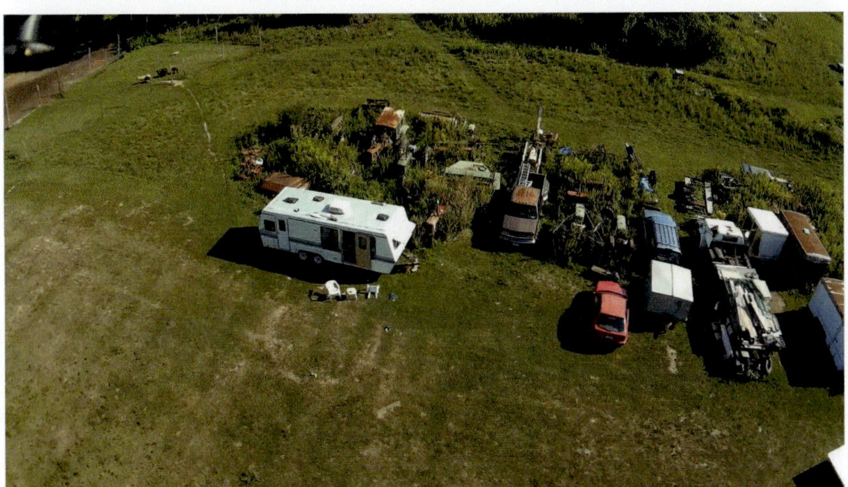

Figures 7.31–7.33 Examples of frames exported from a Mobius camera's video

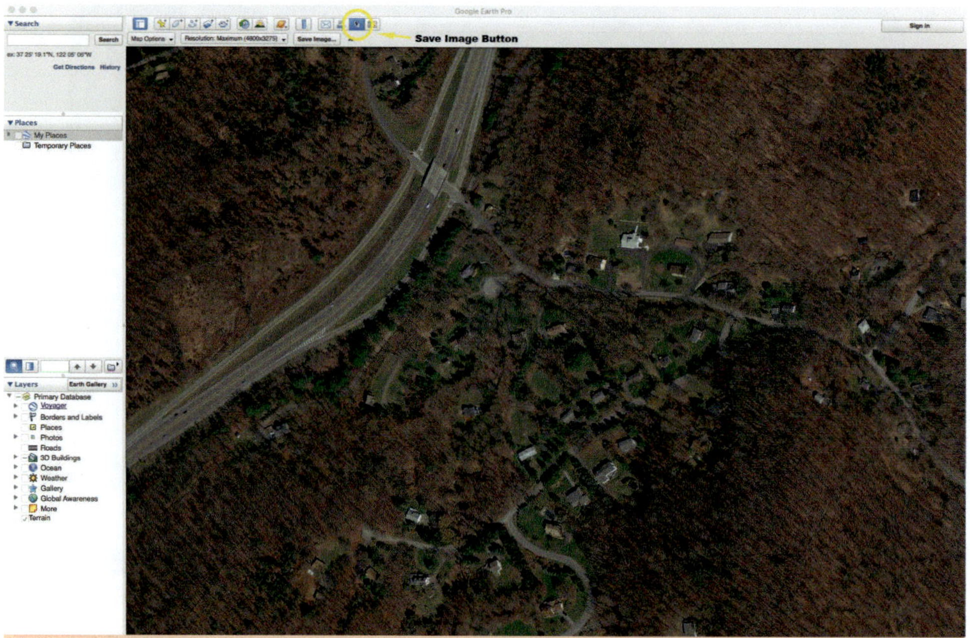

Figure 7.34 Select File > Save > Save image ... or click the Save Image button on the toolbar. The image will be saved with all place marks, borders, or other layer information that is visible in the 3D viewer

Figures 7.34–7.36 demonstrate how to save images as. jpg files in Google Earth Pro.

Overhead Photography

The following techniques, while not exactly aerial photography, will enable you to get overhead photographs of a scene or subject. Since these techniques will put the camera out of your reach, the greatest challenge faced will be how to trigger the camera remotely. This may be accomplished in one of several ways. The use of a long shutter-release cable, a wireless shutter release (remote control), or through a smartphone application connected to the camera via Wi-Fi can be helpful.

The first technique uses equipment that is most likely already in your arsenal. Use a tripod as a boom by extending its legs to their longest lengths without spreading them, then hold the tripod by the legs and suspend the camera over the subject. If you need additional height and there is a ladder available, you can use it for an additional few feet. Be cautious as this setup will be very top heavy and thus unsteady.

A second technique is the use of a painter's pole adaptor to mount a camera atop an extension pole. These poles are commonly available at hardware stores in the tool or painting section and come in various lengths up to 23 feet and longer. Again, use caution as larger cameras will be very top heavy and unstable at long lengths.

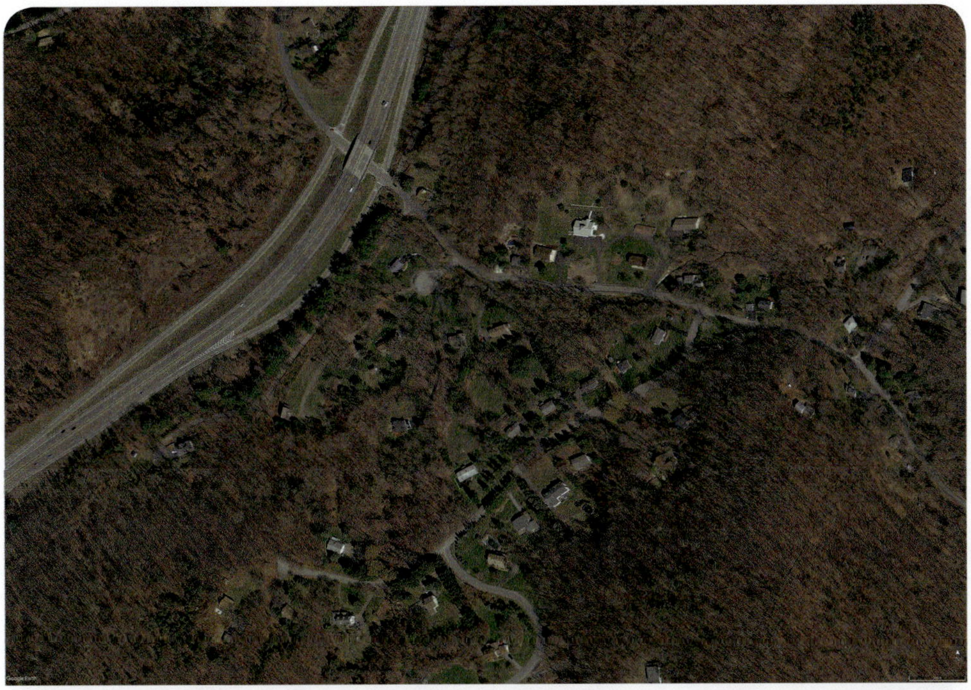

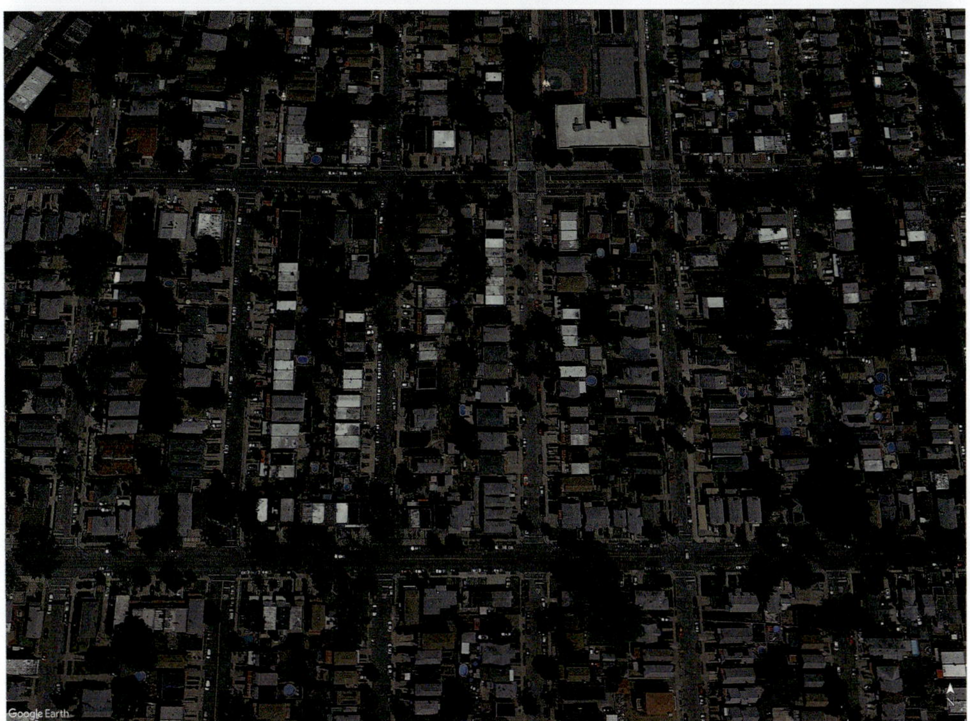

Figures 7.35–7.36 Examples of images exported from Google Earth

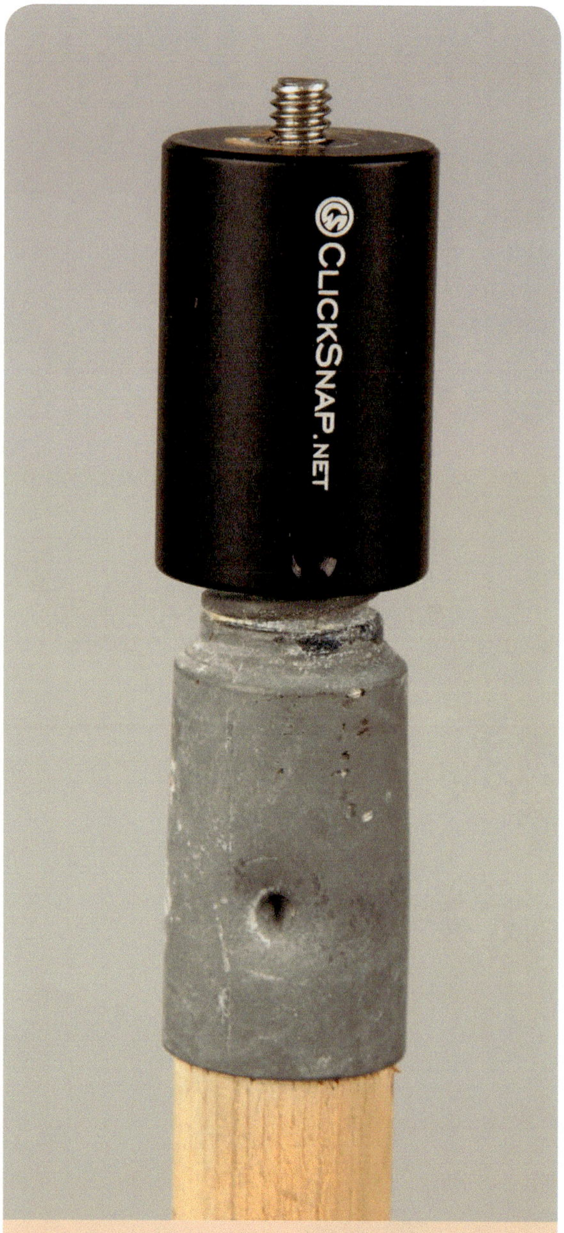

Figure 7.37 An adapter that converts painters pole threads to a standard tripod mount thread

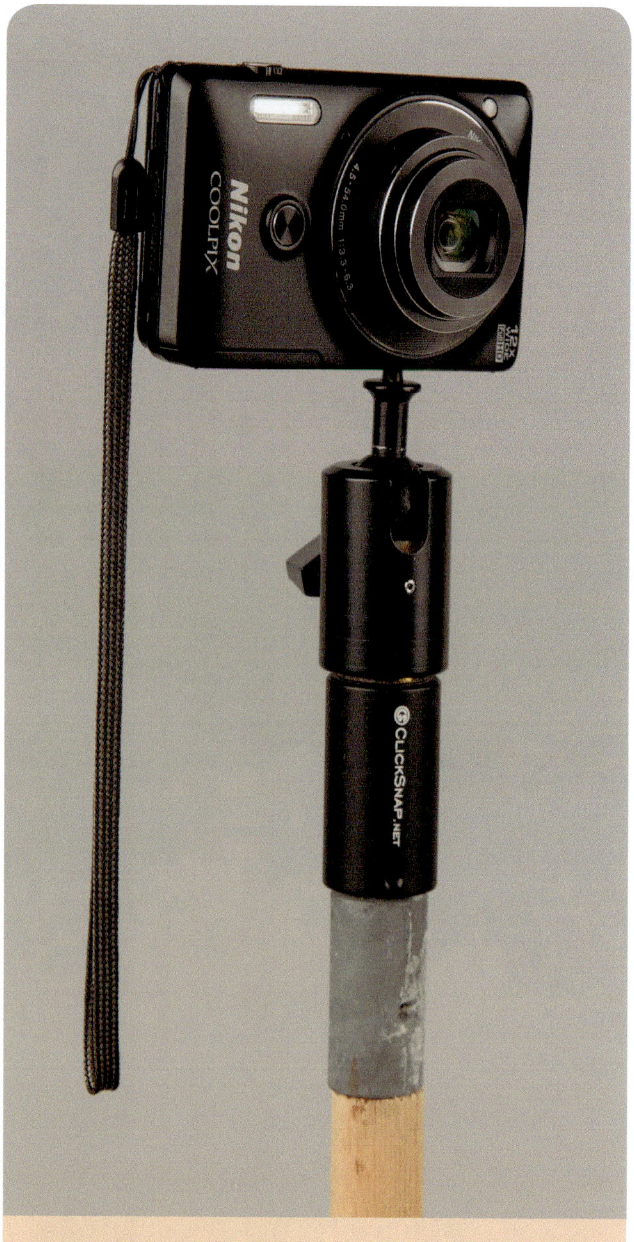

Figure 7.38 A point-and-shoot camera and small ball head attached to the painter's pole adapter

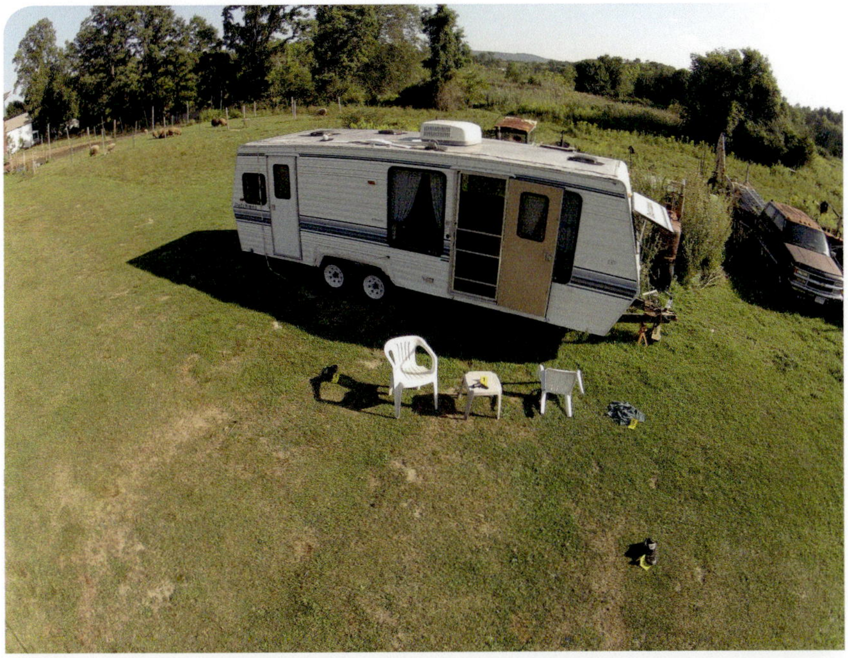

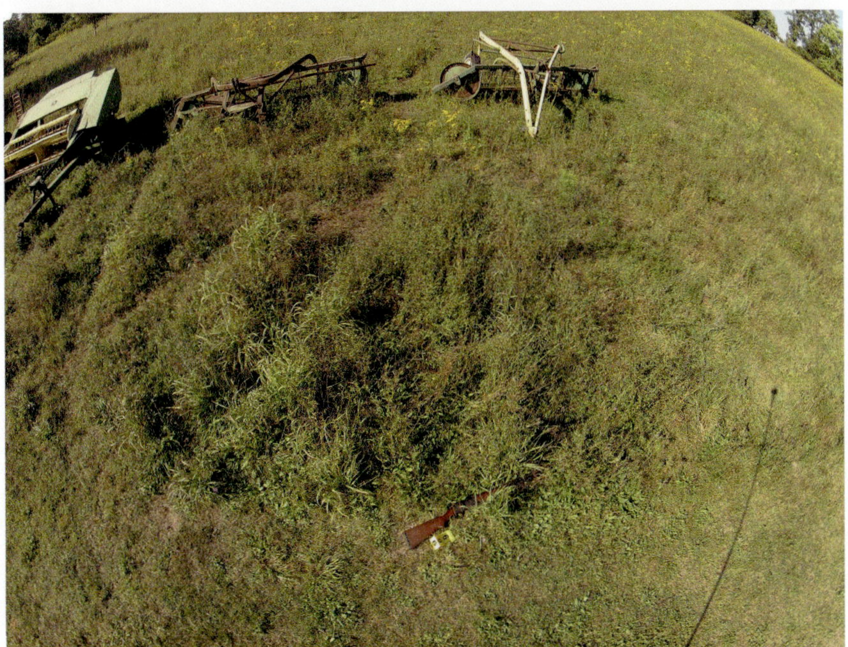

Figures 7.39–7.40 Examples of images shot using a painter's pole adapter and small point-and-shoot camera

Chapter 8 Close-Up and Macro Photography

These two photographic techniques are relatively similar and sometime share the same setup and equipment, therefore it is difficult to define them independently. The close-up photography technique is generally accepted as the capture of images from approximately one-tenth life size (1:10 reproduction ratio) to life size (1:1). Reproduction ratio is calculated on the image sensor, and will be discussed in greater detail later in this chapter. Macro photography is the capture of images from 1:1 to 50x (50 times magnification). Photography that is greater than or 50x is normally considered photomicrography.

Forensic evidence can come in a variety of sizes, ranging from vast landscapes to the minute details found in almost anything. Close-up images are used to document evidence of smaller subjects and specific features. Examples include fingerprints, blood-spatter droplets, shell casings, tool marks, cuts and tears in clothing, and many other subjects.

There are many methods used to create close-up images using basic equipment and a few accessories. One of the key needs in forensic documentation is the requirement to include a measurement device or calibration scale. This is an important factor when taking close-up images since it will provide a size reference to the object within the image. A common statement is "Use the right tool for the job" and that holds true with close-up photography. Using the best equipment that you can afford or have available will aid in documenting evidence gathering and image quality.

Lenses for Close-Up and Macro Photography

Many lenses can be used to create a close-up image; however, a lens designed for close-up photography, such as a macro lens, will provide the highest quality. Close-up or macro lenses are designed for this type of photography and will provide high-quality images with less distortion. Also, it should be noted that some non-macro lenses are not capable of focusing within a certain distance (close-up) to a subject.

There are several choices of close-up and macro lenses for most DSLR cameras. Some are fixed focal length (known as prime lenses) while others zoom. The close-up and macro lenses are designed for this type of photography and will provide high-quality images with significant sample definition. Prime lenses typically provide greater image quality and edge-to-edge detail than zoom-macro lens. This is a result of the complexity of a zoom lens's optical characteristics. The edge-to-edge or flat field functionality of a prime zoom lens is its most important feature. Depending on manufacturer, common focal lengths can be 50mm, 60mm, 100mm, or 200mm typically with a maximum aperture of *f*/2.8.

Lens choice should depend upon the photographer's need. Fixed focal length lenses tend to provide better quality at a lower cost, but a zoom macro may provide more flexibility for a variety of subjects. When choosing a macro lens, focal length determines the working distance, or the distance from the lens to the subject. Lenses with longer focal lengths will require the photographer to be farther from the subject. This may be an advantage when working with small subjects such as shell casings, but will be a disadvantage when working with larger subjects such as footwear impressions. During close-up and macro photography at 1:1 magnification or greater, the working distance will be two times the focal length of the lens.

Keeping distortion at a minimum is the primary target and true macro lenses are designed to produce magnifications of 1:1 (life size) larger while operating at short lens to subject distances. Macro lenses produce excellent edge-to-edge detail across the entire image.

Macro and close-up lenses are more expensive than common photography lenses because of the sophisticated internal mechanical structures where the grouping of lenses within the lens move independently to aid in focusing and documenting evidence at the 1:1, life size, or larger images. To assist in knowing the reproduction ratio of evidence, macro lenses have the reproduction ration annotated or marked on the barrel of the lens. During close-up and macro photography at 1:1 magnification or greater, the working distance and the image distance will be two times the focal length of the lens. The use of a longer focal length lens will provide a greater distance between the camera and the subject. This is useful to be able to use additional lighting and during situations when being close to the subject is hazardous such as contamination, infectious disease, or extreme heat. To use a macro lens, set the desired magnification/reduction and then change the working distance or distance

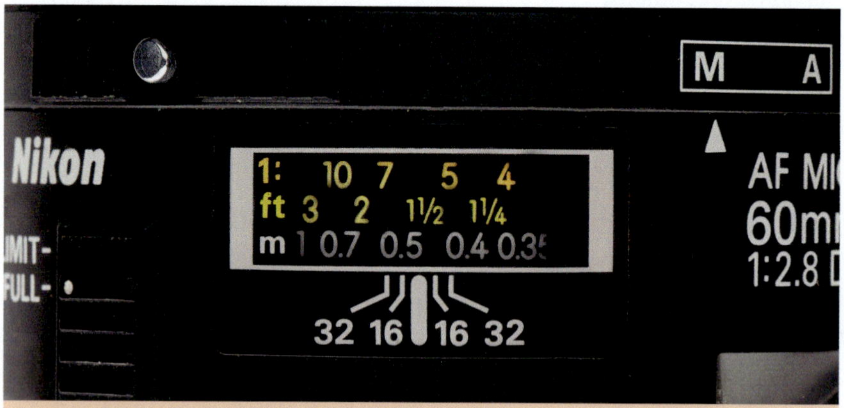

Figure 8.1 Image of a macro lens's macro scale

between the lens and subject. In this fashion, the image size will remain known and constant.

Close-Up Accessories

Supplementary Lenses

Sometimes there is a need to focus at a shorter working distance than a lens will allow. This is because most fixed focal-length camera lenses are optimized for long camera-to-subject distances and they are usually limited in their minimum focus distance. This distance can be reduced and the image size increased by using supplementary or close-up lenses. These lenses are either a single lens or lens group that attaches to lens like a filter. These lenses are also sometimes known as plus lenses or diopters. When used on compact digital cameras, this can be the easiest way to achieve close-up images.

Teleconverters

A teleconverter is a secondary lens that can be located between the lens and camera body. Teleconverters increase the focal length of the lens by a multiplier, creating a larger image of the subject while not affecting the working distance. Teleconverters reduce the aperture of a lens, allowing less light to pass through the lens, which leads to slower speeds. The ability to maintain the amount of working distance is advantageous for forensic photographers because the increased working distance allows for adjustments and composition of the evidence such as arranging lighting while keeping a safe distance from the subject matter.

Teleconverters are most commonly used with telephoto lenses so, for example, a 300mm *f*/2.8 with a 1.4x teleconverter will transform into a 420mm lens at *f*/4. The lens will lose one stop of speed. If a 2x teleconverter is used on the same lens, it becomes a 600mm lens with an *f*/5.6 reducing its aperture two stops.

It is important to consider the type of teleconverter that will be purchased. If the teleconverter is not designed to work with the lens and camera system, the autofocus and other electronic elements may not be able to communicate with one another and will not operate properly.

Teleconvertors may slightly degrade the quality of the image produced when compared to a true macro lens by itself. This degradation is minor and is much less noticeable in macro photography primarily because macro lenses are engineered to create crisp sharp images throughout the entire lens.

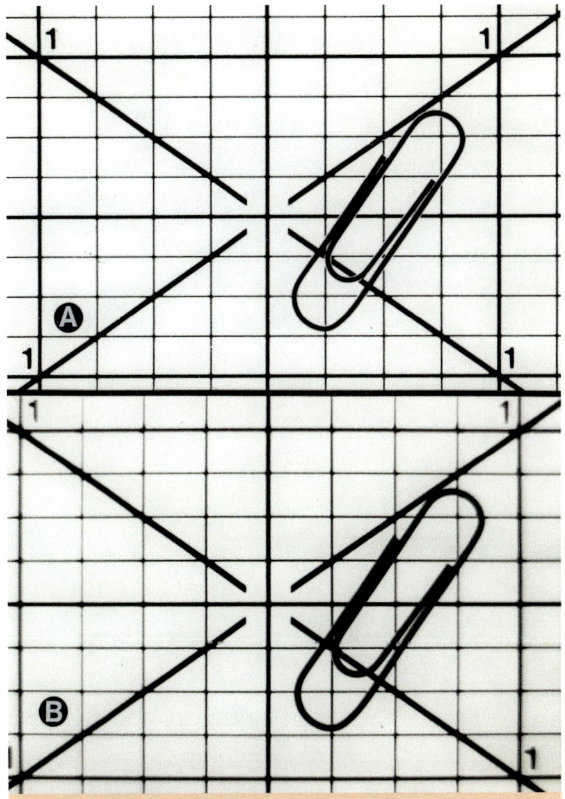

Figure 8.2 This composite photograph reveals the differences between a 50mm normal lens on the bottom (B) and a 50mm macro lens (A) on the top. There are considerable quality differences in the edge-to-edge definition of the image structures such as sharpness and definition

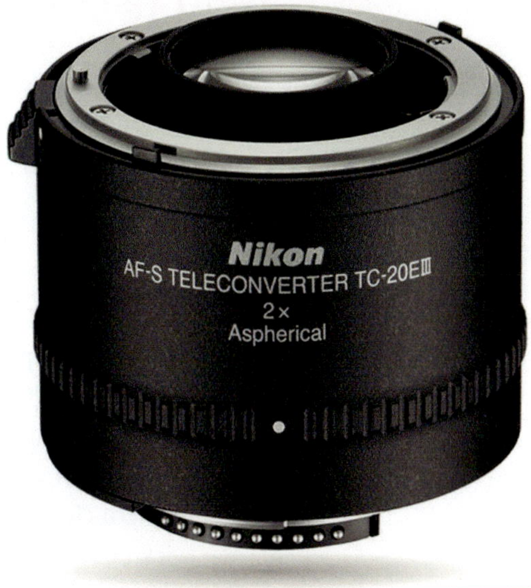

Figure 8.3 Image of a camera-lens teleconverter

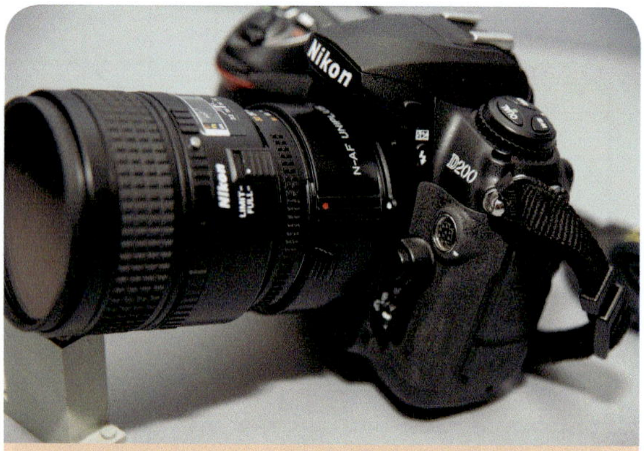

Figure 8.4 Image of a camera-lens extension tube

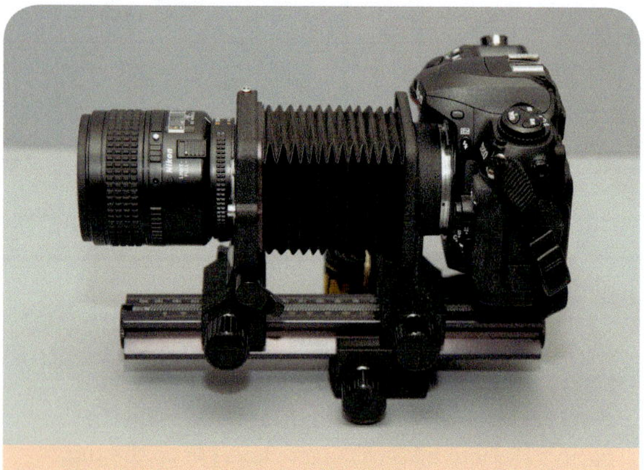

Figure 8.4.1 Image of a camera-lens bellows extension

Extension Tubes and Bellows

Extension tubes and bellows increase the distance between the lens and sensor of the camera. The farther the lens is from the sensor, the closer the focusing distance and greater the magnification.

Extension tubes are made in differing lengths and can be mounted together to increase the length. The most common single extension tube lengths are 12mm, 20mm, and 36mm, though each manufacturer produces additional lengths that can reach 250mm and beyond. Depending upon the type of extension tube, some automatic camera features may be lost.

While extension tubes offer only fixed lengths, a bellows is adjustable allowing varying lengths. The bellows is relatively easy to operate with some practice. Magnification is controlled by the length of the bellows, and focus is controlled by the distance of the lens to the subject.

For optimal quality, it is best to use lenses manufactured for macro and close-up photography since they are designed for the shorter working distances required. A normal camera lens can be used for macro photography by using a reverse mounting ring. The ring attaches to the filter thread on the front of the lens, and makes it possible to mount the lens in reverse.

Creating a Close-Up Image

Close-up and macro photography is a photographic process of its own. As image magnification increases, new challenges arise such as creating the best focus, improving and managing depth of field, and creating sharpness by controlling diffraction formed by the lens aperture.

How to Focus

To obtain proper focus in close-up or macro photography at a specific reproduction ratio, the barrel of the lens should be set to that appropriate reproduction ratio. The autofocus feature on the camera should be turned off. Once established, do not adjust the lens. To focus, change the working distance between the cameras lens and object by moving the camera closer or further from the object. Do this until the object is in sharp focus in the viewfinder. Camera preview or live view screens are also useful in achieving precise focus. The use of a tripod or other support, like a focusing rail, can aid in steadying the camera.

The focusing rail is designed to move the camera and lens position precisely. A focusing rail allows small movements and adjustments of the camera and lens making it ideal for close-up and macro photography. A focusing rail can be mounted on a tripod and permits incremental movements both forward and backward as well as left to right movement without having to move the tripod. When considering the purchasing a focusing rail, look for models that have calibration marks as well as locking smooth adjustment slides.

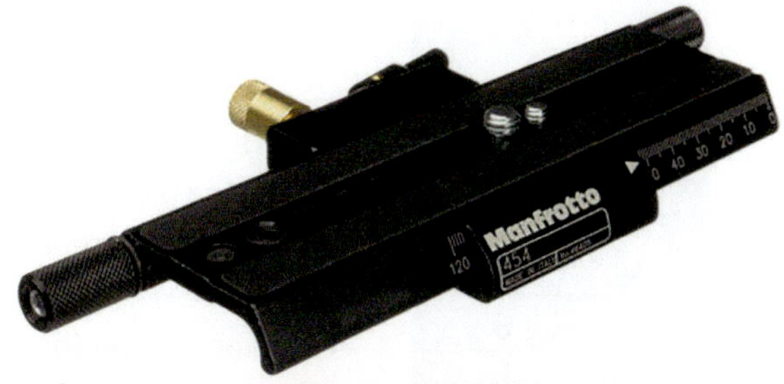

Figure 8.5 Image of a camera-lens focusing rail

Another method for achieving focus of an object is with the use of a scientific lab jack or moveable stage. Side-to-side adjustments in addition to the height adjustment are features to seek when purchasing or using this tool. A focusing stand should have a solid and heavy base that may be needed to keep objects on the device and sturdy.

Another solution to the challenges of achieving a precise focusing is to use an old lens. Attach a clamp or some item to anchor the bottom of the lens to keep it from sliding too freely on the imaging surface. Create a platform for the subject both using a piece of black cardboard or matte black plastic and locate it on the front of the lens. The focusing ring of this upside down lens when rotated will move the subject up and down similar to that way a lab jack goes up and down on its helical screw.

Close-Up and Macro Photography Depth of Field

As discussed in Chapter 2, the depth of field (DoF) of an image is the range of sharp focus from the front or an image or foreground to the most distant region in the scene called the background. As image magnification increases, DoF decreases, therefore shallow DoF is inherent in close-up and macro photography. To maximize the DoF in a macro image, align the camera and lens to the object's primary plane of interest. After establishing the proper reproduction ratio on the lens, align the camera to be parallel to the plane of the subject. Move either the camera or subject to create this alignment. When at an active investigation site, do not touch or move the subject of interest.

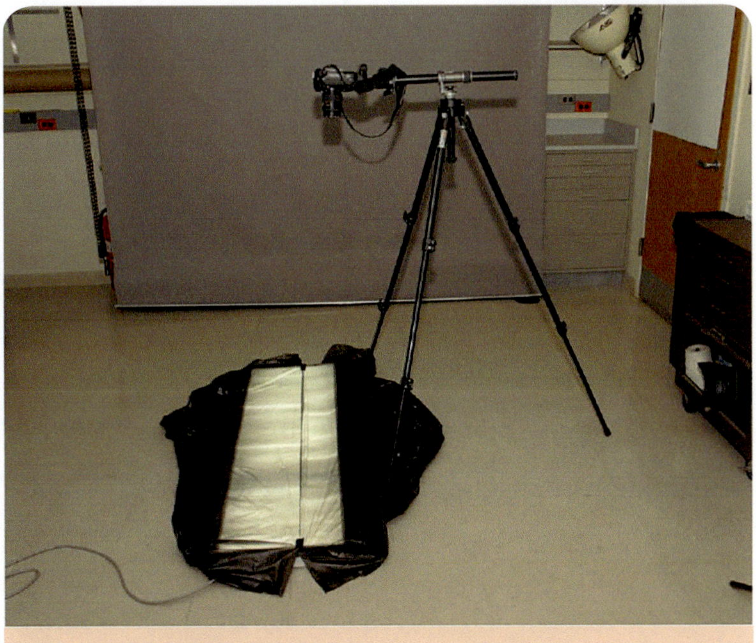

Figure 8.6 Example showing the camera parallel to the subject

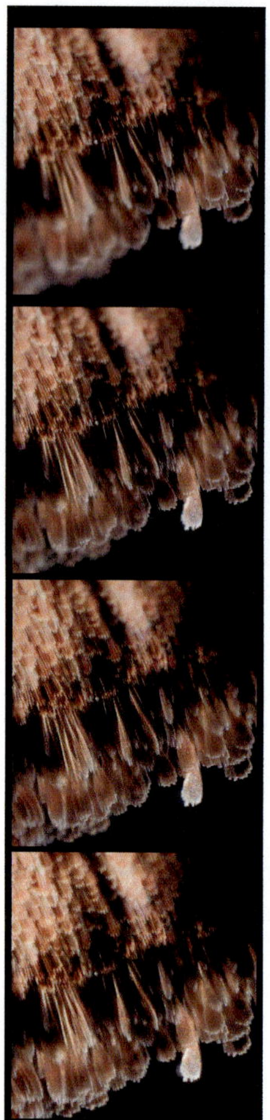

Figure 8.7 Image series of bristles demonstrating diffraction as the aperture size decreases

Close-Up Aperture Selection and Diffraction

Selecting the proper aperture needed for taking close-up images is not the same as is found in routine photography where the DoF is increased by selecting a small aperture. During close-up photography, as you get closer to reproduction ratios near 1:1, the smaller apertures *f*/16–*f*/22 will produce diffraction. Diffraction is dependent upon the characteristics of the object and the total magnification, and leads to softness in the image. Unfortunately, a larger aperture does not provide adequate DoF needed to completely share information about the subject. A forensic photographer must determine the best aperture considering each of these image characteristics when selecting aperture and its role in affecting the image attributes of evidence.

When doing routine photography, the rule of thumb is that two-thirds of the DoF will fall behind the focusing area and one-third will be in front of the focus area. When doing close-up photography, the DoF is nearly an equal distribution of focus in front and behind the selected object focus. This makes selection of where to place focus important.

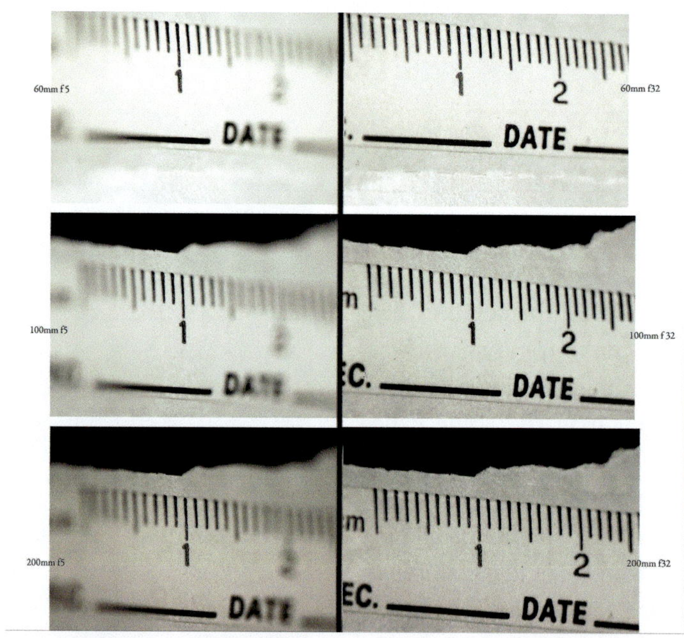

Figure 8.8 This photograph features a ruler where the minimum and maximum DoF possible was formed using a magnification of 1:1 using a 60mm, 100mm, and 200mm focal length lens to demonstrate how the focal length affects the DoF of an image. The left photo used an aperture of *f*/5 and the right *f*/32

Exposure Compensation

When using close-up lenses, extension tubes, or bellows, the increase from the lens to the camera's sensor produces light loss. As the magnification/reproduction ratio increases, light loss also increases and less light is available for composing, focusing, and creation of the exposure. This can lead to images that are underexposed or dark. Modern DSLR cameras have a highly adaptable through the lens (TTL) metering system that adjusts for light loss and determines the correct exposure. Be cautious as shutter speeds can be longer and even subtle vibrations can cause blur in images.

The imaging sensor's location within the camera body can be found by locating the circle θ symbol on the camera body. This is typically located on the top of the camera near the center or rear part of the camera body just before the back.

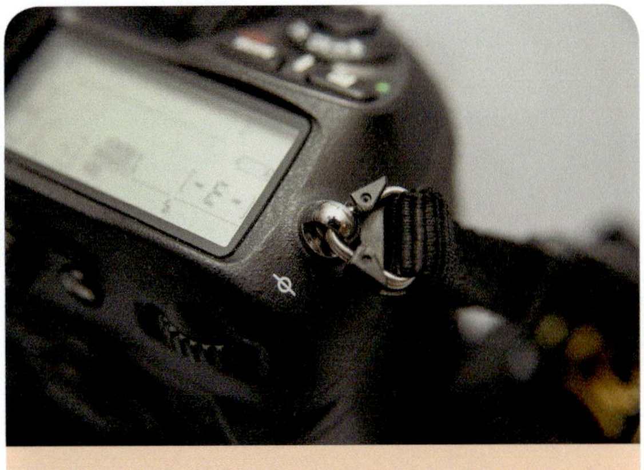

Figure 8.9 Annotation on the camera body designating where the sensor is located by the circle-strikethrough symbol

Image Magnification

Calculating magnification or reduction of an image is done by dividing the image size by the object size. Magnification = image size (i)/object size (o), M = i/o. A second method is to use the viewfinder as a rudimentary scale. Because a full-frame sensor's dimensions are 1 in. (24mm) × 1.5 in. (36mm), there is a built-in 1 in. ruler on the viewfinder's short dimension. The viewfinder can be used to quickly evaluate the object's size and compared to the viewfinder width. Magnification (M) is calculated with the equation, M = i/o. The imaging sensor represents the image (i) and the object (o) is the measured and recorded as

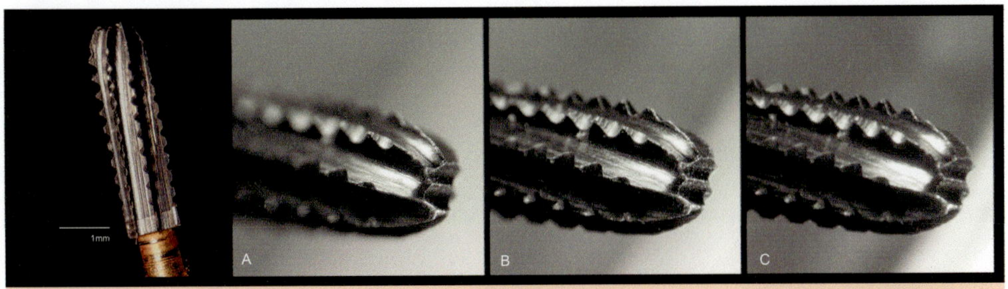

Figure 8.10 This illustration reveals the DoF and sharpness of a dental drill burr photographed with a magnification of approximately 5x. Photograph (A) was made with the lens wide open at *f*/2.0. It shows the lens's least amount of DoF and most resolution. Photograph (B) was made at *f*/11 and reveals a modest gain in DoF at no real expense to resolution. Photograph (C) used the lens's smallest aperture, *f*/22, and reveals what happens to an image's sharpness, negatively impacted by aperture-induced diffraction

(o). For example, if an object (o) were .25 in., and the imaging sensor and viewfinder is 1 in. (i), the equation can be solved this way:

$$M = 1 \text{ in.}/.25 \text{ in.}$$

This situation describes an image magnification of 4. The equation can be calculated using millimeters as well.

Chapter 9 Photomicrography

Stereo Photomicroscopes

A stereomicroscope is quite different from a compound or upright microscope. It has a primary objective and eyepieces but that is where their similarities end. One of the greatest advantages for selection of a stereomicroscope separate from its ease of operation is that the image is oriented correctly to the way it is seen. So, the left side of the object is the left side of the image. When moving an object, or collecting evidence, this orientation alignment can greatly simplify its use. This makes this instrument ideal for trace evidence analysis.

Stereomicroscopes form two optical images because there are two optical pathways in a stereomicroscope. This allows the image from a stereomicroscope to produce true stereopsis or stereovision. The image is said to be 3D. The microscope is typically located on a vertical column that is adjustable. This adjustment allows the microscope to be used for evaluation of objects of various thicknesses. The instrument can be quickly raised or lowered on the column and the objective's working distance can be quickly changed.

There are two basic adjustments on a stereomicroscope. One adjustment mechanism is used for focusing or changing the working distance of the microscope and the other is for changing the microscopes magnification. The focusing knob moves the instrument up or down using a very precise worm gear system. Unlike compound microscopes where the sample is moved, the stereomicroscopes itself is moved. There is only one focus mechanism for a stereomicroscope, unlike compound microscopes where there is a fine and course fine adjustment.

There are actually two ways that magnification is adjusted in a stereomicroscope. The actual magnification is dependent on the microscope's primary objective. Many stereomicroscopes have various objectives such 1x, 1.5x, or 2x as the primary objective lens. These lenses are interchangeable. This objective lens forms the initial stage of magnification. Then it is possible for a magnification adjustment function specific to the instrument. Many stereomicroscopes have a zoom range of approximately 7–12 times. This adjustment is not fixed and allows an operator to have an entire range of fine adjustments available to optimize the just the right amount of magnification. The viewing eyepieces also have magnification. These can range from 2.5x to 10x. When all the various components of a stereomicroscope are factored as possible elements, these instruments can create images with a magnification of 2x up to 250x.

Stereo is achieved as a consequence of the two optical pathways, but the imaging system utilizes only one of these pathways. The photograph produced from a stereomicroscope is not stereo.

Photographing

There are no real unique challenges associated with making photographs using a stereomicroscope. There will be a beam splitter located in the instrument, which directs a portion of, or all, of the image to the camera. The image in the camera will be dimmer than the image observed in the eyepieces since rarely will 100% of the image brightness be directed there. There will always be some light loss in an image when relayed to the camera and away from the viewing eyepieces. Often the image will remain visible in the eyepieces but the focus maybe different. A camera can be attached to the stereoscope just as it would be attached to a compound microscope, which will be described in more detail later in this chapter.

More Magnification and the Microscope

The first microscope was invented in 1590 in Middelburg, Netherlands, by the eyeglass makers Hans and Zacharias Jansen, using collapsible tubes to produce magnifications up to 9x. Improvements to the original microscope were developed by Galileo Galilei the by using a set of aligned lenses, "*occhiolino*," which means "little eye." In 1625, "*occhiolino*" was renamed as a compound microscope by Giovanni Faber and this name continues today where magnifying powers escalated to up to 1,000x to 2,000x since the 1590, 9x magnification.

There are many types of compound microscopes and most contain a light source. Those where the light is in the base are also considered bright field microscopes because the sample is illuminated from below the subject, and observed and imaged from above.

The compound microscope contains many parts each designed for a specific purpose. Figure 9.1 shows an image of a compound microscope with numerous parts labeled. You will notice that a compound light microscope contains ocular lenses known as binocular eyepieces and more than one objective lens on a rotating nosepiece in addition to its own light source.

Microscope Parts and their Locations

Operating a Light Microscope

The microscope is easily operated with a few techniques that will assist with ease of use and ensure that you obtain a great image. Initially turn on the microscope and adjust the

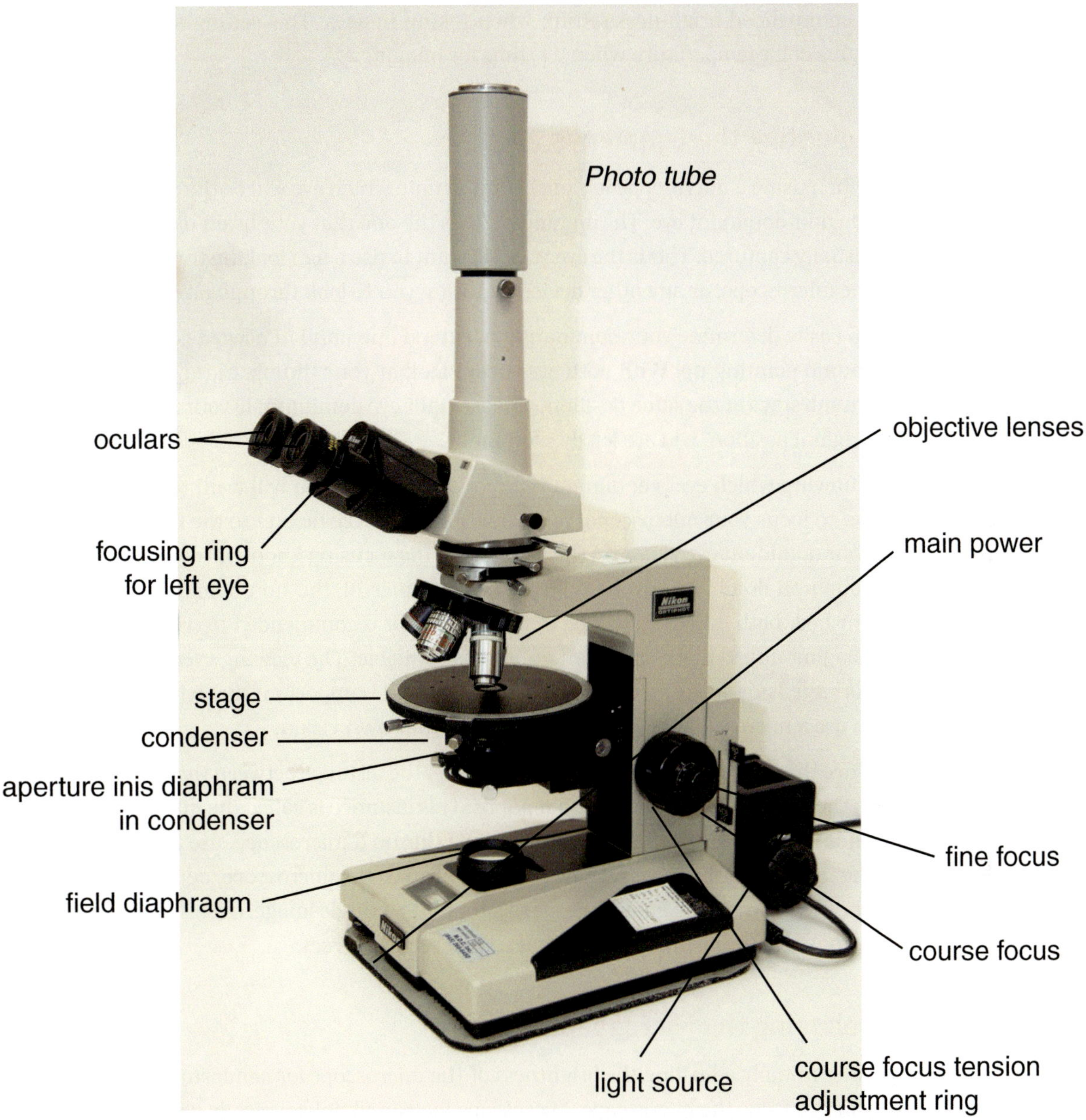

Figure 9.1 This illustration shares the key parts of a light microscope. Knowing where each of the controls are situated on a microscope can enable an operator to improve imaging outcomes in much the same as drivers must know where all the controls for operating an automobile are located. This knowledge might be called "knobology." Never looking away from the sample during evaluation can allow very subtle differences in an image to be evaluated. This might include not blinking

lamp's brightness where you are able to look through the eyepiece with ease. The lamp or light source is usually located at the back of the microscope. The brightness is adjustable with the microscope's voltage regulator or with a polarizing or neutral density filters; however, it is not recommended to adjust the brightness once the imaging-making process has begun. Occasionally photomicroscopes contain a marking or symbol that represents the recommended brightness setting when taking images. This setting also standardizes the lights color temperature when it is time for imaging.

Adjusting the Eyepieces

When using a microscope it is important to note which eye will be the dominant and which the non-dominant eye. The dominant eye is the one that your brain uses to process what is visually captured. This is the eye you will want to use when looking through the eyepiece of the microscope, or any other device requiring you to look through an eyepiece.

To easily determine your dominant eye, extend one hand in a fisted gesture out with your thumb pointing up. With both eyes open, look at your thumb. Close your left eye. If your thumb stays in the same position, you are right eye dominant. If your thumb shifts from its original position, you are left eye dominant.

Knowing which eye is dominant is important because you will want to use your dominant eye to focus your microscope. To start, set the eyepiece diopter to the 0 position and, using your dominant eye, focus on the image with the focusing knob. Once this is adjusted, focus your non-dominant eye by adjusting the diopter of the non-dominant eyepiece. When finished, both eyepieces will be in focus. It is not recommended to use these eyepieces for imaging unless there are no other options available. The viewing eyepieces are not highly corrected nor do they use the best-quality glass. It is important that whenever you sit down to use a microscope, adjust the eyepieces to your own vision.

Once the eyepieces have been adjusted, adjust the distance between the individual eyepieces to the distance between your own pupils. This distance is called the interpupillary distance and is specific to each individual. To adjust this on a microscope, use both hands and hold the tubes of the eyepieces. While looking through the microscope, adjust the tubes inward or outward until the images merge together into a single image. Occasionally you may have to make this adjustment a few times until it seems correct.

Focusing the Microscope

After initially adjusting the brightness of the microscope for comfortable viewing, you will want to focus the microscope. Microscope focusing knobs typically will be below the stage and close to the back of the microscope. See Figure 9.2. Usually on each side of the microscope, there is a large knob that will control the coarse focus and a smaller knob used to adjust fine focus. Also, newer research microscopes can be focused using a control panel on the computer that operates the microscope's imaging software.

Adjusting the focus knobs will move the stage up or down, changing the lens to subject separation or working distance. When using a microscope regularly, it is a help to know which direction the stage moves when rotating the knobs clockwise or counter-clockwise. This will lead to quicker focusing of a subject. Because of very small working distances, you may want to adjust the focus without having to remove your eyes from the eyepieces. To do this, start with the sample closest to the microscope's objective (lens) and adjust the coarse focusing knob while watching the movement while looking from the side of the microscope.

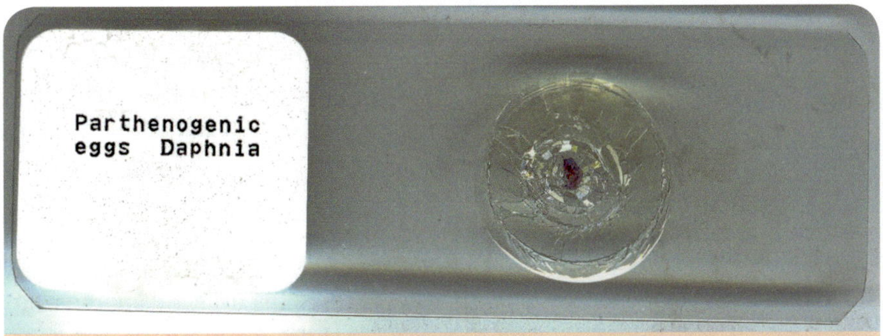

Figure 9.2 When focusing a microscope, it is easy to become disoriented. Not paying attention to how close or far from a slide the objective is can sometimes lead to driving the objective into the slide when trying to focus. Inadvertently placing a slide upside down on the stage can also lead to this outcome

Image courtesy of Lynne Tseng

This will allow you to learn which direction rotating the focusing knob causes an increase or decrease the subject to lens working distance. Perform this assessment a number of times until the working distance travel direction is memorized.

This is a very important exercise because it will enable you to focus on the subject without the fear of driving the objective lens into the sample. Focusing the image in the correct direction will move the subject further from the lens and increase the working distance.

Body Tube

The body tube is the corridor where light travels from the objective to the eyepiece. The body tube keeps external light and ambient light from entering the microscope and enables the image to contain a great amount of detail and good contrast. Using one hand, steady the microscope and gently pull the eyepiece out of the body tube disconnecting the eyepiece from the microscope. With the light turned on, when you look down into the microscope you will see the light from the lamp in the tube. Additionally, you will see the aperture diaphragm near the bottom of the body tube at the rear of the objective.

Turret

The nosepiece or turret of the microscope holds the objective lenses which usually contains four or five lenses of differing focal lengths or magnifications. The nosepiece is able to rotate and lock into place when selecting the desired objective. Advanced microscopes are able to rotate the turret with a computer. Additionally the turret is removable to be able to clean and service the objectives.

Substage Condenser

To obtain proper illumination it is important to know how to operate the substage condenser. The substage condenser moves up and down when turning a small adjustment knob

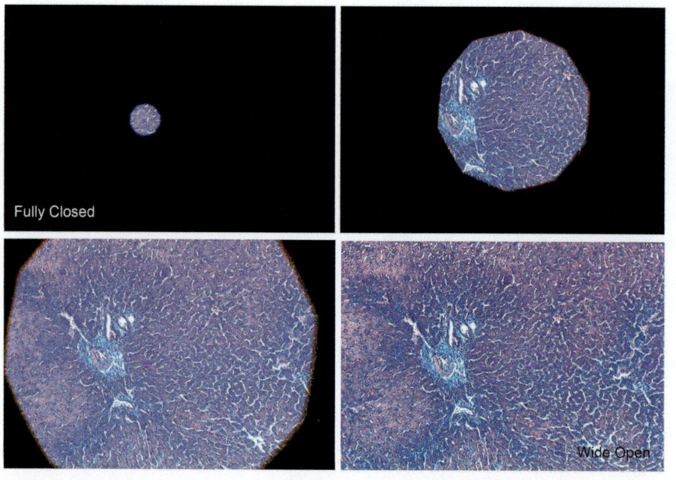

Figure 9.3 The field stop controls the diameter of illumination but not its brightness. In the top left image, the field stop was completely closed and exhibits the same brightness that the image situated in the bottom right includes

Image courtesy of Michael Peres

similar to that of the focusing knob that is located on the side of the microscope. Adjustment of the condenser is necessary to obtain the correct height and illumination for each optical magnification needed to form and control the cone of illumination.

Field Stop

The microscope contains a field diaphragm or field stop that is located directly below the substage condenser in the base of a biological or compound instrument. The field diaphragm controls the diameter of the illumination beam or the width of the beam as it enters the substage condenser. Adjustment to the field stop opens and closes the diameter but does not affect microscope brightness. If the field stop is too small, the aperture blades will be visible at the image, or if the aperture is too large, stray light similar to image flare will be present and may affect the contrast of the image.

Aperture Diaphragm

The aperture diaphragm is a critical control in a microscope. The diaphragm controls the contrast, resolution, depth of field, and intensity of the created image. The diaphragm is located in the substage condenser and its operation is critical in creating the highest quality image. A wide-open diaphragm will provide higher resolution but will result in an image with a shallow depth of field and low contrast. Making the diaphragm size smaller will result in an image with higher contrast and more depth of field, but the resolution will be compromised. The location of the aperture diaphragm will affect the image brightness but should not be used as a control to adjust the image brightness.

Establishing Proper Brightfield or Köhler Illumination

Creating illumination that is uniform and creates or maintains structural information about a sample was first proposed by August Köhler in 1893. Managing the widefield illumination in a transmitted light microscope is important and required for achieving high-quality images. Variances in illumination can be a problem when photographing because any differences in illumination will be amplified by the camera and image. Sensors and the way a pixel discriminates variances in brightness can embellish lighting problems. Since a pixel records data either as off or on, illumination errors will be exaggerated by a sensor. Achieving Köhler with lower power magnification is more challenging than for when making higher magnification images. Some imaging software can correct for shading or illumination errors. The feature is called shading correction.

Steps required for establishing Köhler illumination:

1. Turn on the microscope and set the interpupillary distance.
2. Adjust each eyepiece diopter as required starting with the dominant eye.
3. Focus the image by changing the working distance using the dominant eye. Next focus the eyepiece diotper for the non-dominant eye to bring images to the same focus.
4. Close the field stop fully.
5. Using the substage condenser, focus the image of the field stop until the blades are well defined and at the same plane as the focused image is.
6. Center the image of the field stop using the substage condenser centration screws. The centration should be visible in the field of view.
7. Open the field stop until it just leaves the field of view.
8. Set the aperture diaphragm to the correct setting.

When changing objectives, it is important to re-establish Köhler. Typically, once established, changing of magnifications will require only minor corrections.

How Köhler Illumination Works

1. Set the interpupillary distance.
   First establish a comfortable viewing brightness. Once this has been accomplished, look into the microscope and set the interpupillary distance by adjusting the eyepieces. It is important to have the two concentric images visible at each eyepiece to appear as a single image. Adjusting the height of the chair and locating your eyes directly across from the eyepieces without effort is also a component of this step. The eyepiece diopters must also be properly set at this step.
2. Focus the image of the subject.
   Bring the image into rough focus. Once the rough focus has been achieved, using the fine control critically focus the microscope. At this time make sure the substage condenser is set to the highest setting or most near to the sample. Once you have established these conditions, it may be necessary to tweak the eyepiece diopter settings.
3. Close the field stop.
   Operate the field stop control and close the stop until it is at its smallest size. The field stop is a mechanical device that can be operated by viewing through the microscope or from the side when moving the field stop. Depending on the state of the microscope's alignment, you may not be able to see anything, or the image of the field stop is clear and visible. In either situation, operators may need to close the diaphragm slowly and continue to make minor adjustments while proceeding. These adjustments include centering the image of the field stop using the substage condenser. At this time, it is required to keep the image of the field stop visible at all times.
4. Focus the image of field stop.
   Grasp the substage condenser focus knob and rack the condenser up and down until an image of the field stop is sharply defined in the oculars. The image will be focused when the edges look very crisp and black when focused by condenser. The sample's image *must* remain sharply defined when the field stop image is sharply defined. You may notice color fringes (red or blue) at the edges of the image of the field stop. This

indicates the presence of some chromatic aberration. Chromatic aberration is a lens defect where the various spectral components RGB are all not brought to focus at the same location. Depending on how out of alignment the field stop is, this step of focusing the field stop image could be easy or challenging. See Figure 8.10.

Achieving parfocality of the specimen and the image of the field stop may be a bit more difficult in some situations depending on the state of the alignment or the sample's thickness. Parfocal describes a condition where all the images are in the same plan of focus. It may require that you move very slowly making small adjustments, such as the closing of the field stop or minor height adjustments to the substage condenser. Do not be in a hurry, but rather study the field of view to determine the location of the field stop relative to the edges of the field of view. Once the image has been successfully located, it may be advisable to begin to center the substage condenser, which moves the image of the field stop. Move the substage condenser using the centration tool typically located just below and on the bracket that holds the substage condenser under the stage. Move them gradually and observe what happens to the image of the field stop. Move the image of the field stop roughly into the center of the field of view.

5. Center the image of the field stop.
   Locate the centration screws on the condenser assembly and look into the microscope. Adjust each of the mechanisms individually or together. Move the image of the field stop into the center of the field of view. If the image of the diaphragm is crisp, this condition will have been established; if not, you may have to go back through each of the subsequent steps prior to this point to accomplish this. The goal is to achieve a focused and centered image of the field stop that is superimposed over the focused image of the specimen when looking into the eyepieces.
6. Open the field stop until it just leaves the field view.
   Once the image of the field stop is focused and centered, the final adjustment can be a bit tricky. Looking into the microscope and grasping the field stop, begin to open it. Bring the field stop to the edges of the field of view and, at this location, assess the centration of the image of the field stop to the edge of the field of view. If additional centering is needed, using the substage condenser assembly knobs finalize the adjustment. Once truly centered, open the field stop until it is just outside the field of view and is not encroaching into the field of view. Sometimes this setting will be different for photography and for viewing. It is best to adjust the field stop for the imaging system requirements. You may also notice the image of the field stop will get less defined as it is opened. Focus should be assessed based on the central region of the field of view and not the periphery.
7. Adjust the aperture diaphragm.
   Establishing the proper aperture diaphragm setting is probably the most important adjustment a microscopist can make. The next few paragraphs will share how to create the ideal setting. The aperture diaphragm is located in the substage condenser but visible in the body tube when an eyepiece has been removed. By moving the aperture diaphragm (opening and closing), it can be observed as it moves in the tube. It can be very useful to move the diaphragm through its entire range and observe the brightness and location changes.

The goal is to have the diaphragm just interject itself into the body tube. When the diaphragm is all the way open, the diaphragm is not visible in the body tube and when the diaphragm is all the way closed, it may cover more than 50% of the tube. A general starting point for the diaphragm location would be where the aperture diaphragm is visible in the body tube and where 80% of the tube is open, and where 20% of the tube is covered by the aperture diaphragm. If the aperture diaphragm is outside of the tube, it will have *no* effect on image formation, and if the aperture diaphragm is closed to its smallest size, it will create significant contrast, increasing the image's DoF and diminishing image resolution.

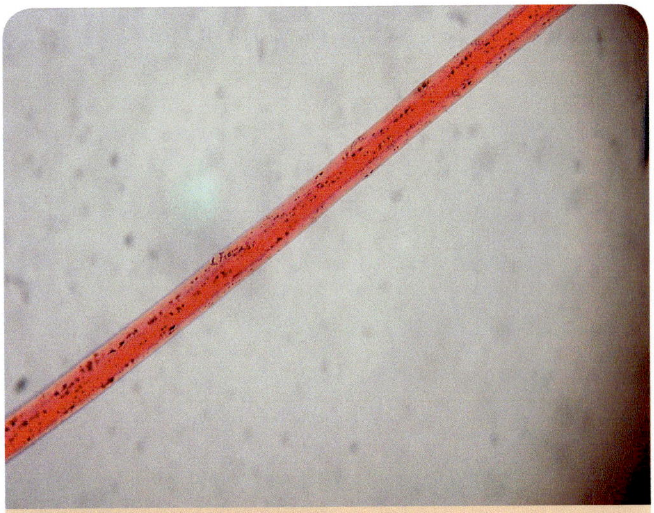

Figure 9.4 Image of Köhler illumination
Image courtesy of Brandi Clark

Determining the Optimal Diaphragm Settings

The two apertures on the microscope are the field stop and the aperture diaphragm. To create the highest quality image it will be necessary to adjust each of them properly. The field stop controls the diameter of the illumination beam and will marginally affect the contrast of the image. The aperture diaphragm affects the depth of field, resolution, contrast, and intensity. The captured image will be highly influenced with the proper use of the aperture diaphragm.

To determine the effects of the aperture diaphragm, use a 10x objective and set up Köhler illumination on the microscope. Choose a faintly stained microscope slide with structural details that are visible without too much difficulty. Remove an eyepiece and look at the aperture diaphragm moving inside the tube at the end of the objective. The image of a bright circle of light and the aperture diaphragm at the outside edge of the tube will be visible when adjusting the aperture diaphragm. Watch how the aperture diaphragm operates when it is rotated throughout its range.

The numerical aperture on the substage condenser is matched to the numerical aperture of the objective when the aperture diaphragm in the tube is set so that its edge is at the edge of the body tube. This doesn't always create an ideal image but is a good starting place to then make adjustments to enhance image depth of field, contrast, and resolution. When the diaphragm numerical aperture matches the objective's numerical aperture there will be minimal effect on image formation. To enhance or degrade the image, the diaphragm must interrupt the illumination pathway.

The aperture diaphragm controls four essential characteristics of an image, depth of field image contrast, resolution, and intensity. The amount of diffraction created by the system will influence each of the image characteristics and is influenced by the specimen's characteristics directly.

Determining the correct aperture diaphragm setting will depend upon the subject and also your individual judgment. If you are just starting out learning about microscopy, it would be beneficial to practice observing diffraction and become skilled in determining where

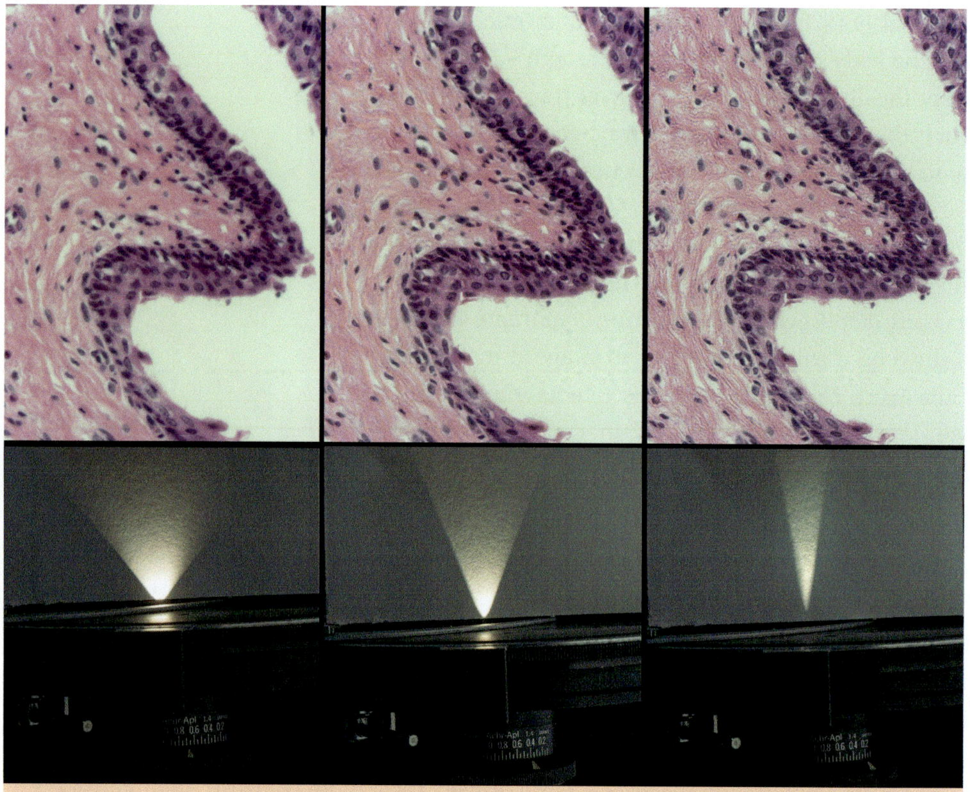

Figure 9.5 In these three photographs, the aperture diaphragm has been set to three different locations. The photographs were each made using a 10x Fl - NA .45 objective and an achro aplanic substage condenser, NA 1.40. The photograph on the left was made with the aperture in its maximum opening for the 10x lens (NA .65) creating the maximum resolution and the least amount of contrast. Notice the angle of light leaving the condenser. The middle image was made with the NA set to approximately an NA of .3, which created the optimum balance between the contrast and resolution potential for the objective. Notice the angle of the light becomes smaller when the aperture diaphragm is closed. The image on the right has the most contrast and least amount of resolution as a consequence the aperture being nearly closed to its smallest setting at an NA of .15. The angle of light is also the smallest when operated in this position

Image courtesy of Michael Peres

diffraction is optimal. You will want to do this by viewing the specimen through the eyepieces and rotating the diaphragm throughout its entire range. There may be times when you must refocus when required to see the effects. While rotating the diaphragm observe the edges of the sample and examine the effects. Depending upon the sample you may be required to re-focus while examining how much depth of field, contrast, and resolution each sample requires.

You will notice, as the diaphragm gets smaller the image becomes darker and shares more contrast having an increase in depth of field. When the diaphragm becomes larger, the opposite is true and the image will get brighter and contain less contrast and depth of field. As the photographer, you must determine the ideal setting for a specimen within the range. Each subject will require a different setting to obtain the highest quality image. As you review the range of the diaphragm, look at the specimen's fine detail and do not confuse contrast with resolution and detail. It is better to capture optical resolution initially and add contrast to the image during image processing. When you are observing the different effects of the diaphragm, this may be a time when you would consider taking multiple images at each diaphragm setting and then determine the best or group that shows the fine details within the specimen.

Image Taking Using a Microscope: Photomicrography

Creating images when using a light microscope is not as difficult as you might think. Images can be acquired by using dedicated microscope cameras or DSLR cameras. It is also possible to use a smartphone for quick snapshots. Ironically the smartphone's simplicity proves to be very advantageous, although consistency and repeatability to create high-quality images is the greatest challenge when using a smartphone for photomicrography. The hardest challenge is to achieve repeated color results and consistent exposures in addition to properly aligning the eyepoint to the camera's lens. There are brackets that can be used to secure the smartphone to the microscope in addition to telescopes.

Dedicated Microscope Instrument Cameras

There are several types of camera systems designed specifically for use on a microscopes. They are operated using imaging software such as Zen® from Carl Zeiss Microscopy or Elements® from Nikon that control the camera's operations. The camera will contain the basic controls such as an electronic shutter and a light meter needed to determine the correct exposure of the specimen.

Other features of an instrument camera include a preview or live view mode, manual or automatic exposure modes, exposure adjustment controls, sensor sensitivity adjustments, white balance, gain, binning, digital resolution (megapixels), and image contrast capture mode or input dynamic range. These cameras are usually compact but contain an adequate resolution and offer numerous features that are useful during low-light situations such as fluorescence applications or other more common applications such as wide field.

Each manufacturer's camera will differ in their specifications; however there are some common features.

To start, microscope cameras are controlled by a computer software or application. The software can be operated to focus the subject using the preview or live-view mode.

Instrument cameras contain two exposure modes, auto and manual. When the manual mode is selected, the photographer must determine the time needed to create an accurate exposure. The time will be dependent upon the brightness of the microscope. The ability to review the image in the camera preview mode and evaluation of the histogram will give feedback to the photographer to determine if a change is necessary to improve the image exposure.

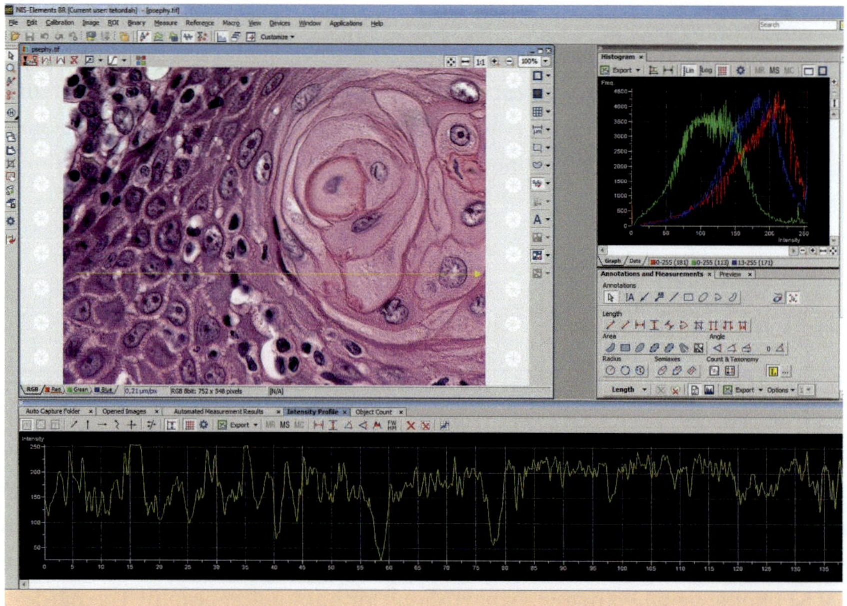

Figure 9.6 A screenshot showing typical camera control software

Image courtesy of Michael Peres

Operating the camera in the automatic mode results in the basic exposure of the specimen being determined by the camera. When performing brightfield microscopy, it may be beneficial to increase the auto exposure by adjusting the exposure compensation control by approximately +1 or +1.5 exposure values (EV). Conversely when operating the microscope with darkfield illumination, decrease the exposure value by approximately –2.0 EV. Because it is possible to view the exposure when using the preview mode, it is possible to optimize the exposure by evaluating the display image. A general rule of thumb is to not overexpose the image and base your exposure upon the brightest region of the sample containing specimen detail. The ideal exposure will contain specimen details throughout the entire range of the tones from the highlight to dark regions.

Correct exposures times will vary and be affected by the sample's contrast and if the sample is very thin and weakly stained or thick and has a very dense stain at the same brightness setting of the microscope. The sample's thickness and concentration or darkness of the stain will determine the internal visibility of the specimen. Sometimes it is useful to adjust the gamma of imaging sensor to better capture characteristics of the sample. This is completed within the camera's software. An increase to sensor gamma is better suited for weakly stained samples with low contrast and thick or contrasty samples will benefit by using a decrease in the gamma of the imaging sensor. Selecting the exposure and contrast setting is a critical step required to accurately capture the maximum amount of detail of the specimen.

White Balancing

White balance creates a color reproduction of a white target that creates equal RGB information. When using a brightfield microscope, the background is the best source target to use for white balancing. The ability to white balance or calibrate the camera sensor is useful when imaging standard samples. White balance can also be completed with software by averaging the entire scene or measuring a specific area of the scene by using the software eyedropper tool. As a reference, a brightfield image's white point brightness of 240 in the RGB pixel data is the goal. When averaging for a white balance, the illumination pathway must be free of the stained tissue. The method chose must be reliable and repeatable to be able to create consistent quality photomicrographs.

Instrument cameras do not have the ability to change ISO like DSLR cameras and in some situations there will not be enough brightness to obtain a proper exposure. The GAIN tool is used to change the instrument camera's sensitivity, though increasing the GAIN can create digital noise in an image. This process should only be contemplated when all other methods to increase brightness have been utilized.

Binning is another way to increase a camera's sensitivity and is done by grouping pixels to work together as one pixel. As a group, the pixels are able to gather more light and create a proper exposure when there is not much light to work with. The concern with binning is that the number of pixels of the captured image will be less by the binning factor. If a sensor has 2048 pixels in the long dimension and the camera is set to the 2×2 binning selection or four pixels, the binned captured image will be 512 pixels and not the original 2048 pixels.

The software instrument cameras use contains features that permit simple image processing such as sharpening. The software also has the ability to annotate images and add bar scales, which is useful when reviewing and evaluating images at a later time. Saving images as a TIF or PNG should be the primary choice because they are a lossless file format. Conversely the JPEG file format is a universal format; however, image information may be lost to artifacts formed through the JPEG file compression.

Mirrorless Cameras

Similar to the DSLR, mirrorless cameras are also effective but will need to be operated differently in the laboratory. They function similar to the DSLR but are more compact and do not use the reflex viewing system. They are useful when travelling and when size matters but at this time they are not a commonplace in the laboratory or when using a microscope.

DSLR Cameras

The DSLR camera is easily used for photomicrography however there are advantages and disadvantages. Advantages of the DSLR include the ability to select a variety of camera settings, which can be used to optimize the imaging sensors ability to capture images.

DSLR advantages include:

convenient to transport and use for multiple imaging possibilities;
adjustable ISO;
high resolution imaging sensor at a cheaper price;
ability to choose a variety of file formats and the RAW image format;

quality color reproduction and color management;
live view and video capture in high-end newer camera systems;
noise management choices;
variable bit depth.

DSLR disadvantages include:

creates vibration when used at high magnification imaging;
difficulty attaching to a microscope;
alignment and setting up or tearing down;
focusing of the viewfinder;
small rear screen compared to a computer to change imaging features in the menus;
battery usage;
delayed shutter during mirror lock-up mode.

Attaching the DSLR camera to a microscope is the first step when considering whether to use this camera system for photomicrography. The DSLR can be mounted on a vertical copy stand or tripod and basically hover over the top of the photo eyepiece or use extension tubes or bellows on the camera to eliminate ambient light which may create image flare and other defects. A rudimentary method is to use a toilet or paper towel cardboard tube lined with black tape or black construction paper to act as the baffle. The DSLR's imaging sensor must be perpendicular to the optical axis and carefully aligned over the eyepiece. The use of a handy smartphone level app or a spirit level will assist with the alignment. The distance between the camera's imaging sensor should be where the circle of illumination produced by the eyepiece will cover the imaging sensor without creating a circular image. To increase the image size, move the camera further from the eyepiece. The increased distance will produce a dimmer image and the circle of good definition will become larger and cover the entire sensor.

Optem® Thales or Spot® Imaging sells couplers for cameras to microscopes and many manufacturers of microscopes such as Nikon or Zeiss also sell adapters for DSLR cameras. The coupler and adaptor is a more secure method to attach a DSLR to the microscope; however, it is important to select the coupler and mount that will match with the specific microscope and camera system you are using. Make sure the coupling and mounting device are of good quality before purchasing because with these items, if you purchase lesser quality products, the optical elements will produce poor quality images. Be aware of the type of imaging sensor your camera contains. Full-frame sensors and cropped sensors will have different magnifications.

When the DSLR is attached to the coupling device, focusing can be done a few ways. First, the image projected from the microscope can be cast directly onto the imaging sensor without the use of a lens for focusing; however, seeing a clear image can be difficult because of the coarseness of the viewfinder glass. It is important to set the DSLR viewfinder reticle similar to adjusting the eyepiece of the microscope by adjusting the diopter dial near the eyepiece of the camera. The camera diopter only affects the image as seen through the viewfinder. Another method that is available on newer DSLR camera systems is to focus on the subject using the live-view mode. This allows the image to be projected directly onto the imaging sensor and conveyed to a computer or monitor for precise viewing to compose and focus the sample. If only using the camera preview window it may be too small and difficult to properly focus while photographing active events. One must be careful because the mirror and shutter could cause vibration when pressing the shutter release button to capture the image.

Parfocalizing a microscope for the image distance and eyepieces can easily be done by first focusing the image in the camera's viewfinder. Once the image has been focused in the camera, re-direct the image back to the microscope's eyepieces. Using the eyepieces diopters only, re-focus the image without changing the working distance. If done properly, both images should be in the same plane of focus.

Vibration

Vibration creates many negative issues when creating a photomicrograph. Vibration can be created by many sources ranging from the camera itself and up to situations near the microscope or at distances far from where the work is being done. Vibration will cause a well-focused subject to appear un-sharp and blurry from the very slightest movement during the imaging process. Basic items such as internal light fans and computers located on the microscopy table can create the slightest vibration to deteriorate image quality. Environmental issues such as elevators, HVAC (heating, ventilation, and air conditioning) systems, or from traffic such as highways, subways, or large trucks near the building can also be a source of vibration. Microscopy anti-vibration tables are available but are very expensive. Vibration reduction lenses and camera settings can reduce the amount of vibration and are a reasonable method to help manage vibration. Image shake and artifacts created by vibration can be removed with image processing but this method is not the best solution.

The camera itself can create vibration simply by pressing the shutter-release button, which can move the camera enough to create image shake. The mirror in a DSLR camera that permits viewing of the image will move out of the way when the focal plane shutter opens and closes to capture the image, and will always cause vibration from the mechanical action taking place. These effects are controllable by using slower shutter speeds instead of shorter exposure times. The longer exposure time will essentially minimize the effect of the vibration by the longer and more static exposure.

Minimizing the camera vibration can be accomplished by activation the camera from a tethered computer using Adobe® Lightroom or other software that has the ability to control the camera. Another method to trigger a camera is to use the camera's self-timer. There is also a remote shutter release where an operator can trigger the shutter without touching the camera itself.

The DSLR mirror lock-up feature is most likely the best tool to control camera vibration. The operator focuses the image first, then the mirror is locked up; the mirror moves out of the imaging path prior to exposure to allow the focused image to be captured directly onto the imaging sensor when the shutter opens and closes. Once the camera relaxes from the mirror movement, the exposure is taken creating a high-quality vibration-free image. It is good practice to take multiple images of the same subject to be able to choose an image that might be a bit sharper than the others.

Advanced Methods to Produce Contrast

Darkfield Illumination

Photomicrographs that contain objects with high contrast and appear white on a field of nearly black are created with darkfield illumination. Hairs and fibers might benefit from using this technique. Darkfield methods require the need to use a special condenser but all other elements of the microscope remain the same. Creating a dark background has some challenges and results are contingent on the sample and its preparation. Everything and anything that ends up in the preparation can glow white in this type of illumination.

Darkfield illumination is created by using an oblique angle lighting technique to illuminate the sample. The illumination comes from oblique angles to the system's optical axis. Light that normally would illuminate the background (zero order) is subtracted from the system using an opaque disk located where the aperture diaphragm would normally be located. The diameter of the background illumination should be equal to or greater than the NA (numerical aperture) of the objective. Anything in the system that is transparent will refract light and will be illuminated, especially dirt. Cleanliness in sample prep is an absolute requirement.

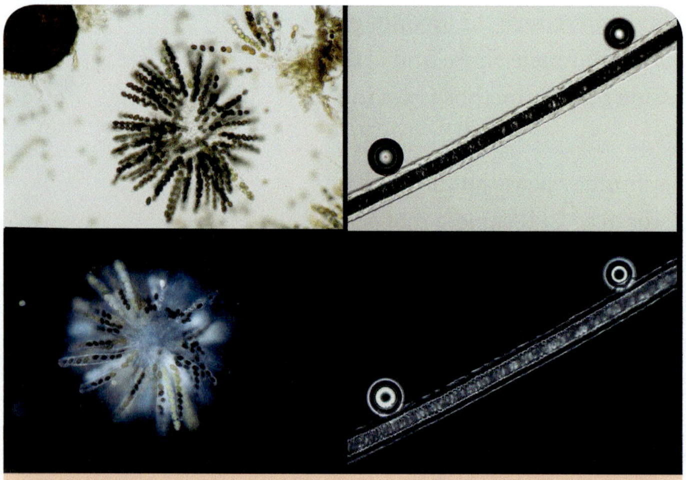

Figure 9.7 This figure on the left shares how Sordaria fimicola will appear in brightfield illumination (BF) on the top and in darkfield (DF) on the bottom. The image on the right features a dog hair and air bubbles examined with BF on the top and DF on the bottom. A 10x objective was used to photograph both samples
Image courtesy of Michael Peres

Differential Interference Contrast (DIC)

Creating contrast makes the near invisible visible. Differential interference contrast is an effective microscopy technique but it is very expensive. DIC is an interference technique that is very useful for examining unstained and living materials for different reasons than darkfield. DIC images will have topography or relief, creating a 3D effect. The technique to create DIC is complex and uses interference to produce images that contain contrast and structural information. The image has a topographical map appearance of the subject. DIC images may appear monochromatic but colors can be created using an additional quartz wedge. A quartz wedge is a special optical element used to create multiple beams of light from one.

Fluorescence

Fluorescence in microscopy is challenging because of the combination of magnification and low-light conditions increasing the problems needed to create images. Fluorescence microscopy uses epi-illumination. Epi-illumination shines light onto the sample from above. A few reasons for the need to come from above the surface absorbs and scatters the light creating a better separation and brightness of the sample.

When working with fluorescence, the sample might be infused with a liquid stain that essentially glows, or fluoresces, when illuminated with high, short-wave energy where the stained material sample absorbs short-wave energy and re-emits it as longer-wave energy or common light. These dyes have a few names such as fluorochromes, fluorophores, probes, or markers. In the forensic sciences, some objects might exhibit fluorescence, which might be a characteristic behavior of a piece of trace evidence.

Polarized Light

It is possible to use any microscope for use as a polarized light by placing a linear polarizing filter on the field stop and another polarizing filter, which is called

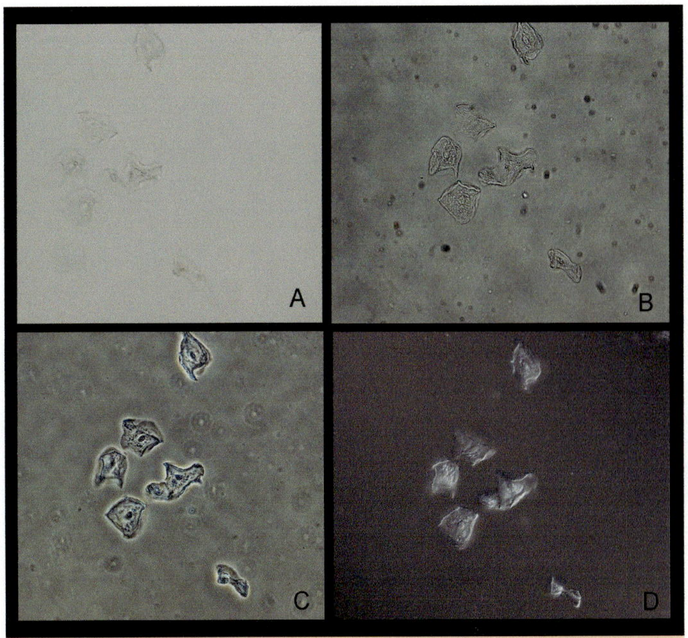

Figure 9.8 This illustration reveals how one subject—cheek cells—will appear when examined using various methods. Image A: unstained cheek cells photographed using brightfield microscope, 10x objective and with the aperture wide open. Image B: the aperture diaphragm was completely closed down. Image C: phase contrast revealing internal structure. Image D: differential interference contrast (DIC) reveals sample topographical information

Image courtesy of Michael Peres

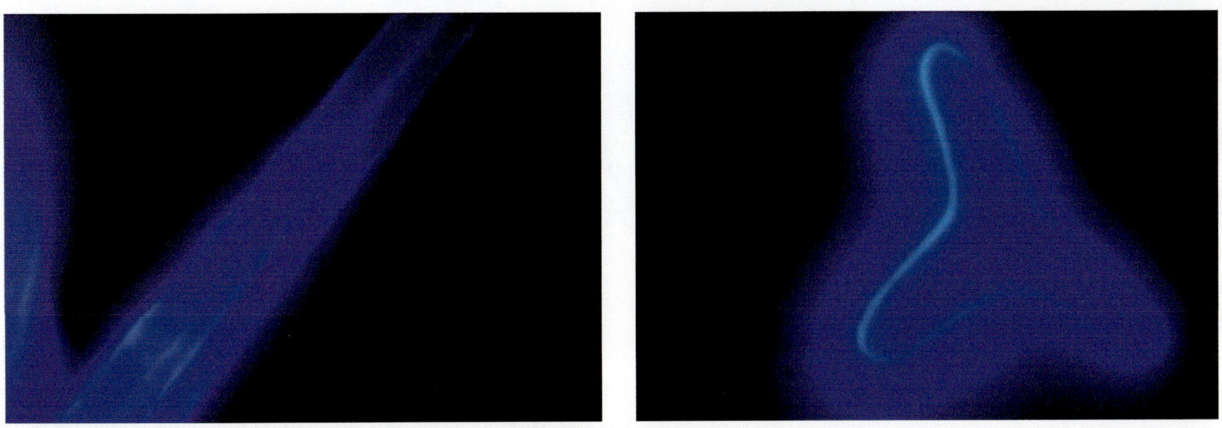

Figures 9.9–9.10 A tri-lobal fiber showing acquired fluorescence as a result of being washed in a cleaner containing optical brighteners

Image courtesy of Jeff Buszka

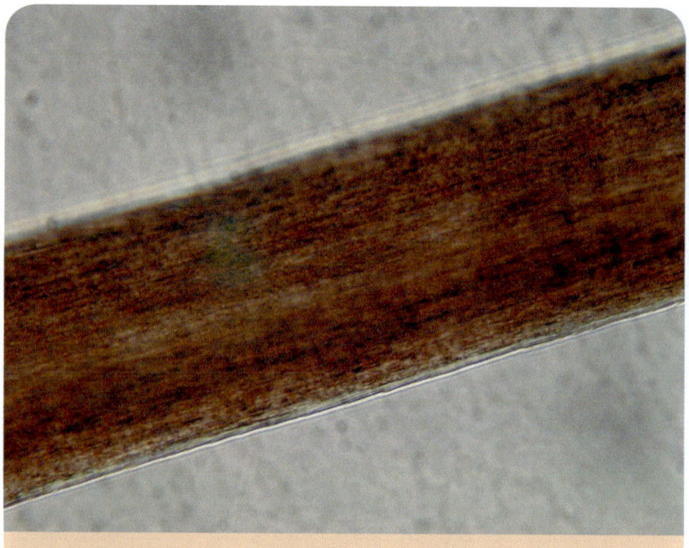

Figure 9.11 Specimen with unpolarized filtration
Image courtesy of Brandi Clark

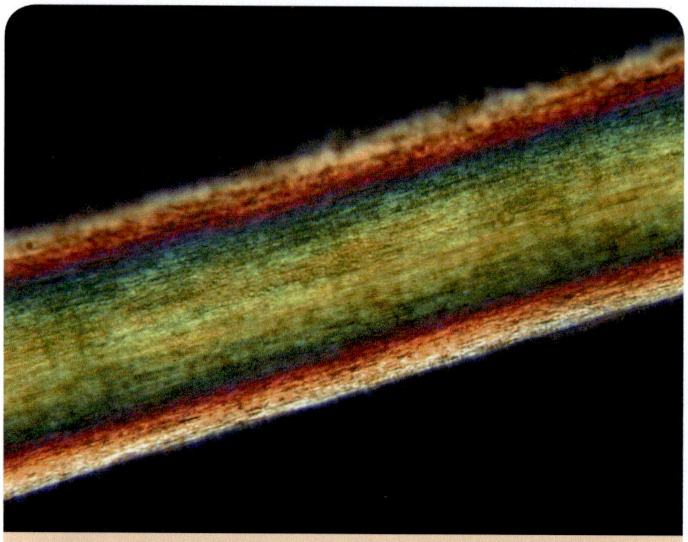

Figure 9.12 Specimen with brightfield polarized light filtration
Image courtesy of Brandi Clark

an analyzer when located behind the objective or in front of the eyepiece. The images from this type of microscope conversion would be qualitative but not quantitative. For true analytical work a true polarizing light microscope is required and one that has POL objectives that are stress-free. This instrument would also have a nosepiece that can be centered and have a circular or rotating stage.

The fundamental advantage for using polarizing light is to evaluate for the presence of birefringence in materials. Birefringence is behavior, where a material that is composed of multiple refractive indices will reveal colors when examined using polarized light. A material with one refractive index would be characterized as isotropic and a material with multiple refractive indices is said to be anisotropic. Glass, water, and air are isotropic. When an object of unknown refractive index is placed in an optical system where two linear polarizing filters are oriented at a 90 degree angle to one another or crossed, the presence of refractive properties can be observed and photographed. Substances that reveal colors and are lit against the black or extinguished background are anisotropic and objects that are black or do not glow are isotropic materials. The colors produced using polarized light can be used to identify materials based on their refractive properties.

Evidence such as hairs, fibers, and glass are often visualized using a polarized light microscope. The McCrone Institute in Chicago is well known for its polarized light microscopy short courses.

Suggested Reading

Alfred A. Blaker, *Handbook for Scientific Photography* (2nd edition), Focal Press, 1989.

Barbara Foster, *Optimizing Light Microscopy for Biological & Clinical Labs*, Kendall Hunt, 1997.

H. Lou Gibson, *Close-up Photography and Photomacrography*, Eastman Kodak Co., 1970.

Lester Lefkowitz, *Manual of Close-Up Photography*, Watson-Guptill, 1979.

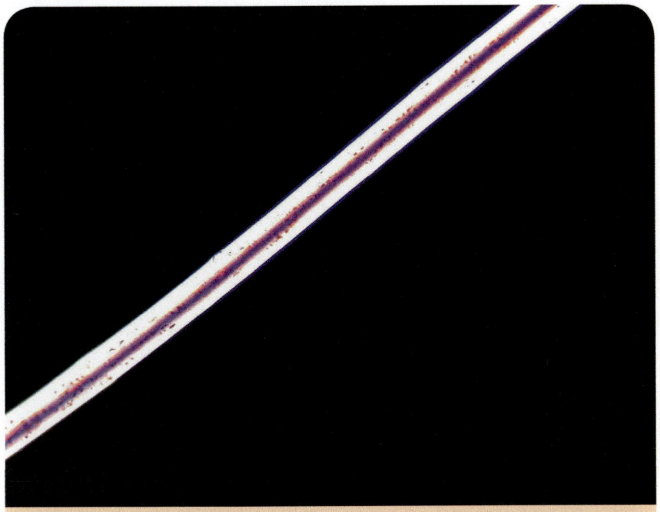

Figure 9.13 Specimen with brightfield polarized light filtration
Image courtesy of Brandi Clark

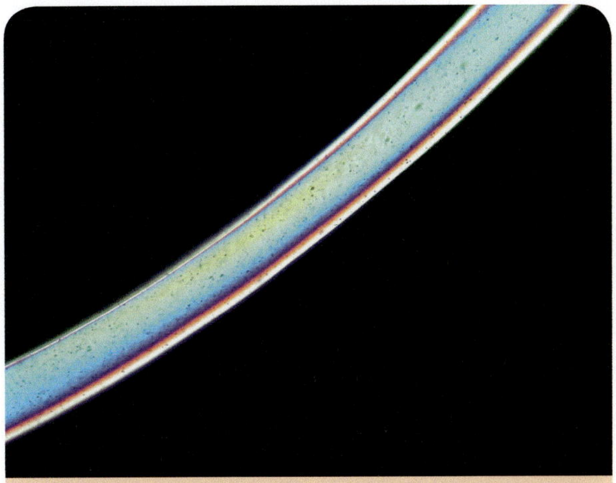

Figure 9.14 Specimen with brightfield polarized light filtration
Image courtesy of Brandi Clark

Douglas B. Murphy, *Fundamentals of Light Microscopy and Electronic Imaging*, Wiley-Liss, 2001.

Michael Peres, *Laboratory Imaging and Photography: Best Practices for Photomicrography and More*, Focal Press, 2016.

Rob Sheppard, *Macro Photography*, Pearson Education, 2015.

Brian Herman Springer, *Fluorescence Microscopy* (Microscopy Handbooks) (2nd Edition), Garland Science, 1998.

John Paul Vetter, *Biomedical Photography*, Focal Press, 1992.

Randy O. Wayne, *Light and Video Microscopy* (2nd edition), Academic Press, 2013.

http://micro.magnet.fsu.edu/primer/index.html

www.olympusmicro.com

www.microscopyu.com

www.leica-microsystems.com/home/

http://zeiss-campus.magnet.fsu.edu/index.htm

Chapter 10 High Speed and Time-Lapse

High-Speed Photography

High-speed photography is a technique of taking pictures of things that happen with very fast action. It may involve either the taking of still photographs that freeze motion, or the recording of an event using video at an increased frame rate sometimes referred to as slow-motion video. High-speed photography is useful for documenting action that is too fast for the human eye to see, such as blood droplets, guns firing, or the impact of an instrument.

Capturing a High-Speed Photograph

Capturing a photograph of high-speed events may be as simple as just using a fast shutter speed; however, many events will require other methods for creating a short duration exposure. The technique that is used will depend largely upon the event itself and what is being photographed. For action that cannot be captured with shutter speed alone, a short duration electronic flash or high-speed strobe must be used. For example, a shutter speed of 1/2500, which is considered very fast as a shutter speed, may be fast enough to freeze the motion of a moving vehicle, though it is not nearly fast enough for a high-speed event such as a moving bullet. Even a slow bullet, will travel approximately 950 feet per second and would move approximately 4.5 inches during that 1/2500 exposure. A portable flash may also not be fast enough to stop a bullet in motion by itself. However, there are many high-speed events that a portable flash is suitable for, like documenting blood droplets in motion, impacts to a surface, or the smoke from a discharging weapon.

Typical handheld flash units at full power represent approximately a 1/1000 second exposure, but at 128th power they may reach speeds of 1/40,000 sec. Even though the light from a flash appears to be an instantaneous event, there is a duration during which the light is on that is shorter at lower speeds. So using a flash at a lower power will generate less light but create shorter exposures.

Stopping the motion of something like a bullet requires an extremely high-speed flash. The premier high-speed flash, the EG&G® Microflash, is no longer commercially available;

however, there are a few types of high-speed flashes still available. The Spot Flash from Prism Science Works is an updated version of the microflash and is capable of freezing the motion of a speeding bullet. The budget-friendly Vela One® flash uses LEDs for illumination and promises 1/2,000,000 second exposures while using only 4 AA batteries for power. Also, plans to build an airgap flash may be found online; however, it should be noted that the capacitors may be very dangerous, so it is not suggested for use unless by a professional or someone versed in electronics.

Triggering the Camera

Once the exposure speed necessary is determined, a way of triggering the camera will be needed. Photographing a high-speed event requires accurate timing in order to synchronize the capture of the intended subject

There are several devices available to trigger a camera and while they all have similar features, there are pros and cons to each device. It is important to evaluate each device based on the individual needs of subject and the environment the work will be performed in. These type of trigger devices feature sensors that react to the action you are trying to record as well as an output to trigger a camera or flash. The following are some different types of sensors available. Sound triggers activate upon detecting a vibration in the air (noise), which are effective for loud events such as a firearm discharging or something breaking. A gate trigger activates when an object passes through a beam and these are useful for capturing objects in

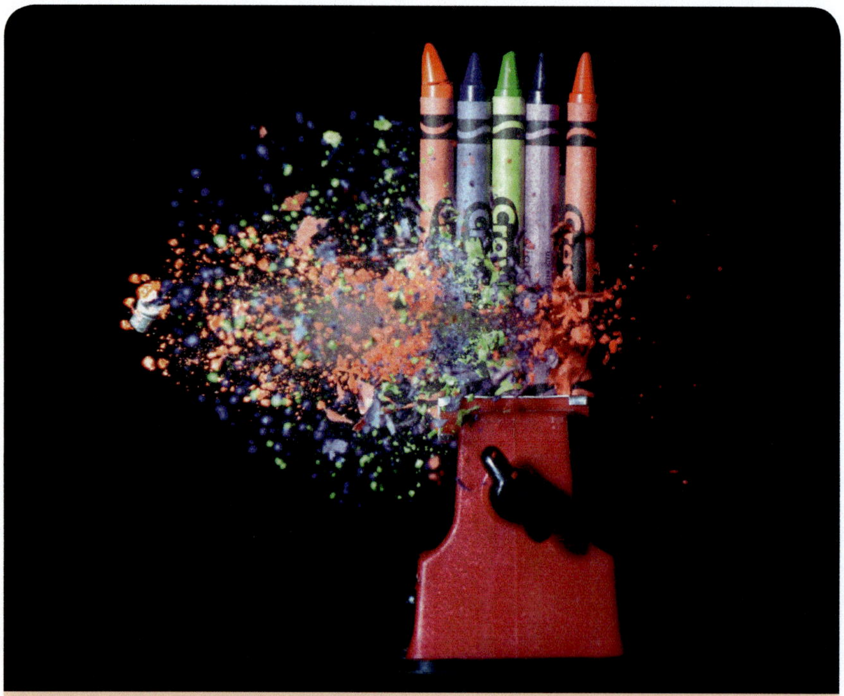

Figure 10.1 A photograph of a bullet at the moment it pierces a stack of crayons. Photographed with a sound trigger and a high-speed flash

motion such as droplets or projectiles. Contact triggers activate when an object makes contact with the trigger, useful for recording an impact. Other triggers include motion, vibration, light-activated sensors, and many more. The device should have adjustments for sensitivity and delay of the triggers as well. Also be sure to consider the speed of the device as some events may require more sophisticated circuitry in order to capture the event. For example, if you want to capture a bullet coming out of the barrel of a firearm, an app-controlled trigger may not suffice

The following is a list of currently commercially available devices, the type of sensors they use, and features:

MIOPS $239: light sensor, sound sensor, gate trigger, combination mode, smartphone controllable.

The Stopshot: a programmable high-speed trigger and intervalometer device featuring three outputs, a sound trigger, gate trigger, and control for multiple other accessories. A drop kit is available for creating droplets from liquid.

The Mumford Time Machine: a programmable high-speed trigger and intervalometer that features sound, vibration, gate, a light sensor, laser and IR cross-beam sensors as well as a ballistic sensor. Other accessories available include a rotary table, drip kit, and flash sequencers ($325 + accessories).

Other similar devices include the camera axe ($185 + accessories) and universal photo timer ($218 including some accessories).

For labs/photographers on a budget, or perhaps a do-it-yourselfer, several high-speed kits are available from HiViz.com. Sound, photo gate, and light triggers are available as well as kits for controlling water drops.

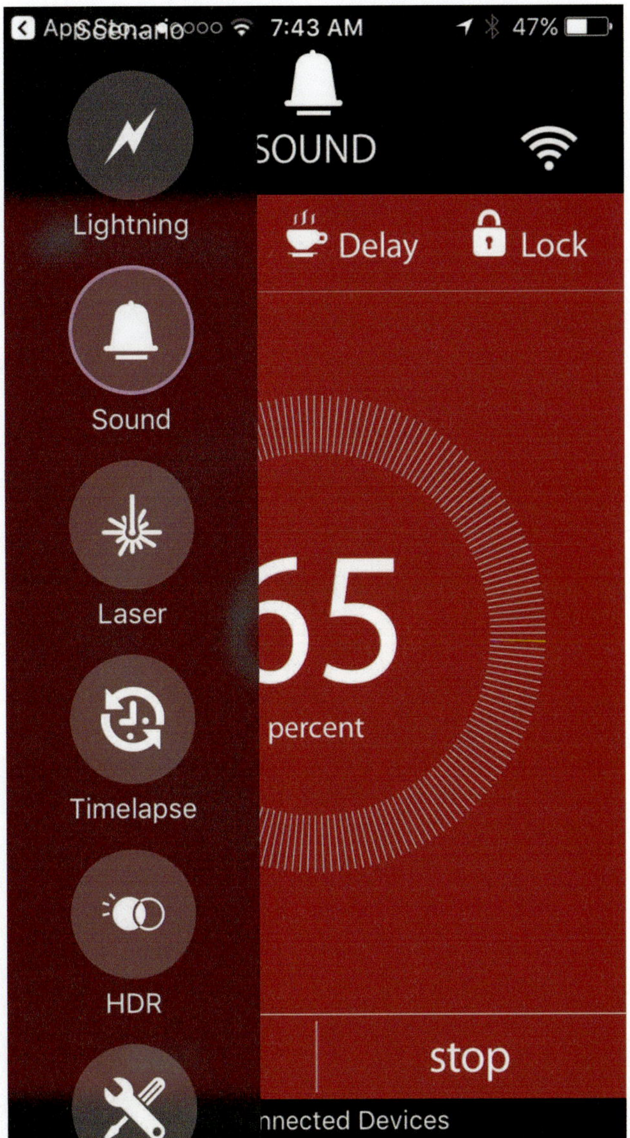

Figure 10.2 A screenshot from the MIOPS smartphone application

Setup for High-Speed Photography

Capturing high-speed photographs may require the assistance of others and it can be useful to have some volunteers around if needed. Find a location that is suitable for the action to be documented. Safety is key as high-speed events such as those using firearms or impacts may pose a danger. Be sure to take precautions to protect yourself, others, and your gear from harm.

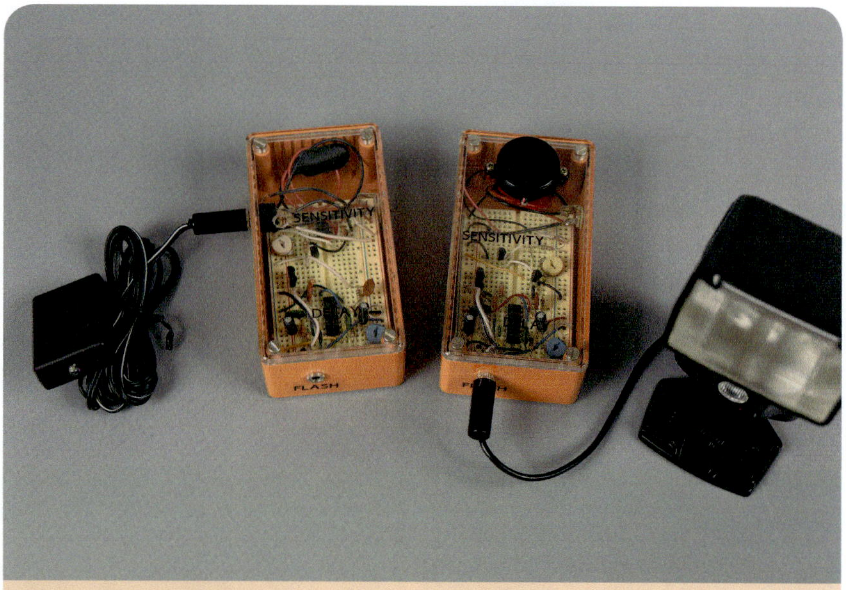

Figure 10.3 Examples of two DIY high-speed trigger kits

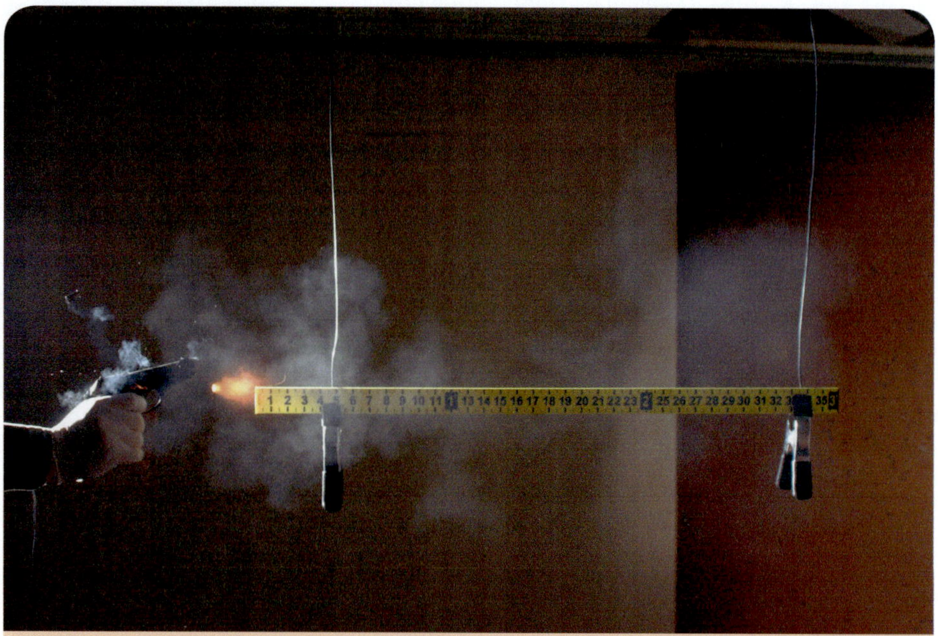

Figure 10.4 A high-speed photograph of a firearm discharging. Photographed using a DIY sound trigger and a portable flash set to low power. This setup is not fast enough to capture the bullet; however, it was fast enough to capture the smoke leaving the barrel. The image was used to demonstrate the distance that GSR (gun shot residue) travels from the gun

It may require several tries to get the shot to your satisfaction, so it is best to ensure the equipment is secured against movement. This usually requires the use of a tripod for mounting the camera, a mount for the flash, and perhaps the action taking place as well.

High-speed photographs typically require a great deal of light because of the short exposure time. If you are using the shutter to stop the action, either a high-speed sync flash or bright studio lights are necessary. To get the maximum brightness from an electronic flash useful for high-speed photography, place it as close to the subject as possible. Compose the image for the area in which the action will take place. It may be necessary to pre-focus the camera and set the lens to manual focus. Using an electronic flash light meter, determine the exposure necessary to capture the image. For flash photography, only the aperture can be used to control the amount of light hitting the camera sensor

Be sure to test the setup, especially the timing, and be sure the event will happen in front of the camera. The timing of the exposure may be adjusted using the delay on the capture device. If the action happens prior to the camera's zone of view activating increase the delay or vice versa. With the use of a sound trigger, the timing may be adjusted by varying

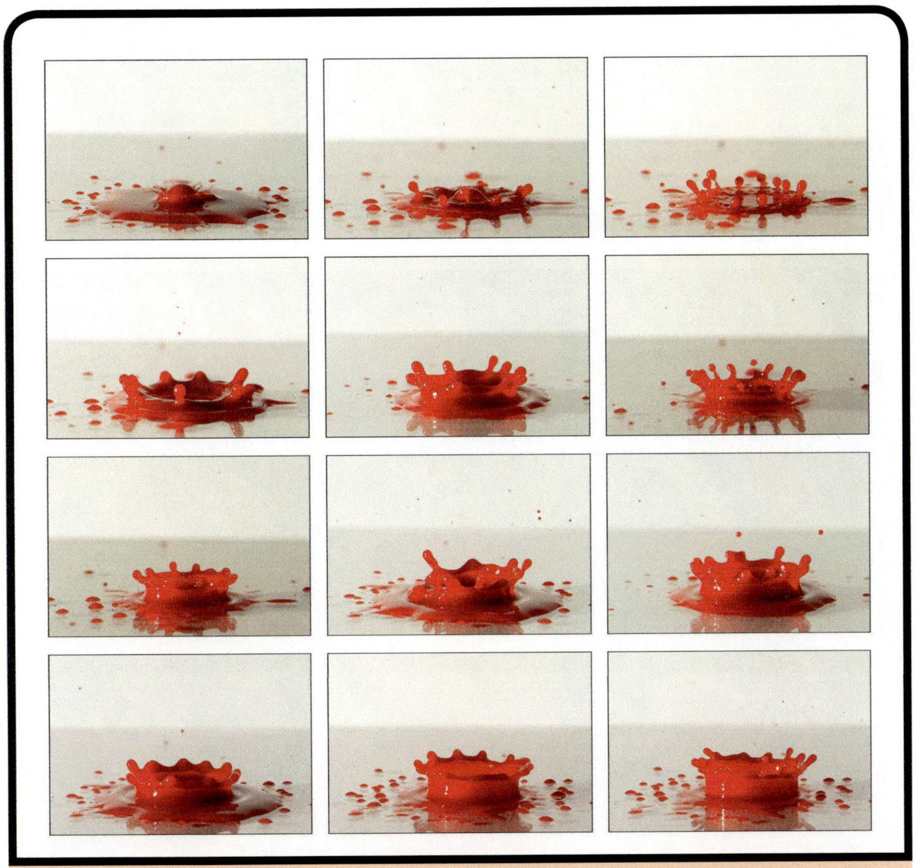

Figure 10.5 High-speed photographs of blood droplets impacting a surface

the distance of the microphone to the sound. The further the microphone is from the sound the longer the delay.

When using electronic flash to capture the exposure, the room should be relatively (if not totally) dark. Once everything is completely set up and ready, darken the room and open the shutter using the bulb setting. Trigger the action, which should also trigger the flash. Once

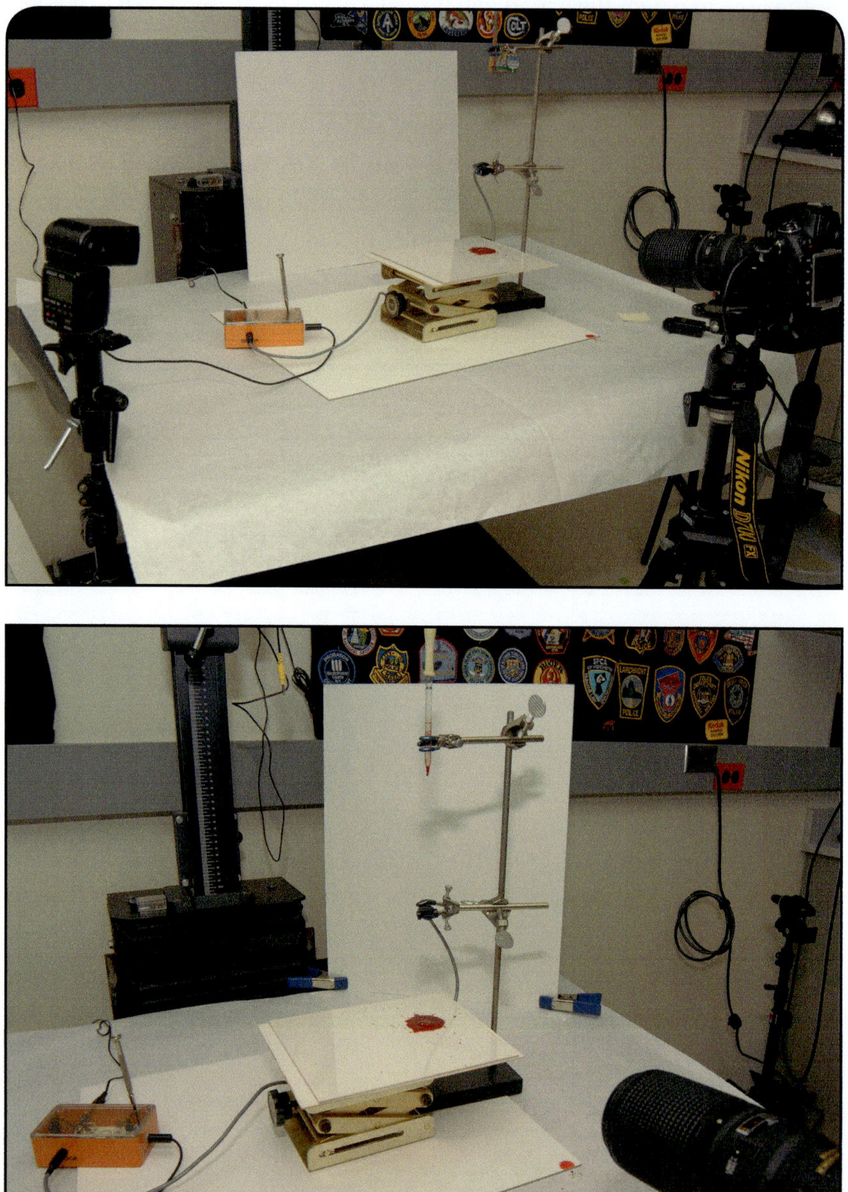

Figures 10.6–10.7 The setup for capturing blood droplets in motion. A photo-gate sensor was used to trigger the flash when a droplet passed through the sensor. The delay was adjusted to capture the precise moment the blood struck a surface. A fair amount of trial and error is necessary for success

the action has completed close the shutter. Evaluate the image and make any adjustments to the timing or exposure as necessary.

High-Speed Video

High-speed video, sometimes referred to as slow-motion video or just slow-mo, is the technique of recording video at high frame rates and playing it back at a slower speed. The typical frame rate used for video is approximately 24–30 frames per second. Slow-motion video is achieved by recording video at higher speeds and playing it back at normal speed. The faster the recording speed, the slower the action can be played back. One benefit of this technique over capturing a high-speed photograph is the ability to visualize action over a period of time.

Cameras

There are several models of high-speed digital cameras available today. High-end cameras are capable of recording thousands of frames per second. As you can imagine, high-end cameras are also much higher in cost. Some may cost tens, or even hundreds, of thousands of dollars. Some cameras are designed for machine vision, or high-speed inspection and require the use of a computer and frame-capture cards, while others are standalone and can record to a flash drive or other storage device. Keep in mind that the more frames per second you are recording, the more storage space required. Manufacturers of high-end cameras include Vision Research, Fastec, and Photron.

Recent additions to the market of high-speed cameras include the Edgertronic and fps1000, both of which were successfully funded through the website kickstarter.com. They are each capable of speeds as high as approximately 18,000 fps (at reduced resolutions). These cameras are much less costly than the high-end cameras above.

Several consumer-grade digital camera models are capable of high-speed video, some up to or over 1000 frames per second. Casio high-speed cameras are capable of 1000 fps at a reduced resolution of 224 × 64px, the Nikon 1 AW1 and J3 through J5 that are capable of 1200fps at resolutions up to 414 × 144px, and the Sony RX1000 V and RX10 III will record at 960fps at a capture resolution of 1136 × 384px.

Many action cameras, like the GoPro Hero or Sony Action Cam, are capable of recording at up to 240 frames per second. As well phones like the iPhone and Samsung line are capable of recording at 240 frames per second. These are certainly not the fastest high-speed cameras on the market, but they may be readily available and may be able to do the job in a pinch.

The best camera for your needs will depend upon the speed of the action you are trying to record as well as your budget

Shutter Speed

Shutter speeds, just like in high-speed photography, play a role in stopping action in a digital video as well. Even while recording at high frame rates, the shutter inside your camera may

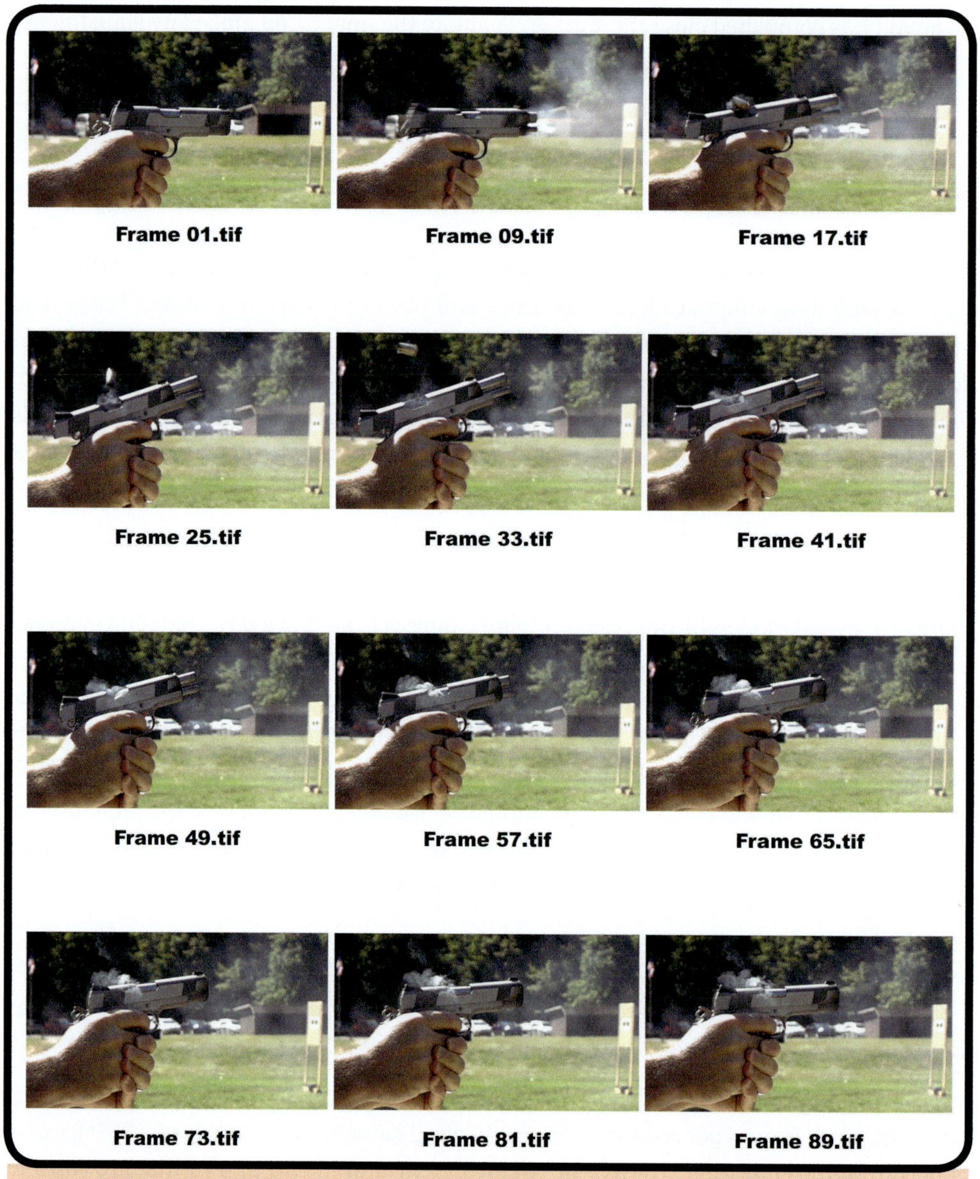

Figure 10.8 Several frames from a high-speed video of a handgun discharging. The video was captured using a Sony RX10 II set at 960 frames per second. Photographer Joseph P. Mancini. The frames were exported from the video using the steps described in Chapter 7, Figures 7.23–7.27. The original video may be viewed at https://youtu.be/q9fu6ByCZA0

still be responsible for part of the exposure. Faster shutter speeds will minimize the motion blur in each of the frames of video.

Lighting for High-Speed Video

A great deal of light is typically required for shooting high-speed video. Upwards of five times more light is required for shooting at 1000 fps than for shooting at 30fps. Since the video will be rolling for some duration, continuous lighting will be needed. Another issue with high-speed lighting is flicker. Lamps that are powered by electricity have a natural occurring cycle which may cause the light to dim slightly. This flicker can occur with tungsten, fluorescent, and even some LED bulbs. To avoid flicker use "flicker-free" lights, either tungsten bulbs over 5000 watts, fluorescent bulbs that use high-frequency ballasts, or LED bulbs that are powered by DC current.

Time-Lapse Photography

Time-lapse photography is the opposite of high-speed photography, as it speeds up an event. Time-lapse photography can be a useful tool when photographing an event that occurs over a longer period of time. An example of an event that can benefit from time-lapse photography would be construction (forensic engineering), a crime scene search or archaeological dig, or a decomposition study. Many times but not always, time-lapse images are displayed as videos that allow the event to be watched in accelerated time.

Prior to making the first exposure, several factors should be considered. How long does the event last from start to finish? Is the process/event linear or logarithmic in its behavior(s), does it have an acceleration or deceleration component, or does it occur at the same rate throughout? And lastly, how long will the video's playtime be? The answers to these questions will influence decisions about the time increment between exposures and how many frames are needed to produce a screen time of the desired length.

If individual single frames of the event will be used for print applications, moving forward is a relatively straightforward. Select the best frames and build a composite.

If the final images will be displayed as a video, you must consider how long the event you are recording will last, as well as how long you want the final video to be. You must also consider the playback frames per second (fps), at the very least 24fps in order to convey smooth motion. Therefore, a ten-second video will require 240 frames if shown at 24fps. If the desired event takes 24 hours from start to finish, and a 10-second video is desired, one photograph would need to be taken each six minutes. Time can be shortened or lengthened in time-lapse photography and events can be speeded up or slowed down by changing the frame rate of display or by changing the number of the individual images captured.

Use the following formula to determine the duration between shots for a particular scenario:

(Desired duration) × (frames per second) = frames needed
(length of event in seconds)/(frames needed) = duration between shots

Setup

The key to success with time-lapse photography is to ensure that nothing changes to the camera settings or to the artificial lighting (if used) during recording of the frames. If the exposure changes during capture, the video may exhibit a "flicker" or brightness variance throughout. This can be very distracting when watching the time-lapse video. When time-lapse work is done using ambient or found light, this flicker or variance of the lighting may be part of the event. If the lighting and its brightness remain constant during the event, it is recommended to use a camera's manual mode to minimize any variances that may be produced by the automatic light measurement features of the camera. It is also recommended that the color temperature be set manually as well. If the lighting does change during the event, then using the automatic camera exposure mode may be more practical allowing for better management of the brightness changes

It is also important that the camera or optics do not move during the recording as well. As such, a tripod or other sturdy mount is recommended to minimize movements to the camera that will produce "jittery" or an unstable appearance in the final video.

Since the vast majority of time-lapse work is shown in video format, the files will – in all probability – be shot in JPEG format. Making hundreds or thousands of TIFF or RAW files that will subsequently require image processing and then video editing may be time- and resource-consuming. It should be noted though that there may be compromises when using JPEGs such as data compression or artifacts. Also important is to consider the output size of the final video. Since digital camera images are typically several megapixels in resolution, but high-definition video resolution is only just over 2 megapixels (and 4k video is just over 8 megapixels), it may be advantageous to take the images at a reduced size

Many point-and-shoot, smartphone, and DSLR cameras are capable of creating time-lapse recordings directly. Unfortunately, every camera, and software program, will have differences in how they are set up and operate for this type of work. It would be impossible to offer specifics for all products, so we will use some examples to address the most global considerations and settings. These suggestions will need to be adapted as necessary to your equipment and applications. Using a DSLR camera can be a very good choice for time-lapse photography applications because of its features, high-quality output, and excellent controls.

Shooting the Still Photographs

Once the camera position has been determined and the various exposure attributes set, it is time to take the individual photographs that will make up the frames of the video. Making a time-lapse movie is the product of many individual exposures. Producing this type of media without automation can be accomplished but it will be fraught with challenges. It is more practical to program an electronic controller to make the exposures using an internal timing application called an intervalometer. This device allows an operator to program a camera to take pictures using specific time increments between exposures as needed. Intervalometers are valuable tools and allow precise and autonomous operation of the camera over a long period of time. An intervalometer can be embedded in camera software or operate as a remote trigger.

Many cameras have a built-in intervalometer, interval timer, or time-lapse mode. If your particular model does not, there are several external triggers available like the Canon TC80N3 trigger, the Nikon MC-36, or the Vello ShutterBoss which is available for several cameras. Regardless of the camera, make a test exposure with it to ensure that all functions work correctly.

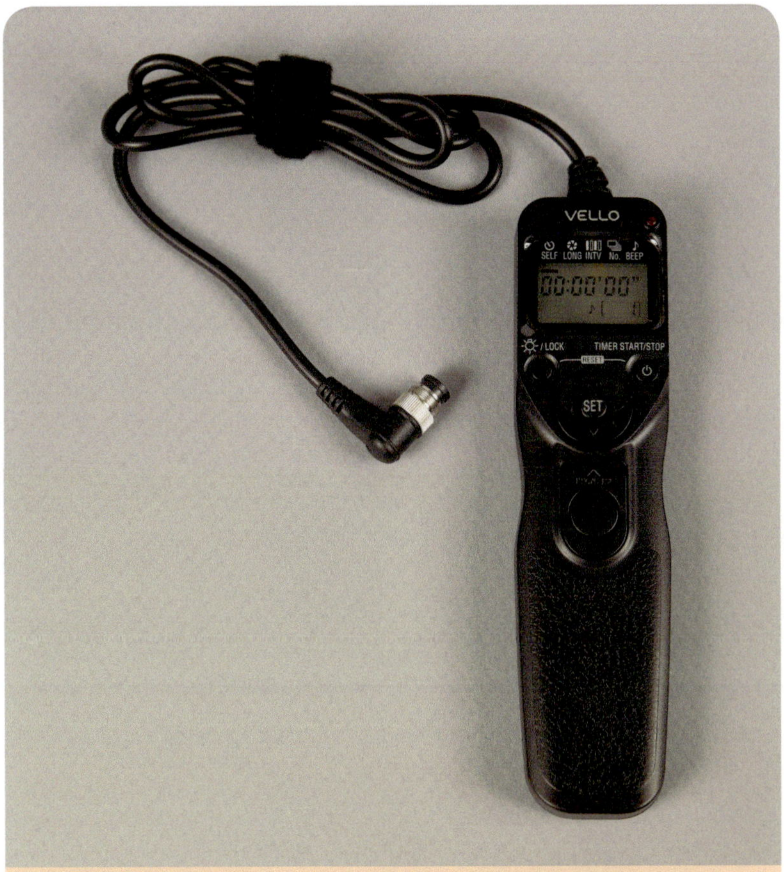

Figure 10.9 An intervalometer for a Nikon camera

Photographing a Time-Lapse Sequence

1. Set the time-lapse shooting function in the camera's menu or on the intervalometer.
   - Set when to begin the shooting sequence.
   - Set time increment between exposures.
   - Set how long the session experiment will last.
2. Be sure there is enough memory available on the memory card. Photographing several exposures over time will create significant amounts of data. It would be a problem if the event could not be recorded from the start to finish because of a lack of storage on a media card.
3. Disable all power consuming settings such as LCD preview, autofocus, and image stabilization on the lens.
4. Reformat the card before exposing a time-lapse sequence. Losing a few critical frames can render the project unusable. Fast cards are also suggested.
5. Set the white balance to the light you are photographing in. Do not use auto white balance settings.

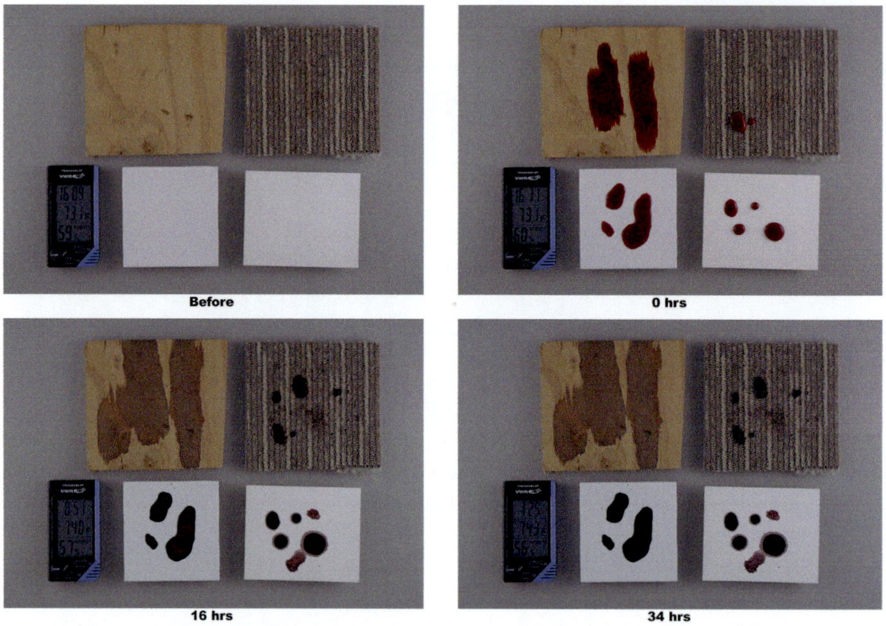

Figure 10.10 A time-lapse sequence of blood drying. The resulting video may be viewed at https://youtu.be/xKnrd4s2W4g

6. Set the camera's exposure attributes including ISO, aperture, and shutter speed. Do not use auto exposure.
7. Be sure there is enough power in your batteries or use an AC adapter if available.

Reducing Flicker in Time-Lapse Videos

The final time-lapse video may exhibit a flicker due to small differences in the exposure of the individual frames. In order to reduce flicker, follow these guidelines:

- Shoot in manual mode; avoid using auto exposure of any kind. If there will be a considerable difference in the brightness of the subject, then it is best to use aperture priority mode.
- Cover the camera eyepiece during shooting if you are using any automatic exposure control.
- Use a continuous light source such as tungsten lights; if you must use a flash set it to manual mode and adjust the power setting for the correct exposure.
- Expose with the aperture wide open or use a manual lens that allows locking in the f-stop. If you are using a newer lens that doesn't lock in the f-stop, it is possible to trick the lens by setting the f-stop, then depressing the depth of field preview button while unlocking and slightly turning the lens. This may cause the camera to display an error message, but it should still shoot in manual mode.

- If flicker is unavoidable, there are programs available to de-flicker during postproduction. Examples of such programs include LRTimelapse, GBDeflicker, and Digital Anarchy's Flicker Free (a video software plugin).

Once considerations for all the above aspects of the process have been finalized, the individual frames can be exposed. Some cameras will produce a series of images that may require a small amount of image optimizing before they are inserted into a time-lapse assembly software. Some cameras are capable of creating the time-lapse movie within its features when attributes are selected from the video modes within the camera itself.

Editing Time-Lapse Images

After the shooting has been completed, there may be hundreds or more image files. The number of images is a function of the settings that were selected. In some instances, there may be advantages to improving the image attributes before merging them into time-lapse video. This might include brightness, cropping, white balance, and so on. Editing each photo one at a time would be time prohibitive but there are ways to batch process the individual files using Lightroom or Photoshop software. Keep in mind that the images produced by a digital camera are typically many megapixels in size, so they may have to be re-sized to fit video standards

Creating a Time-Lapse Video

There are software products that can assemble a time-lapse movie when using cameras that do not have this feature.

Adobe Lightroom

To create a time-lapse movie directly in Adobe® Lightroom, a preset module for time lapse will need to be added to the software. These presets can be found online and downloaded. Once a module has been added to the presets folder, the choices are quite intuitive. There is a frame-rate choice and other export mode choices are also located in the module. It is a relatively easy activity to work through.

Adobe Photoshop

To create a time-lapse video using Adobe Photoshop go to the file menu and choose open. Locate the folder containing the time-lapse files It is important to note that the images must be named in sequential order (Timelapse001, Timelapse002, etc.); if Photoshop encounters a missing number it will not

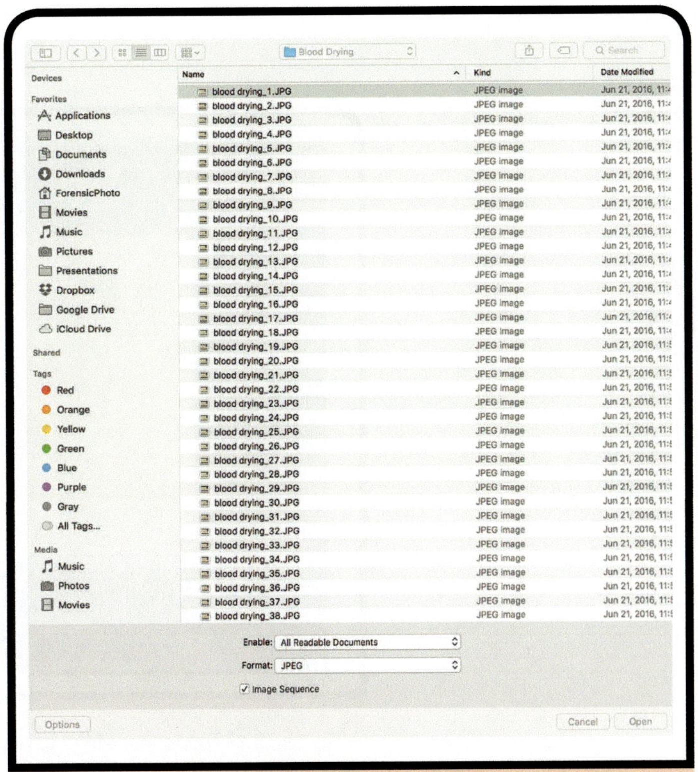

Figure 10.11 The file open dialogue box within Adobe Photoshop

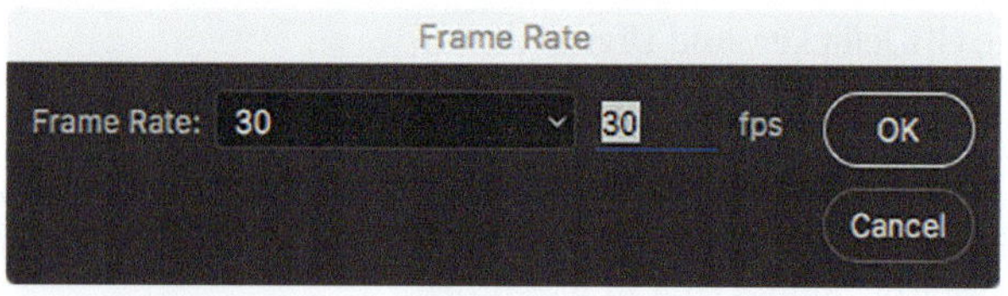

Figure 10.12 The frame-rate selection dialogue box within Adobe Photoshop

continue opening files. Choose the first file in the list, check the image sequence box, and click the open button

Select the desired frame rate and click OK.

To preview the time-lapse, be sure the timeline window is visible then click play on the timeline. Photoshop creates a new layer containing the video, and many of Photoshop's adjustments are available to apply to that video. Keep in mind that some adjustments are applied only to the current frame. Sticking to adjustment layers will prevent that. Saving a time-lapse video does not create the video, it only saves a Photoshop file. To create a video, go to the file menu and choose export > render video

Choose the output format or a preset and then click render to create the video file.

Apple QuickTime Pro

Apple QuickTime Pro 7® software is a very simple and effective choice. It operates on both Windows and Mac operating systems. To produce a time-lapse using QuickTime Pro, go to File > Open Image Sequence

Locate the folder containing the time-lapse files and select the first photo file, then hit the open button.

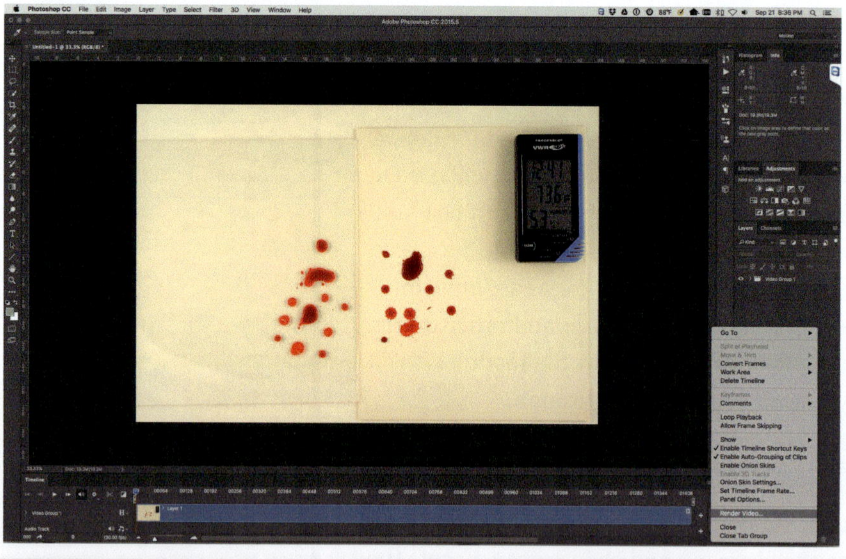

Figure 10.13 The render video option is located in either the timeline panel menu (located in the top right of the timeline window), of in the export menu

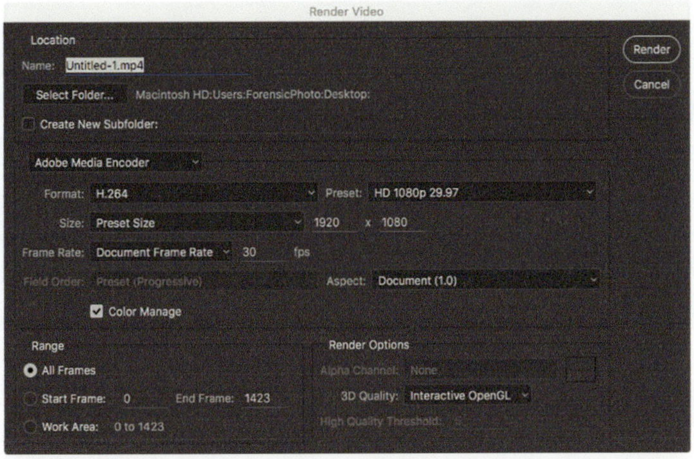

Figure 10.14 The render video dialogue box from within Adobe Photoshop. The resulting video may be seen at https://youtu.be/BRfXCiuKC84

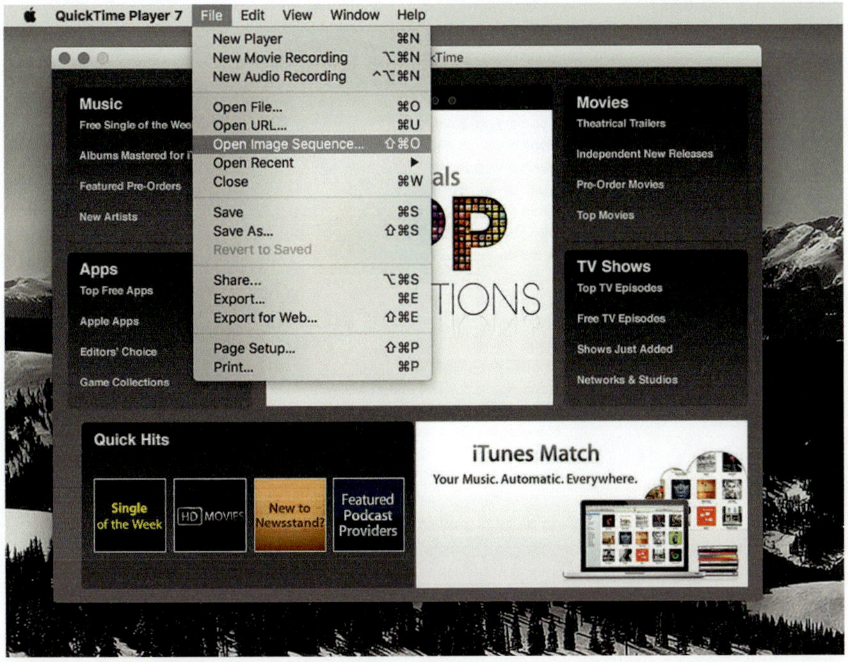

Figure 10.15 Opening an image sequence in QuickTime Pro

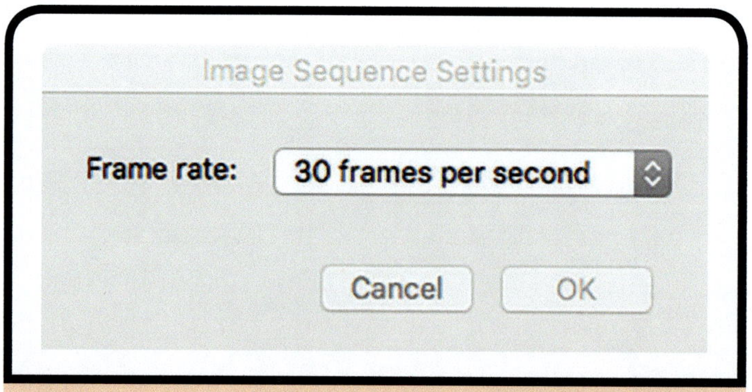

Figure 10.16 The image sequence settings dialogue box within QuickTime Pro

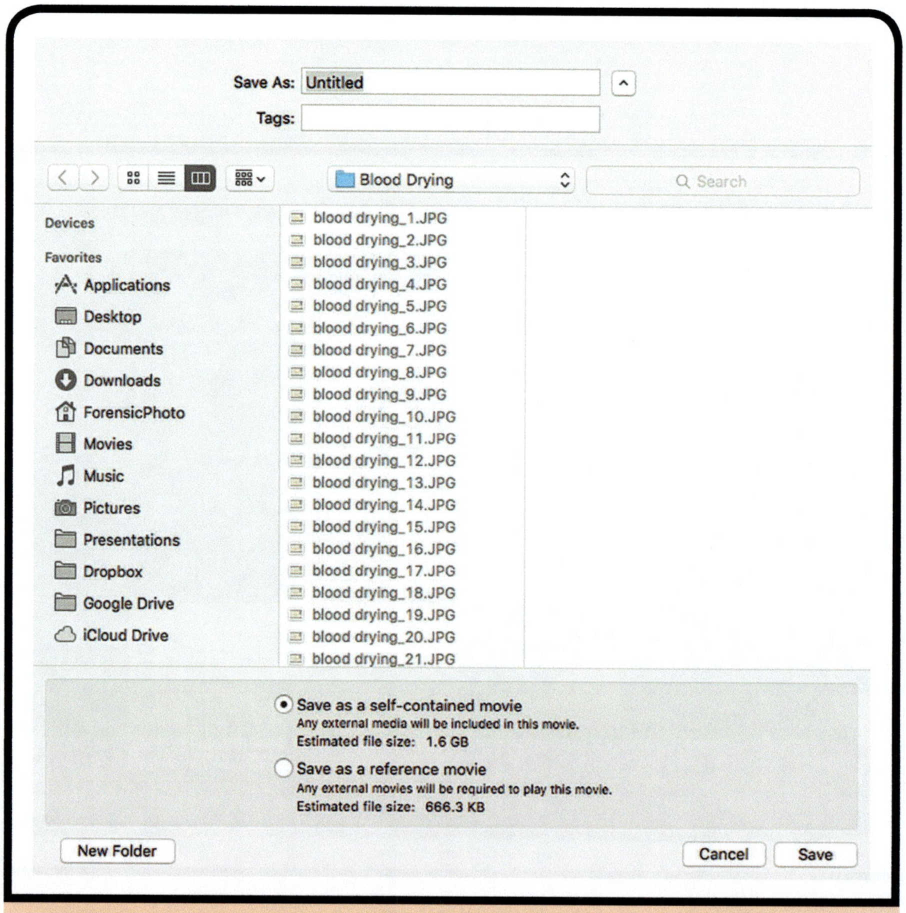

Figure 10.17 The QuickTime Pro Save As: dialogue box.

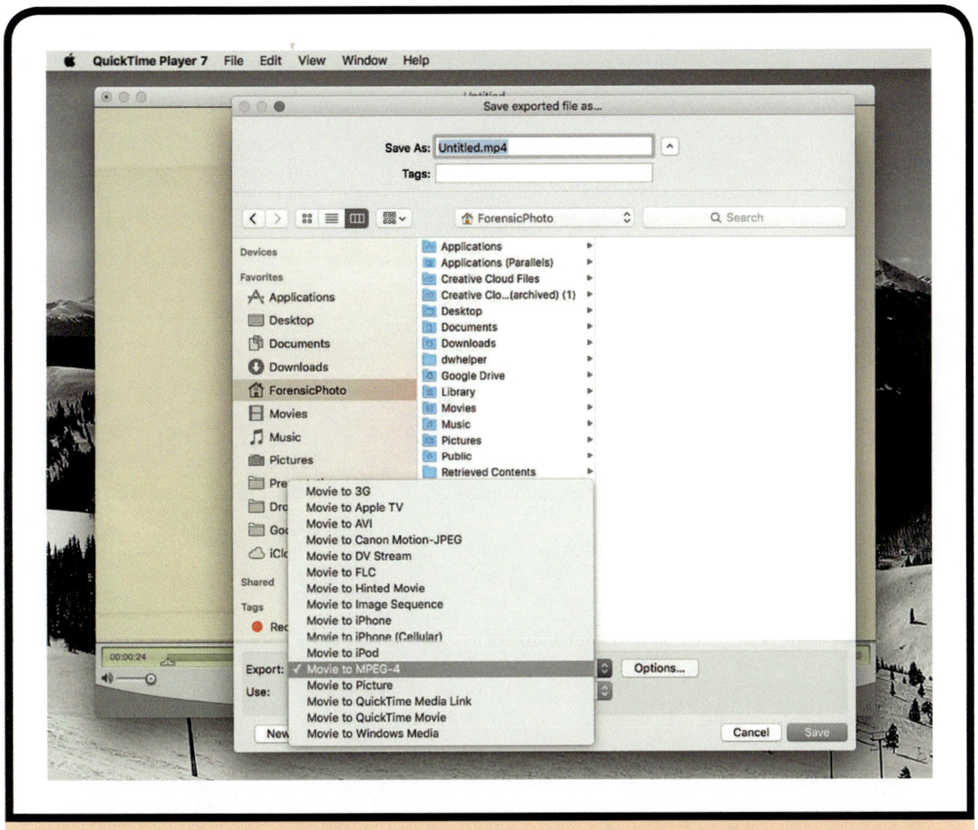

Figure 10.18 The QuickTime Pro Export dialogue box

Select the 30 fps output (or the desired frame rate) and hit OK. The software will compile the individual files into the video at this time. Select file fit to screen to preview video. The video can be trimmed to the desired length by setting the in-and-out points. Once satisfied, export and name the file. Save the file to an appropriate location selecting the desired export settings.

Choose file > save as: to save the video as a QuickTime (.mov) file.

Or choose file > export to save the video as another file type. MPEG-4 is perhaps a more cross platform compatible choice.

Chapter 11 Computational Photography

ADAM HARTLEY

Increased Depth of Field

Many areas of photography and imaging use Depth of Field (DoF) as an aesthetic component, choosing to selectively keep areas in focus or out of focus. However, in science there is little need for out of focus regions of a picture. Although technically there is only a single point in any optical path that is truly in "focus," the area of "acceptable focus" extends 1/3 in front of that point and 2/3 behind it; the total length of this DoF decreases when the lens is moved closer to the subject (increased magnification) to the point where using a microscope results in a DoF being less than a sheet of paper. The relative size of this area can be controlled by the lens's aperture, or f-stop, in an inverse relationship; the larger the f-stop, the smaller the aperture, the greater the DoF. However, there is a cost to using the aperture to increase DoF; smaller apertures reduce the resolving power of the image as well as the amount of light reaching the image plane. Ironically in situations such as high-magnification photography where DoF is at a premium, detail is important, and camera vibration is magnified, long exposures due to loss of light and reduced resolution is not desirable. Many techniques have been developed over time to achieve a greater area of focus and to overcome the limitations of traditional optics. Situations that may benefit from a greater DoF include close-up imaging of a curved surface (see Figure 11.1), a subject with a deep cavity, or a highly textured surface under high magnification.

Very early attempts to increase DoF before the advent of digital cameras and scanners were more hardware-based. A very basic technique utilized, quite literally, was cut and paste. Photographs of a subject were taken at different focus points and printed out at the same magnification. The in-focus areas of the prints were physically cut out and layered on top of each other and then photographed again. The resulting negative would have a subject that was completely in focus. This technique was very time and labor intensive and required a great amount of skill to get a quality product.

Another technique to get enhanced DoF images involved creating an image-capture apparatus. The subject would be mounted on a motorized height-adjustable stage and illuminated with a sheet of light that was narrower than the set DoF of the lens. The camera would be mounted on a stand directly above the subject and focused on the area of the sheet of light.

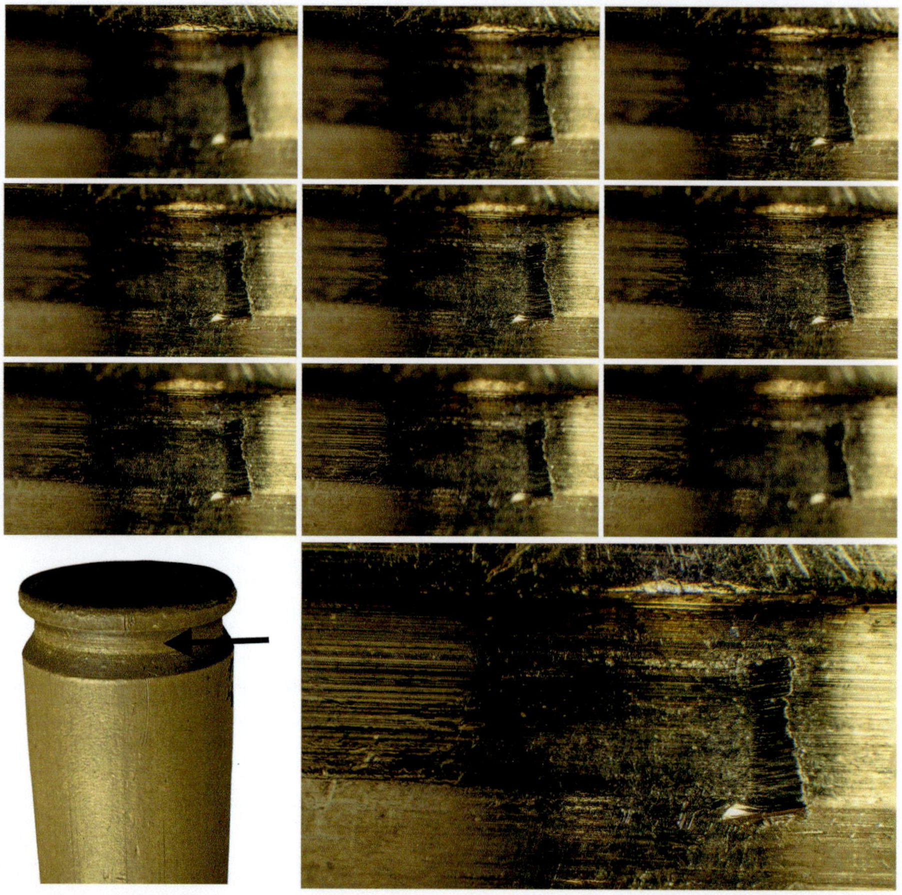

Figure 11.1 When examining evidence at the microscope it is easy to follow small details while racking your focus, but photographically documenting your observations on a curved surface can be a great challenge; the DoF is limited but the detail that needs to be captured is in an area that exceeds the area of focus even at a very small aperture. This is a situation where using an enhanced DoF technique would be beneficial

To capture the image, the room lights would be off and the shutter of the camera would be held open while the subject was moved through the light. Since only the field of focus was being illuminated, only in-focus light would be recorded, resulting in a fully in-focus image. As you can imagine this style of imaging had a good amount of limitations and was also not only labor and time intensive, but also required specialized equipment. It also didn't work on all subjects such as ones that had deep internal cavities where the sheet of light never reached and ones that had areas that were translucent or reflective that illuminated other areas of the subject while exposing.

Once computing caught up with digital imaging technology, some very high-quality but computationally intensive and expensive techniques became available. Deconvolution is a method used in microscopy for sharpening a series of images by using a point-spread function of the optical system; essentially mapping how light is diffused by the lens. By defining how the light is dispersed, the software can reverse the dispersal and create a focused image. However, the pinnacle of enhanced DoF in microscopy came with the invention of the confocal microscope. This is a tremendously complex device but the basic principle is that it only captures in-focus light by blocking the out of focus light with the use of scanning lasers and a pinhole at the focal point.

Focus Stacking

By far the most accessible method of creating enhanced depth-of-field images is through a technique known as focus stacking. This method takes principles from the previous techniques and executes them without the need for expensive software used for deconvolution, complicated equipment such as a confocal microscope, or a great time investment like cutting and pasting different prints together. Focus stacking, as the name implies, uses a stack, of images taken at various focal planes of a subject, calculates the sharpness of each layer, and then combines the sharpest areas into a single fully focused image. This technique has become so popular and widely used that most image-processing applications such as Adobe® Photoshop have the capability included. Microscope manufacturers such as Nikon, Zeiss, Olympus, and Leica have also integrated focus stacking into their instruments so that an enhanced DoF image can be acquired simply by selecting the focus range in the software interface.

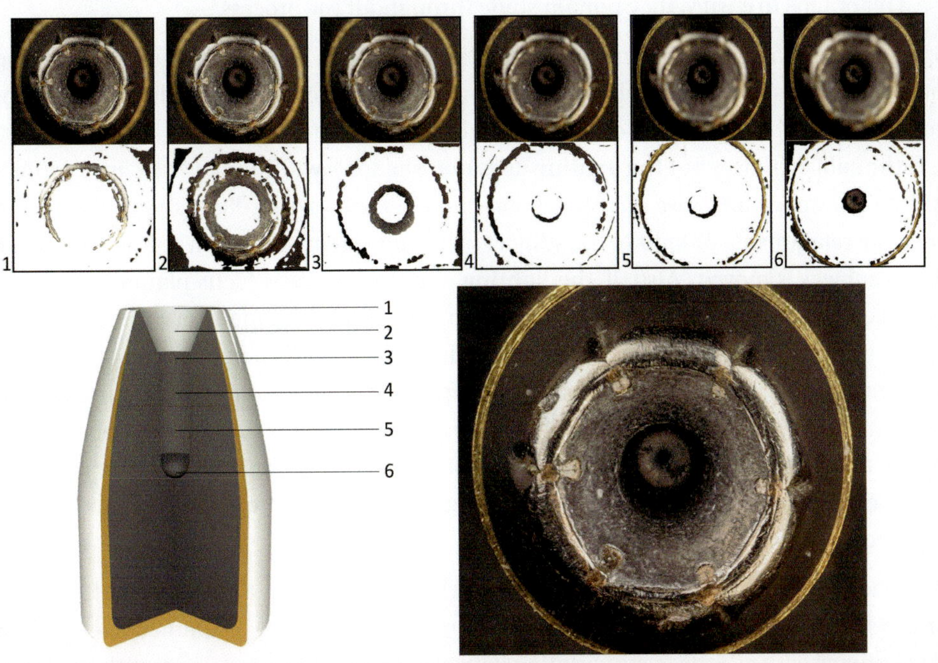

Figure 11.2 Stacking focus: by capturing images at a series of focal planes, the most in-focus areas from each image can be combined into a single composite image that has a greater depth of field than would be possible with conventional optics

The image acquisition phase for focus stacking is the most important part of creating an enhanced DoF image. Although it can be done with as minimal hardware as just a copy stand that is moved up and down in small increment, more consistent results can be had using a simple Kaiser single-axis focusing stage or a Cognisys Stackshot® which is an electronically controlled focusing rail system that can be programed for very small precise focus increments.

When assembling your focus-stacking camera system, it is important to take many factors into consideration to optimize the quality of your images. The first and foremost is stability. When acquiring a series of images, it is vitally important that nothing move in the process. If the camera tilts, the focus ring or zoom of the lens moves, the lighting changes, or if the subject itself moves, ghosting or other artifacts will be visible in the resulting composite image. When photographing items of evidence, wax or clay is often used to keep a subject in just the right orientation. While this works well for a single photo, minute drift or movement of the subject can occur during the acquisition of the focus series that will change the orientation or perspective of the subject (especially under hot copy lights), which will in turn cause problems later on when combining the images. Since it would be next to impossible to reorient the subject into the *exact* position, it is best to start the series over again. When framing a scene, set the camera to *manual* focus because a camera will try to refocus when it moves closer or further from the subject. As you change focal planes it is imperative that either the subject or camera is moved and not the zoom or focus on the lens. Changing either of these would alter the magnification of the image and cause distortions in the final image. If the focus or zoom controls on your lens move very easily, it would be beneficial to use a bit of tape to ensure they remain static throughout the process.

Lighting is also a consideration with focus stacking. While moving the camera to change the focal plane is typical, it is also possible to move the subject through a fixed focal plane. However, that should only be done if the lighting is fixed to the subject and moved with it. If the subject moves but the lighting does not, shadows will change and cause artifacts in the final image. Because of this any on-camera flash or ring-light should be avoided since the relationship of light to the subject will change regardless of whether the camera or the subject is moved. Also, if the lighting changes between focus planes it may be a good idea to start over. Image correction for exposure can be done afterwards, but better results can be had if the lighting is consistent from the start. When selecting an exposure for capturing the image, it is best to use *manual* rather than automatic, aperture priority, or shutter priority. The lighting should be exactly the same throughout, so the exposure should also be the same. Since the metering of the scene may change as areas get out of focus or more in focus, an automated metering system may try to compensate by altering the exposure.

Once the system is fully configured with proper lighting, support, and exposure, the images for the stack, often referred to as a Z-series, can be acquired. It is recommended to take as many photos with as little focus variation between them as possible to ensure that all focus planes are captured. While it would be hard to take "too many" images during this process it is vitally important that you do not capture too few. Missing focus planes in the stack can confuse the software by not having enough information to complete the image or the resulting image will have blurry gaps that look unnatural. If you do find that some focus planes have been missed, the series will need to be discarded as it would be difficult, if possible at all, to go back and insert the missing plane.

After all the images in the stack have been captured, optimally using the RAW file format, they will likely need some pre-processing before they are compiled into a single image. Any processing done to optimize gamma, exposure, contrast, color correction, or the like should be done globally via batch processing. The goal of batch processing your images is to keep the color and tonal range the same throughout the series so that they will blend together well later. You can use the optimized RAW files in Adobe Photoshop® or other focus-stacking applications such as Helicon Focus® as is, but if the software you are using does not support RAW files, you should save your files as a TIFF file rather than a JPEG if possible to avoid image compression artifacts and quality degradation. Another popular software is Zyrene® Stacker can also handle RAW files.

With the captured and optimized series of images, it is time to bring the files into the focus-stacking software of choice. There are many to choose from, with Adobe Photoshop®, Zyrene, and Helicon Focus® among the most popular. There will be differences in the methods and ways they will work, but the concepts will be very similar. The series of images can be selected from a folder or batch-opened as layers into the host application. Once loaded there may be a need to align the images so they are exactly in register. Even the most stable system could have a slight shift from image to image. After alignment the software will analyze the sharpness of each layer and combine the sharpest areas into a derivative image that is totally in focus from top to bottom.

Some may argue that "focus" or "sharpness" is a subjective matter. After all some people may see photos as more or less in focus than other people. However, focus can be quantitatively identified in a digital environment by measuring localized contrast between adjacent pixels. Since contrast is defined by the difference in tonal value, the quicker an area in an image transitions from one tone to another, the higher the contrast. The higher the contrast of an area, the sharper or more in focus it appears. Computers are particularly good at measuring and comparing, so it stands to reason that they can easily detect areas of more or less focus by measuring localized contrast (see Figure 11.3). This concept is used by many image-acquisition systems to either autofocus an automated system or provide a focusing aid in a manual system. Most focusing aids are seen as a gage on the side of the interface that will increase as your image becomes more in focus and decrease when the image or area of the image becomes less focused.

File management or organization is now paramount in an image collection, and thus file-storage requirements have just grown exponentially. In the event of a court challenge it is important that the focus stacked composite image and all of the component images used to create it were saved in addition to the notes on settings and methods for the process. It may be required for a photographer to defend a processed image months or years after it was created. If this is a technique that will be used often, it will be wise to design a naming convention and storage structure than can be referenced later so the image can, if needed, be recreated in court.

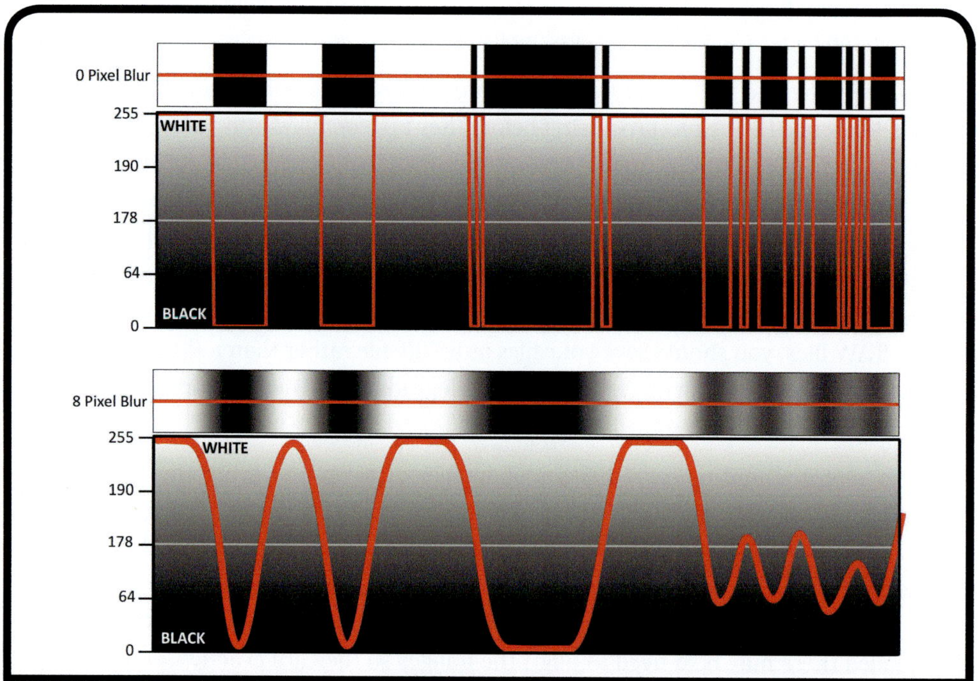

Figure 11.3 Localized contrast analysis: as an image becomes less sharp, the changes from black to white become more gradual, visually having less contrast and more out of focus

Image Stitching

When photographing a subject, you will on occasion find that you will need more subject in the photo than what a camera system is providing. Either your lens isn't wide enough to capture the width of a landscape, or the magnification that is available to get the required view doesn't capture enough of the subject, or a camera system simply doesn't have enough resolution. These are situations where using a technique known as image stitching can help. Image stitching is a process where two or more images are combined to increase the area imaged by using a camera system differently. There are two primary categories image stitching typically fall into: image mapping or panorama. Both types of stitching use the same basic type of image-processing function of pattern recognition and mapping to find common edges and details in a series of images in order to seamlessly splice them together to extend the scene.

Image Mapping

Image mapping can be used to make a seamless mosaic of photos in order to increase the resolution or viewing area of the final image. When using a microscope or a macro lens, higher magnification is used to increase the resolution and fine detail of a subject that lower magnification optics will not capture. The trade-off of high magnification is a very small viewing area. Capturing several high-magnification images from an area of a subject and stitching them together can produce an image with the area of a low-magnification image with the detail and resolution of a high-magnification photo. It is sometimes referred to as wide field—high-resolution imaging.

Another situation where image mapping could be beneficial would be when needing to compensate for a low-resolution camera. Several low-resolution images can be stitched together to create a higher resolution image that would be a high-enough quality for creating large prints for posters or publications. This technique has been performed for many years even before digital technology became readily accessible, but it was laborious, time consuming, and often did not provide optimal results. Every aspect of the process was a manual task from sizing the image to adjusting the tones and brightness. Modern computers now have ample processing power and memory to handle most image mapping projects, although some very high-resolution composites may require higher-end computers. There are also many software packages to choose from ranging from very simple free applications, to built-in functionality in common programs such as Adobe Photoshop, to complicated stand-alone applications, to even web-based utilities. Some instruments and microscopes that have automated cameras and stages may have image-mapping capabilities included in the software package.

Although image mapping is a common technique and is fairly straightforward to accomplish, there are some considerations to keep in mind when acquiring images. Whether using an automated system or photographing a scene with a handheld camera, it is important to be sure there is overlap between the images. This will not only aide the software in aligning and placing the images, but also allow room to fade the two images together to create a seamless transition. The number of images used to create a wide-field composite image is really only limited by your computer's memory and storage space.

Before capturing images, it is important to select the right lens. Despite the goal of capturing a wide visual area, a wide-angle lens is not optimal. Wide-angle and fisheye lenses create a good amount of distortion in the image along the edges. Because of this distortion, the edges of the images will not naturally align with each other. Although most software will correct for this distortion, it is far better to start the process with the most optimized images possible to prevent major artifacts in the final stitched image.

As with all photography, lighting and exposure will be a key element to success. Since a subject or scene will contain a wide range of lights and darks, the camera in any automatic exposure mode will want to adjust for that in each frame. This could cause issues when combining the images together, so it is recommended to use a manual exposure to ensure smooth transition from one image to the next. Asses a scene and select an exposure that will capture tones in the entire area. This is made simpler by using a high bit-depth or RAW file format. If you are particularly adventurous, high dynamic range imaging can be done for each frame of the series, but do keep in mind how many images will be captured by the end; file management and organization will be very important. There will inevitably be some lighting variation if taking photos of an outdoor scene as clouds change and shadows move. Most stitching software can compensate for these slight changes to the lighting although some software will handle this better than others. If the lighting changes drastically while capturing a series for stitching, consider starting again. Different software packages are better at tone matching than others, so as a rule it is better to acquire higher-quality images with consistent lighting and tone than to rely on software post-processing (see Figure 11.4).

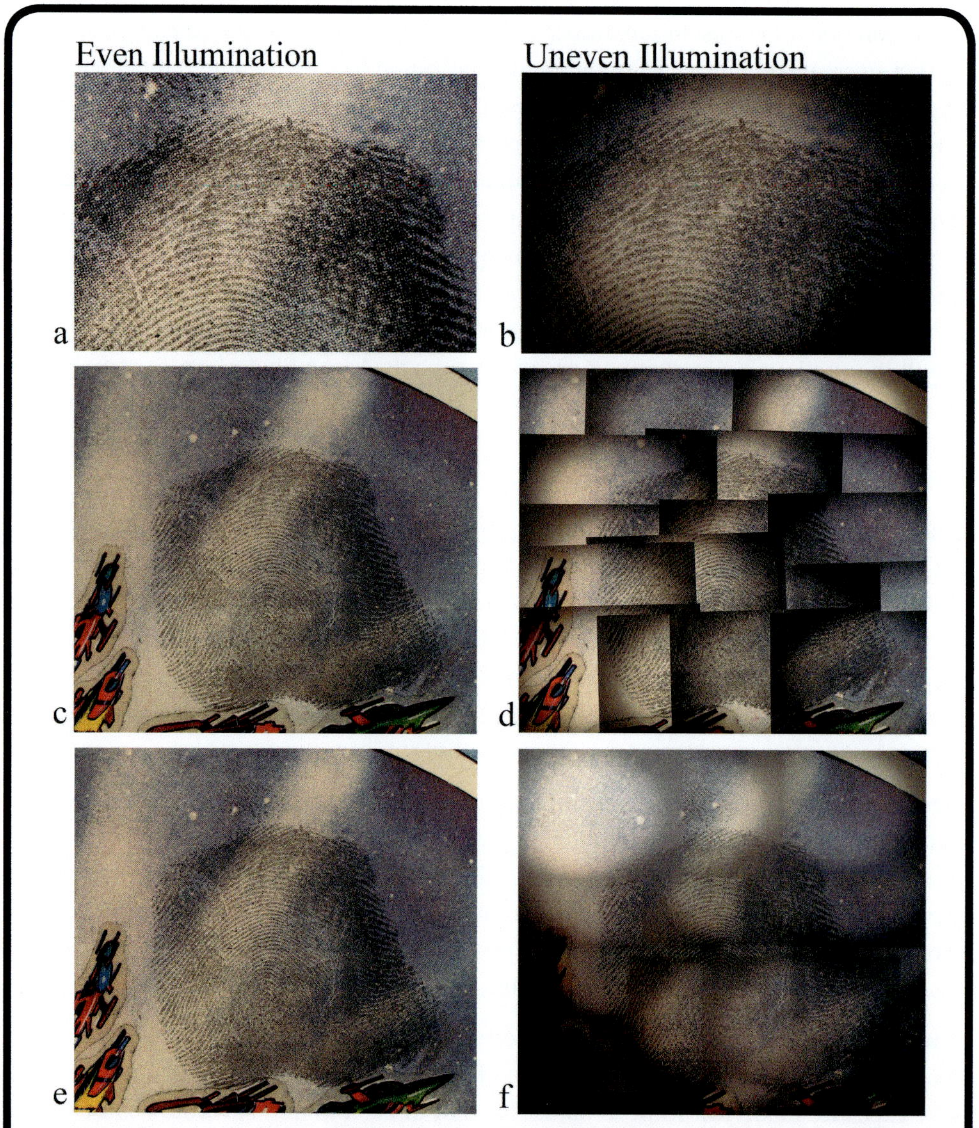

Figure 11.4 Even illumination: although software can compensate some for uneven illumination, it is better to get your illumination as even as possible. a & b show a single frame from a series comparing the same frame with even illumination and uneven illumination. c & d show the mapped images from the two different lighting scenario with no edge or tonal blending applied. The edges on the composite created with uneven lighting shows very obvious edges while the example with proper illumination does not. e & f show that although edge and tonal blending have been applied, the series with uneven lighting is not usable. It is interesting to note that the series with even illumination without any blending (c) produced a far superior composite image than the series with uneven illumination with edge and tonal blending applied (f)

While software can compensate for exposure, alignment, and geometric distortion, it cannot compensate for focus. The focus settings on the camera should be set to manual rather than automatic and then fixed before capturing the series. When the focus changes from one frame to another on an object that spans multiple frames, it can cause noticeable artifacts and the software may have difficulty matching the frames correctly.

Cleanliness is also a factor that should be considered. Unlike other types of computational imaging such as high dynamic range and focus stacking where a series of images are flattened on top of one another, stitching techniques place a series of images adjacent to one another. If your lens or image sensor has dust or dirt on it, that debris will appear on every frame in the same place, creating a pattern over the final image. This dirt may also cause the stitching software to have problems matching the edges of the frame.

Panoramic Imaging

Creating a panoramic image is similar to image mapping but the goal is usually to get a wider field of view rather than gaining image size or resolution. Over the years many methods have been devised to make panoramic images. Most of the earliest methods used non-continuous methods such as swinging lenses or moving film. Although capable of creating high-quality images, the hardware was prone to malfunction and the images were susceptible to camera shake and subject movement during the relatively long exposure time. Using a stitching method with multiple images to create the panoramic allows the use of short exposure times and thus eliminates movement issues but does create some others, the major ones being magnification and perspective.

There are two primary ways of capturing images for a panorama: rotational, the most popular method of rotating the camera on an axis; and transitional, moving the camera laterally to keep the subject the same distance from the camera. When using a rotational method, perspective can be compensated for by using the correct pivot point to eliminate parallax (which will be defined in the next section), but magnification becomes a problem. When rotating the camera in order to take a full image of something straight such as the side of a building or a road, the resulting image will make the straight object appear curved. This is a result of the distance of the subject to the camera becomes greater as the camera is rotated away from the center of the object. As the distance increases, the magnification becomes less, so the ends of the building will be further away, and thus appearing smaller, in the image (see Figure 11.5). If a transitional method is used to capture the images, moving the camera to the side, the issue of magnification is solved but artifacts gained from a change in perspective is evident. Because the camera's physical location is moved, parts of an object, such as the side of a box, would be visible where it was not before (see Figure 11.6). The goal of the panorama should be decided before selecting the type of image capture is used. If the image is going to be used for measuring

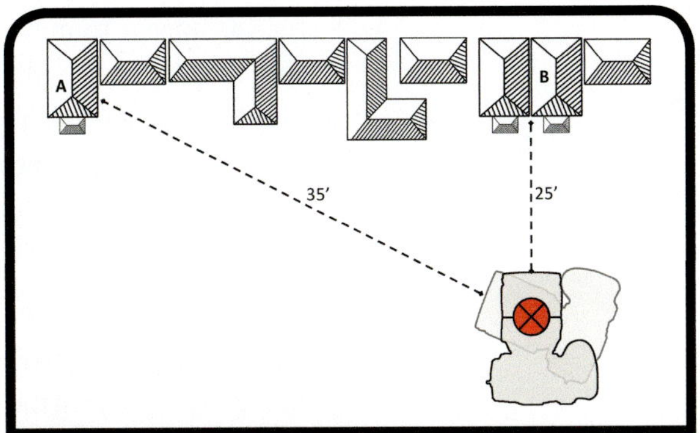

Figure 11.5 Magnification distortion can be seen in rotational wide-field panoramas. As the camera is rotated, objects that are in a straight line will appear to curve away because of the increased distance from the camera to the subject

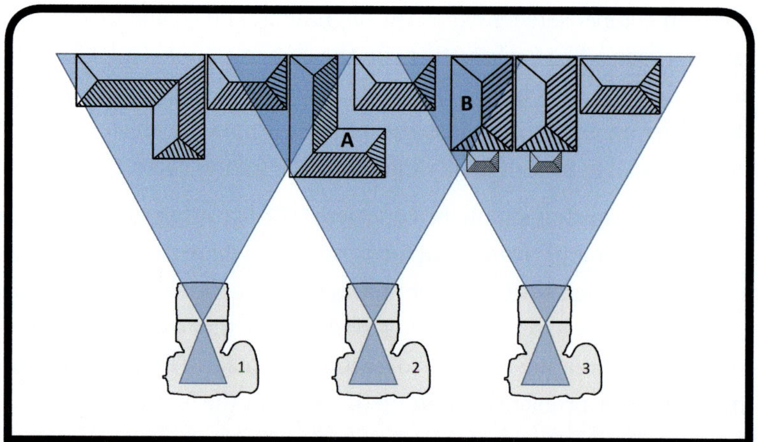

Figure 11.6 When the camera is moved transitionally along the scene, magnification remains constant as the working distance is consistent. However, perspective will change. Camera 1 will capture the left side of object *A* while camera 2 will only capture the front of object *A* and the side of object *B*. Camera 3 will capture the front of object *B* and not the side. Using this method for creating a panorama would produce an image suitable to measure but would have noticeable perspective distortion

or photogrammetry, a transitional approach should be used since the magnification is not changed. If, however, the point of view of a scene from that location is important, then a rotational method should be used.

Parallax

The most important factor that foils most beginners attempting to create a rotational panorama is parallax. Parallax can be seen when the camera is rotated and the foreground objects appear to move at a different rate than the background objects. The effect is that two objects that are aligned at one angle are not aligned at another angle, which can cause great distortions when creating a stitched panorama. To eliminate this type of distortion, the camera needs to be rotated on a specific axis where the ray path of objects to the imaging sensor does not change on rotation (see Figure 11.7). This point of rotation has been referred to as the nodal point, or aperture point. That actual name of this axis has been debated for many years but the location remains the same.

For all practical purposes it can be referred to as the *no parallax point* or NPP. This point can be located by taking the focal length of the lens and measuring that distance from the imaging plane of the camera. Although accurate, this method is inefficient for a few reasons. The first is finding the exact location of the imaging plane. Most professional cameras have it marked on the body using a ϕ; however, many cameras no longer use this convention. In addition, many zoom lenses do not accurately label the focal length at various zoom settings, making it difficult to calculate the NPP. It is much easier to use a practical, rather than quantitative, method to find the exact NPP (see Figure 11.9).

- Mount the camera on a focusing stage that allows the camera to be moved forward or backward while mounted on the tripod. If the tripod mount of your camera is not directly aligned with the center of the lens, you will need a stage that also moves the camera side to side. This is normally found on point-and-shoot cameras (see Figure 11.8). There are many panoramic-specific tripod heads and camera mounts available, ranging from very basic to very full-featured programmable electronic models, for your specific needs. For most situations a simple single-axis focusing stage will do the job.
- Set the tripod to be level with the ground. Many tripods have a bubble level built into the tripod; if not, a carpenter's level can be used on the tripod head. Many smartphones come with a level app as well.
- Mount the camera on the focusing stage onto the leveled tripod.
- Set two poles or sticks in line with each other and the center of the camera. The distance between them is not important, but when looking through the viewfinder of the camera they should be in the center of the frame and directly aligned with each other (see Figure 11.9a).
- Pan the camera to the side so that the poles are at the far side of the frame. At this point the poles will most likely not be in alignment with each other. This is the effect of parallax (see Figure 11.9b).
- Using the focusing stage controls, move the camera backwards until the poles are once again in alignment with each other. This is your no parallax point that should be used to create a panorama. When you rotate the camera from side to side now, the poles will always be in alignment with each other (see Figure 11.9c).

Now that the NPP has been set, the acquisition of images is pretty straightforward, with requirements fairly similar to the image-mapping process. Focus and exposure should be set to manual to minimize changes from frame to frame; since scene composition and distance will change as the camera is rotated, automatic exposure and focus would also tend to change. Although the software can and will modify the exposure of an image in order blend it with the next frame, having consistent exposures initially will prevent losing shadow or highlight detail when tonal corrections are made. When capturing the individual frames, it is a good idea to use landmarks in the scene to make sure there is enough overlap of consecutive images to enable smooth transitions and accurate matching in the stitching software.

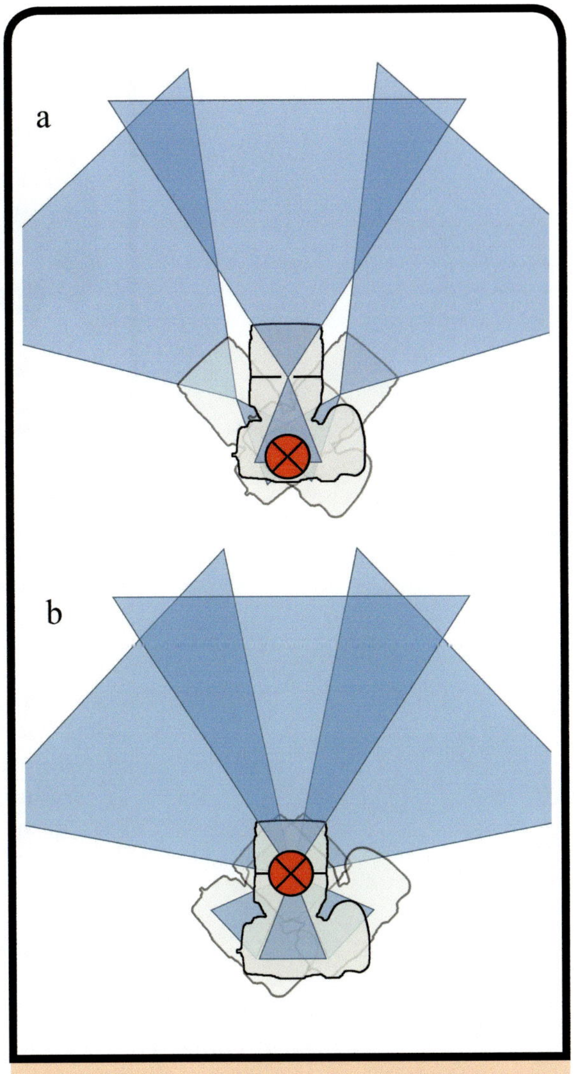

Figure 11.7 (a) Rotating a camera normally on a tripod will change the angle of the optical path from the subject to the imaging plane, making objects in the image change relative positions to each other. (b) Rotating the camera on the no parallax point will keep the angle of the optical path the same, ensuring the relative positions of objects in the image remain the same and suitable for panoramic photography

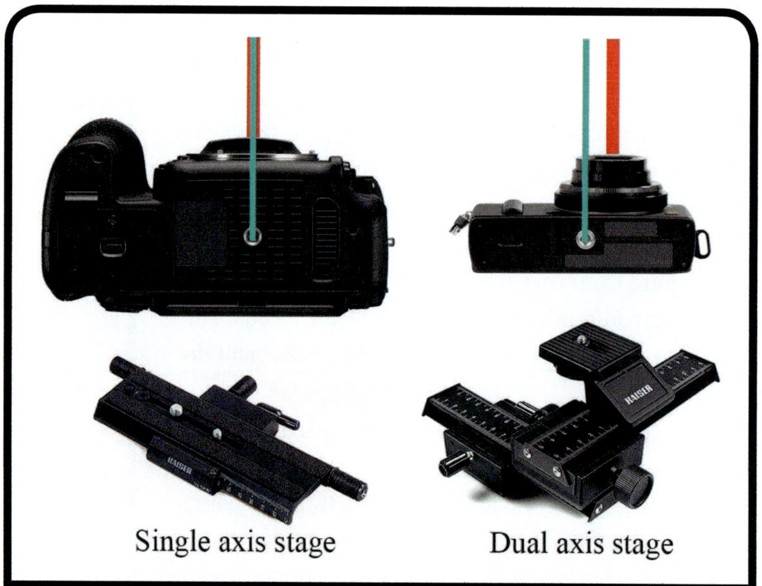

Figure 11.8 Most professional cameras have a tripod mount aligned with the central axis of the lens. Because of this a single-axis focusing stage can be used to set the no parallax point. Some cameras have a mounting point that is not aligned with the center of the lens. This is generally found on non-professional grade and point-and-shoot-cameras. A two-axis focusing stage should be used with these types of camera in order to align the lens and mounting point on the tripod

Stitching

With a series of properly captured images in hand, it is now time to bring the images into the software of choice for stitching together. Whether the goal is to create a panoramic image or a large high-resolution image map, the software and technique are pretty much the same. While a panorama is generally composed of a single row of images, an image-mapped compilation will be composed of a grid of images; however, the technique and options for creating the stitched image are the same. There are numerous software packages, but some popular ones include Panorama Stitcher, Adobe Photoshop's photomerge plugin, and an online utility available at www.dermandar.com. Although these programs may use the term panorama in the title, they are also capable of image mapping. Using these programs is very simple; only a spare few options need to be selected.

The most basic mode of stitching is *reposition*. This method will take the images and attempt to align them the best it can. No rotation, geometric correction, or resizing of the image is done. It can be liked to taking prints a lying them on a table to put them together. However simple this may be, if the source images have been acquired properly it can produce a good quality final image. One step more complicated than a simple *reposition* method is the *collage* option. This is essentially the same with the added feature of rotation. The images are still not resized or have any geometric correction applied to them. Although this seems like

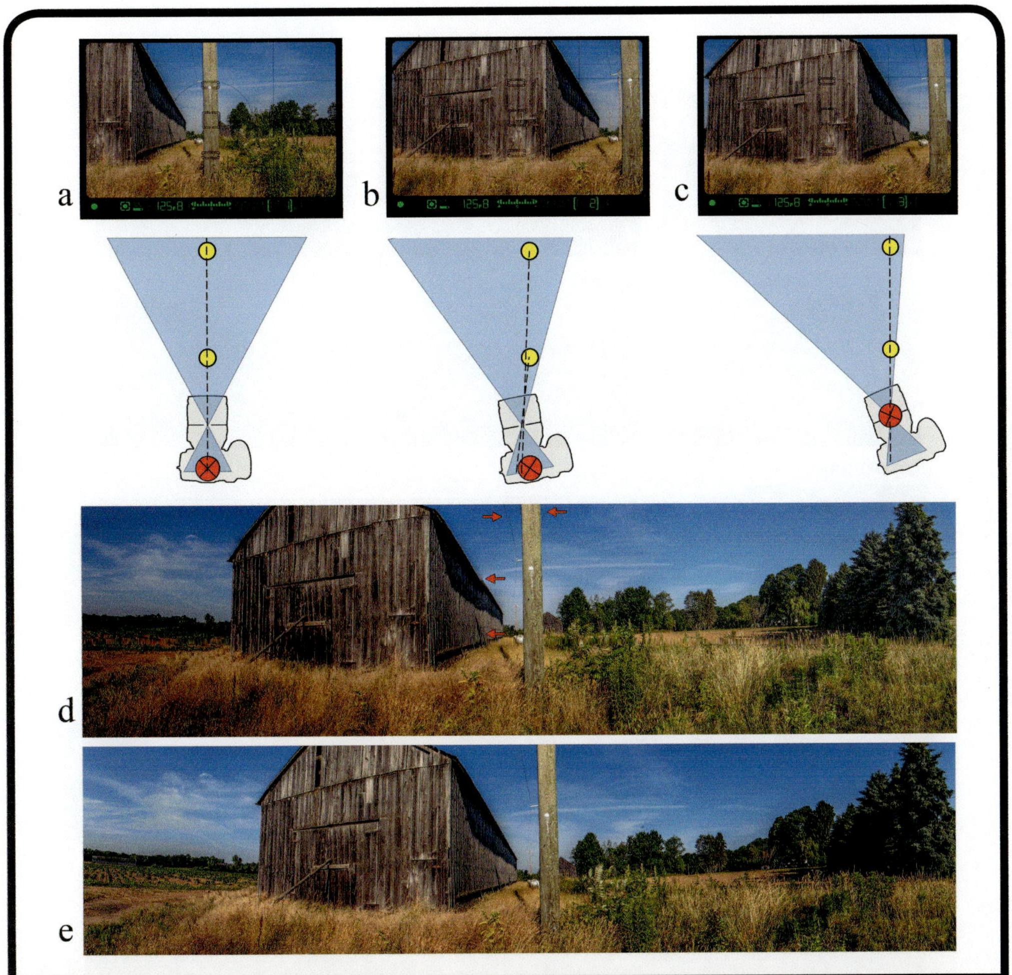

Figure 11.9 Finding the no parallax point. (a) Find two objects that can be aligned with your camera. The closer the first object is, the more obvious the parallax will be. Aligning an edge can be more helpful than the center as the closer object will tend to mask the farther point to the point where it will also mask the parallax. (b) Rotate the camera so that the aligned object moves to the edge of the frame. At this point you should see both objects. (c) Adjust the focusing stage so that the two objects are realigned with each other. The red cross indicates the axis of rotation. Note how this point is more forward than the normal tripod mounting point. (d) Example of a panorama created without rotating on the NPP. Arrows indicate areas that did not align properly in the image due to parallax. (e) Panorama created with the camera mounted at the correct NPP axis. Note that all areas of the image are properly aligned

a small addition, the ability to rotate images may be enough to dramatically increase the quality of the final image.

The most robust mode of stitching includes geometric corrections for size, perspective, and spherical distortions. These corrections can be necessary if the lens used had edge distortions from being too wide, if the capturing angles were not exactly correct, or the panoramic scene was extremely wide. The software will attempt to align all the images in any way possible by resizing, skewing, or compressing parts of the images.

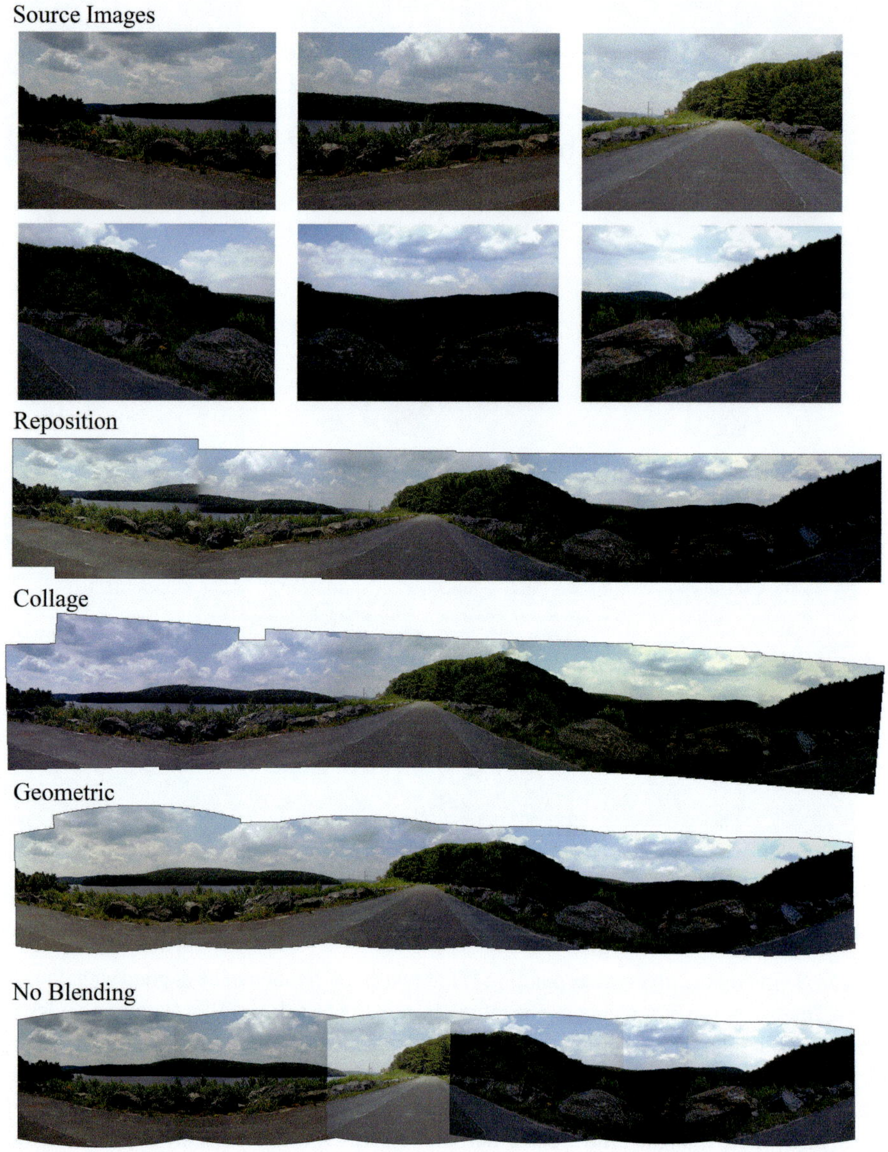

Figure 11.10 When reposition is used, there may be some areas that don't exactly align; however, it doesn't introduce any distortion and requires far less processing power. Collage is similar but adds the element of rotation when aligning neighboring images. Sometimes this is just enough to get better results without much more computer overhead. Geometric correction is the most complicated and processor intensive but has the ability to fix many errors in the source images caused by lens distortions. Blending is used to match the tonality of the image and fade the edges together so there is no stark line where the images begin and end

The final consideration for the stitching process is blending. Blending will feather or blend the edges of the adjacent images together to make the transition as seamless as possible. The tones, brightness, contrast, and color balance will also attempt to be matched when blending is chosen. If the source images were carefully acquired, this will not add much time to the process or cause any artifacts in the final picture, but it will help to add a final layer of seamlessness to the image compilation.

When using these techniques to prepare exhibits for court or to aid in analyzing evidence, be sure to tread carefully. Always be upfront and fully disclose that these techniques were used to produce the images being presented. Be prepared to reproduce the results if requested, which means taking very careful and thorough notes of settings used in the process. Also be fastidious with the archiving and storage of any and all source images used. In some cases, this can include a vast amount of images, so organization is key as you may be called to defend or explain the image months or years after they were created.

High Dynamic Range Imaging

In the course of photographing a piece of evidence or a crime scene you will find that your camera will not always be able to capture both the dark shadow detail simultaneously in the same image as the very bright highlight areas. This often happens at arson scenes where there are important details both in the charred remains and the surrounding areas, when photographing nickel-plated cartridge cases on dark blacktop, inside dimly lit rooms with bright sun coming through a window, or under a car on a sunny day. These scenarios could benefit from using high dynamic range, or commonly referred to as HDR, imaging techniques. In essence, what HDR photography does is take two or more images that were taken using different exposures and combine them to create an image that includes tonal information from both images. Although people often refer to HDR as producing high dynamic range images, what is actually happening is the process takes a *scene* with a high dynamic range, much greater than the capturing device, and compresses that high range into a "normal" range that is suitable for digital image formats.

In recent years HDR photography has gained wide acceptance and popularity, mostly due to increased accessibility and reduced cost of the software, but the challenge of photographically capturing and reproducing these high dynamic range scenes has existed ever since photography was invented. The dynamic range of a photograph or scene is defined by the difference in exposure value (EV), often referred to by photographers as f-stops, between the darkest area and the brightest area. Different films were found to have much different dynamic ranges; Kodak® TMax 100 black and white film had a broad range of ten stops while Kodak® Ektachrome 100 slide film only had a range of six to seven stops. To make the most of the possible range of film, the famed landscape photographer Ansel Adams developed a method of exposing and developing film in a way that would optimize the dynamic range of film to capture both highlights and shadows of these landscape scenes called the Zone System which was developed in the late 1930s.

Once the negatives were developed, another challenge emerged in managing the negative tonal scale. Photographic paper had a wider dynamic range than film but with less flexibility in changing tones. Attempting to do a straight print from a negative, especially one that was not carefully exposed, would result in either the shadows losing detail in order to not lose detail in the highlights or vice versa. In order to compress the tonal range of the negative onto the limited range of the paper, most photographers would use a technique known as dodging and burning. This entailed either blocking small areas of shadow (dodging) in order to properly expose areas of highlights or allowing more light on a localized area (burning) to enhance highlight areas when the shadows are already properly exposed. If you were particularly ambitious and skilled in the darkroom you may try a technique known as *unsharp masking*. Although most people know this term now as an Adobe Photoshop sharpening filter, this film technique created a slightly out of focus and underexposed negative of the original negative to create additional density in underexposed areas of the original negative. By putting these two negatives together, the effective dynamic range of the image was lowered to fit more easily on photographic paper, so more detail in the highlights and shadows could be seen.

The same challenges face digital photographers today in regards to dynamic range. Instead of film with different ranges of dynamic range we have digital cameras with various image-capturing capabilities. Instead of paper, we have printers and monitors that have the same limitation as photographic paper did; with a laser printer the toner will always be blackest black and the paper is always the brightest white, and the brightest white on a monitor depends on the type of monitor and the darkest black is only as dark as the color of the monitor screen when it's not on, which is not usually very black. This is why projection televisions and projection screens tend to look very low in contrast; the darkest area of the image is actually the color of the screen, which is white. The contrast is then enhanced by making the projector brighter to increase the dynamic range. The big difference in digital formats compared to film is that your "negative" is a digital file that has a set and finite number of tones available going from 0 to 255 in an 8-bit image. Some people often confuse dynamic range and bit-depth as being interchangeable. Although in a 16-bit image the tonal range would be 0–65,535, the dynamic range is the same. It would seem that having more tone to work with would increase your dynamic range, the 0 is still the same black, and the 65,535 is the same white as in an 8-bit image. An image with a high dynamic range can have a low bit depth and a high bit depth image can have a low dynamic range. Not to say 16-bit images are not better, they have orders of magnitudes more information, they just don't have more dynamic range. This is why unprocessed 8-bit and 16-bit images look the same on a monitor or when printed.

Digital capture technology has come a long way since it's been available to the consumer market. Most professional DSLR cameras can capture a dynamic range of 10–12 stops and getting better all the time. Lower-level or less expensive cameras often have lower dynamic range but can still take very good photos under the right conditions. The iPhone is an excellent example of this. Many professional photographers have tried to show the quality of iPhone images with fantastic-looking studio photos. This, however, is merely smoke and mirrors. In a studio environment where the scene and its lighting is controllable, a skilled photographer can set up the lighting of a scene to fit within the narrow dynamic range of the iPhone's camera. Attempting to use an iPhone camera in a crime scene scenario, where all elements of scene are out of your control, will result in very poor quality images. It's easy

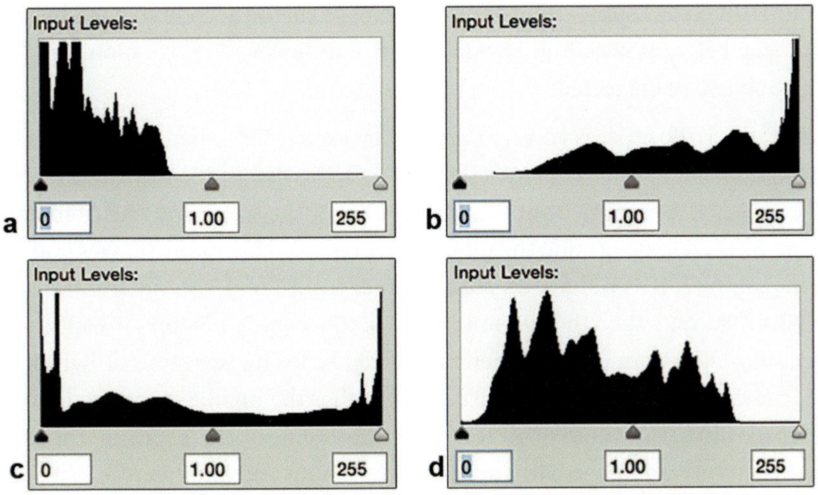

Figure 11.11 Histograms where an abundance of the values go to the edge of the scale indicate a loss of information. (a) An underexposed image will have most of its values on the dark side while having very little on the brighter side. (b) Overexposed images will have the bulk of values on the light side while having little information on the dark or shadow side. (c) Having values that span the entire range with a mass of values on the edges indicates a scene with a higher dynamic range than the camera and cannot be properly exposed to include all available tones. (d) A properly exposed image of a scene that does not exceed the camera's dynamic range will typically have the bulk of values in the middle of the range where the values decrease to 0 on either side, indicating that all information was captured

to tell if a scene had a higher dynamic range than the device that captured it by looking at the tone histogram. Almost all image-processing applications have the ability to show you the tonal histogram of an image (see Figure 11.11). If there are high values at either end of the histogram, there may be tones that are not captured. An optimal histogram will have the majority of the values in the middle. Many cameras will have the option to alert you if your scene is out of range of the exposure used to capture the image by either showing the histogram on the preview screen or by blinking the area of the image that is cut-off.

Capturing Images for HDR Processing

Once you have identified that a scene or object has a higher dynamic range than your camera, there are some considerations to keep in mind when capturing images for HDR processing. Of the most vital importance to the success of an HDR series is stability. Since these images are going to be merged into one single image, any movement can cause artifacts that show up as ghosting or blurring. Obviously if you are capturing an outdoor crime scene there will be factors out of your control such as clouds moving across the sky. In most cases important information will not be in the clouds, so this would be an acceptable artifact. You will have to make a judgment call on whether any important details are moving and would be problematic. It is certainly recommended that a tripod be used; however, if the camera can take the images rapidly enough, you can hand-hold a camera while capturing your HDR series. Some transitional movement can be accommodated by an image-alignment step before processing, but any change in perspective, rotation, or tilting will likely not be able to be corrected.

The basis of the HDR process revolves around exposure. First measure the scene with a handheld light meter or your camera's internal meter to determine the range of exposures that will be needed. A reading from the darkest area of the scene and one from the brightest area can be used to determine the dynamic range and how many images you will need to take. For example, if the shadows require an exposure of 1 second and the highlights require 1/2000 second, then the dynamic range of the scene is 12 stops. If your camera can record ten stops of dynamic range, then you would be losing two stops of light in a single exposure, causing the image to have no detail in either the highlights or shadows. To start your HDR exposures you would want to start in the middle of this exposure range at 1/32. You would then take an image with an exposure +1 stop and another at –1 stop. This can be accomplished by either manually setting the camera's shutter speed at 1/64 and then 1/16 or by setting the camera's exposure compensation to +1 and then –1. It is important to note at this point that you should not use your camera's aperture setting to change your exposure as this will alter your depth of field and cause artifacts in your final image. This will not be an issue if you are manually changing the settings, but if you are using exposure compensation, be sure the camera is set to aperture priority so that the f-stop is not changed for the exposure series. Many cameras have the ability to take these series automatically with either an HRD or bracketing mode. These modes can be preset with a range of exposures you wish to take. If your scene has an even greater dynamic range, simply increase your range of exposures to include +/–2 stops for a total of five images in the series or even +/–3 stops for a total of seven images. Although HDR images can be used to capture a great expanse of scenes, there are some hardware limitations. If the highlights are too bright for any exposure with your camera, you can use neutral density filters to compensate; however, if an area is too dark, your camera may not have the sensitivity to image it at all.

After the images have been captured, combining them into a composite HDR image is a relatively simple matter. There is a wide variety of applications and plugins available to process HDR images ranging from the popular Adobe Photoshop software which has HDR processing built-in, to third-party plugins, to standalone HDR-specific applications, to even free applications such as ImageJ. Each will have different options and capabilities but the fundamentals will be very similar. What any HDR software does is to take the tonal information from each of the images in the exposure series and compresses the total dynamic range into a single digital image by mapping the tones. As mentioned earlier, in a digital image the white and black values are static; no value can be more black or more white regardless of how much tonal information is available. The HDR processing simply maps all the tonal information and scales it between the black and white. Very high dynamic range scenes can look surreal and unnatural because human vision cannot see this dynamic range naturally. The human eye can only see about six stops of dynamic range at one time, but can adapt this range very quickly, almost instantly, so that it seems like a much wider range. Because of this, highly processed HDR images can look flat or lack contrast since you would not normally be able to see details in the dark and light areas at the same time.

Although HDR can be used to your advantage, it is important to know when to use HDR, and when not to. When there is important detail in both highlights and dark shadows such as photographing down a hole in the ground, into the open door of an unlit room, or any black object on a light surface. Any outdoor scene when it is sunny will likely benefit from HDR processing as well. It should not be used if color is important. The blending algorithms used map the tones of several images can have an effect on your color accuracy not only due to the averaging process, but because digital sensors can have very different color sensitive over its exposure range. When looking at HDR images you will start to notice they have a certain characteristic *look* to them. Also, scenes that have a good amount of movement to them are not well suited to HDR processing; if it's windy and your subject is in tall grass, there will be some distortion that may not be desirable.

High dynamic range image processing, whether it be manually done by the photographer or by an automated instrument such as a microscope, is a powerful tool but should be used with caution. To prevent any challenges to your images in court, always disclose that HDR was used in the making of the photograph beforehand when it's originally submitted. Always be prepared to defend the image by keeping the original images that were used to create the HDR image as well as any notes of settings, exposures, software used, and equipment. If asked, you should be able to recreate the HDR image exactly even if months or years have passed. Possibly most importantly, understand the process and be able to explain it to a layperson. There has been precedent where evidence has been excluded because the process used to create it could not be adequately explained.

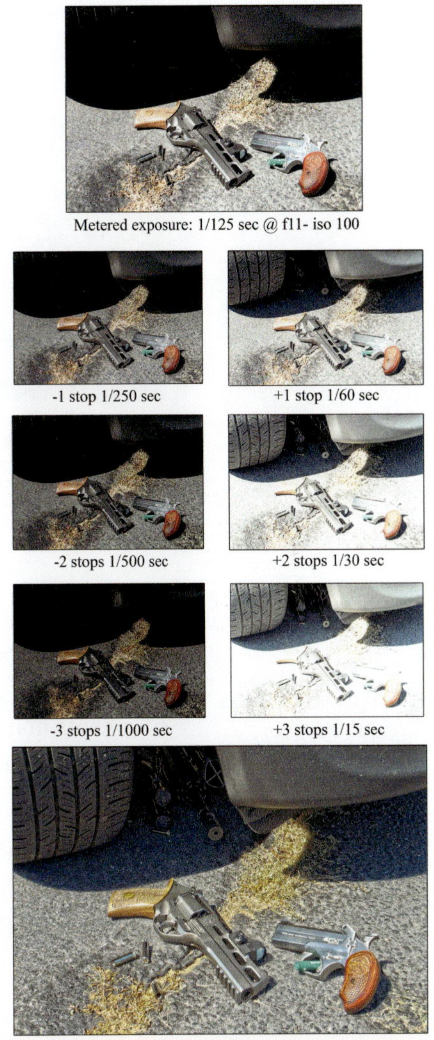

Figure 11.12 Imaging dark objects in deep shadow or shiny objects in bright sun may be challenging on their own for most cameras, but virtually impossible if they are in the same scene. Exposing long enough to capture details in the shadows will obliterate any detail in the shiny metal and highlights, but exposing for the highlights will leave no discernible detail in the shadow areas. Using a camera in any sort of automatic exposure mode in this type of situation would likely result in a compromise that gives poor detail in both areas. By combining the tones from a series of exposures, the useful details from all areas can be preserved and able to be shown in a single image. Understanding the concept behind HDR imaging and being able to explain it would be vitally important when defending an HDR image in court

Three-Dimensional Imaging

3D Scanner Systems

A 3D scanner is a device that collects multiple points of data from a scene that can be used to create a 3D model of that scene. 3D scanners work by emitting a laser to measure several million points throughout the scene. A built-in camera is used to record color information of the objects within the scene.

3D scanners allow investigators to document an entire scene with minimal setup and recording time. They are able to make an infinite number of measurements, with accuracies down to 1/16 inch. Larger scenes may require multiple scans that must be stitched together during post-processing.

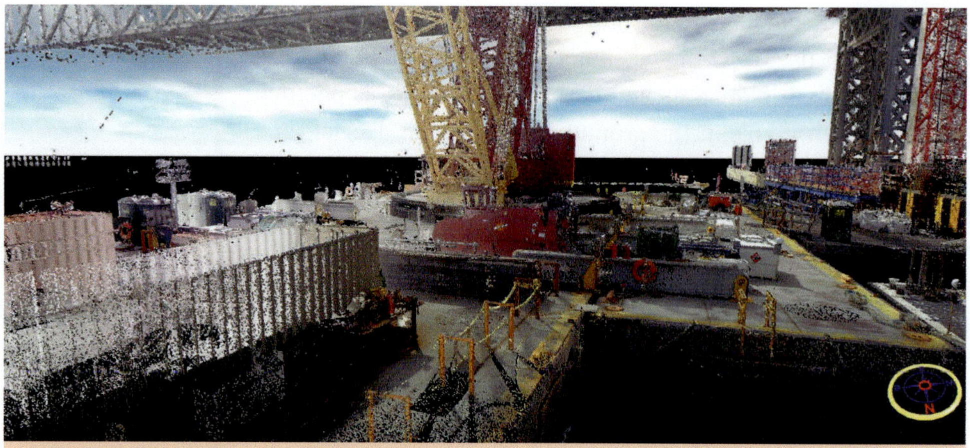

Figure 11.13 An image created from a 3D scan of a bridge construction project
Image courtesy of Detective Donald Palmer, Westchester County Police

Post-processing of the recorded data is required to build the scene, and this may be time consuming depending upon the size of the scene. The result is an accurate 3D model of the scene. The model can be used to create a virtual "walk-through" of the scene. Measurements may be taken of almost everything in the scene. The reconstruction of blood spatter, bullet and other trajectories, and possibly the height of a suspect may be possible as well.

Popular 3D scanners for crime scene documentation include the Faro Focus 3D and Leica ScanStation. Unfortunately, due to their relatively high cost, approximately $100,000 including equipment and training, 3D scanners may be cost prohibitive to some departments.

Photogrammetry

3D models of scenes or objects can also be created using standard digital cameras and special processing software. By taking several shots of a scene or item from multiple angles it is possible to recreate that object in three dimensions. The models are created using software that extracts 3D information from multiple photographs of an object or scene.

While the quality of the 3D model usually relies upon the input quality of the camera used, decent results are possible for very little investment. The technique is even possible using smartphones and relatively inexpensive cameras such as the Microsoft Kinect®.

Photogrammetry software includes Autodesk's Remake, Agisofts PhotoScan, and Photo Modeler.

Autodesk's Remake is available in two versions free and professional. The free version is limited to 50 images and standard quality only. The free version uses the cloud for processing the images, while the professional version supports local processing. The professional version costs $30/ month or $300/ year.

Agisoft PhotoScan comes in two versions, standard and professional, and supports Windows, Macintosh and Linux-based PC's. A free demo is available if you wish to test the software prior to purchasing.

PhotoModeler is available in three different versions that build upon each other's features. The software currently is only runs on Windows computers. A free demo is available of all three versions of the software.

All three photogrammetry software packages work in the same manner. The photographer takes multiple images of a scene or object from several angles. The images are loaded into the software for processing and a 3D model of the scene or object is created. The quality of the 3D model depends largely upon the quality of input images, the number of angles/directions shot, and the processing power of the computer. Some patience and practice may be necessary in order to achieve acceptable results. If the quality of the results are high enough, it may be possible to extract measurements and make conclusions similar to a 3D laser scanner.

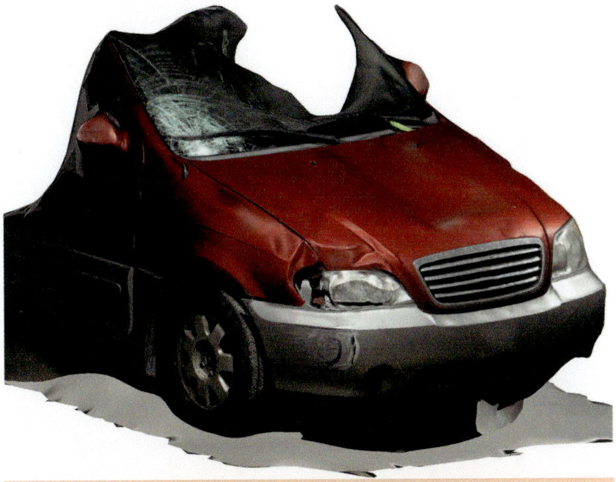

Figure 11.14 This image was generated using several photographs of a vehicle from different angles. The images were then processed using photogrammetry software to create a 3D model

Image courtesy of Keith A. Mancini

The resulting 3D files created by a laser scanner or the photogrammetry method can be used to preserve the condition of a scene for further examination in the future. Accurate measurements may be taken from the model after the scene investigation has concluded, saving time on scene and allowing investigators to release the scene sooner. Virtual "walk-throughs" can be created allowing investigators to show a detailed recreation of a scene to other investigators, attorneys, and members of a jury, without having to return to the scene. Photogrammetry software as well as laser scanners have been used to scan a scene from the air by using drones or aircraft to capture the images. Additionally, the files created can be edited in other 3D software such as Meshlab, Blender, and 3ds Max, and some objects may even be 3D printed to create a physical rendition of the object.

3D imaging technology is an ever-growing field, and technological advances will most certainly bring down costs and shrink equipment. 3D imaging has the potential to bring many possibilities to the field of forensic science and crime scene investigation.

Chapter 12 Digital Image Processing

GEORGE REIS

Image processing is an important part of the forensic photography workflow. Once we take our photographs of a crime scene, traffic accident, or item of evidence, they need to be downloaded, archived, and eventually used as part of an investigation or in court to assist the trier of fact in the case.

Best Practice

Just as there are best practices to follow in forensic photography, there are best practices in the image-processing portion of the workflow. These can be summed up to include:

- Archive the original image.
- Only process duplicates of the original.
- Only use valid processes.
- All processing should be repeatable.

To archive the original images, the image-downloading process should copy the images from the memory card to an archive location that is backed up and secure. If the system prevents the original from being deleted, or from being overwritten, it will assure that the original, unaltered image is always available. A cryptographic hash value can be calculated for the images in the memory card, and in the archive to verify that the archived file is a complete and accurate copy of the original file.

A hash value is often referred to as a digital file's fingerprint. When comparing the hash value of the image on the memory card to the hash value on the archive, one can determine if the files match, and therefore that the file was completely and accurately copied. This process also provides a simple and fast way to verify that your data has not changed over time—that the file in the archive today is the same as when it was archived. There are numerous free and inexpensive hashing applications (such as MD5 Summer, Quick Hash GUI, and Karen's Directory Printer). Hashing is commonly used in the field of computer forensics.

Some image-management systems allow the user to "check out" images to process, clarify, print, or share. These generally provide a copy of the archived image, keeping the original unchanged. This can also be done without investing in a turnkey system by copying files from the archive to a local drive when making adjustments. If significant changes are made to this copy, they should also be archived.

Valid processes are those that affect the quality of the image but do not change the content of the image. For instance, one can adjust the color balance, brightness, and contrast of an image to correct for problems with light sources, exposure, and so on. However, making adjustments that cause the image to no longer represent what it purports to should not be done. It is also important to avoid over-processing, where artifacts become prominent and change the meaning of the image.

When processing images, either the software or the user should take notes to enable the processes to be repeated. Many software applications (including Photoshop, ClearID, and Amped FIVE) have methods for tracking all adjustments made to an image. This can also be accomplished by using features such as adjustment layers and smart filters (a Photoshop example) which can be referred to for the exact settings used for the adjustments. If your software does not track the processing you did, then you should keep notes so that the steps can be repeated by someone else processing the same image to get similar results.

Image Processing

Image processing can be divided into three general categories—corrections, clarifications, and output preparation.

Corrections are made to correct a problem in the image due to a recorded color shift, bad exposure or lighting, excessive image noise, and so on. These are usually minor adjustments.

Clarifications can include the same processes as with corrections when the problems are severe, or they can involve extracting details from an image that isn't due to a photography problem such as dropping out a distracting background from a latent fingerprint, or removing a pattern from electrical interference in a video image, or correcting focus or motion blur.

Output preparation includes operations involving the image size, resolution, or layout. These operations are made to provide the best image for viewing on a monitor or a printed image, or to create contact sheets or court charts.

Category 1 and Category 2 Images

The Scientific Working Group for Imaging Technology (SWGIT) has several documents related to various aspects of forensic photography and image processing available at their website (www.swgit.org). Although SWGIT terminated operations in May 2015, their documents remain some of the only available guidelines and best practice documents currently available. The Scientific Working Group for Digital Evidence (SWGDE www.swgde.org) has taken over some of the responsibilities from SWGIT. There are also two committees in the Organization of Scientific Area Committees (OSAC www.nist.gov/forensics/osac/index.cfm) that deal with areas related to forensic photography, digital images, and imaging processing. These are the Digital Evidence Subcommittee and the Video/Imaging Technology and Analysis Subcommittee.

SWGIT, in Section 11 of *Best Practices for Documenting Image Enhancement*, describes forensic photographs as falling into two categories: Category 1 and Category 2 images. In this document, SWGIT states, "The degree to which procedures used in image enhancement should be documented will depend on the intended end use of the image. Furthermore, the nature of such documentation will depend on the procedures used."

In general, Category 1 images are described as basic documentation images, and Category 2 images are images that are required for additional analysis. But Category 1 images that are determined to need further analysis can become Category 2 images.

In general, SWGIT recommends following basic image-adjustment processes for Category 1 images (brightness, contrast, color) and indicates that these can be a part of a Standard Operating Procedure (SOP) without any additional documentation. Category 2 images may have additional image processing, and some sort of notes (within the software or external to it) should be used so that any adjustments are repeatable.

Destructive vs. Non-Destructive Adjustments

Many software applications work by changing the pixel values of the original image. In these cases, once the file is saved, it is no longer possible to undo the adjustments that were made, and the only way to show the original image is to open another copy of the original image file. These are known as destructive because they overwrite the original pixel values.

Some software applications retain the original pixel values (often in a "layer") and all adjustments are actually sets of instructions that can be turned on or off and can be modified, even after the file has been saved. These are known as non-destructive or re-editable adjustments. In Adobe Photoshop, these are accomplished through the use of adjustment layers and smart filters. In Ocean Systems' ClearID, they are accomplished through the use of their workflow that duplicates image layers and applies the adjustments to those duplicate layers. And in programs like Amped FIVE, the original is always maintained as a separate file.

There is no requirement to use non-destructive methods, but they offer some key benefits, including the ability to show, step-by-step, all adjustments made to an image; and the abilities to re-adjust any process that has been applied to the image. But it should be noted that the original should always be retained in an archive regardless of the types of adjustments made.

Image Corrections

Basic image corrections include adjustments to brightness, contrast, color, and noise reduction. Adjustments to brightness, contrast, and color can often be made with a single tool because the three adjustments are closely related. All three are basically adjustments to the tonal values in one or more of the image's color channels. Equal adjustments to all three channels affect brightness and contrast; adjustments to only one or two of the color channels (or unequal adjustments to all three) affect color balance.

The image-processing samples used in this section will be done with Adobe Photoshop. There are similar tools available in most image-processing software applications, and the approach would be similar.

Color, Contrast, and Brightness Adjustments

Color shifts are usually caused by a color cast created by the type of lighting in the scene. In many cases, our eyes automatically compensate for the lighting and we don't notice the color shift when present, but it shows in the photograph. Examples of this are under fluorescent lights or incandescent lights. Fluorescent lights will often cause a green color shift in our photographs, and incandescent lights will cause a yellow to orange shift. Some lights are more extreme, and we can see the color shift with our eyes, such as under sodium vapor or mercury vapor lights outdoors.

Overexposed and underexposed images are easily corrected by adjusting the brightness of the image. Overall adjustments to brightness affect the entire image in the same way, and all image values retain their same relative relationships.

Contrast adjustments are generally to increase the contrast in an image. Low-contrast images will occur when it is overcast, foggy, or indoors under dim light.

Adjustments to contrast are generally made globally (to the entire image) and thusly affect all aspects of the image equally.

Contrast, color, and brightness are the most frequent adjustments in general scene photographs, and also are often corrected using the same tool.

One of the simplest methods for correcting color in a photograph is to use the "white balance tool" in the software and click on a gray card, or any object that is neutral gray in real life. Neutral gray is not referring to the brightness of the gray, but to the color—one that has no color values in it. In Photoshop, there are white balance tools in several locations, including within the Levels Adjustment, Curves Adjustment, and in Adobe Camera Raw—which is Adobe's application for processing camera raw files, but can also be used as a filter on any image from the Filter menu.

These same tools can be made to correct brightness and contrast. A general rule of thumb is to adjust contrast first, then adjust the mid-range brightness second. Using the Levels tool in Photoshop as an example, one would increase contrast by moving the black and white sliders (under the histogram) toward the center (without clipping important values), then adjust the mid-point slider.

Contrast and brightness adjustments are also often made for the purposes of enhancement—specifically in enhancing fingerprints, footwear, and tire impression photographs, and in forensic video analysis. In those cases, the adjustment is not made to correct problems based on the scene or the photography, but to clarify the image so that details can be better discerned in the image. In these cases, the images would be considered as Category 2 images, and the adjustments may be stronger than made to correct these issues in a Category 1 image. Proper documentation is also highly recommended.

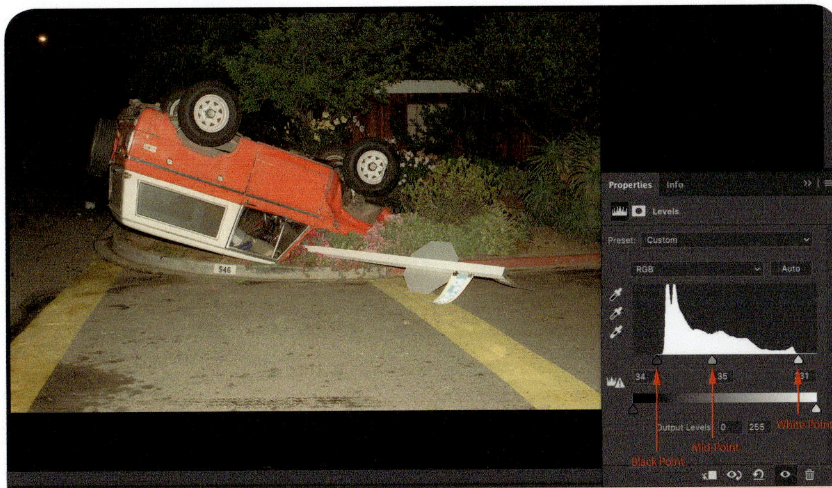

Figure 12.1 Using Photoshop's "Levels" tool to increase the contrast of an image

Noise Reduction

Image noise is a function of high ISO settings, long exposures, poor-quality electronics in the camera system, or very small image sensors. Image noise is equivalent to photographic grain when film was used to capture photographic images. With modern cameras, noise is rarely an issue, and the need for noise reduction is much more infrequent than it was in the early days of digital photography. Image noise will generally be most noticeable in the darkest tones.

When image noise is prevalent in a digital photograph, there are multiple methods for correcting it. Noise-reduction tools generally reduce noise by blurring the smallest areas of high contrast in an image. This results in a reduction in image noise, but also result in a slight blurring of the details in the overall image. Because of this, the goal in noise reduction is to balance between the amount of noise reduction and the retention of details.

Noise-reduction filters often have sliders to control the strength of the filter, the amount of detail preserved, and possibly also to reduce color noise and luminance noise separately. Photoshop's Reduce Noise filter has these options, and a good approach in using this filter is to first eliminate the color noise, then adjust the strength and details sliders in combination to maximize the noise reduction while maintaining detail.

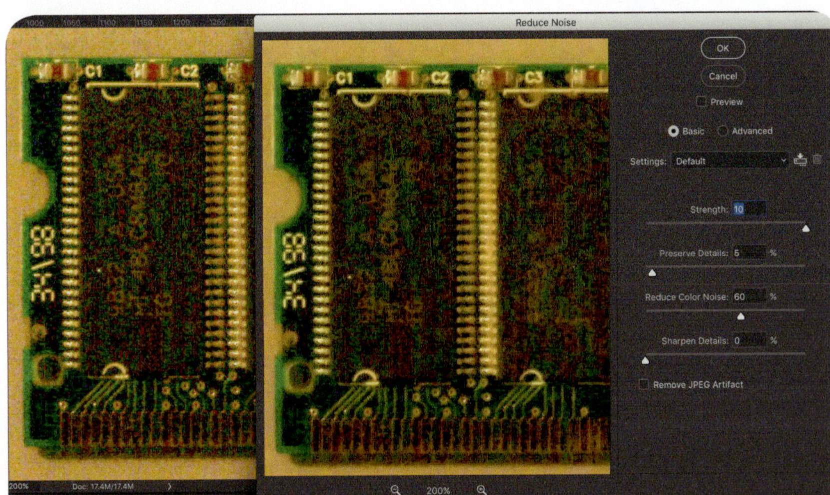

Figure 12.2 Using Photoshop's "Reduce Noise" filter to reduce the noise in an image

A method of noise reduction that does not result in a loss of image quality or sharpness is called frame averaging. This method combines multiple photographs of the same subject (with no camera or subject movement) and combines them. In combining these images, the average value for each pixel position is calculated, providing a reduction of image noise with the retention (and even improvement) of image detail. This is a common practice in forensic video analysis, but can also be useful for scene photographs under low light by taking multiple photos of the same subject with the camera on a tripod, and then applying frame averaging during post processing.

Image Sharpening

Most digital cameras interpolate the image to reproduce a color scene. This process prevents photographs that can be as sharp as possible. If photographing in the JPEG file format, the file is being processed internally, and that likely includes some image sharpening. If shooting in a raw file format, there is no processing done.

There are multiple methods for sharpening images, but the most common are those that increase the contrast along edges of the subject. Higher-contrast areas appear sharper. Sharpening filters, including the HiPass Filter, Unsharp Mask, Difference of Gaussians, or Smart Sharpen work on this general principle. The application is to sharpen enough to provide the sharpness that was lost through the color interpolation, and less than the amount that will show artifacts that can appear as light and dark halos on the edges of objects. Some filters allow one to control these filters with a fair degree of precision.

When using a filter, such as Smart Sharpen in Photoshop, starting with an Amount setting between 100 and 200, and a radius between 1 and 3 is often all that is needed. Subjects for image analysis, such as fingerprints, tire impressions, blurry license plates, and so on, can generally benefit from stronger adjustments than general photographs of crime scenes, traffic accidents, people, injuries, and so on.

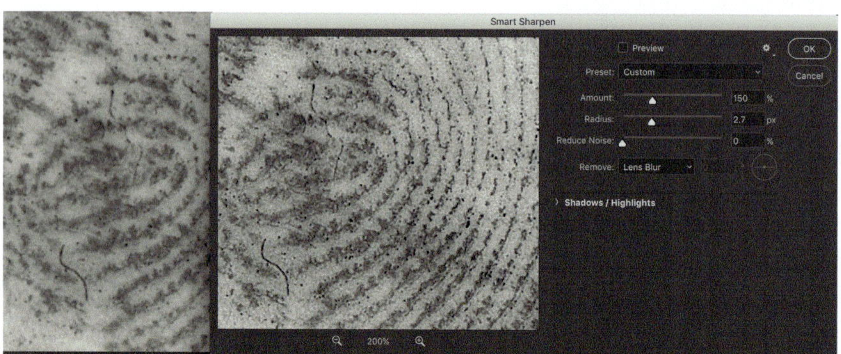

Figure 12.3 Using Photoshop's "Smart Sharpen" filter to increase the appearance of sharpness in an image

Scaling and Resizing an Image

Scaling and resizing care are often thought of as the same thing, but there is a distinct difference. We may resize an image so that we can print an 8 × 10 inch print, and we may scale an image so that we can reproduce it at 1:1. Scaling refers to making our image a specific size relative to the original, and resizing involves changing the size based on how the image will be displayed, regardless of the size of the original object.

Resizing may be done when printing images for court, to deliver to an interested party (detective, attorney, investigator, etc.), or displaying photographs on a monitor or projector. Resizing may be an interim step before bringing the photos into PowerPoint, Keynote, or into a multipage PDF document. Resized images are used for printing and display, and are illustrative.

Scaling an image is often done without changing the number of pixels (without resampling) and generally requires that a scale is included in the photograph that is parallel to both the subject and the camera back. By not resampling the image when scaling it, the full resolution of the image is retained, and no interpolation occurs.

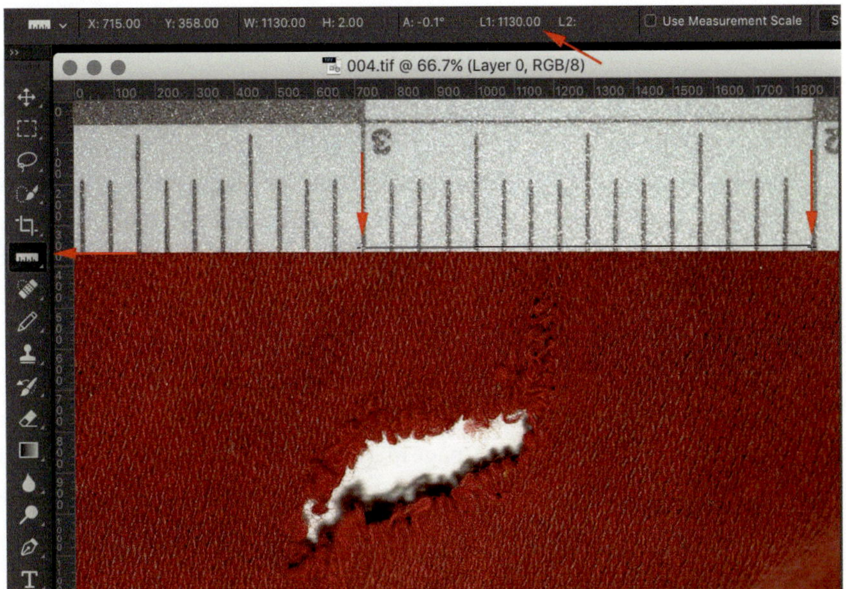

Figure 12.4 Using Photoshop's Ruler tool to measure pixels in an image

A common need for scaling an image is to prepare a fingerprint for an AFIS (Automated Fingerprint Identification System) search, or to prepare a 1:1 photograph of a tool mark, footwear impression, or tire impression for printing for comparison.

To scale the image using Photoshop, the Ruler Tool can be used to measure a known distance (such as one inch) in pixels. The distance is shown in the Ruler Tool Options Bar. In Figure 12.4, one inch has been measured, and the distance is 1130 pixels.

Next, in the Image Size dialog box, the Resample Image box should be unchecked so that the image will be resized without resampling. The measured distance can be placed into the Resolution text box. And, the units dropdown menu should be set to match the scale in the image (cm or inch). In this case, one inch was measured as 1130 pixels, so these dimensions and units were entered, as shown in Figure 12.5.

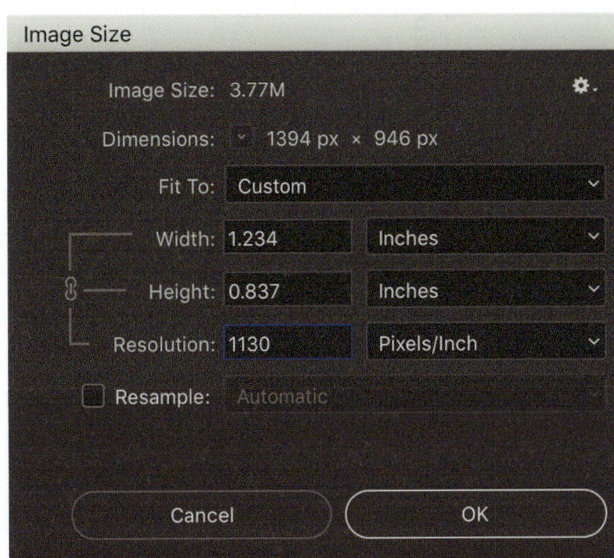

Figure 12.5 Entering the pixel measurement in Photoshop's Image Size dialog box

Interpolation is the process of calculating the values in an image when the same subject is displayed with a different number of pixels. This is necessary when resizing an image, and there are several excellent interpolation methods available in many image editing applications. Interpolation does not take place when scaling an image if the total number of pixels remains unchanged.

Contact Sheets

In the days of film, a contact sheet could be made by laying strips of negatives onto a sheet of photographic paper, and printing it so that all of the photographs on a case, from a scene, or on a given roll of film could be seen in thumbnail size images. Thumbnails is another term that is often used to describe small images that can be placed on the same page to show a sequence of photographs.

The advantage that contact sheets or thumbnail pages have is that they enable one to look at a sequence of images and see where every photograph was taken. For instance in an injury case, the contact sheet will likely show the full person to start, then mid-range photos, followed by close-ups. Looking at a photograph of a specific injury, one simply needs to work one's way back in the contact sheet to see where the injury was located, and who the injury belonged to.

Features for making contact sheets or thumbnail images are common in many image-editing applications. Some will enable the user to choose the size of the images, the layout, whether any caption information should appear (numbering, description, exposure info, etc.), page numbering, title, and so on. Contact sheets can be very simple, with just the series of images on a single sheet, to pages that include the case name/number at the top, frame numbers under each photograph, page numbers, and a footer with descriptive information.

Saving Files

When doing any processing, it may be necessary to save the files for future reference. By working on copies of the originals, this file can be saved as a separate file and compared to the original photograph to show precisely what was done, to answer any court challenges, and to maintain a chain of custody.

Methods that are consistent with your internal policies and standard operating procedures should be followed.

These processed files can go into a separate folder on your archive, or can use a different naming structure for the purpose of differentiating them from the original files. There are simple methods to do this through basic folder hierarchies and file-naming methods, and there are several companies that provide image-management solutions that may automate the process.

A simple manual method is to begin each year with a folder for all photographs for that year. When photographing a new case, create a folder with that case name or number in the correct year. Within that, create a folder called "Originals" and archive all files to that location.

When processing the images, work on copies and save them into a separate folder within the case folder. A folder called "Working" can be used for files that are Category 2 images and contain multiple layers, or notes, and so on. A folder called "Output" can be used for the final versions of all processed files, whether Category 1 or Category 2 images.

A file format should be used for these files that retains the image quality and settings used, etc. For instance, if using Adobe Photoshop, and using adjustment layers, and retaining the History Log-in metadata, the files would need to be saved as TIFF, PSD, or PSB.

INDEX

Page numbers in italics refer to figures. Page numbers in bold refer to tables.

For Product Safety Concerns and Information please contact our EU representative GPSR@taylorandfrancis.com Taylor & Francis Verlag GmbH, Kaufingerstraße 24, 80331 München, Germany